# PRACTICAL MODERN BASKETBALL

## THIRD EDITION

John R. Wooden

**Macmillan Publishing Company**
New York

**Collier Macmillan Publishers**
London

Macmillan Publishing Company
866 Third Avenue, New York, New York 10022

Collier Macmillan Canada, Inc.

**_Library of Congress Cataloging-in-Publication Data_**

Wooden, John R.
  Practical modern basketball.

  Includes index.
  1. Basketball—Coaching    I. Title
GV885.3.W66  1988      796.32′3′077      87-18594
ISBN 0-02-429470-5

Printing: 1 2 3 4 5 6 7 8      Year: 8 9 0 1 2 3 4 5 6 7

# ABOUT THE AUTHOR

John R. Wooden is by far the most successful of a select few basketball men who have excelled as both a player and coach. He is the only person to be enshrined in both categories in the Naismith Basketball Hall of Fame.

He was an All-American high school player from the state of Indiana and a three time all-American college player while at Purdue University, where he also was College Player of the Year in 1932. He has been named to the Indiana all-time high schools and college basketball teams and to the Helms Athletic Foundation all-time college team.

After a very successful high school (11 years) and small college (2 years) career, he taught and coached at UCLA for 27 years where he and his teams set many records that may never be broken.

Here are some of the records that have made him generally recognized as the greatest college coach in the history of the game:

10 NCAA championships, next best 4

7 consecutive NCAA championships, next best 2

38 consecutive "sudden death" NCAA tournament victories, next best 12

88 consecutive victories, next best 60

4 undefeated seasons, next best 1

8 undefeated conference seasons, next best 0

Excellent fundamental execution, superb condition, and unselfish teamwork always have been the trademarks of his teams.

An honor student as an English major with a Master's degree in Education, John Wooden has utilized his vast experience as a player, teacher, and coach to write this book that should be very enlightening and enjoyable to every person interested in the game of basketball and a must for every coach.

# PREFACE

This book presents my ideas on teaching and coaching the wonderful sport of basketball. It covers the fundamentals and style of team play in which I believe.

In this revised edition many things remain the same because they relate to things that do not change. Of course, I have had many new experiences since the first edition, so I've included the things I've learned that may help today's coaches and players. The most significant addition is the discussion on having to adjust for dominant players. I entitled the discussion, "The Alcindor (Jabbar) Adjustment" and included it under General Coaching Concerns. Additional coverage of working with assistant coaches and the managerial staff has also been included. Some new plays have been added and several sections have been refined. At the request of many friends, I've written a few comments about my favorite and championship teams. You'll find these comments at the end of the book.

Although some new photographs have been included, most have been retained. They may appear dated, but the techniques illustrated have not changed. They still adequately depict techniques that, in my opinion, will always be applicable.

This book is based not only on my experiences as player and coach, but also on my study of the publications on playing and coaching the game, attendance at numerous coaching clinics, and talking basketball with many players and coaches. To all the authors of the books and articles and to those who have shared their time and talent with me I want to express my gratitude.

In addition to the many wonderful young men whom I have had the from the floor except that the shooter never leaves the floor. He comes up on his toes to get the necessary follow-through and then settles back to the exact position that he was in before starting the shot. men whom I would like to single out as having had the most influence on my growth and development as a person and coach. It is to them and to my wonderful wife, Nellie, who has been my most loyal and devoted booster since our high school days, that I dedicate this book. In the order in which they affected my life the men are:

Joshua Hugh Wooden, my father—a man who never spoke an unkind word of another person and who was far more interested in character than in reputation. He had many misfortunes, but he never complained nor compared himself with those more fortunate. In my opinion, he came as close to living the philosophy of the Golden Rule as anyone I have ever known.

Earl W. Warriner—my country grade-school principal, teacher, and coach. There were no "stars" or privileged few in his eyes; everyone was given the treatment earned and deserved. He would not compromise his principles for the sake of convenience, but he recognized the right to a difference of opinion and was man enough to admit to being wrong without rationalization or alibi.

Glenn M. Curtis, my high school coach—a brilliant teacher, psychologist, and handler of young men. He had a tremendous talent for getting individuals and teams to rise to great heights. He was a master strategist and tournament coach and a fine teacher of fundamentals.

Ward L. "Piggy" Lambert, my college coach at Purdue University —one of the truly great coaches in the history of the game. He had tremendous success at both the high school and college level and is now enshrined in the National Basketball Hall of Fame and in the Indiana Basketball Hall of Fame. Although a fierce competitor, he was a man of very high principles and refused to swerve from what he considered to be right, regardless of potential personal gain, recognition, or glory. He, too, was a master at teaching the fundamentals and the little details.

Nellie (Riley) Wooden, my wife of almost 53 years and sweetheart of almost 60 at the time of her death on March 21, 1985. She provided the inspiration and support that enabled us to "weather all storms" throughout our high school and college days as well as being a wonderful wife, mother, and supportive friend during all our years as man and wife.

*Los Angeles, California*                                    **John R. Wooden**
*1987*

# CONTENTS

# 1

# MY COACHING PHILOSOPHY

## INTRODUCTION

Webster tells us that, among other things, a philosopher is a person who meets all events, whether favorable or unfavorable, with calmness and composure. Furthermore, among the comments he makes in defining philosophy are such statements as: originally, love of wisdom or knowledge; a study of the processes governing thought and conduct; the general principles or laws of a field of knowledge or activity; and a study of human morals, character, and behavior.

These definitions certainly indicate the necessity of a coach being somewhat of a philosopher and having a philosophy of his own if he is to do well in his chosen profession.

Psychiatrists tell us that two of the possible symptoms of insanity are delusions of grandeur and delusions of persecution. Since all coaches are subject to delusions of grandeur when their teams on occasion may accomplish what did not seem possible and subject to delusions of persecution when every close call and every break seem to go against them, they must be philosophically inclined to accept such events with calmness and composure and continue to make decisions in the clear light of common sense.

Coaches must also be able to react in a philosophical manner to the unpredictable emotional reactions of players, fans, opponents, and all others who have, or think they have, a very personal interest in the participants, the playing, and the scores of the games. The coach must recognize that his profession places him in the public eye and he will, at times, receive both unjustifiable criticism and undeserved praise, and he must not be unduly affected by either. He must also realize that much of his work is being done under circumstances that are likely to be of an emotional and excitable nature involving many immature individuals.

Although it is a most difficult task to specifically explain my philosophy, I believe that the following things constitute a part of my philosophy.

## ON DOING YOUR BEST

A coach can only do his best, nothing more, but he does owe that, not only to himself, but to the people who employ him and to the youngsters under his supervision. If you truly do your best, and only you will really know, then you are successful and the actual score is immaterial whether it was favorable or unfavorable. However, when you fail to do your best, you have failed, even though the score might have been to your liking.

This does not mean that you should not coach to win. You must teach your players to play to win and do everything in your power that is ethical and honest to win. I do not want players who do not have a keen desire to win and do not play hard and aggressively to accomplish that objective. However, I want to be able to feel and want my players sincerely to feel that doing the best that you are capable of doing is victory in itself and less than that is defeat.

It is altogether possible that whatever success I have had or may have could be in direct proportion to my ability not only to instill that idea in my players but also to live up to it myself.

Therefore, I continually stress to my players that all I expect from them at practice and in the games is their best effort. They must be eager to become the very best that they are capable of becoming. I tell them that, although I want them to be pleased over victory and personal accomplishment, I want them to get the most satisfaction from knowing that both they and the team did their best. I hope that their actions or conduct following a game will not indicate victory or defeat. Heads should always be high when you have done your best regardless of the score and there is no reason for being overly jubilant at victory or unduly depressed by defeat.

Furthermore, I am rather thoroughly convinced that those who have the self-satisfaction of knowing they have done their best will also be on the most desirable end of the score as much, and perhaps more, than their natural ability might indicate.

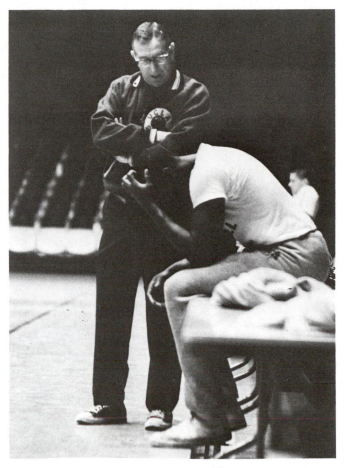

**FIGURE 1-1** Coach Wooden with troubled player at a workout the day prior to a game.

## THE COACH AS A TEACHER

Since the most important responsibility of a coach in regard to the actual playing of the game is to teach his players properly and effectively to execute the various fundamentals of the game, he is, first of all, a teacher.

As a matter of fact, it is unlikely that a teacher of any subject finds it as necessary to follow the laws of learning as closely and specifically as it is for the teacher of the fundamentals of basketball. A fundamental must be explained and demonstrated, the correct demonstration must be imitated by the players, their demonstration must be constructively criticized and corrected, and then the players must repeat and repeat the execution of the proper model until the correct habit has been formed to the point where they will react instinctively in the correct manner.

If the coach is, first of all, a teacher, the following ideas expressed by Mr. John R. Shannon, a brilliant professor of education, and the chairman of my thesis committee, in regard to teachers should also apply to coaches. Although the exact wording has been changed a little, the ideas remain essentially the same.

The coach must come (be present), see (diagnose), and conquer (correct). He must continuously be exploring for ways to improve himself in order that he may improve others and welcome every person and everything that can be helpful to him. A wise motto might be, "Others, too, have brains."

The following ten criteria that he listed as being helpful for a teacher certainly apply to the teacher of basketball:

1. Knowledge of your subject (basketball).
2. General knowledge.
3. Teaching skill.
4. Professional attitude.
5. Discipline.
6. Classroom (floor) organization.
7. School and community relations.
8. Teacher-pupil (coach-player) relationship.
9. Warm personality and genuine consideration for others.
10. Desire to improve.

## THE COACH AS A LEADER

The coach must never forget that he is a leader and not merely a person with authority. The youngsters under his supervision must be able to receive proper guidance from him in all respects and not merely in regard to the proper playing of the game of basketball.

Next to their parents, youngsters spend more time with and are more likely to be influenced by their teachers than anyone else, and the coach is the teacher who will provide by far the most influence. Therefore, it is not only the duty but also the obligation of the coach to be fully aware of and to handle this responsibility with grave concern. The powerful influence of example should be a sacred trust for all of those who are in the position to help mold the character of young people in their formative years.

Mr. Wilferd A. Peterson lists a number of important ideas in regard to leadership in his essay, *The Art of Leadership.* Some of them are as follows:

*The leader is a servant. As the Master of Men expressed it, "And whosoever would be chief among you, let him be your servant."*

*The leader sees through the eyes of his followers.*

*The leader says, "Let's go!," and leads the way rather than, "Get going!"*

*The leader assumes his followers are working with him, not for him. He sees that they share in the rewards and glorifies the team spirit.*

*The leader is a man builder. The more men he can build, the stronger the organization will be, himself included.*

*The leader has faith in people. He believes in them, trusts them, and thus draws out the best in them.*

*The leader uses his heart as well as his head. After he has considered the facts with his head, he lets his heart take a look, too. He is a friend.*

*The leader plans and sets things in motion. He is a man of action as well as a man of thought.*

*The leader has a sense of humor. He is not a stuffed shirt. He has a humble spirit and can laugh at himself.*

*The leader can be led.* He is not interested in having his own way, but in finding the best way. *He has an open mind.*

*The leader keeps his eyes on high goals. He strives to make the efforts of his followers and himself contribute to the enrichment of personality, the achievement of more abundant living for all, and the improvement of all.*

The coach who makes a sincere and determined effort to follow the leadership ideas and ideals that I have taken from the essay by Mr. Peterson is certain to improve his leadership qualifications and enhance the possibilities of a successful team.

A team without leadership is like a ship without a rudder that is certain to wander aimlessly and will probably end up going around in circles and getting nowhere.

Of course, the coach must know the game and know his players to be able to provide proper leadership, but he must realize, welcome, and assume the full responsibility.

## STYLE OR SYSTEM OF PLAY

While it is important that you have complete confidence and faith in the primary offensive and defensive systems that you decide to use, if you are going to be able to teach them with conviction, you must realize that style or system is not the most important thing. There are various excellent and sound systems of play. The important thing is to be certain that both your offensive and defensive systems of play are based on sound, valid principles of play that keep floor balance at all times and with the offensive system requiring continuous movement and drive toward the basket from various angles.

You must firmly believe in what you are doing and that—

**1.** It is not what you do, but how well you execute it if it is based on sound valid principles. There are no real secrets to the game, at least not for very long.

**2.** No system will be successful unless the players are well grounded in the fundamentals and execute them properly and so quickly that they seem to be done instinctively. Almost any system will be successful if it is taught well, stresses positive action with floor balance and is used by quick, aggressive players who are well grounded in the fundamentals, in excellent condition, possess a good team attitude, and keep their emotions under control.

**3.** Team play from both the offensive and defensive points of view comes from integrating well-conditioned players who have mastered the fundamentals into a smooth-working and cohesive unit.

## THE FAST-BREAK MINDED COACH

It is my purpose not to try to sell other coaches on fast-break basketball, but to explain my reason for keeping it foremost in my offensive thinking.

I do not adhere to the philosophy of some coaches who say that they use the fast break because they fast break every time the opportunity presents itself. If you are fast-break minded, you are constantly working to make fast-break opportunities. Most of these opportunities are made in the back court by constant emphasis and repeated drill. You adjust to your set offense in the offensive end of the court after a high percentage shot failed to materialize from your quick thrust from defense to offense.

The principal reasons for my belief in the fast-break game are:

**1.** *To please the fans.* It is my feeling that the fans prefer and deserve to see as much action as is compatible with good play. We are all dependent upon fan interest whether or not we like to admit it. The success of our game is in direct proportion to its popularity with the fans, especially in areas where the climate and other sports are in strong competition with you. When the fans quit attending the game you are coaching, then both you and the game itself are in serious trouble.

The ball-control and stalling type of game can be excellent basketball, perhaps the very best, but I am convinced that the game would gradually, but surely, lose its popularity if all teams used that style of play. It would not occur as soon in areas where there aren't too many things in competition with basketball during the basketball season, but it would come inevitably.

The professionals who openly admit that they are completely dependent upon fan interest for their very existence have done and are continuing to do everything possible to provide more action. This is true of all professional sports and not just basketball alone.

Local fans will usually support the home team very well if they are in the championship class and reasonably well if they are a winning team, but they will most likely support a winning fast-breaking team better than a winning ball-control type of team. Moreover, they are almost certain to support a losing or ordinary team that provides a lot of action much better than they will a losing or ordinary ball-control type of team.

Contrasting styles of play are important to the game and good for the game, but it must never be forgotten that the popularity of basketball came from the fact that it is a game of fast action.

**2.** *To please the players.* I once made a personal survey to determine the style of game that most players would prefer to play. The results of the questionnaire showed that an overwhelming majority of players preferred the fast-break style of offense over any more deliberate or ball-control style of game even though they might fast break whenever they had an opportunity.

This survey attempted to get information from an equal number of players who had participated in the fast-break or ball-control style exclusively: players who had playing experience in each style, players from winning teams, players from losing teams, and players from teams with an average record.

Regardless of the system used or the success of the team, the fast-breaking style of game was preferred by the majority of every group.

**3.** *More players get to play.* As a general rule, more players get an opportunity to play more in the fast-break style of game. This enables more people to derive additional personal satisfaction, including the players, players' parents, other relatives, and friends of the players. It is only natural for those who have a personal interest in a player, through kinship or friendship, to be more pleased when he gets into the actual game competition.

## FIVE BASIC PRINCIPLES

There are many important principles that must be considered when attempting to teach the game of basketball to a group of young men and develop them into a smooth-functioning combination. In spite of the difficulty of accurately selecting a few out of many, I am making a select group of the five things that make up the cornerstones and the heart of the *Pyramid of Success,* a mythical structure devised to help consolidate my own thinking.

**Industriousness.** There is no substitute for work. You and your players must work hard, as all worthwhile objectives are attained only through careful planning and hard work. Perfection can never be attained, but it must be the goal and must be sought by determined effort. You can never reach your goal by looking for a short cut or the easy way.

**Enthusiasm.** You and your players must be enthusiastic about basketball. If not, you should seek some other profession and your players should try some other activity. Enthusiasm "rubs off" on those with whom it comes in contact and the enthusiastic tend to inspire and stimulate others. Your heart must be in your work if you are to progress as it will make you eager to improve and learn more.

**Condition—Mental, Moral and Physical.** The mental and moral conditions of your players are of extreme importance because they will determine the physical condition if the players are industrious and enthusiastic. A player who is not mentally and morally sound will never be able to become well conditioned, because he tears down rather than builds.

The mental and moral example set by the coach can have a strong influence on the type of ball players he produces, and, of even greater importance, on the character of the young men who later leave his guidance and begin to lead others.

**Fundamentals.** Through the teaching of the coach the players must acquire a thorough knowledge of and the ability to properly execute the fundamentals of the game. They must be taught to react properly instantly without having to stop or hesitate and think about what to do. In basketball there is no question about the truth of the statement, *he who hesitates is lost.* The entire foundation for sound play is the quick execution of the basic fundamentals. Fine execution of the fundamentals might overcome an unsound style of play, but the finest system cannot overcome poor execution of the fundamentals. The coach must be certain that he never permits himself to get "carried away" by a complicated system to the extent that he "steals" practice time from the fundamentals.

**Development of Team Spirit.** The coach must use every bit of psychology at his command and use every available method to develop a fine team spirit on his squad. Teamwork and unselfishness must be encouraged at every opportunity, and each player must be eager, not just willing, to sacrifice personal glory for the welfare of the team. Selfishness, envy, egotism, and criticism of each other can crush team spirit and ruin the potential of any team. The coach must be aware of this and constantly alert to prevent such traits by catching them at the source before trouble develops.

## OTHER IMPORTANT PRINCIPLES

**1.** Basketball is a game of habits, and it takes time and patience to develop proper habits and to break bad ones. One of the greatest faults of most beginning coaches is likely to be a lack of patience. Try to convince the players that they must never become careless in practice because they are likely to do in games as they do in practice. Concentration on the objective is a must.

**2.** The coach and the players must never become satisfied, but must work constantly to improve. Have perfection as the goal, even though it can never be attained.

**3.** Remember that it is not so much what you do, but how well you do it. Therefore, it is better for you to teach them to do a few things well than to have so much to do that they might not do any of it very well. Do not give them too much.

**4.** Do not tie them down so rigidly that you take away their initiative. They must have some freedom of movement, but must react to the initiative of a teammate in order to keep floor balance.

**5.** Try to devise a balanced offense that provides each position with an equal number of scoring opportunities over the course of a number of games, but do not confuse them by making it too complicated in an effort to show your own knowledge.

**6.** Do not overlook the little details as it is the little things that may make the difference. Perfection of a few minor details is often the only difference between the winner and the loser.

**7.** You must prepare to win to be a winner, and you cannot prepare others without being prepared yourself. Confidence comes from being prepared and properly conditioned.

**8.** Convince your players that condition is often the deciding factor when teams are evenly matched and properly prepared. However, if the better conditioned team is to be able to take advantage of their condition, they must keep the pressure on early in the game in order for it to pay off in the latter part. Your fundamentals, your poise, and your confidence may leave you in direct proportion to fatigue, so make your opponent reach each stage of fatigue before you do.

**9.** Use the positive approach and develop pride in your own game, defensively and offensively. Prepare for your opponents, but never worry about them. Let them worry about you.

**10.** Stress offense without the ball and defense before your man gets the ball.

**11.** Give public credit to your playmakers and defensive men at every opportunity. The scorers get plenty of acclaim to salve their natural ego, but the others must not be forgotten.

**12.** The coach should do the criticizing, and it should always be constructive. Permit no player to criticize, razz, or ridicule a teammate in any respect.

**13.** Insist that the scorer acknowledge the passer whose pass led to his score and that all acknowledge any teammate who makes a nice play.

**14.** Be constantly analyzing yourself as well as your players and be governed by the result of your analysis.

## ESSENTIAL PERSONAL TRAITS AND ABILITIES FOR THE COACH

The following personal traits and abilities should be possessed by the coach who really wants to reach the top of his chosen profession.

### PRIMARY TRAITS

**Industriousness.** This has been discussed previously.

**Enthusiasm.** This, too, has been discussed in another section, but it might be noted that enthusiasm comes from your heart being in your work.

**Sympathy.** The coach must have a genuine love for youngsters and be very considerate of their needs and feelings. He should be easy to approach by the players concerning their problems.

**Judgment.** The coach must be extremely careful in his judgment and consider all matters in the clear light of common sense. He must have a sense of discretion and tact comparable to that of Solomon. A sense of values in regard to men, games, techniques, and training is a must for him.

**Self-Control.** He must keep his emotions under control to be able to think clearly at all times. He can do this and still be a fighter who lets his players know that he is with them at all times. He must discipline forcefully at times, but be fair and hold no grudge or he will lose respect. He must keep his poise.

**Earnestness.**  A coach must be sincere and honest in every phase of his work. He might lack something in knowledge and technique and still get along, but his fate is failure if he is lacking in honesty and sincerity.

**Patience.**  Lack of patience is possibly the greatest fault of the beginning coach. Don't expect too much. Progress comes slowly in many respects. The formation of new habits and the breaking of old are no quick-change propositions.

**Attentiveness to Detail.**  The perfection of the minor details may be the difference between success and failure.

**Impartiality.**  Make every effort to give every player a fair and equal chance and make certain that they realize it. Give every player the treatment that he earns and deserves.

**Integrity.**  A coach who is not a sound and honest man has no place in the development of our youth.

## SECONDARY TRAITS

**Affability.**  A coach should be a friendly, cordial person.

**Appearance.**  Keep a clean neat appearance. You should make as good an appearance as any person on the faculty.

**Voice.**  Learn to speak clearly and firmly to obtain and hold attention.

**Adaptability.**  Be flexible enough to be able to adjust to the environment and to the occasion.

**Cooperativeness.**  You must be a harmonious co-worker with the faculty, administration, athletic department, team, and community.

**Forcefulness.**  Back up your ideas with firmness, but not "bull-headedness."

**Accuracy.**  You must be accurate in your choice of men, in judgment, in technique, and in your reactions to emergencies.

**Alertness.**  Be alert to note both weak spots and strengths in your opponents and in your own players and quick to make the necessary adjustments to correct or capitalize.

**Reliability.**  Your players must know that they can depend upon you and so must all of your co-workers and neighbors.

**Optimistic Disposition.**  Think positively rather than negatively. Sincere optimism builds confidence and courage.

**Resourcefulness.**  Each individual and each team present a different and separate problem; mentally, morally, physically, socially, and spiritually. Use the proper appeal for each.

**Vision.**  Provide your players with a realistic incentive—a picture of the possible.

These primary and secondary personal traits and abilities, together with the ten criteria listed with the discussion on "The Coach As a Teacher" and the five basic and other important principles that I have listed, have provided some basis for directing my thinking as a coach, and I hope that they may be of some help to others.

Had they not been included in the ten criteria for a teacher, I would have listed Teaching Skill, Discipline, Floor Organization, and Knowledge of the Game of Basketball under "Primary Traits," and Desire to Improve and Consideration for Others under "Secondary Traits."

# THE PYRAMID OF SUCCESS

The idea for this pyramid of success originated from my association with two men during my high school days.

One of my teachers, L. J. Shidler, once asked each student in a class of which I was a member to write our definition of success. A few days later he informed us that he felt that we all disagreed somewhat with his idea of success. He said that we all had agreed with Mr. Webster and defined success in one way or another as the accumulation of material possessions or the attainment of a position of power or prestige. He said that, although these qualifications were very laudable and might indicate success, he did not feel that they were the true criteria. It was his opinion that success could come only from peace of mind, which could only be acquired by the self-satisfaction of knowing that you had

# THE PYRAMID OF SUCCESS

John R. Wooden
Head Basketball Coach
UCLA

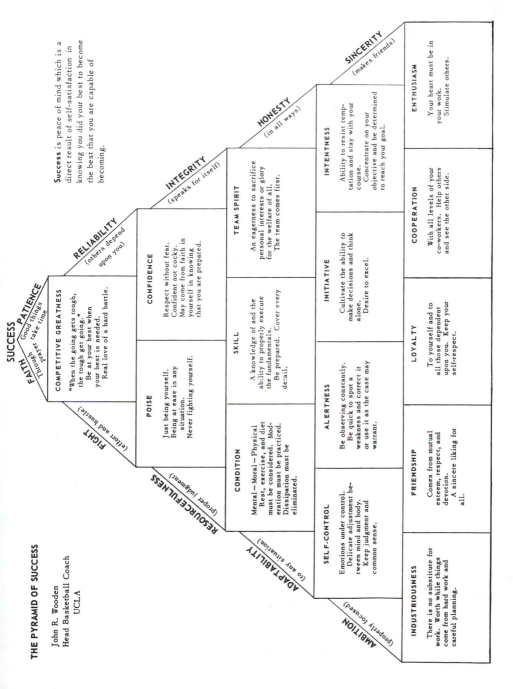

**SUCCESS**

**FAITH** Through prayer take time

**PATIENCE** Good things take time

**Success** is peace of mind which is a direct result of self-satisfaction in knowing you did your best to become the best that you are capable of becoming.

**RELIABILITY** (others depend upon you)

**INTEGRITY** (speaks for itself)

**HONESTY** (in all ways)

**SINCERITY** (makes friends)

**FIGHT** (effort and hustle)

**RESOURCEFULNESS** (proper judgment)

**ADAPTABILITY** (to any situation)

**AMBITION** (properly focused)

**COMPETITIVE GREATNESS**
"When the going gets tough, the tough get going." Be at your best when your best is needed. Real love of a hard battle.

**POISE**
Just being yourself. Being at ease in any situation. Never fighting yourself.

**CONFIDENCE**
Respect without fear. Confident not cocky. May come from faith in yourself in knowing that you are prepared.

**CONDITION**
Mental—Moral—Physical Rest, exercise, and diet must be considered. Moderation must be practiced. Dissipation must be eliminated.

**SKILL**
A knowledge of and the ability to properly execute the fundamentals. Be prepared. Cover every detail.

**TEAM SPIRIT**
An eagerness to sacrifice personal interests or glory for the welfare of all. The team comes first.

**SELF-CONTROL**
Emotions under control. Delicate adjustment between mind and body. Keep judgment and common sense.

**ALERTNESS**
Be observing constantly. Be quick to spot a weakness and correct it or use it as the case may warrant.

**INITIATIVE**
Cultivate the ability to make decisions and think alone. Desire to excel.

**INTENTNESS**
Ability to resist temptation and stay with your course. Concentrate on your objective and be determined to reach your goal.

**INDUSTRIOUSNESS**
There is no substitute for work. Worth while things come from hard work and careful planning.

**FRIENDSHIP**
Comes from mutual esteem, respect, and devotion. A sincere liking for all.

**LOYALTY**
To yourself and to all those dependent upon you. Keep your self-respect.

**COOPERATION**
With all levels of your co-workers. Help others and see the other side.

**ENTHUSIASM**
Your heart must be in your work. Stimulate others.

done everything within your power to become the best that you were capable of becoming.

The other person back of this idea was Glenn M. Curtis, my high school coach, who used what he called *A Ladder of Achievement* in an attempt to inspire the players on his team to improve their play. Five of the seven points that he used in his *Ladder of Achievement* have been incorporated in my *Pyramid of Success*.

Sometime after I had entered the teaching and coaching profession, in an attempt to analyze my own objectives and to find something more meaningful for which the students in my English classes and the players on my teams could strive rather than making an "A" grade or scoring more points than another team, I recalled the ideas of my high school teacher and coach.

There is nothing wrong with striving for a "A" mark and wanting to win a contest, but we must face the fact that we are not all created equally as far as mental and physical ability is concerned, we are not all raised in the same environment, we will not all have the same foundation in English or in athletics, and we will not all have the same facilities with which to work. However, if success and satisfaction can be attained only by making a superior mark in a class or by winning a contest, many students are going to be dissatisfied and, since, as far as the point score is concerned and discounting ties, there is a winner and loser in every athletic contest, one half of all the participants in an athletic contest are going to be unhappy.

Believing these facts to be unjustifiable and invalid, my thoughts on the subject eventually brought about *The Pyramid of Success*.

Before analyzing this structure further, it must be understood that it is based on my definition of success in regard to coaching and playing the game.

## SUCCESS

Success in coaching or playing should not be based on the number of games won or lost, but rather on the basis of what each individual does in relation to his own ability and in comparison with others when taking into consideration individual abilities, available facilities for use, the caliber of the opponents, the site of the contest, and other things of a similar nature.

True success can be attained only through self-satisfaction in knowing that you did everything within the limits of your ability to become the very best that you are capable of becoming. Therefore, in the final analysis only the individual himself can correctly determine his success. You may be able to fool others, but you can never truly deceive yourself, except, perhaps, for a short time.

It is impossible to attain perfection, but that should be the goal. Less than 100 per cent of your effort in every respect toward attaining your objective is not success, regardless of individual honors received or the number of games won or lost.

We are not all identical or equal. Others may have more ability than you have—they may be larger, faster, quicker, stronger, better jumpers, and superior in other physical attributes—but no one should be your superior in such very important qualities and characteristics as team spirit, enthusiasm, industriousness, cooperation, loyalty, determination, honesty, sincerity, reliability, and integrity. Acquire and keep these traits and success is assured.

The diagram of the *Pyramid* that accompanies this should be self-explanatory. However, I want to point out and emphasize a few of the important ideas as I considered them in constructing it.

Any structure must be built on a solid foundation and the corner-stones of the foundation are the most significant part of it. You will note that the corner stones of this structure are *industriousness* and *enthusiasm.* Since they have been discussed under another heading, I shall not repeat it here.

The heart of a body is extremely important and, since architects have been known to stress the heart of buildings that they have created, I have selected three outstanding essentials—condition, skills, and team spirit—to comprise the heart of this structure. They have been discussed as part of five basic principles along with industriousness and enthusiasm in another section, and need no reiteration.

Although a great amount of space could be devoted to any individual heading in the pyramid, I believe that the very brief comments under each should suffice and encourage a person to give the particular point additional thought.

Before discontinuing the explanation I should like to call attention to the top of the structure. The apex is *success* and it must be remembered that it is success according to my definition that preceded this discussion.

Furthermore, success is not easy to attain and the connecting points, *faith* and *patience,* to the apex are meant to indicate this. You must have patience and realize that all worthwhile objectives take time. Things that come easily, as a general rule, are not very meaningful. It is also true that you must have faith if you are to have patience. In the search for success you will constantly find yourself beset with adversity and you must have faith if you expect to reach your goal.

Also, the connecting blocks, *poise* and *confidence,* upon which *competitive greatness* rests are vitally interwoven in the process of reaching the apex. Confidence and poise both come from being prepared and are vital requisites for being a good competitor. Those who lack confidence in themselves are certain to be lacking in poise and will be pressing when the going gets tough. The front runners are easy to find, but all coaches are constantly searching for those individuals who excel when excellent performance is necessary.

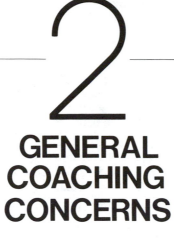

# GENERAL COACHING CONCERNS

## IMPORTANT COACHING METHODS

**1.** *The coach must be a teacher.* He must understand the learning processes and follow the laws of learning. He must be able to explain and provide a demonstration, have the players imitate the proper demonstration, constructively criticize and correct their demonstration, and have the corrected imitation repeated and repeated until the proper execution becomes automatic.

**2.** *He must use and take advantage of all possible teaching aids* and constantly be on the lookout for additional ones. Some helpful aids to supplement the daily practice sessions and used in their proper way are as follows: movies, photographs, diagrams, mimeographed suggestions and material, bulletin boards, lectures or "skull" sessions, rules discussions, pre- and post-game meetings, individual player conferences, statistical charts and records of all objectives and fundamentals, and proper use of information or suggestions from any and all sources.

**3.** *He must be a student of psychology* and constantly make use of the results of his study and experience in working with his players. Each player presents a new and different problem, but experience and study of similar individuals and situations can be of immense value to the effective solution of many problems. The coach must do everything within reason and compatible with good team spirit to "save" a player rather than taking the easy way and sacrificing a player to prove a point. In my opinion, strength and character are built through overcoming problems by desire, determination, and hard work. We must get our players to believe that the best way to improve the team is to improve themselves, and, in doing so, we must not lose sight of the fact that the same principle holds true in regard to the coach.

**4.** *Insist on punctuality and proper dress for practice, meetings, and all occasions* where a specific time is involved, but be understanding and reasonable.

**5.** *Be firm and forceful,* but not "bull-headed" if you wish to obtain respect and cooperation.

**6.** *Insist on strict attention* when instructions are being given and when an explanation, correction, or demonstration is being made. Try to get your players to understand that they should never make it necessary for you to repeat something to them because they were not listening or to someone else because of something that they might have been doing.

**7.** *Permit no "horseplay"* during the practice period. *Have fun without being foolish.* Since a player usually will revert to his practice habits during the actual games, you must be certain that they develop the correct habits.

**8.** *Have patience* and never forget that you are dealing with youngsters in their formative years.

**9.** *Praise as well as censure.* Be careful to avoid harsh, public criticism. A compliment or a "pat on the back" after a severe criticism may take the sting out of it and not cause it to lose any of its effectiveness. However, you must know your players.

**10.** *Encourage teamwork and unselfishness* at every opportunity.

**11.** *Give players* as much individual attention as possible. Have some time set aside each day for players to work alone or in pairs on their individual weaknesses that you have pointed out to them and under your partial supervision.

**12.** *Do not attempt to give your players too much.* A few things properly executed may be more effective than a number of things poorly executed.

**13.** *Do not destroy individual initiative* by restricting their movements too much. Initiative is fine until it becomes an excuse for selfishness.

**14.** *Try to devise an offense that gives each player an equal number of scoring opportunities* over the course of a number of games. Individual skill, ability, hustle, and initiative will enable some to score more than others, but it isn't wise for the offense to be set up to make a scoring star out of any position. That can hurt team play, team spirit, and make it easier for the defense to defend.

It is natural for a player to want to score and I want every player to want to score, but not at the expense of a teammate or the team. If a player tells me he doesn't like to score and that he would rather set up plays or play defense, I immediately tell him that he is either lying or he must be abnormal and I want neither type on my team. I want every player to enjoy the thrill of being called a team player and to derive pleasure from playing defense, but I do not consider it natural to actually enjoy those fine qualities more than scoring. False modesty is not a virtue.

# ASSISTANT COACHES

Assistant coaches should be exactly what their title implies—assistant coaches. They should be ready and eager to assist in every way possible throughout the year.

The role of the assistant coach is a very difficult role and not very glamorous which means that the head coach must be very understanding and very tactful in working with them. Make certain that they feel that they are working with you rather than for you. The head coach must want and be receptive to suggestions from assistants. You will not always agree, but you must always listen and avoid being disagreeable when you disagree. Analyze all suggestions and use logic.

If you make your assistants hesitant or afraid to make suggestions, their value as assistants has become greatly reduced. A head coach does not need a "yes" man to inflate his ego, but someone who will make suggestions. Assistants must, of course, realize that only the head coach must make the final decisions and must not be upset when the ruling goes against their suggestions. Decision making is a lonely position and much more difficult than suggestion making. The head coach must ever keep in mind that it is imperative that you listen to others if you expect others to listen to you, whether it be players, assistants, or others.

In addition to the things mentioned in the section entitled Essential Personal Traits and Abilities for the Coach, which are discussed in Chapter 1, pages 10–12, other desirable qualities or essentials for the assistant coach are:

**Optimism.** A positive, optimistic, yet realistic approach is necessary for an aggressive confident team and the coaches must be leaders in this. Do not waste time complaining or worrying about things over which you have no control and about which you can do nothing. Concentrate on improving the things you can.

**Loyalty.** The assistant may disagree, but must never be disloyal. Lack of loyalty in any group project insures failure to do nearly as well as you are capable. Lack of ability may be excused, but lack of loyalty—never.

**Industriousness and Enthusiasm.** These are the cornerstones of my Pyramid of Success which is discussed in another chapter and are absolutely essential for an assistant coach. All of the qualities discussed in the Pyramid are desirable but these are essential.

**An Understanding Spouse.** Some promising assistant coaches have been handicapped or have left coaching because of the lack of an understanding spouse. The family should come first, but any ambitious coach will perhaps be away from home more than persons in many other careers, so it is important that the spouse be understanding. However, the coach must realize that the spouse also may have adjustment problems. Establishing and maintaining an understanding relationship is important.

**Knowledge.** If the assistant does not "know his stuff," there will be lack of respect from the players and desirable results will be impossible. You cannot bluff your way through with the bright young people of today, especially when you are working with them on a daily basis.

**Pleasant Personality.** Assistants will be in close contact with many segments of the school and community, in addition to the players, and must be warm and pleasant to gain the cooperation of all those involved or interested in the program. A sour disposition will alienate others as will lack of politeness.

**Punctuality.** Assistants must acquire the habit of being on time, keeping up to date on all correspondence and responsibilities, and being well organized.

**Neatness and Politeness.** A neat and clean appearance and a courteous demeanor are essential as the lack of these qualities will be very harmful to your relationship with the faculty, the administration, the media, parents and others whose cooperation you need. "Politeness is a small price to pay for the good will and affection of others."

**Ambition.** Assistants should want to improve their positions and should be encouraged and helped in their efforts or they probably will be doing little more than marking time. Certainly they will not be contributing to the best of their ability. They become like a team that has become satisfied and complacent.

**Desire to Improve.** Every effort must be made to study those who have been successful, to keep up on the techniques of the game, to learn more about the psychology of working with others both as a leader and as a follower, to analyze the strengths and weaknesses of individuals as well as systems of play, to better teach the fundamentals, and to improve yourself as a person.

**An Example.**   Assistant coaches should make a conscious effort to set a proper example for young people as there is much truth in the statement that youth need examples more than critics. They should understand the words of the one who said, "No printed word, no oral plea, can teach our youth what they should be; nor all the books on all the shelves, it's what the teachers are themselves."

Of course these are not all of the qualities one would like in an assistant coach, but they are among the most essential and desirable.

## RESPONSIBILITIES OF ASSISTANT COACHES

This will vary according to the situation. High schools will be different from colleges and the locations, size, budgets, competition, and other things enter into this.

However, regardless of and according to the situation that exists the head coach must decide what the duties and responsibilities of the assistants will be and go over them carefully together. I believe they should be written as well.

Among the things that probably must be covered in either/or the high school and college programs are:

**1.**   Work with the head coach and other coaches in every possible way. Assist or lead as the occasion requires.

**2.**   Assist in the planning of the daily practice program. This should be done at a regular pre-designated time each day.

**3.**   Assist in the daily practice. Specific responsibilities should be assigned when the program is planned.

**4.**   Counsel all players in the planning of their academic schedules for normal progress for their graduation, keep completely informed of their academic progress, arrange for necessary tutoring and extra study programs, and show sincere interest in them as individuals away from basketball.

**5.**   Cover special meetings, speaking requests, and so on.

**6.**   Oversee and supervise the coaching and organization of the freshman or junior varsity.

**7.**   Scouting of opponents and keeping an up-to-date file on them.

**8.**   Recruiting. Compile and keep up-to-date records and needed information about all prospects—class, age, size, transcript, attitude, letters from their own and several opposing coaches, family background, and personal interest in you. Arrange visit to your campus at appropriate time, get films when possible and other pertinent information. See them play if possible. Arrange for the head coach to see them play when advisable.

Always keep in mind that local players are preferred and that you do not want to initiate contact with out of the state prospects. We want them to want us. However, do not lose a local "blue chipper" to an opponent because of lack of effort on your part.

You want quickness in relation to others who will play the same position, but it must be under control, and you want unselfish team players of good character. Do not waste valuable time on bad actors or those who are not going to meet your academic requirements.

**9.** Arrange board and room for players during holiday seasons during the basketball season.

**10.** Arrange for summer jobs for all who need them. Keep an up-to-date file on all potential employees and keep a good relationship with them.

**11.** Keep in contact with as many high school coaches as possible. They are your life's blood.

**12.** Send your schedule to all opponents, get a copy of their schedules, and arrange for the scouting of them.

**13.** Be sure that the basketball office is covered at all times.

**14.** Aid and assist your players in every way within the rules and regulations that is in their and your best interest.

**15.** Organize your film library and keep it up to date with a record of all films. Keep your projector and films in good repair.

**16.** Work with the committee assigned to select your ball boys or ball girls and with your head manager in the selection of new managers.

**17.** Set up a fall term meeting and dates for the physicals.

**18.** Keep an up-to-date file on all coming coaching clinics and new books.

**19.** Make sure that your managers prepare for your visitors and carry out their responsibilities.

**20.** Help your players arrange for housing in the fall and when needed. Be informed about your residence halls and arrange well in advance for rooms.

**21.** Make a special effort to be cooperative and on very friendly terms with everyone in your athletic department—administrators, secretaries, other coaches, other athletes, custodians, all visitors.

## THE MANAGERIAL STAFF

A competent managerial staff supervised by an experienced head manager, preferably a senior who has worked his way up, is of immeasurable help to the coach. However, for better effectiveness, the coach must make certain that the players understand that the managers are to help aid both them and the coaches, but are not to be their servants to run errands and pick up after them. Neither should be demanding of the other, but they must work together in a cooperative manner.

If possible, the head manager should have three freshman, two sophomore, and one junior manager under his supervision. He should organize the staff and assign specific duties and responsibilities to each and should train the junior manager, who will be the next head manager, to take over when necessary.

Some duties and responsibilities are:

## A. BEFORE DAILY PRACTICE

**1.** Make certain the practice floor is clean, the lights are on, and that outsiders are cleared from the practice floor area by the time the players are due on the floor.

**2.** Have the needed player equipment ready for them when they report to get dressed.

**3.** Have available on the floor the required number of properly inflated and clean basketballs, proper colored scrimmage shirts, a few towels, some extra shoelaces, tape, scrimmage charts, spare whistles, free throw chart, and an extra piece or two of all practice gear.

## B. DURING DAILY PRACTICE

**1.** Keep a daily free throw chart for the squad.

**2.** Keep spectators away from the players.

**3.** Anticipate and be ready to distribute or collect balls to or from certain areas when necessary.

**4.** Have scrimmage shirts immediately available.

**5.** Have charts and chart keepers ready when needed.

**6.** Know the practice schedule and be ready to help implement it at all times.

**7.** Have sweat suits ready to distribute when needed, then collect later.

**8.** Learn the needs of the coaches and players and be ready to supply them.

## C. AFTER DAILY PRACTICE

**1.** Collect and store all equipment.

**2.** Have juice ready for distribution.

**3.** Turn over charts to coaches.

**4.** Check shower room, locker room, and lockers.

**5.** Get towels and dirty practice gear ready for laundry.

**6.** Turn out lights and lock up.

## D. HOME GAMES

**1.** Have two managers assigned to take care of the needs for practice of your opponent.

**2.** Have six excellent warm-up balls in bags and in the dressing room of each team.

**3.** Have game uniforms, game socks, supporters, and other necessary gear and equipment ready for use.

**4.** Make certain that all equipment is supervised and cared for before, during, and after game.

**5.** Check with opponent's manager to have everything ready for practice and game.

**6.** Make certain players know the time schedule.

**7.** Get game ball and towels to dressing room of officials and then pick up after the game.

**8.** Get copies of statistical charts to coaches as soon as possible at the half and at the end of game.

**9.** Anticipate and help in every way to see that things go smoothly in regard to equipment, travel, charts, conduct, morale, meals, rest, meetings, and anything else that pertains to the game and the teams.

**10.** If there is a preliminary game, be sure that everything is covered.

### E. ROAD GAMES

In addition to the things that apply for the home games:

**1.** Pack bags for all traveling players and manager.

**2.** Distribute a travel itinerary to all on the trip.

**3.** Check closely with coaches and trainer for any necessary changes.

**4.** Arrange for a scorekeeper to keep your book.

**5.** Check with opponents manager to have everything ready for practice and game.

**6.** Make certain you leave the dressing room in excellent condition.

**7.** Collect equipment and get it properly stored or to the laundry when you return.

### F. PRE- AND POST-SEASON

**1.** Meet with the coaches shortly after the opening of school for instructions in regard to squad meeting and getting everything ready for the first day of practice.

**2.** Have all necessary forms to be filled out ready to distribute at the first meeting and all equipment ready for first day of practice.

**3.** Keep immediately available at all times the up-to-date addresses and telephone numbers of all the players, managers, coaches, trainer, team doctor, and parents of the players and manager

**4.** The head manager must get a notice out for prospective freshman managers shortly after school starts and arrange for a meeting with all returning and prospective new ones.

**5.** Immediately after the close of the season, get a complete inventory of all equipment and the condition of all items. Arrange to get it cleaned and stored.

# THE PRACTICE SESSION

There are so many things that are extremely important in coaching the game of basketball that I continually find myself referring to one particular idea as, perhaps, the most important. However, there are many things that must be emphasized and proper planning of the practice session is one of these.

The coach who has the ability to properly plan the practice sessions from both the daily and the long-range point of view together with the ability to devise the necessary drills to meet his particular needs for maximum efficiency has tremendously increased his possibility of success.

Time and length may depend upon many factors, but the coach must always bear in mind that there is no substitute for work and no short cuts to success. It is also quite important for him to get that idea across to the players.

Since it has been established that the learning processes are closely related to physical, mental, and emotional fatigue, it is not wise to continue past the point where such a condition becomes apparent. This is particularly true once the team has attained good physical condition. In your early season practices it may be advisable to continue conditioning drills a few minutes each day past the point where they are tired, but never try *to teach* past that point.

By carefully organizing your practice sessions after giving a lot of thought to what you hope to accomplish on that particular day, you will be able to accomplish more than you can in a disorganized practice that might extend considerably longer. The players must be kept busy at all times regardless of the length of the practice.

The coach is there to teach during the practice session, and he must give that duty his undivided attention. If you are distracted in various ways, you cannot logically expect your players to give their complete attention to the job at hand. Therefore, all distractions for each should be avoided.

Your early season practices prior to your first game will naturally be longer than those after your season is under way. After our playing season has opened and because most of our games are played on Friday and Saturday, our daily practices usually are patterned with one or two particular things in mind, such as the following.

### Monday

The practice will be thirty minutes shorter and the principal theme will be to constructively criticize our play of the games over the previous weekend and to present a picture of what we can expect for the coming weekend and what we can do about it. We will also work lightly on our fundamental drills and shoot a number of free throws. The players who did not have the opportunity to see much action in the games are usually given a good scrimmage.

### Tuesday and Wednesday

The principal practice days in which you try to devote the necessary predetermined amount of time to the individual fundamentals of both offense and defense and to the development of the team offensive and defensive systems.

### Thursday

This practice will also be thirty minutes shorter than the practices on Tuesday and Wednesday. The principal emphasis will be on reviewing all anticipated possibilities for the games on Friday and Saturday as far as the offense and defense of our opponents is concerned and on brushing up on our own offensive and defensive setups and strategies. We want to finish this practice day with not only optimistic confidence in ourselves, but with complete respect for our opponents.

### SEASON PLAN

It is important to have a general outline or practice plan for the season, taking into consideration such things as: your opponents, the details of your schedule, your gym, your material (size, speed, strength, weakness, and experience), and any other factors that might be of importance.

This is very helpful to you not only in regard to good schedule planning, but it also forces you to review all the factors related to the coming season and keeps you thinking basketball.

### WEEKLY PLAN

Prepare a weekly plan prior to the first practice of the week. This must be somewhat flexible in order that it may be changed from day to day according to the progress made and other things that may have occurred in the preceding days of the week.

## DAILY PLAN

A daily practice plan should be prepared and followed. If you fail to follow the program on one thing, it may affect many others. If you planned poorly, make the corrections for the following day, but never alter your program on a specific day once practice has started. Running overtime can be distasteful for both you and your players and should be avoided. The practice day should end on a high note in order for both coach and players to look forward to the next day with pleasure.

Some important ideas in regard to the daily program are as follows:

**1.** The coach should be on the floor early to make certain that everything is in readiness for practice. I like to have a checklist for the managers to go by, but the coach must make sure. Some of the points on the checklist are: See that the floor is clean; see that the desired number of balls are available and that they are clean and properly inflated; be sure that the scrimmage shirts are on hand and that extra shoelaces and other emergency equipment items are near at hand; have the statistical charts ready for use; and be sure that towels, tape, and anything else that might be necessary to insure a smooth practice are available. Anticipate from past experience and be prepared.

**2.** When the players individually report to the floor, they should on their own initiative warmup with some easy running and stretching, work alone or with a partner on their weaknesses of which the coach has spoken to them, pair up for practice shooting with some passive defense, and shoot a number of free throws. The coach should work with different individuals during this period.

**3.** When the coach blows his whistle to signal the start of the organized practice, the players should immediately and without taking another shot see that the balls are softly rolled, not thrown, to a predetermined spot and then they should run quickly to the position that the coach indicates.

**4.** Start the organized practice with warmup drills.

**5.** End the organized practice with team drills.

**6.** Vary the drills during the day and from day to day to prevent monotony.

**7.** Plan and organize your drills very carefully as to the number participating in order to get maximum results. At times the squad may be equally divided at three different baskets according to the position they play or in teams or merely evenly balanced as to number. They may be working on the same or each group on different fundamentals, but they must be kept busy and accept that responsibility whether or not you are with their particular group.

**8.** Explain the purpose of each drill initially and emphasize the little details. Players respond better and have more incentive when they can visualize the objective. This may be referred to as the whole followed by the part method of teaching.

**9.** Don't continue the same drill too long and have the players move quickly to get in position for the next drill when a change is made.

**10.** Follow difficult drills from either a physical or a mental point of view with easy ones and vice versa, but be aware that drills must also condition your players.

**11.** Use many competitive drills and imitate game conditions as much as possible.

**12.** Give new material early in the practice after the players are warmed up and still fresh as their learning processes will then be most acute; then repeat daily until learned. Before drilling on some new thing, I think it best to explain and demonstrate it a day or two before and, perhaps, have them perform it once or twice just to get the idea. They will absorb enough to make it much easier to teach a day or two later.

**13.** Even though a particular drill may be emphasizing one specific fundamental, other fundamentals in use should not be overlooked. Sometimes players get careless about their passing during shooting drills, which may lead to breaking down one fundamental while building another. The coach must be cognizant of this and try to prevent it, by permitting no carelessness at any time if progress is to be made.

**14.** Fundamental drills take precedence over team drills early in the season with more time being given to team drills as the season progresses. However, you must never forget, take for granted, or neglect the individual fundamentals.

**15.** Stress offense and defense on alternate days. Because the handling of the ball is involved, offense takes more time than defense, but your players must be taught that neither offense nor defense is more important than the other. They must strive to improve and excel in each phase.

**16.** As a general rule, it is a good thought to close each practice on a happy or positive note. It is desired that coach and players are able to look forward to the next day of practice with eager anticipation. If the practice is concluded on a "sour" note with coach and players in an unhappy, frustrated, pessimistic, negative state of mind, it isn't likely that either will look forward to the next day with much pleasure, and thus you will start a practice under difficult circumstances that might have been avoided.

## PRACTICE SCRIMMAGING

Since all players probably like to scrimmage better than anything else, it is important that you give this phase of your practice sessions considerable thought.

This is another flexible thing about which it is most difficult to set down any hard and fast rules. Some teams need more scrimmage than others from the physical point of view, and some need more from the psychological point of view. Condition, experience, size, and individual characteristics are all factors, along with many others, that may determine how much you scrimmage.

Since we usually play our first games at the end of our sixth week of practice and very rarely have a weekend off following that until the close of the season, our scrimmage program follows this general line of thinking:

**1.** During the first two weeks of practice, I try to arrange our daily practice plan so that every player out for the team will get a minimum of twenty minutes of game-condition scrimmage each day. I want each player to get approximately the same amount of scrimmage time as every other player and under the same conditions. Therefore, at various times each will be with a weak, average, or strong team and be competing against a weak, average, or strong team. By the end of the two-week period, each player should have had the opportunity to scrimmage with and against every other player under similar conditions. Since I keep a number of individual statistics to help me evaluate the players, it is important that I have a valid basis for comparison.

**2.** During the third and fourth week of practice, the squad will now be somewhat smaller, and I try to give each player a forty-minute game-condition scrimmage on Monday, Wednesday, and Friday and a forty-minute half-court scrimmage on Tuesday and Thursday. We try to keep the scrimmages under the same conditions as we did the first two weeks.

**3.** During the fifth week of practice, I like to have a forty-minute scrimmage for everyone on Monday, and a thirty-minute half-court scrimmage on Tuesday, Wednesday, and Thursday. On Friday, I want a dress-rehearsal type of intrasquad game with regular officials and spectators.

**4.** Two days before our first game, we will have a critical full-court forty-minute scrimmage halted many times for constructive criticism. I like to have regular officials for this scrimmage, but we will not wear game uniforms or permit spectators.

**5.** After our playing season has opened, we will usually have a thirty- to forty-minute half-court scrimmage every day, but seldom any full-court scrimmage for the players who do the majority of the playing. However, on Mondays we usually try to have a forty-minute game-type scrimmage for the players who did not get to participate very much in the games of the past weekend.

## Analysis of Practice

The coach should make a careful analysis of each day's practice while it is still fresh in his mind in order that he may plan intelligently for the next day. I like to sit down with my assistant immediately after practice and before my shower and briefly analyze and discuss the practice of that day. I make notes at that time to serve as reference help to me the next morning when I plan the practice for that day. If it can be done without being rude or impolite, you and your assistant should be alone and uninterrupted during both the analysis period following practice and the planning period the following morning.

**Progressive in Intensity.**   Your early season practices must be progressive in intensity until the players have reached good physical condition. You must be careful to avoid sore feet in the early practices, because a basketball player can be no better than his feet.

**File of Practice Plans.**   I consider it a valuable asset to keep a record of my practice plans and can refer to our exact practice schedule for any day of the season in the past seventeen years. In a hard-backed, three-hole, loose-leaf notebook I keep a record of our practice programs for each day of the current season and the complete record for the preceding two seasons. Comments and suggestions are made along the side of the record of the practice of the previous day as the practice program for the current day is prepared and filed in the notebook.

**Practice Schedule Reminder.**   In order to adhere closely to the practice schedule for the day, my assistant and I both carry a copy of the day's schedule on a three-by-five card. Occasionally, but not always, I will post a copy of the practice schedule for the day so that the players will know the plan for the day. I also like the head manager to have a copy of the daily schedule so that the managers will know exactly what is coming next and can have any needed equipment ready in the proper floor area without any waste of time.

The following examples illustrate five different types of practice days:

### UCLA BASKETBALL 1961–62
### JOHN WOODEN, HEAD COACH

*FIRST DAY OF PRACTICE:*

**3:00–3:25**   Individual attention as players work on their own. Pay particular attention to the unknowns.

**3:25–3:35**   Floor-length warmup in three lines. Easy running, inside turns, change of pace and direction, defensive sliding, 1-on-1 (cutter), 1-on-1 (dribbler), jumping, imitate rebounding push-ups.

**3:35–3:45**   Dribble and quick stop and turn (4 groups).

**3:45–3:55**   Rebounding and passing combination (4 groups).

**3:55–4:10**  Floor-length three-man lane, parallel lane, pivot, tight weave, normal weave, front and side, long pass (in groups of three).

**4:10–4:20**  Shooting, alternate post, pass and cut for side post shots (4 groups).

**4:20–4:30**  Set offense, guard to post, weak-side post (5 at a time).

**4:30–4:40**  Setup basic principles and floor balance of man-to-man defense.

**4:40–5:40**  Ten-minute scrimmages, six men alternate on each team; 1 vs. 2; 3 vs. 4; 1 vs. 3; 2 vs. 4; 1 vs. 4; 2 vs. 3.

**5:40–5:45**  Short sprints. Sprint from end line to center line, then "coast" to opposite end line. Return in the same manner and continue for the five-minute period.

*NORMAL MIDWEEK DAY OF FOURTH WEEK:*

**3:00–3:30**  All make five free throws at each of five baskets. Individual attention: Slaughter and Waxman—competitive rebounding, Cunningham and Blackman—special shots, Green and Hazzard—side post moves and defensive positions, Rosvall and Hicks—pass and cut options to Stewart, Milhorn and Gower—one-on-one checking out, Hirsch and Miller—increasing shooting range, Huggins and Gugat—defensive position.

**3:30–3:40**  Easy running floor length, change of pace and direction, defensive sliding, one on one (cutter), one on one (dribbler), inside turn reverse to receive pass, reverse turn and drive with imaginary ball, jumping.

**3:40–3:45**  Five man—Rebounding and passing.

**3:45–3:50**  Five man—Dribble and pivot.

**3:50–4:00**  Five man—Alternate post pass and cut options.

**4:00–4:15**  Three-man lane with one and two men alternating on defense, parallel lane, weave, pivot, front and side.

**4:15–4:25**  Shooting—forwards, guards, and centers separately. Footwork to get free for pass, footwork to get open on drive or fake drive, footwork on shot.

**4:25–4:35**  Strong-side defense.

**4:35–4:40**  Ball handling—weak side post attack without shot.

**4:40–4:50**  Offensive pattern—guard to post, guard to forward for strong side options.

**4:50–4:55**  Three-on-two conditioner.

**4:55–5:10**  Team fast break. One-on-one defense.

**5:10–5:25**  Half-court scrimmage—starters on defense and then fast break.

**5:25–5:40**  Half-court scrimmage—starters on offense.

**5:40–5:45**  Free throws at all six baskets.

*DAY BEFORE A WEEKEND CONFERENCE SERIES:*

**3:00–3:30**  Each player makes five free throws at each of five baskets. Special attention: Slaughter for key area shots, Cunningham and Blackman on cutback and "key" block shot, Green and Hazzard on defensive sliding and combating pressure, Waxman on defensive rebounding.

**3:30–3:40** Inside turn, inside turn and reverse to get open, reverse with an imaginary ball, each guard with a ball—working with forwards and centers on reverse and the screen and roll.

**3:40–3:50** Weak-side post options with and without the shot.

**3:50–4:00** Brush up the defense of the "back door" and the center to the weak side.

**4:00–4:10** Shooting—fake drive and set, fake set and drive for jumper. Three groups in competition.

**4:10–4:25** Review and stress important points of our full defensive plan.

**4:25–4:40** Run our offensive patterns and apply a quick press, after we score—no defense.

**4:40–4:50** Review our special set and out of bounds plays.

**4:50–5:00** Team fast break.

**5:00–** Free throws—one team at a basket. Shoot two and move. When a team makes ten in succession, they are through. After they shower, all report to the training room for evening and game day instructions.

*MONDAY FOLLOWING A WEEKEND SERIES:*

**3:00–3:30** Each player makes five free throws at each of five baskets. Work some more with Slaughter and Stewart. Compliment each player individually for his fine play, but also call attention to his mistakes and advise them as to what we can expect on this weekend.

**3:30–3:35** Five-man floor-length weave with a floor shot and team-rebound balance. Use three teams.

**3:35–3:45** Weak-side post attack—keep moving ball in and out with no shooting until I give the signal. Fast ball-handling and sharp cutting.

**3:45–3:55** Shooting—three groups for: lay-up after head fake, hook, lay-back, reach-back, quick stop and fadeaway. Work back and forth from each side of floor.

**3:55–4:05** Run team offense with entire group together and alternating. Mix up options more when we hit forwards on first pass.

**4:05–4:15** Team fast break.

**4:15–5:00** Scrimmage for all those who did not play very much on weekend. None for Cunningham, Blackman, and Green, considerable for Slaughter and a little for Hazzard. Those not scrimmaging work on free throws or special assignments.

*NORMAL WEDNESDAY IN THE MIDDLE OF THE SEASON:*

**3:00–3:25** Loosen up and shoot free throws as usual. Individual attention: Slaughter—moves and shots from key area, Waxman—checking out on defense and keeping hands up, Hazzard and Green against California type pressure by Milhorn and Huggins, Cunningham and

Blackman on special shot areas for the Cal defense. Others as assigned.

**3:25–3:35** Three lines for floor-length easy running, change of pace and direction, defensive sliding, one-on-one variations, reverse footwork to get open, reverse drive with imaginary ball.

**3:35–3:45** Team ball-handling—weak-side post. No shots for five minutes.

**3:45–3:55** Three-man lane—front and side, long pass—vary defense.

**3:55–4:05** Strong side defense.

**4:05–4:15** Three-on-three, start at center line and use a full-court break vs. full-court press when defense gets ball.

**4:15–4:25** Quick shooting—set and jump. Three-team competitive with two balls and two rebounders.

**4:25–4:35** Free throws. Competitive teams. Work for ten in succession.

**4:35–4:45** Defense the California offense as on Tuesday.

**4:45–4:55** Offensive patterns vs. live defense.

**4:55–5:05** Team fast break vs. 2-1-2 defense and 2-2-1 defense.

**5:05–5:20** Dummy scrimmage—starters on defense and fast break when they obtain possession.

**5:20–5:35** Dummy scrimmage—starters on offense and press when they lose possession.

**5:35–** Line up for free throws. Make two in succession or go to the end of the line.

# EQUIPMENT

The coach has the responsibility of providing within the limits of his budget the best equipment possible if he expects maximum results. He also has the further responsibility to see that the players are properly taught to care for the equipment and to wear the items that are to be worn. The appearance and durability of almost every item of equipment can be improved and extended immeasurably with just a little extra effort and cooperation of the players, but the coach must set the example and provide the proper leadership and instruction for this.

It is surprising how many players do not know how to wear their equipment properly and how careless they will become about their appearance if the coach does not assume the proper responsibility in this regard. The wrinkles must be smoothed out of their sock feet, the shoes must be laced snugly but not tightly, the shirt tails must be tucked in, the supporter must be kept smooth, the hair and fingernails must be kept short, equipment must be hung up properly when not in use, the shoes must be spread open to air and dry out when not in use, and the balls must not be misused or abused.

**1.** Personal practice equipment should be the same for all as far as style, condition, and color are concerned and should be kept clean, soft, and flexible. Clean socks, supporter, and towel should be furnished every day and clean pants and shirt if possible. We prefer and supply our players as follows:

**(a)** Pants. A good quality cotton pants with an elastic top and with legs loose enough that they give the thighs complete freedom.

**(b)** Shirt. A good quality sleeveless cotton shirt that will absorb perspiration and wear well. I like for the shoulder straps to be the approximate width of those on our game uniforms.

**(c)** Supporter. A good quality elastic with a mesh pouch.

**(d)** Socks. We like our players to wear two pairs of good quality socks of approximately 50 per cent wool. Next to the shoes, this is the most important part of the players' personal equipment. Players should be shown the proper way to put on their socks to avoid wrinkles.

**(e)** Shoes. We want excellent quality shoes that have the best traction for quick starting and stopping and changing direction and pace, that have a good arch and inner sole construction that make them comfortable and easy on the feet, they have a last construction that permit them to fit snugly without pinching, as light as possible, and as durable as possible. We like the shoes to be a one-half size smaller than the street shoe as we do not want the foot to slide in the shoe when quick stops are made. As far as equipment is concerned, the shoes are unquestionably the most important item as they are essential for quick maneuvering and for keeping the feet in good condition.

**(f)** Sweat suits. We like each player to be issued a cotton sweat suit of good quality, but we do not want it worn except under our direction. Practice conditions and physical condition may determine when it should be worn.

**2.** General equipment for practice.

**(a)** An ample supply of good, clean, properly inflated basketballs. These must be well cared for and kept as new as possible. We like to supplement them occasionally with a new one to be used for scrimmage or half-court dummy scrimmage. Although they are all in use at the same time for only a short time on any day, we like to have twelve good balls available for practice.

**(b)** We like to have a dozen scrimmage vests of the color of our travel uniforms, and about eight each in the color of our conference opponents. They must be kept clean and dry.

**(c)** A dressing room with a large locker for each player and good shower and toilet facilities are very desirable.

**(d)** Each player should be furnished a clean towel every day.

**3.** Game equipment. A neat attractive game uniform can be an asset in the development of pride. The uniforms should be colorful without being gaudy. Some coaches feel that dull game uniforms induce dull play. Although this isn't necessarily true, attractive and well-fitting clothes always seem to add spirit to the wearer.

**(a)** Game pants. I prefer a tackle twill material of excellent quality with an attached belt and an elastic back. They must be full cut and not binding and yet fit nicely. The V-cut on the legs provides more freedom for players with heavily muscled thighs. I like to have the pants trimmed with a contrasting color down the sides and, perhaps, around the leg holes with some contrast on the waist.

**(b)** Game shirts. A fine quality of tightly knit rayon Durene appeals to me a little more than other fabrics. I like a double trim around the neck and arm holes. The numbers and lettering should be of the same tackle twill from which the pants are made. If possible, we try to number our guards from 20 to 25, our centers from 30 to 35, our forwards from 50 to 55, and use 40 to 45 wherever needed. We don't use numbers 21, 31, 41, or 51. Eight-inch numbers are preferable on the back and six-inch numbers on the front.

**(c)** Game warmup. The material for these may be determined by the likely temperatures in the gymnasiums or field houses where you will be playing most of your games. As a general rule the material should meet the following specifications—be warm, be light and flexible, be durable, have a backing that will not cause the skin to itch, and be attractive. I prefer an elastic top on the pants and long, heavy zippers on the legs that won't catch and will permit the player to get out of them in a hurry. As a general rule, I prefer a jacket with a snap or button front. I like a knit collar and cuff with contrasting stripes interwoven and a contrasting stripe down the outside of the leg of the pants. It is a courtesy to the fans and opponents to have the name or number on the back of the jacket and some school insignia on the front.

**(d)** Game warmup balls. We place six new balls in each of two separate ball bags at the beginning of the season and use them as warmup balls for ourselves and the visiting team throughout the year. They are not used at any other time or for any other occasion during the season. These twelve balls will be the primary practice balls that we will use for the start of the following year.

**(e)** Game ball. We usually use a new game ball for about three games and then put it in with our daily practice balls.

## TRAINING AND CONDITIONING

This refers to those practices that prepare the players for efficient performance and healthful living.

Basketball is a tough game and the players must be in excellent physical, mental, and moral condition if they are going to be able to do their best. It is doubtful if any other game is as strenuous because of the emphasis placed on constant movement, quick stops and starts, sudden changes of direction and pace, jumping, reaching, and considerable unavoidable body contact as well as spills and running on a hardwood floor. Furthermore, there is little protective equipment worn.

Therefore, a coach has a moral obligation to see that his players are physically fit and properly conditioned to stand the strain without impairing their health. This obligation is as important as the fact that excellent condition will greatly enhance the chances of individual and team success. Fundamentals and poise leave you in direct proportion to your physical condition. Other things being equal, the best conditioned team will usually win if they have forced the play and kept the pressure on to give their superior condition an opportunity to take effect.

Condition is further discussed under the five basic and other important principles.

Some of the things that should be considered and action taken in regard to training and conditioning are as follows:

**1.** *Medical examinations.*
   **(a)** Every player should have a complete physical examination before the first practice.
   **(b)** Each player should be checked for hernia, heart, lungs, ears, nose, throat, teeth, blood pressure, eyes, and feet.

**2.** *Colds.* More practice time will be lost because of the common cold than for any other reason. Although varying climatic conditions in different sections of the country may necessitate somewhat different methods of prevention and cure, some of the things that we try to consider and do are as follows:
   **(a)** Give the players cold shots as soon as practice opens and vitamin pills daily.
   **(b)** Instruct them about proper dress.
   **(c)** Instruct them to rub down briskly after they shower and to dry their hair well.
   **(d)** Try to get them to eat plenty of fruits and vegetables and to drink a lot of water and fruit juices.
   **(e)** Keep them out of drafts, especially when they are warm.
   **(f)** Try to keep them moving easily for a while after a hard drill.
   **(g)** Keep a close check on their physical condition at all times. At the first symptom of a cold, don't tire them out too much and weaken their resistance.

**3.** *Feet.* The feet take a hard pounding in the necessary execution of all the quick moves required on both offense and defense on a hard floor and must be watched carefully.
   **(a)** Make certain that the shoes are properly fitted and laced as described in another section.

**(b)** The socks should be changed every day and always put on with care. All wrinkles must be smoothed out.

**(c)** The feet should be dried well after the shower and then sprinkled with a good foot powder. The area between the toes should be dried with care.

**(d)** The feet should be carefully toughened and conditioned early. We use Tufskin, tannic acid, tincture of benzoin, and foot powder.

**(e)** The best method of preventing *athlete's foot* is by having clean, disinfected showers and locker room and by keeping the feet clean and dry. Our most effective treatment has been the use of a ten per cent solution of salicylic acid to prevent spreading and daily use of a healing ointment.

**4.** *Floor burns.*

**(a)** Disinfect and insist on cleanliness.

**(b)** Keep them open to the air as much as possible, but use a healing ointment and sterile pad to avoid contact with a dyed material.

**5.** *Blisters.*

**(a)** Do not puncture unless there seems to be infection or too much pressure. If necessary, puncture from outside into the blister area.

**(b)** When they are open, remove all loose skin, disinfect, and keep open to the air as much as possible.

**(c)** When covered, use a healing ointment and a small pad.

**6.** *Ankles.*

**(a)** Cloth wraps properly wound will help prevent sprains and are worth the time and effort.

**(b)** It is wise to tape daily for the rest of the season after a bad sprain.

**(c)** A sprain should be immediately cold-packed, with ice if possible, for about thirty minutes and then wrapped tightly to prevent swelling. Change tape daily and exercise as much as you can. Try to walk without limping, and keep it loose and rotating when you are seated.

**(d)** In case of the least doubt, have a sprain x-rayed immediately.

**7.** *Shin splints.*

**(a)** The best treatment seems to be heat and rest.

**(b)** The use of foot pads and special taping can help.

**8.** *Weight.* Keep a daily weight chart of their weight before and after practice. Once condition has been acquired, the weight in and out should be fairly consistent each day. Some players will normally lose more than others, but as long as each is consistent there is no problem. Investigate any unusual changes.

**9.** *Staleness*—mental and/or physical.

**(a)** Symptoms—lack of pep, irritability, poor appetite, lack of stamina, undue carelessness, haggard expression, poor fundamental execution.

**(b)** Possible causes—lack of sleep, a physical disorder, extra study, worry, irregular or poor diet, family trouble, embarrassment, lack of competition or too much intense competition.

**(c)** Possible cures—a day off from practice, limited practice, improved diet, more sleep, rearranged work and study schedule, talking out the problem, encouragement, varying the daily practice schedule, release the tension.

**10.** *Weight training.* Although I have not been an advocate of weight training for basketball players, as I want their muscles loose and wiry and am concerned that weight training may make them bulgy, in recent years I have become convinced that a carefully planned and supervised program can be helpful. The program must be designed in such a manner that it will not be detrimental to finesse and maneuverability, which constitute the real beauty of basketball.

The coach should seek the advice of specialists in this field and explain specifically what he wants developed. Sometimes the player may become more interested in building the "body beautiful" than in developing areas that will result in improved efficiency as a player. It must be the responsibility of the coach to see that a proper program is devised and followed.

I firmly believe that many of my daily practice drills took care of the development of our jumping ability and were very instrumental in the development of proper timing without which neither strength nor jumping ability can be exploited. In addition to our daily five-minute "ante over" rebound drill, our rebound and pass-out drill, and our contact rebound drills, further development came in the first ten minutes of our daily practice during which we would do approximately fifteen imaginary jump shots, ten imaginary offensive tips, ten imaginary offensive rebounds, followed by one or two "pumps" and then a power shot, ten imaginary strong defensive rebounds, ten imaginary jump ball tips, five finger tip push ups (repeat five times during the practice session), and several quick starts and stops.

**11.** *Other training devices.* Since I believe, for the most part, that you learn the fundamentals of basketball and how to play the game by practicing and playing basketball, I do not use many other training devices. On their own time I encourage some players to skip rope, do some special jumping and running, do some running up and down steps, perform various reaction and agility tests, work on a prescribed weight program, play some volleyball, and some other things that may help them. I do not believe in giving up any of our regular practice time for any of them.

**12.** As it is unlikely that the coach is a doctor, or an accomplished trainer, or a specialist in weight training, he should seek advice and help from experts in those fields when needed as he would in any other. However, the coach must have a general idea about many things and may know considerable about some. Do not be ashamed or embarrassed to seek help. After all, you are interested in getting results in the quickest and best way as long as it is ethical and honest.

## TRAINING RULES

A dogmatic set of training rules is a questionable practice, although some coaches have had good results from them. They might be more practical and enforceable in small communities than they would be in larger cities where there are many more activities. However, a common-sense, reasonable list of suggestions with a few demands that can be followed should be a good practice.

I follow the latter practice, but permit the players themselves to make up the list under my supervision. It has been my experience that they will make up a more restrictive list of rules than I would feel like forcing upon them. Furthermore, I can gain some stature with them by, perhaps, eliminating one or two that they might suggest and by offering them the opportunity of immediately eliminating any one that they feel they can't or won't follow.

In order to keep their respect, you must strictly enforce rules once they have been agreed upon.

Sufficient sleep (at least eight hours), a balanced diet at regular intervals, sufficient water and juices, proper exercises, no smoking or use of alcoholic beverages repeated long enough should produce good physical condition, and will, if there are no constitutional or organic weaknesses.

It is the responsibility of the coach to see that the players get the proper amount of work to be in the best condition to accomplish the most in his system of play, but it is the responsibility of the players to do all the things that they can that are essential to their best efforts. The players must have the desire and will power to make the necessary sacrifices on their own volition and not because of any outside pressure forcing them; however, the coach may be very instrumental in instilling this desire in them.

Copies of each of the following lists regarding condition and the training suggestions and demands that the players helped to prepare are examples that are posted on our bulletin board and given to each player after the final squad has been selected and the ideas have been agreed upon. Each player again must agree on them or drop from the squad.

### UCLA BASKETBALL
### JOHN WOODEN, HEAD COACH

*RE: CONDITION*

1. Success is built on fine condition. Fundamentals and form leave you as you begin to lose condition. Train and obey the rules as conscientiously as possible. Be honest with yourself and with all who are depending upon you.
2. Never think of your bruises or fatigue. If you are tired, think of how "all in" your opponent may be.
3. It is the hard work you do in practice after you are "all in" that improves your condition. Force yourself when you are tired.

4. Make it your personal objective to be in better condition than any opponent that you will oppose.
5. Condition is attained by what you do both on and off the floor.
6. Your mental and moral condition will determine your physical condition, if you are industrious.

**UCLA BASKETBALL**
**JOHN WOODEN, HEAD COACH**

*TRAINING SUGGESTIONS:*

1. At least eight regular hours of sleep each night.
2. In bed by 10:30 the night prior to a game.
3. In bed as soon as possible after a game, when we are playing the following night.
4. Eat balanced meals, at regular hours, with a minimum of eating between meals.
5. Drink plenty of water, milk, and fruit juices.
6. Relax for a while after eating.
7. Take care of your health—mental, moral, and physical.
8. Force yourself to keep running and working hard when you are tired in order to improve your condition.
9. Earn the right to be proud and confident of your condition.
10. Practice moderation with good judgment in all ways.

*TRAINING DEMANDS: Denial of privileges will be the penalty for failure to comply.*

1. No use of alcoholic beverages, drugs, or steroids of any kind.
2. No smoking.
3. No use of profanity.
4. Be polite and courteous to everyone.
5. Be on time whenever time is involved.

Success can only come to you as an individual from self-satisfaction in knowing that you gave everything to become the best that you are capable of becoming. Perfection can never be attained, but it must be the goal.

Others may have more ability than you, they may be larger, faster, quicker, better jumpers, better shooters, but no one should be your superior in respect to team spirit, loyalty, enthusiasm, cooperation, determination, industriousness, fight, effort, and character.

# SELECTING THE SQUAD

This is always an important task and usually one of the most difficult that a coach must do.

## DETERMINING FACTORS

There are many things to consider before definitely deciding on your final selection, but I believe that five are most important.

**1.** Determining your best players.

**2.** Determining the proper position for each player.

**3.** Determining the correct combination to make up your strongest unit.

**4.** Determining the first-line replacements and possible realignment of positions to maintain the strongest team strength when changes are necessary.

**5.** Determining the proper players and the exact number necessary for the best results.

## INDIVIDUAL CHARACTERISTICS TO CONSIDER

These may vary according to your system of play, but the following are always important:

**1.** Quickness and speed in relation to those who will be playing the same position. I consider controlled quickness to be the most important physical attribute of any athlete.

**2.** Size and jumping ability. It isn't how tall you are, but how tall you play.

**3.** Coordination and balance.

**4.** Experience.

**5.** Fight, determination, courage, desire.

**6.** Ball-handling and -shooting ability.

**7.** Industriousness.

**8.** Enthusiasm.

**9.** Cooperation and team attitude.

**10.** Self-control.

**11.** Alertness.

**12.** Remaining years of eligibility. You must prepare for the future without sacrificing the present.

Be completely impartial and give every player the chance that he deserves and the opportunity that he earns.

Consider team spirit and morale. The five best players seldom make the best team.

Keep as many players as possible. Too small a squad can be a handicap as well as too large a squad.

Be constantly alert for the players who play well under pressure and those who cannot take pressure.

**FIGURE 2-1** Henry Bibby (#45), a six-footer, challenging Artis Gil-more (#53), a seven-footer, on a drive against Jacksonville in a NCAA championship game.

Be alert for potential troublemakers and get rid of them before they infect others if you cannot correct them within a reasonable period of time.

Although the final decision for selecting the squad must be the re-sponsibility of the coach and the coach alone, he should use every possible method to aid him in making the correct decision. Do not be reluctant or too proud to seek helpful information from every available source. In addition to taking into consideration the previously men-tioned items and characteristics, I look for additional help in the follow-ing ways:

**1.** Keeping complete statistical charts of every scrimmage and analyzing them in a comparative manner. (Examples of two of these statistical charts which we also keep for our games will follow this section.)

**FIGURE 2-2** Dave Meyers (#34) expressing his determination against Kentucky in the 1975 Championship game.

**2.** Discussing and rediscussing every candidate for the squad with my assistant coaches and co-workers.

**3.** Obtaining as much information as possible from previous coaches of the players.

**4.** Having the squad rate each other and themselves in comparison with all other squad members. (An example of this rating chart will follow this section.) I make a composite rating chart from the results of the entire squad and compare this composite against my own individual rating chart and those of my assistants. In compiling the composite, I discard any obviously far-out-of-place ranking and substitute for it what is the average.

# AWARDS

The selection of the award winners is another important and difficult task that the coach must perform or supervise. He must not lose sight of the fact that these awards have great meaning to the youngsters. Whether or not it is right, the fact remains that among the young people of our school society, the awards earned in athletics carry a certain amount of prestige.

The coach is obligated to be accurate, fair, and impartial in the making or supervising of these awards. He also has the responsibility of teaching his players to place the proper value on the awards and to accept them with pride and yet in a humble manner.

The players must be taught to understand that no special privileges go with an award. The award in itself merely serves as concrete evidence of a job well done. However, all players should be participating for the pleasure that they themselves receive from the game, and not for any tangible evidence to prove something to others or to themselves.

Participation in athletics should be a privilege, not an obligation. The players should be helped to understand and appreciate the fact that, although they may be encouraged, they are not compelled to try out for a team but are permitted to do so. Their satisfaction from the game can never be very genuine if their principal reason for being a member of the team is due to social, parental, coach, or self-imposed pressure. Unless the desire to play comes from the personal enjoyment and satisfaction that they receive from participation in the activity itself, they should seek some other extracurricular activity regardless of any tangible awards.

A few suggestions that can be helpful in the selection of award winners are as follows:

## LETTER OR MONOGRAM AWARDS

**1.** Have a definite awards system recorded and follow it.

**2.** The system should provide some leeway for seniors who have been on the squad in previous years and have failed to accumulate the required amount of playing time.

**3.** The system should specifically state the amount of required playing time for each particular award.

**4.** The system should permit the consideration of extraordinary circumstances in special cases.

**5.** The coach must be consistent in his consideration of all factors that are of a subjective nature.

**6.** Keep the major award a cherished one and try to avoid every possibility that might cheapen it.

## SPECIAL AWARDS

These can get out of hand through the interest and efforts of well-meaning friends and alumni if they are not carefully administered.

**1.** Although the coach should serve in an advisory capacity, he should have no hand in the actual selection of the special award winners.

**2.** If there is no concrete or objective way in selecting a winner, it is wise to permit the squad to have a strong hand in the selection. At least their opinion should be one of the determining factors. However, I believe it wise to make their voting by secret ballot.

**3.** There should be awards for abilities and traits other than scoring.

**4.** In addition to having his name engraved on a permanent-type trophy that will remain on display, each winner should be presented with a smaller duplicate or something concrete to have, to hold, and to keep.

**5.** Any trophy that immediately limits the opportunities of any position to earn it is not desirable.

**6.** Possible ideas: most valuable player, most unselfish player, best free-throw shooter (require a minimum number of attempts), best defensive, best first-year man, most improved from a previous year, leading rebounder, leader in combined offensive and defensive assists.

These are merely ideas and do not imply that there are not other good ones or that you should use all of these.

# PUBLIC RELATIONS

## ADMINISTRATION

You must have the cooperation of those in administrative positions if you are to accomplish all that you should. Be loyal to them and they will be with you. Remember that an ounce of loyalty is worth a pound of cleverness. Your success or failure will also reflect on them and you would not have the job if they were not with you.

## FACULTY

If you want to be accepted on equal footing with the rest of the faculty, earn that privilege. Too many coaches in the history of athletics did not warrant that acceptance and that fact has hurt the entire profession. You are no better or worse than the other members of the faculty, but the very nature of your profession puts you in the public eye. Your fellow members of the faculty can and will be of immeasurable help to you, if you cultivate their friendship.

## FELLOW COACHES

There is no greater compliment for a coach than to be held in high esteem by his fellow coaches. Furthermore, there should be something that you can learn that will be of help to you from everyone and especially from fellow coaches. Although it is important to avoid cliques, certainly you should find much pleasure and satisfaction in the association and friendship of your fellow coaches.

## PARENTS OF THE PLAYERS

The better you know the parents of your players, the better you will be able to understand and help your players. Also, the parents can be of much help to you if you can get their cooperation. Remember that both of you are vitally interested in the performance of the player. Be careful that you play no favorites among the parents just the same as you must play no favorites among your players.

## THE PRESS—SPORTSWRITERS AND SPORTSCASTERS

It will be to your advantage to go out of your way to cooperate with the press. Work to gain their confidence and they will keep yours. Your administration, the players, other coaches, and all must do their part, but it is the responsibility of the coach to see that it is done. Never condemn the press as a group because you might occasionally find one who will betray a confidence. Coaches, too, make mistakes, and you should not judge nor be judged by the mistakes of others.

## OTHERS

Never lose sight of the fact that you are just a person who has been employed to do the best job that you are capable of doing in the position for which you have been hired. However, unlike many positions you are in the public eye more than most and must act accordingly. You can be helped or hurt immeasurably by your acceptance and treatment of other people.

In addition to those in the administration, the faculty, your fellow coaches, parents, and the press, you are either closely associated or dependent, in many respects, on the secretarial staff, janitorial staff, and almost every person in town who has an interest in your school, your players, and in you yourself. If you will follow the principle of The Golden Rule, you will not only enhance your chances of improvement, but you will be doing the same for others at the same time.

Respect must be given where respect is due and appreciation must be acknowledged when it is due, but the coach who attempts to follow the "Rank Has Its Privileges" philosophy is, in my opinion, a poor example of what we need to help shape the character of the youth of America.

# GAME ORGANIZATION

## PREPARING THE TEAM MENTALLY

A team must start a game in the proper frame of mind if it is going to be able to come close to doing the best it is capable of doing. I want our players to respect every opponent but fear none. I want confidence that can come only from the knowledge that they are prepared and in good condition, but I do not want cockiness or overconfidence. However, I must admit that I would rather have a team a little overconfident than afraid and lacking in confidence.

Our players are told over and over again that I am not worried about our opponents, but about what we will do ourselves. They are told that everything will be fine if, at the end of every game, each boy can honestly answer to himself that he did his best to be prepared for the game and did his best in the game.

In preparing for an opponent we go over their style of both offense and defense, determine what their strengths and weaknesses will be against us and how to counteract or exploit each, and try to be prepared for anything, offensively and defensively, that might be needed.

I emphasize my ideas on how we should attempt to control the game of our opponents and how our game will work against them. Patience is stressed in order that they will not panic if things do not go well early in the game. It is my theory that I want our opponents to have to worry about stopping us and our concern to be mainly in the development of our own game.

In other words, I believe in the positive approach and do not want our players to think negatively.

They are conditioned to keep the pressure on their opponents at all times. I want them to sincerely feel that they are in better condition than any opponent, but they must make their opponent work hard for the first three quarters of the game in order that such superior condition will have an effect in the last quarter of the game, which is the time it really counts.

Since I believe that for every mental, emotional, and physical peak there will be a corresponding valley, the coach should not attempt to get the players too high for any particular game. The importance of the game itself should be enough stimulation and any artificial method used by the coach is not likely to have a positive effect that will not be negated by a corresponding negative effect.

In my opinion, a team will stay closer to their level of competency if a conscious effort is made to avoid both peaks and valleys than when an occasional effort is made to arouse them to a special height.

Furthermore, if the players have been aroused too many times during the regular season, it will be most difficult to have them at near peak efficiency for tournament play at the end of the season when the quality of the competition will require their being at that level for several games in succession. Sudden death tournament play permits no valley.

## PREPARING THE TEAM PHYSICALLY

The daily practice sessions will largely determine the physical condition of the players providing you have also placed sufficient emphasis on their mental and moral condition.

Since our game schedule usually has us playing every Friday and Saturday, our lightest workouts are on Mondays and Thursdays and our hardest workouts are on Tuesdays and Wednesdays, once our regular playing season has opened.

**Monday.** We go over the mistakes in our games of the previous weekend; discuss the strengths, weaknesses, and game plan of our next opponent or opponents; do considerable shooting, ball-handling, and running, but have very few, if any, contact drills; and have a good game-condition scrimmage for those who did not get to play very much the previous weekend. The players who played the majority of the time may scrimmage a little, but will all shoot a number of free throws while the others are scrimmaging.

**Tuesday and Wednesday.** These will be hard practice days, and we will do considerable half-court scrimmaging to prepare us both offensively and defensively for our coming oponents. We will also work on the perfection of all phases of our game—the fundamentals, our regular offense, our regular defense, our press, our counter for the press, our zone attack, our game for protecting the lead, our fast break, jump-ball situations in all circles, offensive and defensive foul-lane assignments, and out-of-bounds and other special plays.

**Thursday.** Review our game plan in regard to our opponents' offense and defense, considerable shooting of all kinds, work on our lead-protection game, work on our plays, use several running drills but have very little contact work. Work to perfect timing in our team play.

The players are told to get in bed early on this night and are instructed to do a minimum of basketball talk with their friends.

We do very little full-court, regular-game scrimmaging after our playing season has opened, except a good scrimmage each Monday for those who do not get to play very much. I feel that too much competitive scrimmage during the week may take the competitive edge away from the boys who do the majority of the playing when it really counts, and I want them mentally, emotionally, and physically ready and eager to play in the games.

I try to keep as close to our regular routine as possible at all times without placing any unnatural or artificial stress on the playing of the games. That should come naturally and need no excess stress or prodding from the coach.

## PREGAME PROCEDURE

**Eating.** Many coaches differ in regard to when and what to eat, and I am very doubtful as to what is the best procedure. However, I have been fairly well satisfied with the results from feeding our players a substantial meal to be completed four hours prior to the start of the game.

This meal usually consists of a ten-to-twelve-ounce steak broiled medium or an equivalent portion of lean roast beef, a small baked potato, a green vegetable, three pieces of celery, four small slices of melba toast, some honey, hot tea, and a dish of fruit cocktail.

Occasionally, I let a player eat as he thinks best.

**Resting.** After eating, I want our players to take a ten-minute walk and then get off their feet until it is time to leave for the game. I prefer them to lie down in a darkened room to try to sleep and forget about the game. If they cannot sleep, I still want them in a darkened room, and they are not to read, study, watch television, or do anything that will strain their eyes during this period. They may have a roommate, but I do not want them visiting with anyone else during this period.

Prior to meeting for the pregame meal, they are on their own for the early part of the day. However, they are requested to stay off their feet as much as possible and to try and eat a substantial breakfast at about ten o'clock. It is my feeling that these two meals are enough for them before they play on a game day. I am thoroughly convinced that they are better off on game day to be underfed rather than overfed.

**Reporting Time.**   The players are to report to the dressing room in time to get their necessary taping done and to be dressed forty minutes prior to game time, but not to be there before then. I would rather that they rest until the last moment.

When we are playing at home, I usually permit them to arrive in time to watch the last ten minutes of the first half of the preliminary game, but they go directly to the dressing room when the preliminary teams return to the floor at half-time.

I want them to dress quietly and to go to our pregame meeting room and get off of their feet as soon as they are dressed. During this period I like to have the lights low, and we may have some soft music, which will be turned off as soon as I come in to give the team their pregame instructions. I always talk to different players individually prior to addressing the team as a group.

They should take care of any lavatory needs before my group talk and there should be neither a hilarious or morbid atmosphere. I want them business-like and serious, but not stern, gruff, or sour.

**Pre-Game Talk.**   For ten minutes before we take the floor, I review our overall game plan and answer any questions that they may have. Earlier I have been talking to specific individuals about their individual assignments.

Their defensive assignments are repeated and briefly discussed, the opening tip and our out-of-bounds setups are reviewed, they are reminded to accept the decisions of the officials in the proper manner and to raise their hands on personal foul calls, bench conduct is reviewed and they are reminded to do nothing but cheer their teammates and to study the game in order to be ready when and if they are called upon, the warmup plan is reviewed, and they are reminded that all I expect is for them to be able to answer to themselves when the game is over.

This is definitely not a fight or a pep talk, but a constructive briefing for the game. We will not leave the room until the floor is clear and will go out calmly and quietly, although quickly, without a lot of commotion and false chatter.

### Warmup

**1.** Pair up in groups of three and pass the ball for about two minutes to get the feel of it. Start rather slowly and finish snappily.

**2.** Start the cutting drills that have been assigned. These should consist of passing and cutting from each side, and from the front for fast-moving shots underneath and then for various jump shots.

**3.** Some dribble drives for both underneath and jump shots.

**4.** Two starters take the free-throw line with one shooting and the other retrieving. The others pair up according to their position and work on the types of shots that they have been getting in game competition.

As soon as the free-throw shooters get their rhythm and feel confident, they move out and designate the next ones to take the line. The starters and those others who play the most should be the first ones on the free-throw line.

There should never be more than three men to a ball, preferably only two, but no player should have a ball to himself while the entire dressing squad is warming up.

Usually, we do not leave the floor before the start of a game, but will have only the starting team, and perhaps one other, shooting alone for the last three or four minutes before the start. At this time each player may have a ball.

### DURING THE GAME

There are a number of things that must be taken into consideration during the progress of a game if the team is to perform as efficiently as their ability warrants, and the wise coach will be alert in regard to them.

**Players on the Bench.** They must be taught to cheer, encourage, instruct, warn, and advise their playing teammates on occasion, but refrain from making remarks to the officials, opposing players, or spectators. They should study the game and pay particular attention to the man that they are most likely to guard, the man who is most likely to be guarding them, and all situations from which advance knowledge may enable them to do a better job if and when they are called upon. They are not to be spectators, but students of the game.

**The Coach.** He must keep his wits about him and be alert to make any criticism or corrections necessary to improve the play of his team and the individuals on his team.

He should constantly be encouraging his team by word and action, but refrain from making personal remarks to the officials or the opponents. He must keep his self-control, but must let his players know by example that he is fighting for them at all times.

Players and coach must not expect or desire any favors, but should insist on their rights and fight for them. Know the rules and never argue or complain about something that you are not certain of yourself. When you are not certain, do not be too proud to ask and find out. Remember the moral of crying "Wolf" all of the time. Nothing can be gained from questioning a decision of judgement.

**Substitutions.** Do not substitute haphazardly. Know what you are doing when you make a change and do it for a purpose. Give a substitute confidence when he enters the game, but tell him it is best for a cold man to handle the ball once before taking a floor shot. Make a place for the man coming out to sit next to the coach in order that you may explain your reason for the substitution and help him.

The following situations or factors may call for a substitution.

1. To instruct a specific individual.
2. To rest a tired player.
3. To replace an injured player.
4. To improve the defense on a player who is hurting you.
5. To replace a player who is not doing well.
6. To develop reserve strength.
7. When a "pinch hitter" or special talent is needed.
8. To develop team morale and give all players a chance to perform when the outcome of a game is reasonably certain. Replace regulars one or two at a time.
9. To provide the best defense, offense, rebounding, ball control, or pressing team as the occasion demands.
10. For disciplinary reasons.
11. To match up, counteract, or offset the substitutions of an opponent.
12. To save a player in danger of fouling out.

**Time-Outs**

1. Reasons for:
   (a) To stop a rally by the opponent.

**(b)** In case of injury.
**(c)** For instructional purposes.
**(d)** To rest certain individuals.

**2.** Position. I have conflicting ideas about this, but usually have the playing five form a semicircle in front of me with their hands on their knees. The trainer wipes off the back of their necks with a damp towel, and the manager cleans the soles of their shoes. The other players form a semicircle behind the playing group.

I want the undivided attention of the players and want no one else to talk to them at all.

Occasionally, I have the playing five take seats alongside each other, and I face them with the others standing behind them.

**Assistant.** My assistant sits beside me and makes notes of things I mention, keeping a record of the personal fouls on the individuals of each team and the time-outs by each team, as the game progresses.

These notes are used during time-outs, during the half time, and for later reference.

## HALF-TIME PROCEDURE

The half-time procedure is divided into five periods as follows:

**1.** *Getting from floor to dressing room.* The players go quickly from the floor to the dressing room but take care of any lavatory needs on the way. The coaches look over the first-half statistics in private and discuss the plans for the second half before entering the dressing room. The managers get the equipment and hustle to open the dressing room and to get the oranges ready for the players, as we quarter a dozen oranges for the players to suck during the half-time period.

**2.** *Rest.* The playing group lie down or assume a restful position as soon as they get to the dressing room. The manager will pass the oranges as the trainer tends to the playing group. He checks them for injuries, rubs them off with a damp and then a dry towel, and gives their legs, arms, shoulders, neck and back a light massage. The players should be reasonably quiet, although they may quietly discuss any helpful facts of the first half. No outsiders are permitted in the dressing room.

**3.** *Correction.* The coach and his assistant talk to the players individually and make necessary corrections and suggestions. The criticism must be constructive. The assistant may use the board to diagram anything that may be needed next.

**4.** *Planning.* The coach now talks to the group as a team and makes corrections, suggestions, and criticisms of the first half. He must also commend the good things. Do not try to cover too much, but make certain that you have covered the pertinent things adequately. Announce the starting line up for the second half.

**5.** *Returning to the floor from the dressing room and getting ready to start.* The coach makes sure that the starters have all reported to the official scorer, checks the starting line up of the opponents, and reports the defensive assignments to each of his starters.

The coach must not be a raving maniac at half-time, but must keep his poise and make constructive criticisms of the first-half play and sound plans for the second-half play. There should be no fight talk. You may arouse them just prior to the tip-off, but not in the dressing room.

Be certain that your criticism is constructive and do not be reluctant to give praise where it has been earned.

## POSTGAME PROCEDURES

**1.** See the opposing coach and congratulate him in a nice manner if you lose, or make yourself available to graciously accept his congratulations if your team was the victor.

**2.** See your players for a moment and give them a "lift" or get their "feet on the ground" as the occasion demands. Also check any injuries. Have your assistant take over the supervision of the dressing room for the next few minutes while you step outside to meet with the reporters.

**3.** Meet with the reporters and cooperate with them to the best of your ability. On occasions you may have to see them before you see your players because of the deadlines that they have to meet. However, if it is at all possible, I believe that a coach should see his players first, if only for a minute, as they are his first responsibility. In many cases, however, you will be doing an injustice to your players if you fail to go out of your way and beyond the call of duty to cooperate with the press.

Do not permit defeat to make you bitter, critical, caustic, or sarcastic and do not let victory make you overbearing, conceited, arrogant or vain in anything you say or do.

Answer their questions according to the facts and knowledge that you have and not according to the way that you might think that they expect or want you to answer. If you give an honest opinion to all questions, you will seldom have cause to feel sorry afterward. Be yourself and do not try to be a comedian.

**4.** After the players have showered and dressed, I have a short meeting with them to give them their instructions for the night and whatever else they need to know before I see them again. These instructions vary according to whether or not we play the next day, whether it is a school day, and other similar factors.

The game is not rehashed at this time, although a few things may be briefly brought to their attention for them to think about.

I try to keep the team on an even course and tell them I do not want anyone to be able to tell the result of the game by their conduct or actions. If they have done their best, there should be no head hanging in defeat and no extra exuberance in victory. I want their heads up always.

Other reasons for keeping them for a while are to give the fans a chance to disperse, to give their hair a chance to dry, and to make certain that any other needs have been considered.

**5.** Since the players have eaten five or six hours earlier and are undoubtedly hungry, we have a sandwich, an orange, an apple, and some milk or a cold drink for them. However, we do not want them to have this until they have showered and are dressed. We hope this snack will take the edge off of their appetite and will encourage them to get to bed earlier than otherwise.

If we are on the road or are keeping the players in a hotel because of playing again the next night, we have a meal (soup, steak sandwich, large orange juice, fruit cocktail, ice cream, and milk or hot chocolate) set up for them when we get back to the hotel or to a convenient restaurant.

If we are at home and not keeping them in a hotel or are on the road and not playing the next night, we will give them money to eat on their own. However, on the road they must never go alone and are given a designated time to be in bed. They must be in bed with the lights out at the designated time, even if they cannot sleep.

**6.** Outsiders are not permitted in the dressing room before or after a game, although reporters may see the players after they are showered and dressed.

# SCOUTING

Since I probably scout opponents as little as any college coach in the country and definitely a lot less than any of the coaches in our own conference, my ideas may be a little different in this regard.

Although I would like to have a recent scouting report on every team we play, I like to have a scouting report on my own team several times a season. This report must not be from a friend or close acquaintance, but from a source that has no interest in my team except to provide an unbiased and neutral report.

I feel that there is a strong possibility of overlooking many things in your own team that may be obvious to an impartial scout. It has been said in one way or another that being too close to the scene may prevent you from "seeing the forest for the trees," and I feel this may happen in regard to your own team, but might be corrected by an impartial report.

Scouting means much more than merely getting information about the style and individual play of an opponent. It also means making an analysis of the information in relation to the effect that it will have on your own team. It is possible to have a wealth of information available, but be lacking in the ability to make sound analytical use of it.

I like to keep a record of the general style of play, offensively and defensively, of all of the coaches whose teams we are likely to play and then to supplement it each year with information mainly in regard to the personnel, although not forgetting that team style may also change some. However, I have noticed that most coaches make gradual changes in their team game, and, although their style may be considerably different from what it was ten years ago, it was never much different from one year to the next. It is rather easy to keep an up-to-date file on your conference opponents, as you see them so often and, since my principal emphasis is on conference play, this idea works well for me.

If convenient, I like to see each conference opponent before we play them, but, if it is not convenient or possible, I rely on a scouting bureau or a high school coach from the area where a game that I want scouted will be played. Since I truly believe that high school coaches, as a general rule, do a better job of coaching than do college coaches, there is reason to believe that they will do a good job of scouting, and they do.

## INFORMATION WANTED

There are a few specific things in which I am interested rather than a long complicated report. I would rather spend time preparing my team for a few pertinent things than having a great number of them. I consider it better to attempt to perfect the play of my own team in relation to the general style and a few individual habits of our opponents than to consider the complete detailed picture of the opponent.

For playing a nonconference opponent and any conference opponent the first time in any season, I am content with the following information.

### Team Offense

1. Are they a fast breaking team?
2. Do they ever try to make or take advantage of fast-break opportunities?
3. If they fast break, how do they prefer to start and finish the break?
4. How do they set up for their set offense?
5. What is the strength of their set offense?
6. Briefly describe the general style of their set offense.
7. Attempted variations.

## Team Defense

**1.** Is it man-to-man or zone?

**2.** If man-to-man, where is it tight and where is it loose?

**3.** If it is zone, what type of zone is it and how far out do they extend it?

**4.** If they press, what type of a press is it, and what is the general plan?

## Team in General

**1.** Can the guards take pressure?

**2.** Do they favor one side of the floor on offense?

**3.** Will they free-lance much or stay close to their regular pattern?

**4.** Diagram:
  **(a)** Their offensive positions.
  **(b)** Any set and out-of-bounds plays.
  **(c)** Their defensive positions.

## Individual Characteristics of Each

**1.** Physical—name, number, height, weight, position, speed, condition, temperament, right- or left-handed, poise.

**2.** Other characteristics.
  **(a)** From where does he score the most, on what type of shot, and how does he get open?
  **(b)** Is he more dangerous as a driver or as an outside shooter?
  **(c)** Does he favor driving to one side or the other?
  **(d)** How does he rebound?
  **(e)** Can he be faked?
  **(f)** Can he be pressed?
  **(g)** Briefly discuss his pet moves, strong points, and weaknesses.
  **(h)** Discuss their pivot man and his moves.
  **(i)** Do they reverse you and can they be reversed?
  **(j)** Any item of particular interest regarding any part of their play.

# TRIP ORGANIZATION

## PRELIMINARY PREPARATION

Before we make our first trip, a meeting is held with the entire squad and they are given instructions as to what will be expected of them on every trip. It is hoped that there will be no necessity for repeating them later and they will not be brought up again unless their actions make it necessary.

The following items are discussed.

## Personal Conduct

**1.** Since they are representatives of our school, and the school itself will be judged by their conduct far more than their play, they should conduct themselves as gentlemen at all times.

**2.** They are encouraged to have a good time and enjoy the trip, but to refrain from hilarity, loudness, wolf-whistling, or anything else that violates good manners and might annoy other traveling companions or hotel guests and bring discredit on their school or themselves.

**3.** They are expected to be very polite and courteous to everyone with whom they are in contact and especially so to traveling companions, bell boys, elevator operators, waitresses, and all other employees of the hotels or travel agencies.

## Dress

They are instructed to wear clothes that are clean and neat and appropriate for the anticipated weather conditions. There was a time when I required shirt and tie, suit or sport jacket and slacks, but this changed in the 1960s.

## Property of Others

**1.** They are cautioned to not be tempted to take any hotel property, such as towels, silver, ash-trays, etc. They may consider it as merely souvenirs, but it is actually stealing, and we want none of it.

**2.** They must treat the property of hotels, restaurants, and other schools as if it were their own, and pull no destructive tricks or do any roughhousing that may lead to property damage.

## Punctuality

**1.** They must be on time for buses, meals, meetings, and any other occasions where we get together as a group or they are asked to be individually. Plan to be a little early in order that something unforeseen or unexpected may not make you a little late.

**FIGURE 2-3** The 1965 NCAA Championship team. Note the clothing which was the acceptable dress at that time.

## Eating

**1.** They are told that they will be fed well and they must not eat between meals without checking with the coach or trainer.

**2.** When toast, butter, celery, and other foods are served family style, take only your proportionate share and do not be greedy and operate on a "first come, first get more" basis.

## Equipment

**1.** Each player must take proper care of his own equipment. Hang it up properly and do not leave it wadded up on the floor when you go to shower, fold it neatly and pack it properly in your traveling bag, spread it out to dry in your hotel room.

**2.** Except for during the time that you are in the game, you are responsible for your own equipment. The manager is not your personal valet, but merely to help as are the coaches and trainer. It is easy to lose equipment if you do not care, but very little will ever be lost if you do care.

### Dressing Rooms

**1.** Assist the manager and coaches in leaving our dressing and shower facilities in even better and cleaner condition than when we came.

**2.** Be sure that showers are turned off, soap is properly racked, the toilets are flushed, the dressing fixtures are in their proper places, and that there is no paper, tape, orange peels, or other refuse on the floor.

**3.** Be sure you place your towel in the proper container or place.

### Rest and Cooperation

**1.** Cooperate with the trainer, coach, and manager 100 per cent in all of their instructions or discuss it with the coach if there is some reason for deviation.

**2.** Have no guest in your room at any time when you are supposed to be resting.

### Study

**1.** Before leaving on a trip, be sure to discuss your impending absence from class with each professor and make satisfactory arrangements for the work that you will miss. *Make these arrangements in advance; do not wait to tell them after your return.*

**2.** Take some textbooks with you as there will always be some time for study.

**3.** Remember that basketball is an *extracurricular* activity, and your studies are the only real reason for your being in school, even though basketball may be providing you the necessary wherewithal.

### General Instructions

**1.** No poker playing or gambling of any type will be permitted at any time.

**2.** Do not visit with strangers and always be with at least one other teammate when you are outside your room.

**3.** No telephone calls will be permitted in or out of your rooms. All incoming calls must be cleared through the coach.

### SOME RESPONSIBILITIES OF THE COACH

**1.** Give each player a complete itinerary of the trip a day before you leave, but make certain that he understands the time and place of departure.

**2.** Keep the players occupied and together as much as possible, but give them some free time. Too much regimentation can bring on boredom and resentment. You must have some faith and confidence in them.

**3.** Provide proper entertainment for relaxation at the proper time.

**4.** Clear all incoming and outgoing phone calls of the players.

**5.** Be a leader, and set a fine example for the players in regard to dress, conduct, and manners.

**6.** Pair up the players for rooms to the best advantage. You should know your players and have specific reason for placing certain ones together and keeping certain ones separated. It may help prevent cliques from getting started by alternating roommates frequently where it can be done.

## DAY PROCEDURE

**Day Before a Game.** If we arrive at the hotel in the early afternoon the day before we play, and we try to do that, we may follow the following procedure:

**1.** Go directly to our rooms, get settled, and wash.

**2.** Stay in the rooms until notified the time to report in the lobby to leave for practice.

**3.** Go to the gym for a workout of an hour, which will consist primarily of shooting, getting the feel of the floor by running and dribbling drills, and brushing up on the timing and teamwork of our fast break and set offense.

**4.** After returning to our hotel, the players go to their rooms until it is time to report for dinner.

**5.** After dinner, we usually take a short walk and go to a good movie if one is available. If the players prefer, they may stay in the hotel and study, but they must not leave or have any visitors in their rooms.

**6.** After the show, we return to the hotel and go directly to bed.

**Game Day.** Assume the game is at 8:00 P.M.

**1.** Have the players called at 9:15 A.M.

**2.** Meet in the lobby, properly dressed, at 9:55 and go to the dining room for breakfast at 10:00. Breakfast menu: large glass of orange juice, choice of cereal (preferably oatmeal) with half milk and half cream, two eggs to order, bacon or ham, three slices of buttered toast per person with side of jelly, and a drink of coffee, tea, hot chocolate, or milk.

**3.** After breakfast the players are excused until 12:30. They must be with at least one other teammate at all times.

**4.** At 12:30 the players are to be in their rooms to be off their feet until they report to the lobby at 3:30 to proceed to the dining room and complete their pregame meal four hours prior to game time.

The procedure on game day from and including the pregame meal on has been discussed earlier in this chapter and need not be repeated here.

# STRATEGY

The coach who believes that he can consistently outsmart his opponents or that he is a master strategist and can depend on strategy to win his ball games is fooling himself. Assuming that the material is adequate, there is no substitute for the three essentials—proper execution of the fundamentals, good condition, and proper team spirit. However, there are certain conditions and situations occurring constantly that may be handled best by a change of strategy.

I have heard many basketball coaches say that they believe in following the three principles of: forcing the opponent to play your game, doing what your opponent does not want you to do, and being prepared to meet any emergency. John Bunn discusses these points in his book, *Basketball Methods.*[1]

It seems to me that you would have nothing to worry about if you were able to live up to the third principle of being prepared to meet any emergency. However, the catch is in being able to meet every emergency successfully. Of course, this is impossible to do all of the time, but it is a very worthy goal. Fundamentals must come first, followed by the development of team play in your own particular system, which must be quite flexible, before trying to successfully prepare for all emergencies.

Time will undoubtedly prevent the successful accomplishment of all of this, but the players must have some knowledge of how to attack or defend against any new situation with which they may be confronted in order to maintain poise and avert panic.

## SOME STRATEGIES OR TACTICS THAT WE USE

We try to fast break each time that we get possession of the ball, then usually set up in a single-post offense that features the pass and cut and change of direction and pace more than screens when our fast break is stopped. Our defense is man-to-man that keeps pressure on the ball and has zone principles, plus a mixture of a man-to-man and zone press.

1.  Pressing defense against:
    **(a)** A big slow team.
    **(b)** A mechanical team that wants to use a ball control type of offense and go through specific patterns.
    **(c)** A team not well conditioned.

[1] John Bunn, *Basketball Methods.* New York: The Macmillan Co., Inc., 1939

**(d)** A zone press against teams that like to advance the ball by dribbling.

**(e)** A team with inexperienced or poor ball-handling guards.

**2.** Using a specific set play following a time-out and after every intermission from play.

**3.** Use our screening attack more against a close guarding or tight man-to-man defense.

**4.** Zoning a man in the key area against a strong post attack.

**5.** Floating deep against the teams that want to drive and tight on those that prefer, and can, to shoot from the outside.

**6.** "Hawking" a star scorer all over the floor.

**7.** Playing the strong points and weaknesses of the individuals as well as the team.

**8.** Changing our defense occasionally for a few minutes to some other type and occasionally using a double-post offense.

**9.** Playing a style of game to which we are best adapted, providing we know what we are doing.

## SOME STRATEGIES EMPLOYED AGAINST US

**1.** Many of the ones that we use as just mentioned when they apply.

**2.** Playing a slow deliberate ball-control game in an effort to slow the tempo and control our fast break.

**3.** Jumping in front of our fast-break receivers from the blind side in an effort to draw charging fouls.

**4.** Two-timing us on the defensive board in an effort to stop our fast-break outlet pass.

**5.** Playing two men back on defense most of the time to be protected against our fast break.

**6.** Using a weave or many screens to counter our man-to-man defense.

## THE ALCINDOR (JABBAR) ADJUSTMENT

When Lewis Alcindor (Kareem Abdul Jabbar) made his decision to enroll at UCLA, I felt fairly confident of several things:

**1.** As long as he was physically capable of playing to potential, UCLA was going to be very difficult to beat, providing that I could come up with an offense that could best utilize his talents and still bring out the best of his teammates.

Since I had never had a truly big man, much less an unusually tall and talented one, I was inexperienced in that area. However, I also knew that I could experiment during his freshman year, as freshman were not eligible for varsity competition at that time.

**FIGURE 2-4** The tall and talented superstar, Lewis Alcindor (#33). Adjustments had to be made to utilize the superstar without the other players on the team losing their identity.

**2.** Much would be expected of me with little credit for winning and tremendous criticism when we lost. However, the Bible tells us that "to those to whom much is given, much will be expected" and I certainly would find no fault with that.

Nevertheless, I was well aware of the fact that Kansas was supposed to be certain of three consecutive NCAA championships when Wilt Chamberlain entered there and they failed to win even one; Ohio State was expected to win three when Jerry Lucas, John Havlicek, Mel Nowell, and some other fine players were there, but they won only one; DePaul won none with the great George Mikan, the player selected as the greatest in the first half century; and USF won only two with Bill Russell, the most dominant player of the era, and a fine supporting cast.

Therefore, I knew that there would be many obstacles to overcome if we were to be able to accomplish the expected.

**3.** We were certain to face a number of collapsing zone defenses and stall offenses for which we must be prepared. After considerable discussion we decided that no change in the High-Low Post or One-Three-One Offense that we had decided upon would be necessary as long as we played with patience and utilized the proper options. However, we did decide to use a 3-1-1 Trap Defense with some variations to counter the stall.

**4.** Team morale must be carefully nurtured as Alcindor was certain to be so outstanding that other players would be lost when compared to him. He was sure to receive most of the publicity and the most sought after for interviews. I felt that he could handle this without difficulty, but was not sure of all of his teammates.

**5.** I needed a strong rugged player to contest Alcindor in practice and help him bridge the gap in regard to the roughness of college play in comparison to high school play.

Since he was reputed to be a very sensitive person as well as intelligent, this would necessitate careful planning and management.

This situation was taken care of by the enrollment in our graduate school of Jay Carty, a big, strong, rugged and intelligent player against whom we had participated during his undergraduate days at Oregon State University.

We worked out a special set of drills for him to use while working with Alcindor each day of practice and I am certain that this proved of invaluable help.

Jerry Norman, my varsity assistant, and Gary Cunningham, who coached our 1965–1966 freshmen, and I spent much time discussing, planning, diagramming, and reviewing every area we could think of in an attempt to determine the best method of working with this potentially great player and the best offense and defense to bring out the best of him and his teammates.

Since my varsity failed to win our conference in 1965–1966 for the only time from 1962 through 1975, there were many who felt that I neglected them by being more concerned with the possibilities of the next three years with Alcindor. Although there may be some justification for this criticism, I know that a study of the records will show that we had more problems with sickness and injury to key players at critical times than in any other of my 27 years at UCLA.

It was decided to stay with my man-to-man defense, but attempt to keep Alcindor near the basket area while gambling with other players much as Phil Woolpert had done so successfully with Bill Russell at USF.

This left us with deciding on a defense to use against those teams who would be using a stall offense.

## The Three-One-One Trap (Diagrams 2-1 and 2-2)

After experimenting with a number of different ideas, we decided on a variation of the "Three-One-One." Alcindor would be left under the basket in the #1 protector position, a forward would be placed in the outer half of the foul circle, and the other three would be evenly placed across the floor between the hashmarks.

The object would be to open up the corners and encourage or force the ball into a corner. The assignments of the players would be as follows: Alcindor would protect the basket, the player in the outer circle would be a "trapper" when the ball went into the corner and a deterrent to a pass into the key area prior to that, the middle man out front would always be an "interceptor" when a trap was applied in either corner,

The Three-One-One Trap Defense.

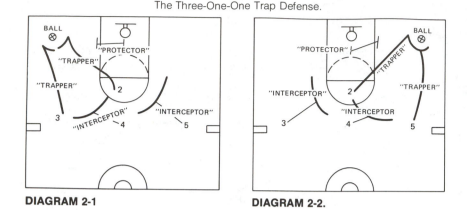

**DIAGRAM 2-1**         **DIAGRAM 2-2.**

the player nearest the hashmarks would be a "trapper" double teaming with his teammate coming from the foul circle when the ball went into the corner on that side and an "interceptor" with the center man in the out line when the ball went into the corner on the opposite side of the floor.

Whenever the trap was evaded and the ball was passed out success-fully, we wanted no frantic rushing around but to calmly set up and force the ball into the corner again.

When properly executed this worked very well for us and we capital-ized on interceptions for some very easy baskets.

It must be remembered that this was used only when the opponent was in a "stall" type of game and reluctant to take shots from the cor-ners. We also found it to be effective at times when teams used the "Four Corner" offense or were attempting to protect a lead.

## The High-Low Post Offense

This is the offense that we eventually decided to use with Alcindor against either zone or man-to-man defenses.

There is not enough movement to suit me, but it kept Alcindor near the basket which usually necessitated leaving someone open in order to help against him, it enabled us to capitalize on some special strengths of teammates, it could be kept very simple and thus easier to perfect essential timing, and no major adjustment was required be-cause of the type of defense used against us.

Alcindor (Jabbar) has been quoted since becoming a pro that the UCLA offense did not permit him to shoot from the outside and that he liked the pro style better. This reminded me of my answer to a reporter when I was asked if he was a good outside shooter. My reply was, "I do not know and do not intend to find out as I consider it much better for smaller players (Warren 5' 10", Shackleford 6' 4") to do the outside shooting and my taller players doing the rebounding rather than the other way around."

The accompanying diagrams illustrate the principal options of our High-Low Post or One-Three-One offense although there were some other variations used on occasion.

**1.** *Normal Set Up* (Diagram 2-3). This shows how we moved from our two guard front to the one-three-one alignment.
As 5 passed to 4, 3 cut toward the basket and then moved with a quick change of pace and direction to the key.
4 fakes away and comes back to receive the ball from 5 without having to use a dribble.
This can be originated on either side of the floor with 1 moving to the opposite side if 2 was to come to the key area.

**2.** *Occasional Set Up* (Diagram 2-4). Occasionally we would have both post men line up low with either one free to break to the key as the ball was exchanged out front.

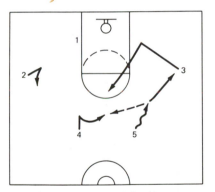

**DIAGRAM 2-3** Normal Set Up.

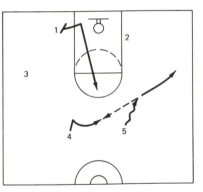

**DIAGRAM 2-4** Occasional Set Up.

**3.** *Point to HiPost* (Diagram 2-5). 4 passes to 3 and moves out to either side of the key, but is to stay busy. 3's first look is to 1 making a move underneath, then for 2 and 5 cutting through a gap, and last to 4. Of course, 3 has the option of a quick drive or a shot from the key if left open.

**4.** *HiPost Screens for Point* (Diagram 2-6). If a defensive person floats back from 4 and makes it difficult to pass to 3, 3 comes on out to back screen for 4 and then rolls aways to protect 4 may get a jumper or have a pass to 1, to 5, to 2, or out to 3.

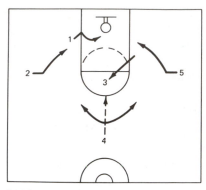

**DIAGRAM 2-5** Point to High Post.

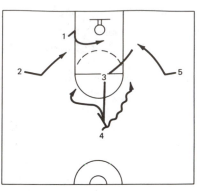

**DIAGRAM 2-6** High Post Screens For Point.

**5, 5A, 5B.** *Point Passes to Right Wing and Cuts Off Post* (Diagrams 2-7, 2-8, 2-9, 2-10)

**5.** 4 passes to 5 and cuts off screen by 3 for a return pass from 5. 3 turns back on 4 when pass is made to 5 to force 4 to run his defense into 3 to get free. This type of screen helps prevent fouls and encourages the cutter to use a screen more properly.

**5A.** 4 passes to 5 and cuts, but does not receive a return pass. 5 passes to 3 at the side post who fakes down with the away foot and then faces 5 for a pass. 3 first looks for 1 underneath, then for 4 coming out off screen by 5 who, after following pass to 3 with two steps, then cuts for the basket looking for a pass and forming a screen 4.

**5B.** Starts the same as 5 and 5A, but 5 passes back out to 2 who has come out to protect from opposite wing. 2 may pass to 1 coming to side post for a two on two, or to 4 coming off screen by 3 and 5, or to 1 who comes back to side post after failure to receive the pass earlier.

**6, 6A.** *Point Passes to Right Wing and Cuts Outside.* (Diagram 2-11)

**6.** 4 passes to 5 and cuts outside and receives a return pass. 2 comes out as the protector. 4 looks for 1 coming across underneath, then for a lob pass to 5 who starts across floor and then cuts for basket off screen by 3 (occasionally 2 will cut back off 3 and 5 will come out). If these aren't open, 4 will look for 3 on the high post or back out to 2, who may have a side post play with 5 coming to post.

**6A.** 4 passes to 5 and cuts outside, but does not receive a return pass. 5 passes to 3 and cuts down to screen for 4 coming back after having gone on under. 3 looks first for 1 underneath, then 4, then out.

**7, 7A, 7B, 7C, 7D.** *Point to Left Wing* (Diagrams 2-12, 2-13, 2-14, 2-15, 2-16)

**7.** 4 passes to 2 who passes to 1 underneath. 1 looks for hook to left or short board shot to his right, or passes to 2 faking in and going toward base line, or to 3 cutting away down lane, or to 5 coming off screen by 3.

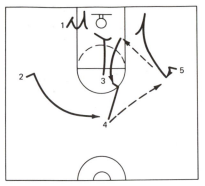

**DIAGRAM 2-7**  Pt. to Rt. Wing to Cutting Point

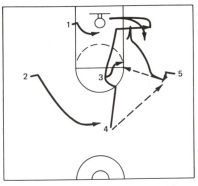

**DIAGRAM 2-8**  Pt. to Rt. Wing to Hi Post.

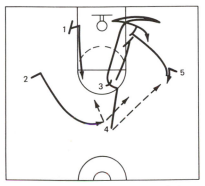

**DIAGRAM 2-9**  Pt. to Rt. Wing to Safety.

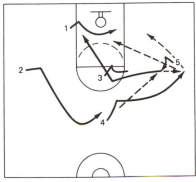

**DIAGRAM 2-10**  Pt. to Rt. Wing—Cut Outside.

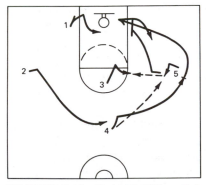

**DIAGRAM 2-11**  Pt. to Rt. Wing—Cut Outside.

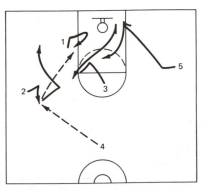

**DIAGRAM 2-12**  Pt. to Left Wing to Low Post.

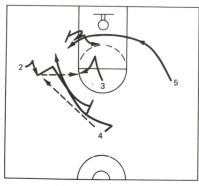

**DIAGRAM 2-13** Pt. to Left Wing to Hi Post.

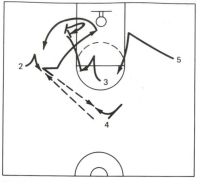

**DIAGRAM 2-14** Pt. to Left Wing to Pt.

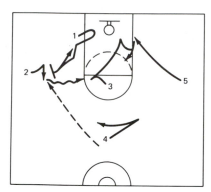

**DIAGRAM 2-15** Pt. to Left Wing (Lo Post Screen).

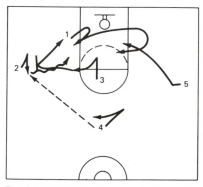

**DIAGRAM 2-16** Pt. to Left Wing (Hi Post Screen).

**7A.** 2 passes to 3, fakes down and comes out to provide screen for 4. 3 looks for 1 underneath, for 5 coming off screen by 1 underneath, for 4 coming off screen by 2, or out to 2.

**7B.** 2 passes to 4 who works with 5 on side post, or passes back to 2 who has cut down and comes back around off double screen by 3 and 1.

**7C.** 1 comes out and screens for 2 and rolls for basket. 2 drives off screen and looks for 1 rolling, for 3 going away down lane, to 5 coming around screen by 3, or out to 5.

**7D.** Same as 7C except 3 screens for 2 and rolls and 1 reverses around screen by 5.

**8.** *Reverse* (Diagram 2-17). 4 dribbles hard toward 5 who reverses for pass, short posts as a second option, then goes on under off double screen by 1 and 3 if 4 passes back out to 2. 2 looks for 4 coming to side post, then for 5 coming

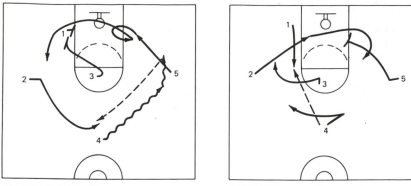

DIAGRAM 2-17  Reverse.                  DIAGRAM 2-18  Special "Backdoor."

around double screen by 1 and 3, then back to 4 on side post who has gone back under and come back again.

**9.** *"Backdoor" Special* (Diagram 2-18). 1 cuts up the lane quickly to receive pass from 4, 2 cuts for pass from 1 going under or off screen by 5 on opposite side, 3 cuts off 1 as in a semi-side post play, while 4 fakes and works outside.

**10.** *"Call Deep" Special.* (Diagram 2-19) On the call of "Deep" by 4, 1, or 3, 1 and 3 stay deep and 4 passes to 2 or 5 and cuts down center to come off screen on base line to either side. 2 or 5 dribble out toward center of floor and looks for 4 coming off screen.

Since the Alcindor-led teams won three consecutive NCAA championships and finished with an 88 and 2 record, I feel that our special preparations produced near maximum results. Even so, we only did what was expected and, even though it is often more difficult to do the expected, there isn't the great satisfaction that comes from doing the

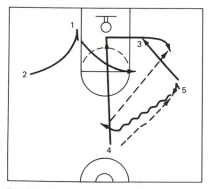

DIAGRAM 2-19  Special—Call "Deep."

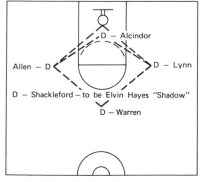

DIAGRAM 2-20  The Diamond and One Defense.

unexpected. Therefore, it was rather nice the next season to get back to the idea of merely trying to do our best without the added burden trying to keep from losing.

Alcindor not only possessed great height and physical talent, he also was one of the most unselfish, intelligent, and hard working players that I ever had under my supervision. He also was a fine student and the most self-sufficient and least demanding super-star that I have ever known.

## The Diamond and One for Houston

After losing (71–69) a memorable game to a great Houston team in the Astrodome, before over 55,000 frenzied spectators, we were a little disappointed but truly hoped that we would get to play them in the NCAA tournament at the close of the year. This seemed quite probable as we were almost unanimously considered the two finest teams in the country and both were undefeated before our meeting in the Astrodome. As a matter of fact, that defeat broke a string of 47 consecutive victories for us.

Houston was led by Elvin Hayes, who had one of the finest individual performances against us that I had ever seen. However, he was not alone since they had a number of other truly outstanding players including Cheney and Spain. Even so, their victory was somewhat "hollow" in the eyes of some as Alcindor, our great star, played with vertical double vision after having been hospitalized in a dark room for a week with an eye injury and had by far the poorest shooting percentage (4/18) that he had in the 88 games he played for us.

I knew that if we did meet them in the NCAA tournament later on that they would be determined to show that their first victory was not lusterless. They were confident that they were a better team than we were and, I think, also hoped for another chance to prove it.

Although I felt quite certain that we would handle them if we met again, I wasn't positive that my players might not be a little tense if that happened and I was looking for something of a motivational nature to help bring that about.

One of my greatest coaching disappointments resulted from this game and it had nothing to do with our defeat. Through an unfortunate misunderstanding, or a poor choice of words on my part, or a failure to communicate, an outstanding player and fine young man, Edgar Lacey, dropped from our squad. Even though this may have helped to solidify us into what many have considered to be the finest of all college teams, it was a great shock and personal disappointment to me.

I won't go into the reasons for this coming about, but will say that it surely could have been avoided had it been handled in a more judicious manner. I failed to understand the deep pride of this fine young man and the period he was going through.

Jerry Norman, my assistant, wanted me to work on a "box and one" to use if we met them again. I have never favored zone defenses and definitely was against using a "box and one" because it might take Alcindor away from the basket. However, our discussions continued and we finally settled on a "diamond and one."

Although I felt we would not have trouble with Houston again since Alcindor would be back to par, I decided that this might be the kind of motivational "gimmick" for which I was looking.

We placed our starting players, as shown in Diagram 2-20, on the "diamond and one defense." Alcindor (7' 2") was to be the deep point of the diamond and stay near the basket at all times. He was the intimidator against drives.

Mike Warren (5' 10") was to be the front part of the diamond. He was float back to discourage passes into the post since we did not fear the outside shooting of Cheney, who would probably play the point for them, and we did want to limit Spain from receiving the ball too much in the post area.

Lucius Allen (6' 2") was to play the right side of the diamond and was to help on Hayes whenever Hayes was on that side.

Mike Lynn (6' 7") was to play the left side of the diamond and was to help on the post and was expected to be strong on the defensive board.

Lynn Shackleford (6' 4"), probably our weakest defensive player, was given a most difficult assignment. He was to "hound" Elvin Hayes at all times and try to prevent him from receiving a pass. When Hayes did get the ball, "Shack" was to play him very tight and not give him room to operate. If Hayes got by Shack toward the base line, he would be coming into Alcindor, and, if he got by toward the key, any one or all of our three men were to harass him. We took the gamble that Hayes would not pass too well.

We worked on this for a few minutes every day for about a month before the tournament and for several minutes every day after the regional when we knew we were going to face Houston in the semi-final game for the NCAA championship.

This tactic worked out far beyond our highest expectations. Shackleford did a tremendous job on Hayes and really rose to the occasion and Alcindor was "fired up" to a degree that I had never seen him before. Warren, Allen, and Lynn all played superb basketball and what everyone thought would be a tremendous game turned into a rout.

The final score was 101–69, but we had led by as much as 44 points before I broke up our combination. It was truly a great team victory, not only on defense but also on offense, where our five starters all scored from 14 to 19 points. The championship game the next night against North Carolina was very anticlimatic as we won by a wide margin with limited enthusiasm.

## WORKING WITH YOUR PLAYERS

The strategy or psychology of working with the various individuals on the teams is probably one of the most difficult and important things that a coach has to do. Every player is different from every other player and will require different treatment in some respects. Team morale or team spirit, as well as getting the most out of the individual, will be determined to a great degree by the ability of a coach to understand and correctly work with the various individuals who make up the squad.

Many of my ideas in regard to this have been discussed in Chapter 1—"My Coaching Philosophy," earlier in this chapter, and will be evident in later chapters. As a matter of fact, the proper treatment of the players should receive careful consideration in everything that is done in connection with the coaching of the team. The discussion of "Preparing the Team Mentally" earlier in this chapter is a part of working with the players.

One of the first things I do with the players is to try and direct their thinking as to why they are out for the team. It should be for the personal enjoyment and pleasure they can derive from such participation, and it should be pointed out that their greatest satisfaction can come from knowing that they have done their best to improve themselves and help the team.

I want them eager to become outstanding basketball players individually and yet to earn the pride that comes from being referred to as a team player. Many players seem to feel that a good team player can never receive acclaim as an outstanding individual player and that a fine individual player has trouble receiving recognition as a good team player. They must try to excel in both aspects on both offense and defense.

A few important methods or ideas of working with the players, some of which may have been mentioned previously, are as follows:

**1.** Be completely impartial and show no favoritism, but remember that no two are alike and that each must be treated according to his own individual personality.

**2.** Be easily approached by the players and sincerely interested in all of their personal problems, successes, and failures.

**3.** Have one team of which all squad members are a part. Never refer to them as regulars and substitutes or in any way that might be embarrassing to some. Try to develop the feeling that the player who may be called upon very little for actual playing time may be very important in the overall picture and he must be ready when he is called upon.

**4.** Be very careful about publicly criticizing an individual. Usually follow severe criticism by a "pat on the back" or referring to some particular thing that he may do well. Approval is a great motivator.

**5.** See that the defensive players and play makers who do not make the headlines receive appropriate praise and commendation in front of the others. Work to get the cooperation of the press to help on this.

**6.** Permit no criticism or razzing among teammates. They must help each other.

**7.** Jealousy, egotism, and selfishness must be prevented.

**8.** Earn the respect and confidence of the players.

**9.** Respect and study the individuality of each boy.

**10.** Teach loyalty, honesty, and respect for the rights of others and a sense of responsibility.


## Letter to Returning Players

I consider it good policy for the coach to keep in contact with all returning players between seasons just as I believe the coach should make every effort to keep as close a relationship as possible with players who have graduated and are no longer under your supervision. You must let them know of your interest and of your concern for their future.

There will be different personalities and different conditions every season that will present different problems that must be faced. Therefore, the coach must constantly be on the alert for ways and means to eliminate or at least minimize them.

It was my practice to stay as close as possible to all returning players in the off season, although I never wanted them to feel that I was invading their privacy and, in addition to other contact, I usually sent them a team letter in the middle of the summer.

When you have a number of returnees from an unusually successful and, perhaps, unexpected national championship team, there always is the possibility of some complacency. Therefore, it is necessary to find ways to motivate without making it too obvious.

Such was the case for my 1970–1971 season at UCLA. We had just won a national championship the previous year, which was somewhat unexpected since it followed three consecutive championships and the loss of Lewis Alcindor and some other fine players. Quite naturally, we had not been expected to win again. However, the 1969–1970 team had a great amount of pride and were determined to show the basketball world that they could win without Alcindor. When they accomplished this most difficult task, it was quite apparent that some were quite pleased with themselves and they had a right to be.

This attitude, I knew, would make it more difficult for us to measure up the following year. Since I strongly believe that the worst enemy of physical talent is lack of a proper mental attitude, I immediately began looking for ways to counter possible complacency.

The following letter was composed and sent to all returnees and other potential squad members on July 7, 1970:

Dear Sidney:
> "Remember this your life time through,
> Tomorrow, there'll be more to do,
> And failure waits for all who stay,
> With some success made yesterday;
> Tomorrow, you must try once more,
> And even harder than before."

Although the regular school term ended a comparatively short time ago, it has been almost four months since our basketball season came to a close. It was a very successful season, but it is now history and we must look toward the future. The past cannot change what is to come. It is what you do each present hour that can influence your future, and I sincerely hope that you are looking to an equally successful 1970–1971 season and are eager, not merely just willing, to make the necessary personal sacrifices to reach that goal. All worthwhile accomplishments require sacrifice and hard work.

It has been said that a true leader is always interested in finding the best way to accomplish something rather than having his own way and I hope that I come under that category. We must work together in a harmonious manner if we are to measure up to our potential and anything less than that means failure to some degree.

However, in every group activity there must be supervision and leadership and a disciplined effort by all or much of our united strength will be dissipated by pulling against ourselves. If you discipline yourself toward team effort under the supervision of the one in charge, even though you may not always agree with his decision, much can and will be accomplished. Your lot is certain failure without discipline.

Recorded history shows that the underlying reason for the failure of every civilization or cause has been because of the breakdown from within and I deeply believe that most potentially great athletic teams that did not measure up to what seemed possible and logical failed because of friction from within. Let us not be victimized in such a manner.

My experience in teaching and coaching over many years has naturally caused me to become somewhat opinionated in certain areas, but even most of those who are inexperienced will agree that experience is a good, although sometimes hard, teacher. The coach must be far more interested in the overall welfare of the team than in any single individual player and, therefore, must be as accurate as possible in the decisions that must be made in regard to the selection of players and their proper use. He is the one who eventually will be hurt the most by poor judgment in those respects. Some of you will disagree over various decisions, but you must not permit your disagreement to become cancerous and affect your effort to make the most of your abilities. When you disagree, try not to be disagreeable.

I am intensely interested in each of you as an individual, but I must act in what I consider to be in the best interest of the team for either the moment or the future. Your race or religion will have no conscious bearing on my judgment, but your ability and how it works into my philosophy of team play very definitely will. Furthermore, your personal conduct and adherence to standards that I set up undoubtedly will be taken into consideration, either consciously or subconsciously.

It may appear to you that I practice double standards at times as I most certainly will not treat you all alike in every respect. However, I will attempt to give each individual the treatment that he earns and deserves according to my judgment with what I consider to be in the best interest of our team. You must accept this in the proper manner if you are to be a positive contributing member of the team whether you are one who plays either much or little. If I do not feel you are capable of contributing in some way, I would want you to spend your time in something more productive for yourself. Although I prefer to go too far with a player rather than not far enough, I will drop you if I feel you are wasting your time.

We will have a meeting for all potential squad members about two weeks before practice starts where a number of things will be discussed. For press and picture day on October 14, with regular practice starting on October 15, you should:

**1.** Have your feet tough and in condition to run without the danger of blisters.

**2.** Wear no mustache, beard, or goatee; have no bushy or unusually long sideburns; have your hair of reasonable length.

**3.** Remember that you are representatives of UCLA and your personal appearance and conduct should not reflect discredit in any way upon yourself or upon those whom you represent. Cleanliness, neatness of appearance, and good manners are qualities that should be characteristic of those who are in position to be of great influence on youth and you should set a proper example.

**4.** Be determined to accomplish what is expected of you by yourself and by those who are responsible for you and the team.

Please come in and chat with me whenever you feel like it, but remember that it isn't necessarily lack of communication if we fail to agree on your position or the position of another on the team. I am and always will be interested in you and your problems, but do feel that one should never become too dependent upon others for the solution of personal problems. Talking them over, however, to a friendly ear can be of help. I have found prayer to be the most helpful when I am troubled, and believe that all prayers are heard and answered, even though the answer is no.

Have a pleasant and productive summer.

Sincerely,

Coach Wooden

# INDIVIDUAL OFFENSE

Before discussing the individual offensive fundamentals, without which it is impossible for a team to have any degree of success, and the systems of play, I want to emphasize strongly an extremely important part of offensive basketball that seldom is as deeply ingrained in the players as it should be.

## OFFENSE WITHOUT THE BALL

Perhaps the most important part of offensive basketball is the part played by each man without the ball. This does not minimize the importance of being able to shoot, pass, dribble, pivot, and rebound, as all of those are important fundamentals and must be mastered to the best of each individual's ability in order to have an effective offense.

However, since only one of the five offensive players may have possession of the ball at any one time, 80 per cent of your players are playing without possession at all times. As a matter of fact, it is more than 80 per cent, because there is a time when you have taken a shot that, although no one is in possession of the ball, you are still on offense, at least theoretically, and all five players must be taking care of their particular offensive rebounding assignments.

Some of the responsibilities of the offensive players who do not have the ball are as follows:

**1.** Work to get open to receive the ball in an advantageous position where you are a threat to shoot, dribble, or pass. When any one of these options has been eliminated, then your total offensive strength has been minimized by that much.

**2.** Be alert to make yourself available for a screen to enable the man with the ball to improve his position or to enable another teammate to get open to receive a pass in an advantageous position.

**3.** Be ready to run your defensive man into a screen by alert fakes and feints whenever the opportunity presents itself.

**4.** Be in a position to make your defensive man turn his head away from the play in order that he will not be able to bother one of your teammates who may have eluded his own man or to intercept a pass thrown by a teammate.

**5.** Be alert to react to any sudden move that the man with the ball might make. Your actions are usually governed by the moves of the man who has the ball or by the man who just passed the ball.

**6.** Be quick to change from offense to defense when possession is lost in any manner.

**7.** Be ready to cover the logical rebounding position when a shot is taken or become the protector if that should be your assignment.

**8.** Constantly study the moves of your defensive man and the habits of other defensive men who might shift to you in order to decoy them or set them up for your own moves or the moves of your teammates.

**9.** Be alert to fill the proper lanes for your fast-break attack.

**10.** Be extremely alert on all situations in regard to out-of-bounds, jump balls, free throws, sudden presses, becoming a trailer, or executing any maneuver that can help your team.

In the final analysis, it doesn't make much difference how capable you might be with the ball, if you are not able to get possession of the ball in the area where you are a threat. Furthermore, that can not be done efficiently unless it is through team effort. You must work together as a unit at all times as well as keeping in mind that one of the very best ways to improve the team is to improve yourself.

## INDIVIDUAL FUNDAMENTALS

A sound knowledge of and the ability to execute both quickly and properly the various fundamentals of the game are absolutely essential for successful play, keeping in mind, of course, that the ability to properly execute them leaves you in direct proportion to fatigue, self-control, and team spirit.

There is no system of play that can be effective unless it is based on sound execution of the individual fundamentals. It isn't what you do, as long as it is basically sound, but how well you do it. A great percentage of every practice session must be devoted to the perfection or the improvement of the individual details. If something has to be neglected, never let it be the individual fundamentals.

## BODY BALANCE

Body balance is controlled by the extremities of the body (head, feet, hands) and the joints, but they are controlled by your mental and emotional balance.

Body balance is essential for an individual to be able to execute a fundamental successfully the vast percentage of the time. Although you may be able occasionally to be effective when out of balance, the percentage is stacked against you. However, the coach must realize that what is poor balance for one player on a particular fundamental might be quite satisfactory for another. Therefore, you must study the individuals carefully, and permit deviation from the standard when it is more natural and effective for that individual. (See Fig. 3-1.)

**1.** The *head* should remain directly above the midpoint between the two feet. This will help to keep the body under control as the mere weight of the head can throw you off-balance. Keep the chin up and do not lean.

**2.** The hands should be kept above the waist and close to the body. The fingers should be well spread and the palms toward the ball. When you have the ball, it should be held close to the chest with the elbows out. When you are a potential rebounder, the hands should go above the shoulders with the fingers pointing upward and the palms forward.

**FIGURE** 3-1 Good body balance—hands above waist, chin up, feet at shoulder width, joints relaxed, head above the midpoint between the feet.

**3.** A slightly crouched position should be maintained with every *joint* relaxed and ready for a sudden move or change.

**4.** The *weight* should be evenly distributed on the full soles of both feet, or perhaps a little toward the ball of the foot, not back on the heels or way up on the toes.

**5.** The *feet* should be neither too close together nor too wide apart. They should be comfortably spread, generally about the width of the shoulders.

## BALL HANDLING

All offense is predicated on adept handling of the ball as shooting, passing, receiving, dribbling, pivoting, making a quick stop and turn, ball-faking, and rebounding are all, in reality, handling the ball in one way or another.

**1.** Maintaining or exchanging possession of the ball with a teammate with accuracy is essential, as loss of the ball without getting a good shot is a cardinal sin of basketball.

**2.** Quickness must be stressed over all things except accuracy. I constantly strive for accuracy with maximum quickness.

**3.** The ball must be handled above the waist and kept close to the body. Generally, we pass, dribble, or shoot *through* or *by* the defense rather than around or over it. (See Fig. 3-2.)

**4.** There is more sensitivity in the fingertips; therefore, it is logical to assume that the ball should be controlled by the fingertips (ends of the fingers to the

**FIGURE 3-2** A guard ready to pass, drive, or shoot.

first joints) and, although it might be touching, it should not be resting on the palms or heels of the hands. This should promote better control and quicker movement of the ball.

**5.** Wrist and finger movement and snap are stressed at all times. Keep the fingers spread and relaxed but firm.

**6.** The elbows should be relaxed and kept close to the body. Protect the ball by rotating the wrist and fingers rather than trying to hold it away from you.

**7.** In faking with the ball keep it close to the body and fake it by merely rolling or snapping the wrists. Use many head fakes.

**8.** The knees, hips, and other joints must stay relaxed to prevent tenseness, and yet not so loose as to encourage carelessness.

**9.** The chin must be kept up not only to help maintain balance, but to increase the peripheral vision.

**10.** Constantly emphasize that you must strive for quickness and cleverness without any conscious resemblance to fancy or "showboat" play.

## PASSING AND RECEIVING

Passing is probably the most important part of all the individual offensive fundamentals and receiving is, in a sense, a continuation of the pass. Some will say that shooting is the most important, but I consider shooting as a pass to the basket. Furthermore, without passing, there wouldn't be very many good shots as a great percentage of the good shots are set up by a succession of passes. The basic idea of any offense is to get a good shot at the basket every time you obtain possession of the ball, and, generally, the team with the best passing attack will obtain more good percentage shots and thus score more unless they lack initiative or play a ball-control type of offense.

It might be logical for a poor shooting team to work very hard to improve their offense by spending more time on the perfection of their passing game in an effort to work the ball in closer for higher percentage shots. This could very well improve their ability to shoot at the same time. Furthermore, if you can not handle the ball well enough to get good shots, it doesn't make much difference whether you can make them or not.

Deception and timing are very important aspects of passing. The defense must not be able to diagnose where and when you are going to pass. Quickness and accuracy must be developed without telegraphing the pass. You must see your potential receiver without staring at him. The potential receivers must fake their defensive man in order to get open to receive the pass in the right place at the right time and

**FIGURE 3-3** Sidney Wicks (#35) moving to get open after passing to deep post. UCLA vs. USC, March 1969.

keep their man so busy that he can not "read" the man with the ball. A potential receiver—and any player without the ball should consider himself a potential receiver—should keep the ball within his vision at all times. The eyes should follow the flight of the ball all of the way into your hands, and then they should be directed forward with all possible peripheral vision.

The man with the ball should instantly and always be looking for the opportunity to advance the ball to a teammate in better position. A crisp pass without too much spin should be used as slow or lob passes are easily intercepted and passes that are too hard or have too much spin on them are more likely to be fumbled. We try to increase the crispness as much as possible for a successful completion, as the harder the pass the less likely it is to be intercepted and the quicker the pressure is placed on the defense.

The target area for straight passes is the area above the waist and below the shoulders on the side away from the defensive man and the target for bounce passes is above the knees and up to the waist. If the bounce pass is thrown properly, it can not be thrown too hard as the floor will absorb the shock. The forward spin for tight quarters and the reverse spin when the receiver is given more of a lead must both be mastered.

Once the technique is understood, most passing drills should have the passes made from moving men or after coming to a quick stop to moving receivers or to receivers in their normal offensive positions.

The coach should make every effort to get his players to develop pride in their passing and encourage all scorers to acknowledge the passer who led to the score by a nod, a smile, a wink, or a word.

The coach must also continually stress that the passing game consists of two parts—passing and receiving. Therefore, proper receiving and getting open to receive must be taught and given as much consideration as seeing the open man and hitting him with the proper pass.

The receiver should block the flight of the ball with the hand away from the defensive man and with the fingers well spread, but relaxed. This hand acts as the gloved hand of a first baseman and the other hand tucks the ball into the blocking hand.

## Types and Methods

There are many types of passes that must be mastered if a player is to become a finished basketball player. Although a player should first master the passes that are most commonly used for the particular position that he plays, he must also be able to execute other passes as well. Offenses are so flexible in the game today that no player is confined to one particular position as was the case a number of years ago and he must be able to move the ball in the quickest and best possible manner for any situation that may arise.

Basketball is a moving game, a game of constant action, and a majority of the passes that are made usually are made from a moving man to a moving man or at least with either the passer or receiver moving. Therefore, once the proper technique of making the pass is established, then practice drills should be devised to imitate game conditions as nearly as possible.

The following types of passes are the ones that we feel are the most important and, consequently, the ones to which we give the most attention in our drills:

**1. The Straight Pass.** This pass should be thrown very crisply, with the ball staying parallel to the floor, and reach the receiver above the waist and below the shoulders. It may be thrown with any type of one-handed or two-handed pass and is used advantageously from any position on the floor. It is the pass to use whenever possible as it is the quickest for getting the ball safely away from the defensive board and advanced down the floor, against a press, against a zone, or in almost any part of your set or breaking offense.

**2. The Bounce Pass.** This pass is almost always thrown with the two-handed or one-handed push. It should hit the floor approximately two-thirds of the distance to the receiver and reach him at a height above his knees and below his waist.

Generally, the bounce pass cannot be thrown too hard, if it is accurate and reaches the receiver at the proper height, because the shock will be absorbed by the floor.

A reverse spin on the bounce may be used effectively at times as it will permit giving the receiver a longer lead and still enable him to handle the ball. A forward spin is also valuable at times as it may enable the passer to pass through a narrow opening and get to the receiver quicker. The forward spin bounce requires more pin-point accuracy, but is well worth developing.

The bounce pass is very effective at times as the pass to a cutter breaking for the basket on a fast-break situation, to pass under a defensive man, to a cutter on a quick reverse, into the post man, from a post man in a tight situation to a cutter, through the front line of a zone, and on many out-of-bounds plays.

**3. The Lob Passes.** This is a dangerous pass to use as it takes longer to get to the receiver and may permit floaters to intercept or get into position to cause the receiver to charge. It is also a little more difficult to throw accurately.

However, it is a valuable pass to use from a distance to a post man coming up to meet it, to a post man reversing a defensive man who is playing in front of him, occasionally to a reverser when the floor is clear in front of him, and as a lead pass to man out front on the break. It is also used to inbound the ball or some out-of-bounds plays.

It is usually thrown by the one- or two-hand push method, but the baseball pass and the hook pass may also be used on occasion.

**4. The Flip or Hand-Off.** This is the pass that is usually used by a post man or by a player who has just completed a quick stop and turn to give the ball to a cutter coming close by.

On the flip or hand-off there should be no spin on the ball and it usually should be given to the receiver at waist height. It must not be thrown up at the receiver nor should it be dropped at his feet. The passer must release the ball with a quick flip directly into the hands of the receiver. He should not make the receiver take it off of his hand, but should flip it and get his hand out of the way. His off hand and arm help protect the ball. The wrist and fingers follow through, but usually the arm will not be extended. The passer must be holding the ball firmly and must not release it too soon as he may want to fake the pass, if a defensive man is moving over, and then be prepared to give the cutter a de-layed pass.

A head fake and slight ball fake *down* followed by a one- or two-handed flip pass over the shoulder on the same side, and a head fake and slight ball fake *up* and a quick flip bounce under and by the defensive man on that side into the path of the cutter are both effective ways of hitting the close cutter at times. As a general rule, a *high* fake will be followed by a quick low pass on that side or a high pass on the opposite side and a *down* fake will be followed by a quick flip over the shoulder of the defensive man on that side or a bounce pass under him on the opposite side. A flip pass over the shoulder should be shoulder high to the receiver.

Post men must receive a lot of practice on the various methods of passing off or handing off to cutters, but we also want all players to get considerable practice at this. All men, and especially the guards, often have to make quick stops and turns with the possibility of handing off to trailers. Furthermore, our weak-side attack on our set offense usually has a forward, but occasionally, a guard, coming up to the side post and becoming a post man.

**5. Push Pass— One- and Two-Handed.** This has been and continues to be the most used pass in basketball to advance the ball down the floor and to initiate your set offense and to hit a cutter from most positions except from the post.

Most players can develop the ability to use it successfully up to a distance of 20 feet and need to do this from almost any position on the floor.

For the *two-handed pass* the ball is held about chest high with the fingers spread on each side and the thumbs directly behind, but a little toward the top of the ball and pointing toward each other. The elbows should be in close to the body and the ball released with a quick snap of the wrist, fingers, and elbows. The long extension of the arms is no longer advised, as it is quickness and snap that we want. The wrist and finger snap should give the ball a normal rotation and not an exaggerated spin.

The body should be slightly crouched and moving forward as the pass is made. A right-handed man will usually be stepping forward toward his target with his right foot and pushing off of the left while the left-handed man will be stepping forward with the left foot and pushing off of his right one. (See Fig. 3-4.)

The pass should be a crisp straight pass if possible, but the bounce pass may also be used. Normally, the straight pass should stay parallel to the floor and reach the receiver above the waist and below the shoulders and the bounce pass should hit the floor two-thirds of the distance to the receiver and come to a height above his knees but no higher than his waist.

Generally, the bounce pass cannot be thrown too hard, if it is accurate and comes to the receiver above his knees and below his waist, because the shock will be absorbed by the floor. A reverse spin on the bounce may be used effectively at times as it will permit giving the receiver a longer lead and still enable him to handle the ball while a forward spin may enable the passer to pass through a narrower opening and get to the receiver quicker. The forward spin requires more pinpoint accuracy.

The bounce pass is very effective at times as the pass to a cutter breaking for the basket on a fast-break situation, to pass under a defensive man, to a cutter

A

B

C

**FIGURE 3-4** The quick push pass.

on a reverse, to a post man, through the front line of a zone defense, and on many out-of-bounds plays.

The use of the *one-handed push pass* embodies the same fundamentals and principles as the two-handed push pass. The ball is held and passed the same way except that it is released from one hand with the opposite hand merely helping to hold and protect the ball prior to its quick release. It is fairly accurate to say that it is usually a two-handed pass when it is released from in front of the body and becomes a one-handed pass when released from the side of the body.

## 6. Two-Handed Overhead Pass.

This is an excellent pass from every position on your set offense. The guards often use it to pass to the post man, the forwards also use it to hit the post or a guard cutting off the post, and the post men use it effectively after receiving a pass on the high post and turning to face the basket. It is frequently used by tall players and by players who have just received a high pass and want to make a quick return or pass off.

The hands are on the sides toward the back of the ball with the fingers pointed upward and the thumbs on the back of the ball pointing inward toward each other. The hands go straight up, not up and back over the head. The elbows are slightly flexed and the ball is released by a quick snap of the wrists and fingers and usually a slight step forward with the foot on the strong arm side. (See Fig. 3-5)

A        B

**FIGURE 3-5** The quick overhead pass.

**7. The Shoulder Pass— One- and Two-Handed.** This pass is similar in nature and use to the two-handed overhead pass except that it is thrown with one or two hands from over the shoulder and close to the ear on either side.

The ball is held firmly in the normal manner, but when the ball is on the right side, the right hand is back of the ball with the palm forward, the fingers upward, and the thumb near the right ear, and the left hand is in front of the ball and slightly under it with the palm facing back through the ball toward the right palm, the fingers pointing upward, and the thumb near right cheek. The position of the hands is reversed when the ball is on the left side.

The ball is released with a quick wrist and finger snap by both hands on either side or by the right hand from the right side and the left hand from the left side.

The straight, bounce, and lob pass may all be used with this as well as the flip pass on specific occasions.

**8. The Hip Pass— One- and Two-Handed.** In general, the principles that apply to the shoulder pass also apply to the hip pass.

The ball is held close to the hip with the elbows bent and is released with a quick wrist and finger snap. The ball does not get behind the line of the body. The palms of the hands face each other from opposite sides of the ball with the fingers pointed down and the thumbs outward. The right hand is behind the ball when on the right side and the left hand is behind the ball when it is on the left side of the body. Each hand is equally important regardless of whether the ball is released by one or two hands.

This pass isn't used as often as many of the others, but it should be given some attention. It is used occasionally from guard to forward and forward to guard and somewhat more often from guard to guard.

**9. Baseball Pass— Right- and Left-Handed.** Although some time will be devoted to the practice of this pass with the off or weak hand, as a general rule, it will be used only with the strong hand.

The ball goes high above the side of the head with the passing hand behind the ball and the other hand in front of and slightly under the ball with the fingers of each hand pointed upward and the thumbs pointing inward over the head. The off-side hand is very important in maintaining control and balance of the ball and adjusting it for quick throwing.

This is a very valuable pass for getting the ball away quickly from the defensive board and for long lead passes to cutter. Although a little more arm movement is used in this pass, the main impetus should come from the quick wrist and finger snap. The long lead pass occasionally may be a bounce pass with reverse "english" that waits for the cutter.

**10. Hook Pass—Right- and Left-Handed.** This pass is used effectively when the passer is being crowded on one side, but there is no pressure from the opposite side. Tall men use it effectively from the board and it is occasionally used from a pivot. The fast-breaking team that features the long-pass attack uses it and the baseball pass rather extensively.

The true hook is thrown with a sweeping motion and a comparatively straight elbow, but we also use the bent-elbow hook, which is more like the throw a second baseman may make to first for a double play.

As a rule you take a cross-over step to get away from pressure, jump, turn, hook, pass, and land facing squarely in the direction the pass was made. You should land on both feet with them spread and relaxed, hips down, knees bent, and ready to move quickly.

The ball is released high with the wrist and finger snap and the fingers pointing toward your target. The off hand must help protect, balance, and direct the ball with the passing hand providing all of the impetus as well as helping with the other parts.

**11. Tip Pass— One- and Two-Handed.** This is merely a controlled deflection without catching the ball. It is seldom used, but when used properly in the proper situation may mean a score because of the quick exchange.

The palm or palms face the ball with the fingers well spread and then turn toward the receiver with a quick flip of the wrist or wrists and fingers as ball contact is made.

**12. Roll Pass— Right- or Left-Handed.** Although this pass isn't used very much, it does have some uses and it is wise to have a drill or two in which it is used. It can be of benefit in helping players to learn to crouch and handle low passes and help in learning to retain or regain good body balance. It may be used by the guards to get the ball into the post or to the forwards at times against certain defensive men and occasionally to get the ball to a receiver when you are under high pressure.

The hands are held in the same position as they are on the hip pass and the ball is released with a quick snap of the wrist and fingers with the elbow extended. The ball should be received with a block and tuck almost as an infielder would field a ground ball.

**13. Behind-the-Back Pass.** I do not advocate the use of this pass except for an occasional player under certain situations. It should never be thrown if another pass can be used at the time. However, to break the monotony or release tension in practice, on occasion we will work on it from a circle formation or by hitting the post with a bounce pass behind the back while moving across the floor in front of the post.

When we do use it, I want the ball kept close to the back with the elbow bent, the fingers pointed down, and the thumb pointed toward your back. It is released with the quick wrist and finger snap that we try to follow in the use of all passes.

**14. Post-Man Passes.** In addition to all of the previously mentioned passes, and especially the flip and hand-off passes, we have our post men work on all types of passes that they might be able to use to cutters. They must learn to protect the ball from their defensive men and from other defensive men floating around them and to get the ball to cutters under crowded conditions.

Quick flip passes, quick bounces, quick fakes followed by a delayed pass over or under, back-hand flips, cross-overs and various other methods are used by the post man. We try to give our post man some passing from the post under crowded conditions almost every day and permit him to use his own initiative and use whatever may be best for him. As long as he can get the pass completed, we are not concerned as to how it is accomplished.

## Passing and Receiving Suggestions

**1.** Our goal is a perfect, accurate pass. Poor passes lead to loss of ball, loss of confidence, and loss of game. Make every pass good.

**2.** Pass quickly, but don't sacrifice accuracy. Don't wind up to pass. You pass through or by a defensive man, not over or around him.

**3.** Look before you pass without staring or telegraphing it.

**4.** Be sure, never careless, with a pass. Carelessness is a major sin.

**5.** Judge the speed of the receiver and lead him properly.

**6.** Do something after you pass—cut quickly, fake, screen, protect. Hesitation after a pass is a major fault. You get no place standing still.

**7.** Passes must be crisp—neither too hard nor too easy and without too much spin.

**8.** Receivers must keep their eyes on the ball all the way into their hands and must not back away from a pass.

**9.** Receivers should block the ball with an open hand and tuck with the other hand. Let the wrists and elbows give with contact.

**10.** Seldom pass to a man going toward the sideline or directly away from you. Seldom pass to corner or sideline "huggers."

**11.** Passer and receiver must time themselves with each other. It is the responsibility of both.

**12.** When the passing is good, the catching is easy. Remember the passer's target is usually on the side of the receiver away from danger.

**13.** Fake to closely guarded receivers as they should reverse quickly to get open when they are being overplayed.

**14.** Proper passing habits are developed in practice.

**15.** Cross-court passes and lob or soft passes are easily intercepted.

**16.** It is very dangerous to pass across under your defensive basket.

**17.** The quick passing and moving team make it very difficult for the defense.

**18.** Look, break, and pass or drive quickly after an intercepted pass.

**19.** Get the ball to the man in the best offensive position, as soon as possible.

**20.** Use the eyes and head for deception and increased peripheral vision.

**21.** You can't pass the ball until you have it and you will pass better when you have balance.

**22.** Be clever, not fancy. The clever passer will receive praise while the fancy one will be ridiculed.

**23.** Develop pride in your passes and work hard to perfect all types of passes.

**24.** Keep hands above the waist with fingers spread and relaxed and give the passer a wide palm target on the side away from danger.

**25.** Work for the ball, do not stand and call for it.

**26.** Passers from the right side of the body usually have the left foot forward and vice versa.

**27.** When the pass comes back out look forward to the weak side immediately.

**28.** Use more quick fakes and bounce passes when in close quarters, but protect the ball.

**29.** The passer should always anticipate a receiver getting open in an advantageous position and be ready to hit him with a pass, while all potential receivers should be anticipating the ball at all times.

**30.** Be neither careless nor overly cautious. Get the pass completed quickly without fear or worry. He who never makes a mistake never accomplishes anything.

## Some Causes of Fumbling

**1.** Receiver takes his eyes off ball coming to him.

**2.** Receiver is not being alert and not expecting the ball.

**3.** Receiver fights the ball. Not relaxed, too tense.

**4.** Receiver loses poise or self-control.

**5.** Receiver is mentally or physically tired.

**6.** Receiver tries to shoot, pass, dribble, or turn before he has possession.

**7.** Receiver misjudges the pass.

**8.** Receiver does not have his hands up and ready.

**9.** Receiver does not have balance.

**10.** Receiver does not have strong wrists and fingers.

**11.** Receiver runs away from the ball.

**12.** Passer makes a bad pass by passing too hard or too easy, having too much spin on the ball, passing too high or too low, giving the receiver too much or not enough lead, or surprises a receiver.

**13.** Receiver is not catching the ball properly. Proper hand work for receiving requires:

**(a)** Fingers spread and relaxed.

**(b)** Hands reaching toward ball and recoiling upon impact.

**(c)** One-hand blocking and the other tucking in a somewhat funnel shaped position.

**(d)** Blocking hand has fingers pointed up and palm forward in a pass waist high or above and fingers pointed down with palm forward on a pass below the waist.

**(e)** Tucking hand has fingers down and palm inward on a pass below the waist and fingers forward and palm upward on a pass above the waist.

**(f)** On a bounce pass, the top hand blocks the ball on the way up and the underneath hand tucks. The top hand has the fingers forward and the palm down and the lower hand has the fingers forward and the palm up.

## SHOOTING

Regardless of how well you do everything else, if you can't "put the ball through the hoop," you are not going to win many ball games against the teams that can. Therefore, shooting practice must be covered every day.

Shooting practice drills, however, must be carefully devised so that every individual will be practicing the type of shots that he is most likely to get in games. Although every player must try to master every type of shot, your particular offense probably produces a certain amount of specialized shots for each position. Furthermore, each individual usually has his own individual moves that may enable him to get more of a particular kind of a shot. These facts must be taken into consideration in your shooting drills and in other practice drills.

I believe in having some shooting drills in which the entire squad will be working on the same types of shots although they may be in smaller groups at several baskets. These drills should cover all of the various types of shots from the different positions and in the manner in which they are most likely to occur. Then I believe in having separate specific drills for the guards, forwards, and centers that specialize in the types of shots that are most common for each particular position. It seems logical that the time spent in practicing and developing certain types of shots should be in near direct proportion to the percentage of the types of shots that they are most likely to get in game competition. It seems foolish to spend a great amount of time in attempting to develop a type of shot that a player will rarely have an opportunity to use. If very much time is devoted to the development of such things, it will take so much time away from other things that the profit will not exceed the loss.

It is very important that a player exercise good judgment in his shooting. Knowing when not to shoot is as important as knowing when to shoot. A player should honestly recognize his shooting ability and should not take a shot unless he is in a good percentage area for him and no teammate is open in a higher percentage area. This does not mean that a player should not take a shot unless it is from a very high percentage area, but means that good judgment must be used. The percentage area doesn't have to be as high when you have a rebounding advantage as it should be when your opponents have a definite rebounding edge. Although a hope shot must never be attempted, a player should feel free to take a shot when he gets one in an area in which he has confidence and when he is sure of good team rebounding balance. However, the score and amount of time left play a very important part as to the percentage shot you should take.

While it is important for a player to spend some time in the development and improvement of his "off" hand for comparatively close-in shots, it is almost impossible to become as proficient with it as with your "strong" hand. Therefore, a player should always shoot with his "strong" hand if it is at all possible. The "off" hand should be used only in those rare cases when you are not able to use the "strong" hand and yet you are in a good enough position to have a high percentage shot with your "off" hand.

Although I do not feel that a player should take a shot when he is off balance, I have found out that some players may be in good balance for a particular shot when they appear to be off-balance. Since a good shot for one particular player might be a poor shot for almost every other player on the squad, each player must have good individual judgment. The coach must study very carefully the shooting characteristics and abilities of each player and be governed by his findings. He must make all of the players understand why one player may be able to take a shot that others should not attempt.

A player must have confidence in his ability to make a shot if he is going to be a good shooter. I feel that a player should always be free to take a shot that he feels he can make, providing a teammate is not open for a better shot and we are not protecting a lead and taking only the sure or almost sure shot.

There are many psychological and physiological factors that may influence a player's ability to shoot well and the coach constantly must be trying to analyze and correct them as well as teaching the proper technique of the various types of shots.

Some psychological factors that may affect shooting are: lack of confidence, stage fright or nervousness, loss of self-control, hurrying the shot, lack of real desire or determination, worry, fear, superstition, being overconfident or self-satisfied, carelessness, lack of concentration, and things of a similar nature.

Some physiological factors that may affect shooting are: physical condition, improper warmup, injuries, lack of sleep, staleness, poor eyes, fatigue, poor hands, lack of practice, and lack of ability.

Some material factors that may affect shooting are: improper lighting, slippery ball, improperly inflated ball, improper ventilation, strange background, change from a rectangular to a fan-shaped board and vice versa, change from wooden to glass boards and vice versa, lack of driving space underneath, slippery floor, and the defense against you.

Basketball is a mental game and this fact probably is more apparent in shooting than it is in any fundamental. Good shooters must have confidence in themselves, but must realize that the best will occasionally have an off night. The coach, too, must realize this and do nothing to destroy their confidence when it happens. A short rest with a few minor corrections and a pat on the back may be all a player needs. Try to build up confidence in all of your shooters. Once a smooth, natural style is selected for an individual, there should be little experimentation. Do your experimentation first to find the best style for a player who may be having trouble and then work on it to perfect accuracy. If a player shoots fairly well and his style is such that he will be able to get the shot away, merely work to speed up and improve the accuracy.

Ten important fundamental techniques in regard to shooting that can be taught are as follows:

**1.** For the jump or set shot try to keep a straight line from the foot, to the knee, to the elbow, to the shooting hand, with the forearm close to the body and perpendicular to the floor. Release the ball *up* toward your target not *out* toward it with the head following the hand and the wrist, elbow, and knees extending at the same time.

**2.** Work for quick wrist and finger action for the release of the ball. The forefinger has the greatest sense of touch and should be the last finger to provide impetus.

**3.** The head should provide the follow-through up and toward your target.

**4.** The target for the eyes is that unseen spot barely over the top of the metal rim that is closest to you for all but the under-the-basket shots.

**5.** Most shots should have a medium arch with a natural reverse spin on the ball.

**6.** Use the board on almost every under-the-basket shot.

**7.** The ball should be held firmly without tenseness and with the first joints of the fingers and thumbs providing the pressure. The rest of the hand should exert no pressure on the ball even though some part might be in contact with it.

**8.** That necessary balance with the head remaining above the midpoint between the feet should be maintained as much as possible.

**9.** After releasing the ball, the shooter must land in balance ready to rebound, provide a press, intercept a careless pass, get back on defense, or remain in the play for any advantageous move. You usually should land slightly forward of the spot from which you took off.

**10.** The scorer must always acknowledge the pass that led to the score by a smile, a nod, or a wink and all players should encourage and build confidence in their teammates by such remarks as, "Nice shot, Gary," "OK., Pete, you'll get the next one," "Beautiful pass, Walt," "Great tip, Bob," "Sorry I missed you, Bill. I'll see you the next time," "My fault, Fred" "Great fake, John," and other brief comments in an admiring tone of voice.

## Types and Methods

There are a number of different types of shots as well as various methods of shooting them. However, there are certain basic things that must be kept in mind for almost every type of shot regardless of the individual characteristics of the shooter and the method that he may be using.

I believe in working on shooting from the inside out. In other words, we first try to teach the various types of shots that will be used from close in and then gradually work our way out to the maximum distance from which we feel that a player should shoot.

We do not have any specific shooting drills from any distance exceeding 25 to 30 feet. Although we will have an occasional player who can shoot with acceptable accuracy up to 35 feet, we do not encourage it. Some players may work on their own time to increase their range past 25 or 30 feet, but we will not devote any of our regular practice time to it. Any time that a player has to strain to get the ball to the basket from an outside shot, the distance is too great. This is true for both the set and jump shots and for any player who likes to "dunk" the close-in shots.

Since a high percentage of game shots in almost every type of offense in the game today are jump shots, it seems advisable that a high percentage of the shooting practice should be spent on the development and improvement of the jump shot.

**1. The Set Shot.** We consider the set-shooting area to be from a distance of 25 to 30 feet. Of course, that doesn't mean that exact number of feet, but from within a few feet of that distance from the basket.

If a team has no dangerous outside shooters, the defense will mass closer to the basket and make it extremely difficult for any offense to get the close-in shots. A driving player who can hit from outside becomes more effective as a driver because he draws the defense closer to him, which makes it easier to get by the defense. A driving game draws the defense back and sets up the good percentage jump and set shots and a good outside shooting game sets up the drives. Good outside shooters also prevent their defensive men from floating and helping out on defense as much as they would against poor outside shooters.

The one-handed set shot was used almost exclusively on the Pacific Coast at one time, but it is now used extensively in all sections of the country at every level. The East Coast continued the use of the two-handed set shot longer than other sections of the country, but it is rarely used now in any section of the country. The two-handed set shooter has now become the oddity that the one-handed set shooter used to be.

After having had considerable experience in different areas of the country playing with, coaching, and observing players who excelled in one or the other type, I have come to the conclusion that the one-handed set is better up to the distance (25 to 30 feet) that I want my players to shoot, while the two-handed set might be better for shots from a greater distance. However, this may vary with individuals. I also believe that the one-handed shot is a little quicker and thus a little more difficult to defend.

(a) *Two-Handed Set from Chest.* The ball should be held properly and firmly close to the chest and under the chin in good position to pass, dribble, or shoot. The fingers are well spread on the sides and slightly in back of the ball with the thumbs in back pointing toward each other with their ends only about an inch apart, although this may vary a little according to the size of the hands. The elbows should be close into and slightly brushing the body. The chin should be up and the head should be directly above the midpoint between the two feet.

The feet should be spread to about shoulder width with the weight slightly forward toward the balls of the feet with the knees slightly flexed and the hips and other joints relaxed. I prefer to have the right foot slightly advanced for a right-handed player and the left foot slightly advanced for a left-handed player. I feel that this is more natural and provides better balance and a better opportunity to fake and move; however, there are many coaches who believe in keeping the feet parallel or together.

The ball is released by a quick extension of the elbows and a flick of the wrists and fingers. The hands should follow through with the forefingers pointing up and toward the basket practically parallel at the same height and with the thumbs almost touching each other. The forefinger should leave the ball last for improved direction. The other fingers and thumbs provide balance and impetus. The weight comes up high on the toes and you may leave the floor slightly, but be sure to go up, not out, and land in practically the same place from which you take off.

I like the head to go up and toward the basket with the shooter rather imagining that he is throwing his head through the basket.

At the conclusion of the shot the set shooter should almost always be moving forward toward his target and then to the long rebound area at the top of the key.

*(b) Two-Handed Set for Over Head.*  This shot is at times used effectively by high post men when they turn and face the basket, by forwards out of the corner or on the sides of the floor, and by some guards from out front.

Since the ball is held in the same manner as for the two-handed overhead pass and then released in the same manner as the two-handed set starting from the chest, it isn't too difficult to teach.

As a general rule, a player will not have quite as much range as he will have with the two-handed set from the chest and, except for the overhead or high pass, he is not quite as dangerous for the pass and cut or for the quick drive when he starts with the ball over his head.

*(c) One-Handed Set.*  Except for the fact that the impetus for the shot comes from only the strong hand and the other is merely used for control and balance, most of the principles that apply for the two-handed set from the chest also apply to the one-handed set. (See Fig. 3-6.)

The ball is held close to the chest and underneath the chin with the shooting hand a little more toward the back and slightly under the ball and the other hand moving a little toward the front but cupped and slightly under the ball.

The fingers and thumb are well spread with the split between the forefinger and the middle finger almost in line with the nose or the middle of the face. The fingers and thumbs on each hand are well spread with the palms almost facing each other when the ball is released. The hand, forearm, elbow, knee and foot should form a straight line. If the elbow gets out to the side, the rotation of the ball is changed and may cause it to curve, and if you start to reach forward instead of upward toward the basket before your release, you will be throwing or pecking the ball instead of shooting it. In both cases the accuracy of the shot will be diminished.

A

B

C

D

**FIGURE 3-6** The quick set shot.

**E**

**FIGURE 3-6** *Continued.*

the shot. Since the forefinger has the greatest sense of touch, it should be the last to touch the ball, which forces the palm to turn slightly outward upon release.

The body is slightly crouched with the knee bent, the joints relaxed, and the head up and directly above the midpoint between the feet. The weight comes up high on the toes of the forward foot and you may leave your feet a little as you get the quick push and upward thrust of the rear foot. (See Fig. 3-7.) Throw the head up and through and land slightly forward of the position from which you take off.

In the one-handed set shot I feel that the right foot should be forward for a right-handed shooter and the left foot forward for the left-handed shooter. This enables you to keep the opposite foot ready for the quick pivot or push off for the quick start when either might be an advantageous move.

Instead of having the shoulders squared off and more or less parallel to your target as you should in the two-handed set shots, the body should be turned and angled slightly for the one-handed set with the shoulder on the shooting-hand side forward toward the basket and the opposite shoulder slightly back. The head is turned slightly toward the shoulder or arm on the shooting side.

A

B

C

D

**FIGURE 3-7** Side view of the quick set jump shot.

E          **FIGURE 3-7** *Continued.*

**2. The Jump Shot.** This shot is very similar to the one-handed set shot, but is usually from the move or a quick movement following a quick stop. The ball should be held in the same manner and brought up to shooting position and released in an almost identical manner. Remember that the hand, forearm, and elbow are in a straight line up the body. (See Fig. 3-8.)

I have come to the conclusion that I and many other coaches of my acquaintance used to place too much emphasis on height of the jump. In doing so, I believe we made it more difficult to maintain good ball control and coordinated rhythm for the shot. I now believe that you should get all of the height possible that comes naturally without undue strain. The shot is obtained through quickness in getting it by the defensive man rather than straining to outjump him. The defensive man can not jump or leave his feet until the shooter has committed himself, and then it should be too late to bother the shot if the shooter has kept the ball close to his body for protection and shot quickly. (See Fig. 3-9.) The ball should leave the hand of the shooter as the arm reaches full extension of the elbow and at the peak of or just immediately prior to reaching the peak of the jump.

The takeoff is from the opposite foot from the shooting hand and the finish, after the follow-through, should be the same as the one-handed

**FIGURE 3-8** Side view of excellent jump-shooting form in an actual game.

set shot, except that you will be higher in the air for the jump shot. You strive for height, not distance, on the last step, but do not strain to get unusual height. The knee of the leg on the shooting-hand side comes up quickly for protection, power, and balance. Remember the movement is up toward your target, not out toward your target and, although you are moving forward some, you should land only slightly forward of the position from which you took off.

Practically every player should release the ball quickly at the maximum height of his jump or just prior to and not after starting his descent. Some players seem "to hang" at the peak of their jump, but it is really an illusion because of their movements. The ball should be re-

**FIGURE 3-9** Front view of excellent jump-shooting form in an actual game.

leased with a quick wrist and finger snap and with the forefinger probably last to leave the ball as the palm turns slightly outward. (See Fig. 3-
10.) The forefinger should finish pointing toward the target, the head
toward the same direction, and you should land on the floor in balance
with the feet spread and ready to move to your rebounding position or
make any necessary adjustment.

In addition to the takeoff from the move where we push off the back
foot and bring the forward knee upward for the shot, we work in two different methods of taking off after making a stride stop.

**FIGURE 3-10** Actual game jump shot, showing good height, body control, eye concentration, and fingertip control of the ball just before extending the elbow and snapping the wrist to release the ball.

In the first one, we make a quick stride stop and then quickly bring the forward foot, which will be the right foot for a right-handed shooter and the left foot for a left-handed shooter, back to the rear foot, tuck slightly, and spring up quickly for the shot. (See Fig. 3-11.)

In the second one, we make the stride stop in the same way, but use a rocker movement by merely bringing the head and shoulders back without bringing the front foot back and then springing upward and

A         B

C

**FIGURE 3-11** Quick takeoff, ball release, and good landing balance of a quick jump shooter.

forward for the shot. We may use this move from a straight drive at the basket, and from a baseline or across the key drive when the defense prevents us from going on in but they are moving quickly. The shot after the stride stop from a drive toward the baseline or across the floor necessitates your changing your body angle and head toward the basket for the shot. Although your momentum has been toward the baseline or across court, we want it toward the basket when the ball is released. Most players should not take the shot unless they can make the head follow straight toward the basket.

We use some form of the jump shot probably more than all of the other types combined, because of our emphasis on fast break and a sharp cutting set offense. As a result it naturally follows that we must devise a number of drills to give us game-condition work on the type of jump shot that each individual, according to the position that he plays, may be getting.

I should like to re-emphasize a fact in regard to all one-handed shots that the "off" hand is used to help adjust, protect, and control the ball until the split second before the shot is taken. The success of the shot is equally dependent upon the use of both hands the vast majority of the time.

**3. Under the Basket or Close-In Shots.** There are several different types of shots that a player should learn and be able to execute well from close in around the basket. Almost any player at any competitive level should be able to make the basket if he is wide open underneath, but it is very seldom that a player gets wide open in that area. Therefore, it is imperative that he learns to get the ball in the basket from a hard drive under pressure, from a little too far underneath, from a twisting off-balance position from either side or in front, or from any position from which he might be able to get a close-in shot if he has a quick move.

I feel that all short shots, particularly from the side, should be banked off the backboard if it is possible to do so. If a man gets open coming directly down the foul lane, I want him to go to one side, preferably his strong side, and lay the ball off the board with his strong hand, as I feel that this shot is more accurate than trying to lay it over the front rim. However, we do some practice on the lay-in, directly over the front rim without using the board for those occasions when they are forced into using by being pressured or squeezed from each side.

Not too many years ago I frowned on the use of the "dunk" shot as I did on the use of the behind-the-back pass, but now I favor every player using the "dunk" shot when he is in position to do so, providing that he can dunk the ball easily without undue or extra strain or effort. It is now my opinion that it is the surest shot of all for the player who can reach that height without straining.

I try to devise drills that will help the players to learn to shoot the close-in driving shots at the end of a dribble drive, from a return pass after a pass and cut, after receiving a pass from a normal cut, and after receiving a long pass. We also work some on receiving a pass high around the basket and putting it in the basket before coming down. We also like to work on the quick stop underneath from a hard drive, using a head and slight ball fake up, followed by the quick jump for the shot.

I stress proper landing after taking a shot and getting back into the play quickly. Quite often we have the driving shooter try to get back and catch the ball before it hits the floor, regardless of how fast he may be moving. It is my opinion that this helps in various ways, such as: helping him to high jump rather than broad jump on that last step; helping him to lay the ball against the board more softly; helping him to get back on defense sooner; and helping him to realize that there is always something to do after taking a shot.

(a) *Ordinary Layup.* As the takeoff should be on the opposite foot from the shooting arm and the push should be up toward the basket and not out in broad jumping style, good judgment must be used as to when to leave the feet. (See Fig. 3-12.)

The ball should not leave the hand until near the peak of the jump, but definitely before starting to come down. As a general rule, there should be very little spin on the ball. It should hit the board so softly that it goes through the basket without touching the metal rim.

The opposite hand should be used to help protect, adjust, and control the ball and bring it into position for the shot. Although we do some practice with each hand on each side of the basket, I favor a player always using his strong hand from either side if he possibly can. The ball must be kept close to the body on the way up.

The shooting hand may be behind and slightly under the ball with the fingers spread and pointing upward or the hand may be under the ball with the fingers spread and pointing forward and the ball released by quick upward flip of the wrist, fingers, and elbow. We work on both and permit a player to use the method in which he has the most confidence.

In our practice drills for this shot we stress a head and very slight ball fake to the opposite side away from our shooting just prior to moving up for the shot. This causes even a good defensive man to hesitate at times and gives the shooter the split second he needs to get the shot away unmolested.

**FIGURE 3-12**   Keith Wilkes making a quick drive for the basket against Arizona State.

(b) *Close-In Shot Following Quick Stop.*   For this we work on exactly the same shots and with the same execution as has been described under the jump shot following a quick stop. The only difference is the distance from the basket. The idea is to get the shot away before the defensive man can recover from your quick stop. You may use the stride stop followed by the fadeaway or rocker stop and then shoot.

We also work on getting the ball in the basket quickly after making a quick head and slight ball fake-up. The jump stop is usually used before this move although it can be equally effective following the stride stop.

(c) *The Short Hook.*   This is used when the player crosses over or is too far under to use the regular layup. The takeoff and pivot are made on the opposite foot from the shooting arm.

There are two rather acceptable forms for this shot as far as the shooting arm is concerned. In the first one the ball is held up high with a bent elbow and the body is turned so that the chest is almost facing the basket when the ball is released quickly across the line of the body above the head. I favor this method whenever the shooter isn't crowded too much. In the other method, the ball is released following an almost straight-arm pendulum swing across the top of the head with the body more sideways toward the basket.

In the first method the wrist and fingers release the ball with a little twist to make it take off the board quickly and in the second method or pendulum swing the ball is released softly with a natural flick of the wrist and fingers up toward your target.

The disadvantage of the stiff-arm sweep method is that it is far more difficult to land in good balance and get back into the play and a defensive floater coming back in may be able to bother you a bit as the ball is extended out away from the body. However, it enables you a little better to get the shot away over an inside man, as the other method is dependent upon the timing and quickness against an inside man.

We do not practice on long hook shots as I never permit my players to use them. I feel that they usually are for big men only and I do not like to see any man take a shot from outside and then be going away from the board. This feeling is particularly true in regard to our taller men whom we want on the board. However, if I were going to work on long hook shooting, I would immediately get in touch with "Tippy" Dye, who had great success in developing long hook shooters at Ohio State and at the University of Washington. Bob Houbregs, Bruno Boin, and Doug Smart formed a succession of long hook shooters for "Tippy" at Washington that helped make his coaching tenure there most enjoyable while making it somewhat less than that for many opponents.

(d) *The Lay-Back.*   This shot is often used in place of the short hook for players who have difficulty in mastering the hook shot with the "off" arm. However, there are players who prefer to use it regardless of their "off" arm ability.

The shot is made quickly over the end-line shoulder with the strong arm. In other words a right-handed player would use it instead of a left-handed hook when crossing under the basket from the right to the left

A

B

C

D

**FIGURE 3-13**   Proper left-foot takeoff for a driving right-hand "layback" shot.

E                              **FIGURE 3-13** *Continued.*

while the left-handed player would follow the same principle when going under from left to right. The shoulder line remains almost at a right angle with the face of the board.

The palm of the hand faces the basket with the fingers up and well spread and the thumb pointed toward the end line. A quick flip of the fingers and wrist should give the ball a natural reverse spin. (See Fig. 3-13)

The takeoff should be from the opposite foot from the shooting hand. However, I occasionally find a player who prefers to take off from the foot on the shooting hand side and permit him to do so providing he hits and it seems more natural to him.

(e) *The Reach-Back.*   This shot is used when a player can not get the near-side shot and is forced so far under the board toward the end line that he can not use either the hook or the lay-back. The left hand is used when driving from the right and the right hand is used when driving from the left.

The shooting hand is extended back inside the board line very quickly with the palm of the hand under the ball and the thumb pointing in toward the center line of the court.

The ball is released with a quick outward twist of the wrist and fingers with the thumb rolling back toward the ear. This will naturally

A

B

C

D

**FIGURE 3-14** Proper right-foot takeoff for a driving left-hand "reachback" shot.

E

**FIGURE 3-14** *Continued.*

cause a pronounced spin on the ball to carry it up and in the basket from the lower part of the board, but it should not be overly exaggerated.

The takeoff is from the opposite foot from the shooting hand with a quick twist of the pivot foot and body. (See Fig. 3-14.) This twist of the body should have the shooter almost facing the basket when he lands.

Although many players have some difficulty in mastering this shot, I have found it to be a very valuable asset. Since the end line is four feet from the face of the board, the opportunity to use this shot may come up several times during the course of the game. It is a shot that helps develop touch and may result in a comparatively easy score for the player who has mastered the shot, while the player without this particular shot would be no threat from that position.

**4. Offensive Rebounding and Tipping.** The most important detail in regard to rebounding, offensively or defensively, is getting position. I believe in constantly and continuously emphasizing that every player must assume that every shot will be missed if he hopes to have an opportunity to rebound missed attempts. The player who waits to see if the shot is missed and then tries to get position will get few rebounds.

The hands should be shoulder high whenever a player is in the rebounding area with the fingers pointing upward. The elbows should be out and the fingers should be well spread.

The timing should be such that the ball is tipped just prior to reaching the peak of the jump. It is impossible to have much control of a ball that is tipped after the player has started the descent from his jump. If the ball rebounds over three or four feet out from the basket, it is better to play for possession rather than trying to tip it into the basket.

The hands and arms should shoot straight up and the tip made with a flick of the wrist and fingers. Bringing the hand in back of the head and slapping at the ball provides very little chance of success and should not be tried for a goal, although it may be used to get the ball to a teammate or away from the defense.

The player should be in good balance and well spread to take up as much space as possible. He should be slightly crouched, in a position ready to jump with the elbows out and the hands at shoulder height.

Next to getting position, the most important detail is to time yourself with the ball. Jumping too soon or too late will do you no good. The ball must be watched in flight toward the basket and rebounding angles must be studied. Find out by constant study the most probable rebounding areas for the flat shot, the arched shot, the long shot, shots from the side, and other peculiarities of a shot.

It takes considerable jockeying and faking to get good position as the defense will usually be inside and in a better position. Be careful not to get caught so far under that you can do nothing more than catch the ball if it comes through; this is as much a fault as being caught too far away from the basket.

On almost every set, push, or jump shot, we should have triangular rebounding underneath with the shooter moving to the foul line to cover the long rebound area and a fifth man back as a protector.

On driving shots from underneath, we try to have triangular rebounding underneath and a combination long rebounder and protector. The driving shooter is to get back into the play as quickly as possible. We try to develop this during the practice drills on driving shots by having the shooter attempting to land properly and get back and catch the ball before it hits the floor.

The long rebound area is not quite as important on driving shots because the ball is not likely to rebound as far out as it may from a missed shot from outside. However, many balls may be deflected out from off the hands of the man battling underneath and I like my players to be alert for these at all times. The quick, alert man is invaluable in the long rebounding area as he can take chances with a protector in back of him and regain possession of many temporarily loose balls. A small quick man is quite often more valuable in this position than a larger, slower man.

**5. Free Throws.**  The free-throw shot can be entirely different from any other shot because the conditions under which it is taken are entirely different. There is no hurry for fear of having the shot blocked; it is always from exactly the same distance and same position; and there can be no yelling, arm waving, or movement to disturb the shooter. The two-handed (chest or underhanded) free shot is seldom used now, but it is not completely obsolete and is used with success by many who practice it.

I believe that the free throw should be practiced so that it becomes such a complete habit that it is almost reflex action. A player should be able to close his eyes, once he has his position, and go through the movement very easily and naturally.

(a) *One-Handed.*  This is shot exactly like the one-handed set shot from the floor except that the shooter never leaves the floor. He comes up on his toes to get the necessary follow-through and then settles back to the exact position that he was in before starting the shot.

(b) *Two-Handed Chest.*  This is also shot exactly the same as the two-handed set from the floor without leaving the floor.

(c) *Two-Handed Underhand.*  This is the shot that I advocate in spite of the fact that practically every college player uses the one-handed set. I have found it quite difficult to change a player who has been using the one-handed shot all through his previous play to the two-handed underhand shot; therefore, I merely try to perfect and improve the shot he has, providing he shoots reasonably well and there is nothing radically wrong with his technique.

However, I insist that if I were coaching high school ball again my players would use the two-handed underhand shot almost exclusively. In several years of high school coaching when using this method, my teams were outstanding free-throw shooters. Our season percentage was always at or near the top of the high school list and usually better than most of the colleges. I attribute this to the fact that the player never attempted any other style and had supreme confidence in this method.

For the technique of this shot I like to have the shooter hold the ball firmly and close to the body in front of the thighs with the elbows slightly bent. A slight knee dip is taken and the ball is brought up close to the body and released up and out in front of the eyes by a quick extension of the arms and elbows and a flip of the wrists and fingers. The flip gives the ball a back or reverse spin that is necessary for final feel and control.

A medium arch of about three feet above the basket should be used, although individuals will vary this. Some shoot better with a higher arch and some like a flat shot.

The weight comes high on the toes as the heels come off the floor and the knees are extended fully just as the ball leaves the hands. After the ball leaves the hands, you settle back down in perfect balance as you were before the shot.

The head does not lean forward, but remains directly above the mid-point between the two feet at all times.

The feet should be spread about shoulder width with the left foot slightly forward for a right-handed player and the right foot slightly forward for a left-handed player. I believe this provides better balance than when the feet are parallel with each other.

The ball is held with the fingers well spread to the sides and a little underneath the ball and with the ends of the thumbs pointing forward from slightly back of the top of the ball. At the conclusion of the shot the forefingers are pointing toward the basket from the same height and the thumbs are pointing toward each other.

## General Suggestions Regarding Free Throws

**1.** Early in the practice season each player should shoot at least fifty free throws each day. Many shots should be taken in succession to develop rhythm and form.

**2.** As the season progresses, fewer shots should be taken in succession until eventually a player very seldom takes over two shots in succession. If a player hits a slump, he may again shoot many in succession until he starts hitting well.

**3.** Divide the players at the various baskets where they shoot as a group, each player moving after two attempts. The others are lined up along the lanes and keep moving clockwise as a new shooter moves to the line.

**4.** Use a competitive drill by having each group change baskets as soon as any group make a designated number in succession. The balls are left when the players move from basket to basket in order that they will not be using the same ball all of the time.

**5.** Get the ball at the back of the circle before you move up to the foul line. Line yourself up at the back of the circle, get the ball, and move directly up to the line.

**6.** Loosen up by flicking the ball with the wrists and fingers and by bouncing it.

**7.** On a two-shot foul hold your position if you make the first one, but step back and come up again if you miss the first one. A teammate should try to retrieve the ball after the first attempt of two and pass it to the shooter with a word of encouragement.

**8.** Do not stare at the basket. Get the ball, line yourself up, walk up to the line and get your position, glance at the basket, bounce the ball a couple of times, and look up at the basket as you shoot.

**9.** Do not take too much time once you are in position to shoot. If you do not feel right, step back and come up again, relax, and shoot.

**10.** Do not lean forward and try to guide the ball. When the ball leaves your hands, settle back in your starting position and be alert for rebounds or to move into your defensive position. Do not reach, lean, or move sideward.

**11.** Develop an easy rhythmic movement with which you feel comfortable and have confidence.

**12.** Do not permit anything to disturb your concentration on your shot. Nothing can bother you.

**13.** Do not worry over a missed shot. Your percentage of making the next one increases with every one you miss providing you do not worry.

**14.** As the season progresses, free-throw drills should be held at various times during the practice session—when the players are fresh and at various stages of fatigue.

**15.** A player should not experiment on the free-throw line, but should be serious and work hard.

**16.** Keep the head directly above the midpoint between the two feet with the feet at approximately shoulder width and the left slightly in advance for a right-handed shooter and vice versa.

**17.** The ball should have a natural reverse spin or rotation and a medium arch.

**18.** Concentrate on a target that cannot be seen because it is down over the top of the front rim ten feet high.

**19.** Keep daily free-throw records for each individual as well as game records.

**20.** A nice trophy for the best season percentage in games provides incentive. A minimum average of one attempt per game should be required.

**21.** An excellent time for some free throw practice is during the 5 on 5 work which constitutes 25 to 30 per cent of our practice and comes near the end. Each player not in the 5 on 5 would make a pre-designated number (6 to 10) free throws in succession and then move in to the 5 on 5 work in a pre-determined manner at the first break in the action. This continued automatically through the duration of the drill without having to stop.

**6. Special Shooting Drills and Moves.** The time and place to use these various shots depend upon your individual abilities, your general offense, and how you are being defensed. The use of these shooting drills also requires practice on various other offensive fundamentals, such as—passing, receiving, faking, quick stops, quick starts, pivoting, dribbling, balance, and ball-handling.

### (a) For Pivot or Post Men

**1.** Receive pass at post and step quickly toward the basket to your right or to your left and drive under for an underneath shot. Throw the inside arm toward the basket as you start your drive.

**2.** Receive ball on post, use head fake to one side and show the ball over that shoulder, turn quickly, and drive the opposite way. The inside arm and inside leg will lead the way.

**3.** Receive the ball on post, take a quick step toward basket to the right or left, hesitate or stop and pull back, then drive quickly the same way. This change of pace may free you.

**4.** Receive the ball on post, make a cross-over turn or a reverse turn to face the basket, then: Fake a drive, step back, and take a push, set, or jump shot; fake a drive to one side, hesitate or stop, then drive that way; fake a drive to one side and drive to the opposite side; fake a drive to one side, pull back, and fake a set shot, then drive under to right or left; bring ball overhead for a two-handed overhead shot.

**5.** Receive ball on the post, take a quick step away, turn to face the basket, and get a quick shot. (See Fig. 3-15)

**6.** Receive ball on the post, drive toward the basket just outside the lane or either side, and take a hook shot; or make a quick stride stop, and pull back for a quick fadeaway or jump shot.

**7.** Work on set and jump shots from all areas where you might be expected to shoot. (See Fig. 3-16)

**8.** Free throws.

### (b) For Forwards

**1.** Receive ball on the side and reverse-drive quickly to the outside for an underneath shot, or a quick stride stop and a fadeaway or jump shot when you get within 5 to 15 feet of the basket.

**2.** Receive ball on the side, cross over or reverse turn to face the basket, and use same fakes as post man, to get same types of shots—underneath, across the key, or by driving baseline. (When a right-handed man receives the ball on the right side of the floor, we like him to face the basket by making a reverse turn to the inside using the left foot as the pivot foot. When he is on the left side of the floor, we like him to face the basket by crossing over with the right foot

A

B

C

D

**FIGURE 3-15** Right-handed post man receiving pass on post and swinging the right foot back to face the basket. (He may also cross over on the left foot to face the basket, as in the instance of a forward on the left side of the floor.)

A

B

C

**FIGURE 3-16**  Post man showing good ball control and release for quick jumper.

and using the left foot as the pivot foot. A left-handed player would merely reverse the foot movements in order that he might keep his right foot as the pivot foot. See Fig. 3-17.)

**3.** Receive ball on the side, turn to face the basket, bring the ball up quickly for a pass to the post, and cut across the top of the key or toward the baseline for a return pass and shot.

**4.** Receive ball on the side, turn to face the basket for a set shot, a fake drive and pull back for a set shot, or a fake set shot and drive.

**5.** Set and jump shots from all set- and jump-shot areas.

**6.** Fake receiving pass on the side, and reverse quickly with an inside turn to receive a pass for a shot.

**7.** Receive pass on the side post and work on all the moves and shots that the post men use from the post.

**8.** Free throws.

## (c) For Guards

**1.** Set and jump shots from all set- and jump-shot shooting areas.

**2.** Fake set shots from various spots in your area and driving right or left all the way for the various shots underneath or the quick stops for the jump or fadeaway shots.

**3.** Fake drive and pull back for a set shot, or fake set shot after pulling back and driving for a shot.

**4.** Come around a cross-screen from a guard or a forward for a quick set or jump shot.

**5.** Pass to the post or forward and cut for a return pass for a quick jump or driving shot or faking a cut after passing and pulling back for a return pass and quick jump shot. (See Figs. 3-18 and 3-19)

**6.** Dribble drives all the way underneath for the various shots and for quick stops at the top of the circle for jump shots.

**7.** Pass to the side post and cut off of him for return passes for the various shots.

**8.** Receive pass on the side post and work on the various shot possibilities from that position.

**9.** Free throws.

## General Shooting Points To Consider

**1.** Take no wild, chance, or hope shots.

**2.** Shoot with confidence—in case of doubt, don't shoot.

**3.** Practice for perfection from the spots where you get the most shots.

A                                    B

C

**FIGURE 3-17** Right-handed forward coming from under to receive pass on the side post, faking a return pass to the cutter, and crossing over on his left foot to face the basket. (The forward may also swing the right foot back while pivoting on the left foot to face the basket.)

D

E

F

**FIGURE 3-17** *Continued.*

A

B

C

**FIGURE 3-18** Forward coming from underneath to receive the ball on the side post and returning it to the cutter.

D

E

F

**FIGURE 3-18** *Continued.*

A

B

**FIGURE 3-19** Post man setting screen for guard who has passed to the forward, then faking in and getting open for a pass from the forward after the guard has cut by.

C

D

**FIGURE 3-19** *Continued.*

**4.** Never shoot carelessly. Concentration is a golden asset.

**5.** Use a reasonable arch, natural spin, and have the head follow through up and toward the basket.

**6.** Practice as much as possible under game conditions once your form is determined and as the season progresses.

**7.** Use competitive drills and be quick without hurrying.

**8.** Work on all types of close-in shots. Develop various driving or twisting shots from underneath, but never take an "off"-hand shot when it is possible to use your "strong" hand.

**9.** Study rebound positions and angles. Know where to go after you shoot or when a teammate shoots.

**10.** Don't keep experimenting—practice and develop your own natural form, but work for rhythm and coordination in all of your shots.

**11.** Analyze and study your shots—know why!

**12.** Eye the rim or the spot on the board and get a follow-through toward your target, rather than toward the side or away from the target.

**13.** High jump, don't broad jump on your driving and jump shots, but don't strain so much for height that you lose shooting rhythm.

**14.** Hit the board softly on driving shots without too much spin on the ball. We like to try to have the ball come off the board down through the basket without touching the metal rim. The shot that is a little too hard to do that will then still have a chance to hit the metal rim and go down through.

**15.** Keep the ball close to the chest with the elbows in. This enables you to shoot quickly over the defensive man with the ball protected.

**16.** Work to develop quickness with accuracy. You must not only be able to shoot accurately, but you must also be able to get the shot away.

**17.** Do not hurry, but do not hesitate when you have a good shot. Shoot with confidence when you are in position and no teammate is open in a better position.

**18.** Practice close in shots first, then gradually increase your distance in direct proportion to your accuracy.

**19.** Shoot when "on," pass more when "off."

**20.** Be unselfish. Compliment the scorer even though he may have missed you on a pass.

**21.** Be determined and yet relaxed without being tense.

**22.** Most fine shooters seem to shoot a light ball.

**23.** Keep ball in position to pass, dribble, or shoot—chest high, close to the body.

**24.** Know when to use the board—on most under-the-basket shots and from certain angles on the side.

**25.** Keep your courage, poise, and self-control. Let nothing disturb you.

## DRIBBLING

This fundamental is a great weapon that has always been much abused, misused, and overused. When properly used it can mean much to any team, but improperly used it can definitely wreck any team from both a morale and a technical point of view.

Entirely too many players have a tendency to fancy themselves as dribblers when in reality they are only bouncers of the ball. A good dribbler must not only be able to control the ball well, he must also be a fine, alert passer who is always heads up and can get his pass away in a fraction of a second. He must have wide vision and see the whole floor and not be looking at the ball.

Years ago, before the ten-second rule was adopted, an expert dribbler could often maintain good possession in the "stall" game as his teammates had plenty of floor space to spread out and give him ample opportunities for outlet passes whenever he got in trouble. That is much more difficult in the game today because of ten men being congested in half of the court and the necessity to penetrate as the rules now demand. However, the dribble is still a very important part of the "stall" game as well as the other offensive parts when used properly.

### Types and Techniques of the Dribble

**1. Low or Control Dribble.** This should be used to get the ball out of a congested area when you can not pass, to drive by a defensive man on a move for the basket, or to advance the ball.

The fingers should be well spread and relaxed with the joints slightly bent and the hands slightly cupped. (See Fig. 3-20.) The elbow should be kept almost in contact with the body and the forearm parallel with the floor.

The ball should be pushed away by the wrist and fingers and kept slightly in front of the body on the best protected side.

The knees should be bent and the body in a crouched position, but with the back straight and the head up and kept directly above the midpoint of the two feet.

In the control dribble the ball should not come up over knee high and frequently not higher than half-way up to the knee. The closer the defense, the lower the dribble, but always keep the head up and be ready to pass. When a defensive man reaches for the ball use the very low bounce.

In the quick drive by a defensive man, the inside arm and leg should lead the way and the low bounce with a change of pace and (or) direction used.

Head and shoulder fakes are better than ball fakes to set your man up for your initial move to get away from the defense. However, we do work on ball fakes with quick movement of the ball by the wrists and fingers while *keeping the elbows in contact with the body.*

**2. High or Speed Dribble.** The high dribble (waist high) may be used to best advantage when you get out in front of the defense or in the open and are driving for the basket or advancing the ball until you get close to the defense when there is no one open in front of you to whom you could pass.

When using this dribble you are not as crouched but are running in a more upright position, ready to pass to an open man or quickly go to the control dribble when needed. The ball is pushed farther away from you to make more speed forward. The ball goes to and comes off the floor in a much greater angle than in the control dribble.

A

B

C

**FIGURE 3-20** The dribble.

The hand, forearm, and elbow are out in front of the body as you are now after speed and must push the ball out away from you. If you permit the ball to come too high or too low, it may slow you down, cause a violation, or cause you to lose an advantage.

**3. Cross-Over Dribble.** This is used in conjunction with either the control or speed dribble and a change of pace and direction to elude a defensive man or get a better position on him.

The dribbling hand flicks the ball to the opposite side by pushing it from slightly outside the ball and the opposite hand continues the dribble.

The ball should be quickly flicked over from close to the body as the foot on the flicking-hand side comes forward to cross over for protection. The flicking hand also leads the way.

When you are crossing over from a fast dribble when the defensive man is moving fast and has passed you, the high bounce can be used on the cross-over. However, when used for a quick start to gain an advantage, perhaps after a fake, a control or low bounce is used and then brought higher if you were successful in getting the step on the defensive man. Never use the high crossover when there is a chance of the defense bothering you that could have been avoided with the low bounce.

**4. Behind-the-Back Dribble.** Although I never want a player to use this when he can use the cross-over, the same as I never want a player to use the behind-the-back pass when he can use a front pass, there is a place where some players can use it to advantage. Furthermore, it can be used for psychological effect at times as well as for the physical advantage that might be gained. Therefore, I believe in spending a little time for drilling in the proper use of it.

There are occasional periods that come up during the practice session when the boys may enjoy a respite from your regular drills and this time may be used to advantage by working on the behind-the-back pass and dribble. They usually get a lot of fun on working on these. The main problem in regard to this is to make certain that they are never used carelessly or for show and only when it is the best and, perhaps, only move for the occasion.

The ball is flicked close behind the back by a quick flip above the back of the knee and across the back of the thigh as the opposite leg moves forward. This keeps the opposite foot and leg out of the way as the ball hits the floor and permits the ball to come up under the opposite hand for a continuation of the dribble.

**5. Off-Hand Dribble.** Although I do not believe in using the "off" hand for dribbling when you can use your strong hand, I do believe that it is extremely important to develop all the dribbling styles, except the behind-the-back dribble, with the "off" hand.

I think it is possible to become almost as proficient with the "off"-hand dribble as with the strong hand and it can prove very valuable for every position. It is more valuable for guards than for forwards, and for forwards than for centers, but every player will find a valuable use for it in almost every game. Therefore, we must not neglect its development.

Some effective uses of the dribble are as follows:

**1.** Short drive for the basket when in the open.

**2.** To advance the ball when the defense is back and when teammates are covered.

**3.** For a quick getaway with an intercepted pass.

**4.** Combined with fakes and pivots to get free.

**5.** As an offensive threat to keep the defense from playing too tight.

**6.** In the fast break when there is no open man ahead.

**7.** To get away from the man-to-man pressing defense.

**8.** To get the ball away from the defensive board and out of congested areas.

**9.** To pick off a guard on a screen.

**10.** To kill time and control the ball in your "stall" game.

Some additional facts and ideas in regard to dribbling are:

**1.** Too much dribbling hurts team play and morale by causing selfishness and resentment.

**2.** Look first, dribble last. Pass ahead whenever you can.

**3.** All dribbles should be driving or with a purpose of setting up something, not just bouncing the ball. Never be guilty of receiving a pass and then just bouncing the ball or using your dribble without a purpose.

**4.** Do not pound the ball, but push it away firmly and quickly with the wrist and fingers.

**5.** Keep the head up at all times and the ball close and under control.

**6.** The body should be crouched with the knees bent and the head directly over the midpoint of the two feet.

**7.** Keep away from sidelines and corners. Stop and pivot when driven to these areas and get the pass away quickly.

**8.** A dribbler should always have a trailer ready to come by at the right time when a dribbler is forced into a pivot. He should come late and fast. There is a tendency for a trailer to come by a pivoter too soon rather than too late.

**9.** Always be able to conclude a dribble with a good quick pass, shot, or stop and turn and pass. Get rid of the ball quickly—as soon as you have used up your dribble.

**10.** Keep the ball low, close to the body, with the elbow in contact with the body, the forearm almost parallel to the floor, and the ball on the protected side when in congested areas. When out in the open and speed is needed, use a waist high dribble and keep pushing the ball out away from you.

**11.** The change of direction and change of pace are very valuable with the dribble.

**12.** If you can't pass, you can't dribble.

**13.** Learn to control the ball with either hand and learn to cross over without carrying the ball, but use your best hand whenever you can.


## STOPS AND TURNS OR (AND) PIVOTS

This particular section deals with the turn made when a player is in possession of the ball. Movements without the ball will be discussed under cutting and faking, which will be the next offensive fundamental to receive attention.

Many coaches prefer to discuss this under footwork, but I believe that footwork is an essential part of every offensive and defensive fundamental. In all probability, footwork is the most essential part of every fundamental because it is necessary for body balance and very little can be accomplished without balance.

**1. Stops.** Before any pivot or turn can be made, a good stop is necessary. In most cases, I prefer the two-foot jump stop with the feet parallel, according to the direction you are going, and well spread to shoulder width or a little wider. However, we also use the stride stop with one foot advanced—preferably the right foot for a right-handed player and the left foot for a left-handed player.

It is very important to get a low body position in good balance with the hips low, the knees bent, the head up, and the ball close to the body and protected from the defensive man. The head should remain above the midpoint of the two feet with the chin and eyes up and with the back neither arched nor bowed.

In the two-foot jump stop the feet should hit the floor simultaneously with the entire surface of the rubber sole contacting the floor, although the forward part of the foot will carry the most weight. The feet must be well spread to shoulder width or wider and the knees and hips relaxed to withstand the sudden shock.

In the stride stop the rear foot hits the floor first and becomes the pivot foot with the other foot following. The pivot foot should be the left for a right-handed person and the right for a left-handed person. Low body balance must be maintained in each type of stop. I should make special emphasis of the fact that *we use the two-foot jump stop when the defense has forced us so closely that we will have to turn immediately after making the stop* and *the stride stop is used more frequently in jump-shooting territory when the defense isn't forcing us so much that we will have to turn immediately upon completion of the stop and may permit us to get a good shot.*

**2. Turns or Pivots After the Stop.** Every stop and turn or pivot is made necessary by the defense forcing the man with the ball away from the line toward the basket and toward the sideline or corner when he has no forward outlet for a pass, although there are some occasions when a man is forced to stop in the middle of the floor.

With that fact in mind, I have tried to concentrate our work on one particular type of stop and turn to serve in practically all situations. Since the terminology differs among various coaches, I will attempt to explain them according to my particular terminology. As a general rule the word *turn* will be used when the player has used his dribble and the word *pivot* will be used when he is free to dribble.

(a) *Inside Turn.* This is the turn that is used almost exclusively by our boys when the defense is forcing you from the middle of the floor and forcing you to make a quick turn immediately upon completion of the stop.

The two-foot jump stop is made with the ball brought close to the hip away from the defense and the turn made by turning on the inside foot and swinging the outside foot and the body backward around the pivot foot. The completion of the turn should have you facing the defensive basket with the feet well spread, the body in good balance, and the ball close to the hip away from the defensive man who forced the stop and turn. As soon as the turn is completed and both feet are again on the floor, shift a little extra weight to the side of the defensive man in order to prevent a slight bump from causing you to lose balance and, perhaps, travel with the ball.

Additional fundamental details of the two-foot jump stop have been described in earlier paragraphs.

(b) *Outside Turn.* The two-foot stop is used and the outside foot becomes the pivot foot with the inside foot crossing over toward the sideline. As in the inside turn you will be facing the defensive end line with the feet well spread and parallel to it when the turn has been completed.

The weight shift, balance, and other fundamental details are the same as before.

This turn should never be used when your stop has been made near the sideline. It is often used by a defensive rebounder to get open for the outlet pass.

(c) *Reverse Turn.*   The stride stop is used with the possibility of getting a good jump shot. When the defense closes in and prevents the shot and there is no opening to pass forward, the front foot crosses over quickly and the back is turned toward the defensive man.

The fundamental details of the stride stop and balance are followed.

**3.   Pivots from the Post and Side Post.**   The moves for these turns were explained under the special shooting drills and moves for post men and forwards and need not be repeated here. However, I would like to reiterate that quickness is essential for effectiveness.

**4.   Pivots from the Forward Position.**
(a) *When Defense Is Tight.*   When a forward receives a pass in his normal position on the side and his defensive man was playing him high and reaching, he pivots quickly on the inside foot and swings the outside leg backward toward the basket, and drives.

(b) *When Defense Is Loose.*   When a forward receives a pass in his normal position on the side and his defensive man is playing him loosely or at arms' length, he pivots to face the basket.

Since we prefer a right-handed player to keep his left foot as the pivot foot and a left-handed player to keep his right foot as the pivot foot, we try to adhere to the following principles: When on the right side of the floor, a right-handed player, upon receiving the pass, pivots on his left foot and swings his right foot backward to the inside to square off facing the basket. (See Fig. 3-21.) The left-handed player on the right side uses his right foot as the pivot foot and swings his left foot across over toward the center of the floor to square off facing the basket. When you are on the opposite side of the floor, the same principles are applied to keep the desired pivot foot when you have faced the basket. (See Fig. 3-22.)

Special points to consider in regard to stops and turns or pivots.

**1.**   As practically every turn or pivot comes at either the end of a dribble drive or the start of a dribble drive, combination drills emphasizing each fundamental are essential.

A

B

C

D

**FIGURE 3-21** Right-handed forward on right side of the floor receiving pass from guard and then swinging the right foot back to face the basket.

E      **FIGURE 3-21** *Continued.*

**2.** Keep the ball close to the body and keep the body between the ball and the defensive man.

**3.** Keep low with the feet spread, knees bent, and tail down, but keep the chin, head, and eyes up.

**4.** Keep in good balance with the head directly above the midpoint between the two feet and the weight fairly well distributed on each foot, but, perhaps, with a little extra bracing on your defensive pressure side. A wide foot spread is necessary.

**5.** If you let the head get forward or sideward as you make your stop, you are likely to lose your balance and travel.

**6.** Combine with dribbling and shooting drills once proper form is established.

**7.** There should always be a trailer ready to come by late and fast to receive a hand-off from a dribbler who makes a quick stop and turn. This requires excellent timing and must be practiced.

**8.** Use the full sole of the shoe to get the best traction for a good stop.

**9.** Stop and pivot when driven toward the sideline or corner.

**10.** Do not start your turn before you have completed your stop.

**11.** Get rid of the ball as quickly as possible after you have completed a dribble and turn or pivot.

A

B

C

D

**FIGURE 3-22** Right-handed forward on left side of the floor receiving pass from guard and then crossing over on the left foot to face the basket.

E                 **FIGURE 3-22** *Continued.*

## FAKING AND FOOTWORK

The ability to make your opponent commit himself by making him think that you are going to do one thing and then doing something differently is one of the most important fundamentals of the game.

This calls for excellent footwork, but it must be remembered that the feet take the body only where the mind directs them. Instantaneous reaction to opportunities is necessary as the opportunity may be there for only a fraction of a second. The slow-reacting player who has to "stop and think" will not be very successful in the quick-reacting game of basketball. A lost opportunity by any individual is a loss to the team.

Faking and feinting are generally thought of as being used primarily on the offense, but such moves are also very necessary and valuable to the defensive player. On offense they apply to the man both with and without the ball and a good fake is always followed by a quick move of some sort—perhaps a pass, a shot, a step back, a reverse, a screen, a dribble drive, a pivot, another fake, a cut, or some other advantageous move.

I emphasize head, body, shoulder, foot, and eye fakes much more than ball fakes, because they can be used with and without the ball. However, we do use ball fakes, but hope to keep in mind the principles of ball-handling and keep our elbows in contact with our body while making these fakes with supple and quick wrists. By using this type of ball fake we never have to bring the ball back from outside the body line in order to move quickly with it in another direction.

Various combinations of all of these fakes should be used in attempts to mislead our opponent and draw him out of position or off-balance. At other times we merely try to lull an opponent into a false sense of security and gain an advantage by a quick start, change of pace, or change of direction at a time when they are expecting a fake.

The type of fake or fakes used depends upon a number of things, such as: your position on the floor, whether or not you have the ball, where the ball is if you do not have it, the passing and shooting ability of the man who has the ball, your particular abilities, your offense or defense, and the particular abilities of the man guarding you and perhaps the ability of a man who might shift to you. For example, a Bill Russell playing defense back in the key area may cause the offense to consider many things.

Every player should be constantly studying his individual opponent and the general defensive principles of the opposing team to find out the individual habits, strong points, weaknesses, or any peculiarities that can be used to your advantage.

I have repeatedly pointed out that basketball is a mental game and quickness is probably the greatest physical asset a player can have. These qualities certainly go hand in hand as it takes mental alertness to put your quickness into action and at the proper time. Every physical movement must be directed by the mind. Good judgment is also necessary if your quickness is to be utilized to the fullest extent. It is impossible to get the jump on the ball or an opponent without it. However, make sure your moves are with a purpose. Merely moving quickly with no particular purpose or aim will get you no place and accomplish nothing worthwhile.

Quickness of thought and action, then, is a characteristic that stands out very prominently in the star performers. Basketball is a game of habits and reactions and the players who can not react instantaneously to situations will be the second-raters because they will lose so many opportunities. Good judgment is necessary, of course, but hesitation, like carelessness, is one of the cardinal sins of basketball. Doing nothing for fear of being wrong is far worse than doing something wrong. Reaction after a mistake can help atone for it, while nothing can make up for doing nothing.

*Change of pace* and *change of direction,* with and without the ball, are two of the finest assets a player can have, but they are ineffective unless they are performed with quickness. I try to develop these by attempting to create the habit of moving lightly on the forward part of the feet, slightly crouched with every joint flexed and relaxed, keeping the hands open and above the waist, keeping the eyes on the ball (when you do not have it), changing pace and direction frequently, and making the changes in angles rather than in arcs. The length of the step may vary with the individual and the situation, but short, choppy steps are better for quick acceleration.

For a change of direction I teach pushing off the foot on the opposite side from the direction we wish to go, taking a short step with the other foot, and then throwing the push-off foot and the arm on that side quickly toward the direction we wish to go. In other words, we push off the right foot to go to the left and off the left to go to the right. (See Fig. 3-23.) We also try to throw the head sharply to lead the way.

The change of pace follows the same principle with a hesitation, perhaps a head fake-up, and a quick push-off of the back foot.

Faking and proper footwork are emphasized in every individual and team drill that we use. By constant stress of these little things in our fundamental drills, I hope to make them become automatic. The players receive practice on the different fakes and types of footwork by changing the drills and working from various positions on the floor. As a result, they are receiving attention during every passing, shooting, pivoting, dribbling, fast break, set formation, set play, defensive, and every other drill that is used. They will probably be developed in direct proportion to the emphasis placed upon them.

Once the individual technique of a fundamental is fairly well understood so that the players do not have to think about the little details, I try to combine as many fundamentals as possible in a limited number of drills, some similar to actual game conditions, and then vary the drills enough to prevent them from becoming monotonous.

In addition to the general type of faking and footwork that are in constant use, there are certain specific types necessary according to a particular position. I believe in giving our players the following list of individual offensive moves that each position should know. This list encourages them to ask questions and do some individual thinking about their play.

## Centers

**1.** Getting open on a high or low post position to receive a pass from a guard or forward.

**2.** Feeding all potential receivers from post positions.

**3.** Getting open for your various shots.

A

B

C

**FIGURE 3-23** Forward on right side of the floor pushing off left foot for a quick inside turn on reverse to get open for a pass.

**4.** Screening to both the strong and weak sides.

**5.** Setting double screen with guard or forward.

**6.** Setting up your man to be screened and working off the screen.

**7.** Getting rebounding position.

**8.** Keeping your man busy when you are on the strong or weak side in order that he may not help out and that you may get open.

## Guards

**1.** Passing to all potential receivers—center, forward, guard, reversers.

**2.** Getting open for a pass from your other guard.

**3.** Getting open after a pass to the post or to a forward.

**4.** Keeping your man busy when you are on the strong or weak side in order that he may not help out and that you may get open.

**5.** Getting open to receive a pass out from a forward to start your weak-side post play.

**6.** Working with the side-post man on the options—pass and cut, dribble by, dribble off screen and roll, hit him with a pass in a reverse, fake a cut.

**7.** Setting up your man to be screened and working off the screen.

**8.** Getting open on dribble drives ending with your various shots, pivots, and passes.

**9.** Setting double screens with center or forward.

**10.** Advancing the ball under man-to-man or zone pressure.

**11.** Getting open on cuts from weak side.

## Forwards

**1.** Getting open to receive pass on side or side post.

**2.** Passing to post and cutting or screening.

**3.** Passing to cutting guard and cutting or screening.

**4.** Passing to protecting guard and double-screening with center.

**5.** Setting up your man to be screened and working off the screen for a shot or pass.

**6.** Reversing from the side with and without the ball.

**7.** Screening and rolling for a pass.

**8.** Side-post options with the guard.

**9.** Getting rebound position.

**10.** Facing the basket properly after receiving pass on the side.

**11.** Getting open on a drive from the side-baseline or across key—and getting a shot, pass, or pivot.

**12.** Keeping your man busy when you are on the strong or weak side in order to prevent him from helping on defense and that you may get open.

### General Ideas

**1.** Filling the proper lanes, crossing over, and screening on the fast break.

**2.** Getting open on jump balls.

**3.** Getting open as a trailer.

**4.** Getting open or checking out on the free-throw lanes.

**5.** Getting open for fast-break outlets.

**6.** Getting open for outlets when being pressed.

**7.** Getting open on special set and out-of-bounds plays.

**8.** Getting open for an outlet pass when we are protecting a lead.

**9.** Keeping the floor spread when we are protecting a lead.

**10.** To execute properly any of the fundamentals.

## SUMMARY

It has been my purpose to try to emphasize that individual offense is nothing more than mastering the individual offensive fundamentals of the game. There are certain fundamentals that must be mastered by each individual regardless of the position he might play, and there are also specific fundamentals that must be emphasized according to position. In other words, the pivot men, the forwards, and the guards each have specific things that they must learn to do especially well that might not be essential to the other positions. However, positions interchange so much in the offenses of present-day basketball that it is wise for a player to be able to adjust himself fairly well to any position, although it is logical to assume that he should be better drilled in the fundamentals most common to the position that he will be playing the majority of the time.

Therefore, as the season progresses, some time should be allowed almost every day for the guards to be working in one group, the forwards in another, and the centers in another. I consider this as necessary as having the guards and forwards working together; the guards, forwards, and post men working together; and the forwards working with the post men. A natural progression of all of these units should follow until all five positions are working together as a team.

Properly grounding the individuals in the proper execution of the fundamentals of the game is the first objective of a coach, and the integration of these individuals into a smooth working unit is the second objective. Basketball is primarily a team game, but every individual must be an offensive threat in order to relieve pressure from his teammates and because each game presents numerous opportunities for individual initiative.

Each player must have the proper mental outlook and mental attitude. It is natural for a player to want to score and none should be criticized for it, but I want no player to attempt to score if he has a teammate in a better position. Not only should the players be unselfish, but they must want to see every teammate do well. I want our players to come to believe from their own experience the truth of the statement, "real happiness begins where selfishness ends."

Each player must have an intense desire to improve. He should be studying and working toward further development at all times. In the majority of cases, the only difference between the truly star performer and just a good player is merely the perfection of a few minor details or fundamentals. This doesn't occur by chance or by accident, but by determination, study, and industriousness.

There is no substitute for being prepared and preparedness can be acquired only by concentrated study, determination, and hard work. Those who are prepared are never lacking in courage and confidence, and it is real, not false. They do not have to "whistle in the dark" and they will have no regrets when an opponent scores more points.

The good offensive player as well as the good defensive player is studying his opponent at all times. He should not be moving aimlessly, but should maneuver with a real purpose in mind. The peculiarities of an opponent may determine what you may be able to set up by some special maneuver.

Since I do not believe in restricting the team with too much of a rigid or set pattern and permit a great amount of individual initiative, it is natural for me to place particular emphasis on individual fundamentals and manuevers. Further discussion of this will be made under team offense.

I want to reiterate and particularly emphasize that I consider quickness to be the most important physical attribute that a player can have for the successful execution of any fundamental. Quickness without hurry is essential. Therefore, we must place special emphasis on quick starts, quick stops, quick changes of direction and pace, quick passing, quick shooting, quick jumping, quick adjustment from offense to defense or from defense to offense, quick reacting to every situation, and in the execution of every fundamental. *Execute the fundamental properly and accurately with maximum quickness.*

In many instances, the fundamentals have not been taught properly or adequately until the execution of them is by habit or reflex. This takes time and demands patience, that invaluable asset to any coach and especially to the beginning coach.

# 4

# TEAM
# OFFENSE

## GENERAL IDEAS

In the discussion of individual offense, it has been pointed out that team offense results from the integration into a unit of the individuals who have been well grounded in the fundamentals of the game.

There are many different styles or theories of offense, but I have long been convinced that it isn't so much what you use but how well you execute it that makes for success. Of course, this is providing that it is predicated on sound principles that keep the floor balanced both offensively and defensively, that the players are in good condition, that they have been properly drilled in the execution of the fundamentals, and that all possess a fine unselfish team spirit. I like the floor balance to usually provide a strong-side cut, a weak-side cut, a cut across the top of the key, triangular rebounding power underneath, a man in the foul circle area to cover long rebounds, and a protector.

I feel that the offense should not be so stereotyped that the players are forced to follow such a set pattern that their individual initiative and freedom of movement are limited too severely. There should be enough options and freedom of movement to eliminate any possibility of the defense or you yourself knowing exactly what each player is going to do. As any offense that becomes too mechanical can invariably be more easily defensed, flexibility is essential.

Another extremely important essential in forming a smooth-working unit is the acquiring of proper timing. This can be acquired only through working the boys together enough so that they will react to the particular peculiarities, physical abilities, and movements of their teammates. All plays are based on timing to some extent and this can be affected by individual characteristics until the players become accustomed to each other. Getting open for a pass, making a cut, getting into position to rebound, taking advantage of a screen, and practically every other offensive move require split-second timing according to the position of the ball and the movements of your teammates.

Development of the offense takes time and requires considerable patience as does the mastering of the individual fundamentals. The first step in the development, naturally enough, is the devising of fundamental drills that are a part of the offense. A picture of the finished offense should be fixed firmly in the minds of the players and they should be able to see the relationship of the drills to the ultimate objective. The drills and number of men used in the drills should be progressively worked out until a five-man team functions as a unit in the execution of the full offense.

This may start out with a guard and forward or a center working together. Then a forward or center is added to make a strong-side unit. Later the weak-side forward is worked in and then the weak-side guard is added to form a complete team unit. The individual parts are worked on first and then put together until you have the whole or finished product.

The maneuvering of the weak-side men or the men away from the ball must never be neglected, as their movements are just as vital for team play as the work of the strong-side men. Too often they may acquire a tendency to feel left out and become "spectators," which permits their defensive men to float and help prevent your strong-side offense from functioning efficiently. This tendency also may keep the weak-side men from being alert to move into the play properly when the strong-side offense is stopped.

A coach must have confidence in his particular style of offense if he expects to instill confidence in his players. If either coach or players are lacking in confidence, the success of any offense is very questionable.

However, although it is a sign of weakness to be constantly changing your offense and may create doubt in the minds of your players, it is an equal fault to stand still and not progress with the game. You must be prepared to meet any and all emergencies and to make the necessary changes that a changing defense might demand. I personally feel that your primary offense should be flexible enough to meet any type of defense reasonably well, get the most out of different personnel with varied strengths, and provide the necessary balance without requiring any radical or extreme changes, but you must be ready to make the little adjustments whenever needed.

With the firm conviction that the ability to properly and quickly execute the fundamentals of the game, having aggressive players in ex-

**FIGURE 4-1**  Excellent example of getting into position to set-up offense.

cellent condition (I want our players to sincerely feel that they are in better condition than any of our opponents), the development and maintenance of an unselfish team spirit, the necessity of constant penetrating movement from spread and balanced areas, and the development of confidence in the players are the heart of any successful offense, I have attempted to permit those ideas to be the most influential in the development of a satisfactory offense. I might add that most of those ideas also apply to team defense.

Furthermore, I am convinced that the offense should not be too complicated, but as simple as possible and still cover the essentials. Too much to do may often result in not doing anything very well.

## PRINCIPAL UCLA OFFENSES

Before discussing and diagramming the principal fast-break and set-type offenses that I use at UCLA, I should like to point out one particular point that is an important part of my philosophy.

In both our fast-break and set offenses, I strongly emphasize the importance of all five men on the floor and try to get each player to feel that when he fails to make the proper move or fake he may cause his team to lose a scoring opportunity.

By encouraging the weak-side men and the protectors and complimenting them for their contribution whenever a play away from them culminates in a score, I try to instill more team spirit. A scorer must always compliment the players who made the pass that led to his score and all the players must compliment or acknowledge a scorer, a passer, a teammate who makes a nice defensive play or gets a clutch rebound or makes some other valuable play. This compliment or acknowledgment is not to be done with a great display, but by a nod, a smile, a wink, or some other gracious word or gesture.

When mistakes are made such as missing an easy shot, making a bad pass, not seeing an open man, making a defensive error, or something of a similar nature, I insist that the players must never criticize or show open displeasure at a teammate, but encourage the offender so that it won't be so likely to happen again. However, be careful not to encourage him in a patronizing manner as that, too, can cause resentment. It is up to the coach to do the criticizing and he should always make it constructive.

Our combination fast-break and set offenses has tended to equalize scoring opportunities for each position. As a result our scoring is usually well balanced, which is especially good for team spirit and morale. One of our conference championship teams that alternated seven different starters found them closely bunched in scoring at the end of the season with averages between 8.96 and 9.91 points per game. Another year found the unit that usually started the game averaging from 8.98 to 10.1 points per game with eight different players having been the leading scorer in at least one game. These are rather extreme examples, but our scoring through the years has usually been exceptionally well balanced in comparison with most teams.

If a player has the ability to make more scoring opportunities for himself or is a better shooter with more drive and individual initiative and, consequently, scores more, the other players won't be so likely to be envious of him or upset because they have been taught to believe that our offense will generally equalize scoring opportunities for the heads up, alert, aggressive, hustling players. Therefore, the leading scorer is usually earning his points rather than getting them through an offense that might tend to make a scoring star of certain positions or individuals.

**FIGURE 4-2** Zip goes the UCLA fast break! Bill Walton (#32) passes the ball downcourt.

## FAST BREAK

There are various styles, systems, and ideas in regard to fast-break basketball, but this particular discussion will primarily emphasize the style that I use and my reason for using it.

Inasmuch as it is generally recognized that fast-break basketball has more appeal to the spectators and to the players than the slow-break and ball-control game, I feel that it is the responsibility of the coach to keep both groups as happy and satisfied as possible. Basketball is essentially a game of fast action and the fast-break attack is the best medium for providing action and quick scores.

Therefore, by teaching the fast break and always trying to make fast-break opportunities rather than waiting for a fast-break situation to present itself, I feel that several important objectives are being accomplished: We are attempting to please both spectators and players; the necessary drills that must be practiced incessantly are very conducive to good physical condition; it helps develop quickness and speeds up reactions in the execution of the fundamentals; it helps players to learn to maintain good balance even when forced to make a quick physical adjustment to a situation; and proper morale and team spirit are greatly enhanced by playing a style of game that the players like and that will probably provide an opportunity for more players to see game action.

It must be kept in mind, however, that there will be more mechanical and, perhaps, mental errors made in this style of game because of the increased tempo of play. This fact again necessitates that the coach must have an abundance of patience. If he does not have the patience to keep his self-control and poise until the players gradually cut down their mistakes, he can not expect to have any degree of success. They will need encouragement and constructive criticism to reach the stage where the results will be worthwhile.

The players must be drilled to near perfection on quick ball-handling on the move; quick shooting from the likely fast-break opportunity areas; recognizing the good percentage shot and not finishing the break with a hope shot; various fakes, feints, and cross-overs with proper footwork to get open or to advance the ball properly and quickly to the man in the most advantageous position; quick reaction whenever you gain possession of the ball; and the proper handling of the two-on-one and three-on-two situations in particular.

I stress getting the ball down the floor and midpoint between the two sidelines as soon as possible and hope to have it there when the potential good shooting area is reached; having a cutter on each side with one being slightly ahead of the man with the ball and one slightly behind being desirable; having a trailer ready to come by the middle man with a good change of pace and direction in case of a pivot or quick stop; and having the fifth man coming down the floor as the protector backing up the play. This type of setup provides the possibility of a good shot from every angle, should give proper rebounding balance, and takes care of adequate protection.

Since possession of the ball is acquired the greatest percentage of times from the defensive board or out-of-bounds underneath after an opponent has scored (the latter being a most undesirable method of acquiring it), I shall illustrate our basic fast-break patterns from possession by those means. However, an attempt is made to follow the same basic ideas or get the ball advanced with the men and the ball in the same relative positions if we gain possession by interception, from a jump ball in the defensive end of the court, from normal back court out of bounds, or in any other manner.

There must be different options to advance the ball quickly to the desired area, as the continuation of any one method would soon be completely blocked by the defense. The problem is to drill the boys enough so that they will react quickly whenever and however we may obtain possession of the ball and are able to shift to the logical option when the defense stops one pattern. If they have to hesitate to think about what to do, they have not been drilled enough and many opportunities will be lost. Whenever you force the defense to make a change to stop you, you have an immediate psychological advantage; so capitalize on it.

Fast-break opportunities are almost always made in the back court by quick reaction immediately upon gaining possession of the ball. The object is to get the defense outnumbered or, at least, out of position in the scoring area and maneuver quickly and properly to get a good percentage shot before the defensive man or men caught out of position can recover and provide adequate defensive balance against you.

The various patterns from which we work to get our fast break functioning will be illustrated in the following diagrams. The players must learn that the defense may block certain lanes and react quickly without losing momentum when that happens. The lanes must be filled as soon as possible and balance must be maintained. They can learn to adjust only by being drilled enough against various defenses that force them to adjust.

I believe in constantly stressing to our players that we must try the fast break *every* time we obtain possession of the ball. Put the pressure on immediately. Many times the application of instant pressure creates a successful break when it did not appear to be possible. The defense will occasionally relax when it seems that they are in position as they are moving back and the quick thrust may cause them to be outmaneuvered.

**Fast Break #1—Deep Middle Man Rebounds Ball** (Diag. 4-1). 1 to 2 to 4 to 5, who drives the ball down the floor and makes the logical play from the top of the foul circle if he gets that far.

The idea is to keep passing ahead if you can and to dribble if no receiver is open. We hope to get the ball to the top of the offensive foul circle with a cutter on each side, a trailer, and a protector.

Each passer will usually go behind the man to whom he passes to fill a lane, but every man must be alert to fill any logical lane by a quick adjustment in case his first choice is filled.

Please note that if 1's initial pass out should be to 3 instead of to 2,

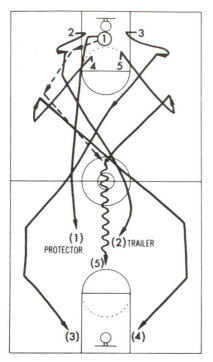

DIAGRAM 4-1 Fast Break #1—Deep Middle Man Rebounds Ball.

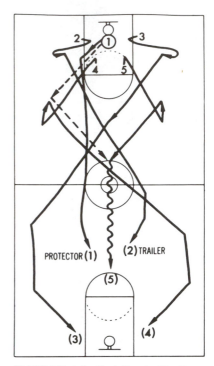

DIAGRAM 4-2 Fast Break #2—Deep Middle Man Rebounds Ball.

the play would proceed the same with 2 and 3 exchanging assignments as do 4 and 5.

**Fast Break #2—Deep Middle Man Rebounds Ball** (Diag. 4-2). 1 to 4 to 5 who drives the ball down the floor. The play proceeds with the same idea as in Diagram #1.

**Fast Break #3—Deep Middle Man Rebounds Ball** (Diag. 4-3). 1 rebounds ball and turns quickly and dribbles straight out, then passes to 4, who drives the ball down the floor. There would be an easy adjustment if 1 passes to 5 instead of 4 or if he kept driving it down the floor himself.

**Fast Break #4—Deep Side Man Rebounds Ball** (Diag. 4-4). 2 rebounds the ball and passes to 4 to 5 who drives the ball down the floor. Note that if 3 should rebound the ball, 3 and 2 exchange assignments as do 4 and 5.

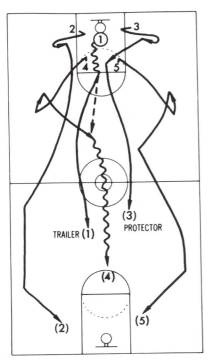

**DIAGRAM 4-3** Fast Break #3—Deep Middle Man Rebounds Ball.

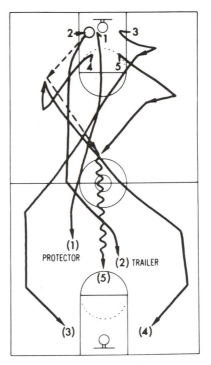

**DIAGRAM 4-4** Fast Break #4—Deep Side Man Rebounds Ball.

**Fast Break #5—Deep Side Man Rebounds Ball** (Diag. 4-5). 2 rebounds the ball and passes to 4 to 3 who drives the ball down the floor. Note that if 3 should rebound the ball, 3 and 2 exchange assignments as do 4 and 5.

**Fast Break #6—Deep Side Man Rebounds Ball and the Defense Closes the Outlet to #4** (Diag. 4-6). 2 rebounds the ball and passes to 3 (sometimes direct to 5 if 3 is covered) who passes to 5 who looks first for 4 breaking down fast and then to 5 who drives it down the floor. Normal adjustments if 3 starts the play instead of 2. We are always looking for this type of initial attack when we find out that the defense try to close the side outlet.

**Fast Break #7—Front Man Rebounds Ball** (Diag. 4-7). 4 rebounds ball and passes to 2 who cuts out and comes back, 2 passes to 5 who breaks straight down to the center circle and comes back to meet ball,

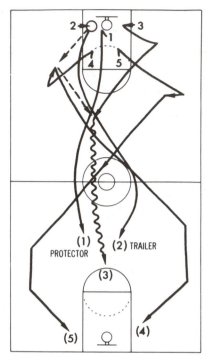

**DIAGRAM 4-5** Fast Break #5—Deep Side Man Rebounds Ball.

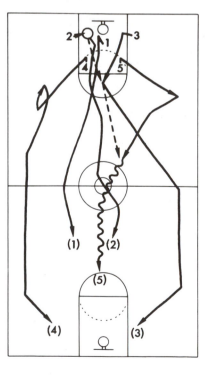

**DIAGRAM 4-6** Fast Break #6—Deep Side Man Rebounds Ball and the Defense Closes the Outlet to #4.

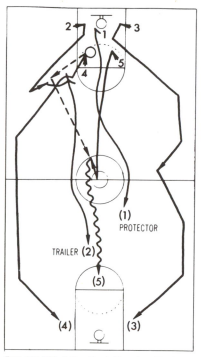

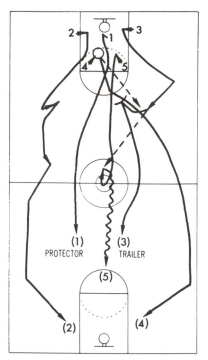

**DIAGRAM 4-7** Fast Break #7—Front Man Rebounds Ball.

**DIAGRAM 4-8** Fast Break #8—Front Man Rebounds Ball.

2 screens for 4 after he passes to 5. Note that if 5 should get the rebound and start the play, 5 and 4 exchange assignments as do 2 and 3.

**Fast Break #8—Front Man Rebounds Ball** (Diag. 4-8). 4 rebounds the ball and passes to 3 instead of to 2. Then the play proceeds the same as in Diagram #7 except from the opposite side of the floor.

**Fast Break #9—Front Man Rebounds Ball** (Diag. 4-9). 4 rebounds the ball and turns quickly and dribbles down the middle of the floor. The lanes are filled and everyone moves hard. If 5 initiates the play instead of 4, they exchange assignments as do 2 and 3.

**Fast Break #10—After Opponent's Field Goal** (Diag. 4-10). 1 (the closest man to the ball) takes ball out-of-bounds and passes to 2 who fakes to get open. 2 passes to 4 who fakes down toward center line on

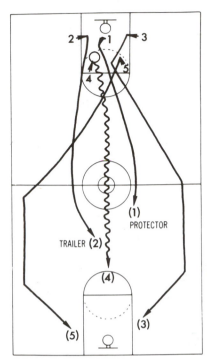

**DIAGRAM 4-9** Fast Break #9—Front Man Rebounds Ball.

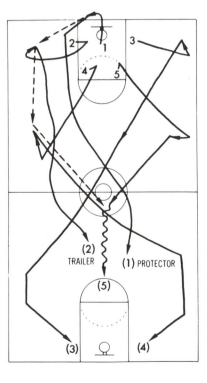

**DIAGRAM 4-10** Fast Break #10—After Opponent's Field Goal.

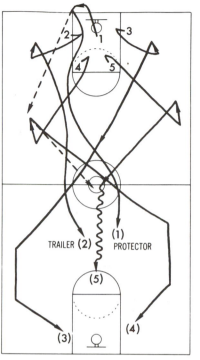

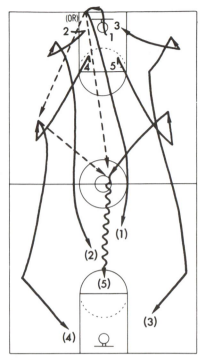

**DIAGRAM 4-11** Fast Break #11—
After Opponent's Field Goal.

**DIAGRAM 4-12** Fast Break #12—
After Opponent's Field Goal.

strong side and comes back to meet pass. 4 passes to 5 who is cutting toward the center of the floor. 5 drives the ball down the floor as the lanes are filled properly.

If 1 should make his pass in to 3 instead of 2, 3 and 2 would exchange assignments as would 4 and 5.

**Fast Break #11—After Opponent's Field Goal** (Diag. 4-11). 1 takes ball out and passes over 2 to 4. 4 then passes to 5 and the play is the same as in Diagram #10. Throw in from either side with the same idea.

**Fast Break #12—After Opponent's Field Goal** (Diag. 4-12). 1 takes ball out and makes long pass in to 5 who drives as 3 and 4 fill outside lanes. Throw-in from either side the same idea.

**Fast Break #13—After Opponent's Successful Free Throw** (Diag. 4-13). In this case the man in the 2 spot will always be our center and he will line up inside the strongest rebounder of our opponents. When

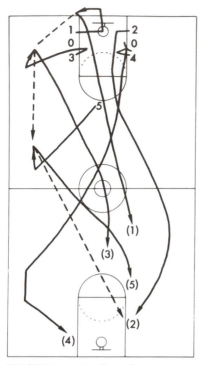

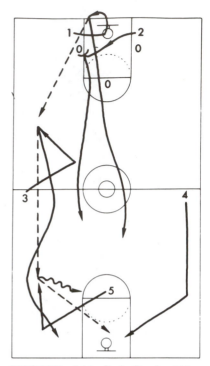

**DIAGRAM 4-13** Fast Break #13—
After Opponent's Free Throw.

**DIAGRAM 4-14** Fast Break #14—
After Opponent's Free Throw.

the shot is made, 1 takes the ball out and passes in to 3 or 5 who looks for 2 who has raced down after a screen by 4.

If 1 passes in to 3 as is shown in the diagram, 3 may pass to 5 or directly down to 2.

**Fast Break #14—After Opponent's Free Throw** (Diag. 4-14). 1 takes ball out and passes to 3 meeting the ball. 3 then passes to 5 who turns and passes to 4 if he is open or turns and dribbles toward the top of the circle.

**Fast Break #15 and #16** (Diags. 4-15 and 4-16). In order to vary the break after a successful free throw, we occasionally have the center take the ball out-of-bounds and then run the break as shown in these diagrams. Each man, of course, must stay alive to cut back and help out.

In #15 the center inbounds the ball to the short man (4) who has

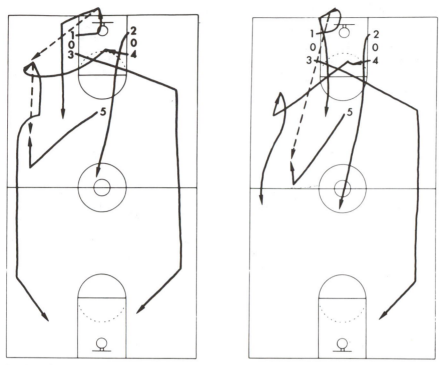

**DIAGRAM 4-15** Fast Break #15.　　　　**DIAGRAM 4-16** Fast Break #16.

come across from the opposite side of the lane after rebounding the front and taking the shooter, while in #16 the center inbounds the ball to the long man (5) who lined up at the top of the key and then broke to the center line and came back.

In either case the receiver turns inside to pass to the open man ahead or to drive the ball down the floor as the lanes are being filled.

## The Finish of the Fast Break

In the preceding diagrams of the fast break the man designated as *trailer* may be either the trailer or the protector and the man marked *protector* may be either the protector or the trailer.

As a matter of fact either of them on occasions may be one of the cutters from the side and one of the designated cutters might be a trailer, protector, or the man in the middle with the ball.

We know that diagrammed plays seldom work out exactly as diagrammed when they come up in competition. However, we try to get the idea of filling lanes and moving down the floor properly without defense and then bring in some defense to teach them to adjust as the occasion requires.

Although the diagrams show considerable dribbling, usually, after the first two passes, we do not want the dribble whenever we can pass safely forward or into the middle of the floor.

We realize that we will seldom get the absolute layup shot so we try to work on the type of finish that we feel that we will get in games.

If we are successful in getting the ball down the floor to the top of the key with our proper floor balance we have the following possible finishes (Diags. 4-17 through 4-24):

**1.** The middle man may pass off to a cutter on either side. If he does, he takes one step toward the receiver with his hands up, chin high, and ready for a quick return pass, but ready to rebound behind the driving cutter if he shoots. The cutter on the opposite side stops and gets position to rebound his side, the trailer comes in to rebound from the broken line of the foul circle area, and the fifth man is the protector between the foul and center circles. The driving shooter gets back into the play as quickly as possible.

**2.** The middle man passes off to a side man who stops up quickly about 15 feet from the basket. The middle man stops quickly and forms a screen for the trailer who cuts down the lane on the strong side. The receiver may get a jump shot, pass to the man who passed to him for a possible shot in foul circle area, or pass back out to the protector. The cutter from the opposite side gets position to cover his side. If a jump shot is taken, the jump shooter rebounds the foul-line area.

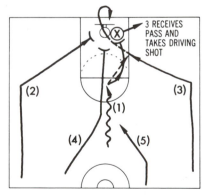

**DIAGRAM 4-17** Fast-Break Finish #1—Middle Man to Flanker Underneath.

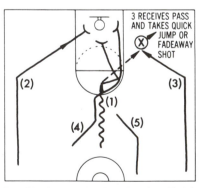

**DIAGRAM 4-18** Fast-Break Finish #2—Middle Man to Flanker for Jump Shot.

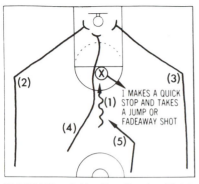

**DIAGRAM  4-19**  Fast-Break  Finish #3—Middle Man Shoots from Key.

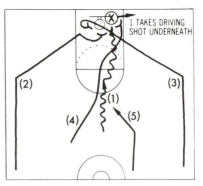

**DIAGRAM  4-20**  Fast-Break  Finish #4—Middle Man Drives Underneath.

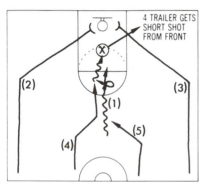

**DIAGRAM  4-21**  Fast-Break  Finish #5—Pivoter to Trailer.

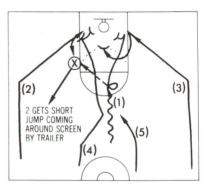

**DIAGRAM  4-22**  Fast-Break  Finish #6—Pivoter to Flanker off Screen.

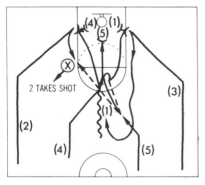

**DIAGRAM  4-23**  Fast-Break  Finish #7—Pivoter Back to Safety.

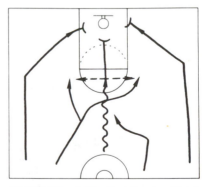

**DIAGRAM  4-24**  Fast-Break  Finish #8—Middle Man to Trailer for Jump Shot.

**3.** The middle man gets a jump shot or quick stop and fadeaway shot from the foul-circle area. In this case each side cutter rebounds his side, the trailer rebounds the short front, and the shooter rebounds the foul circle area.

**4.** The middle man makes a good fake and uses a change of pace or (and) a change of direction and drives down the foul lane on either side. The cutter on the side he comes may screen for him and rebound that side or he may go on through and rebound the opposite side with the cutter or the opposite side moving to rebound the short front and the trailer rebounding the driver's side.

**5.** The middle man pivots and hands off to the trailer who times himself with a good change of direction and (or) pace to set up his man. He may get a short jump shot from in front or from the side of the circle. Side cutters cover their sides and trailer and pivoter cover the short front and long front areas depending upon where the trailer got his shot.

**6.** The middle man pivots and fakes a hand-off to the trailer going by. He then may get a jump shot from the foul-circle area or may pass to a side cutter coming back around a screen set by the trailer when he did not get the pass going by the pivoter. If the pivoter shoots, he covers the foul-circle area, the trailer covers the side on which he screened, the cutter for whom the trailer screened covers the short front area, and the cutter from the opposite side covers his side.

If the pivoter passes to the cutter coming around the screen by the trailer who went by, the passer covers the short front or screens for the opposite side cutter and exchanges coverage with him and the shooter covers the foul-circle area.

**7.** The middle man pivots and fakes a hand-off to the trailer who goes by, passes out to the protector, and turns and goes down the opposite lane from the trailer to screen for the cutter on the opposite side. The protector looks for both side men coming back off the screens, passes to the one that gets open, and cuts hard down the middle. The screeners rebound the respective sides on which they screened and the side man coming back who did not get the pass comes on back as the protector.

### Important Fast-Break Suggestions

**1.** You must have more than a normal amount of patience and expect more mistakes, but drill and drill to reduce them to a minimum. A hard-working, fast-breaking team will often make more mistakes than their opponents because they are aggressively playing the game and attempting to do more and thereby will have an opportunity to accomplish more.

This is what Ward "Piggy" Lambert, the great coach of Purdue University in the 1920s and 1930s, meant when he would frequently say, "The team that makes the most mistakes, particularly on offense, will probably be the winner." The statement must be analyzed and not taken at face value to be clearly understood.

**2.** Unless a good percentage shot is obtained from the break, the players should pass out and set up but continue their movement. The fast break becomes "race horse" or "fire wagon" basketball when the players have not been drilled enough to recognize the good percentage shot and take any kind of "heave" at the basket.

However, players have become so adept at the jump shot that it now may be not only permissible but also commendable for them to take it from distances that would have meant a seat on the bench a number of years ago. Furthermore, many coaches now believe that the offense has a better chance of rebounding if they and the defense are both moving in to the rebounding areas than when they go into set offense and the defense are more in position.

**3.** The players must be taught to react quickly and aggressively *every* time they gain possession of the ball in the back court. Many fast-break situations have been created where they did not appear possible by putting on the pressure immediately. Make your opportunities; don't wait for them to be presented to you. Every man must really hustle to get the lanes and areas filled to provide the needed options.

**4.** Much time must be spent on drills emphasizing the two-on-one, three-on-two, and four-on-three situations in order to get the good shot before the defense recovers.

**5.** Various quick shooting and fast ball-handling drills must be devised and used until the players become accurate as well as quick. We can not sacrifice accuracy for speed, but want maximum speed with control. Hard driving shots under pressure and quick jump shots must be properly executed.

**6.** Defensive rebounding and getting the ball out quickly must be stressed, since more opportunities for possession will come up in this manner than in any other. However, we must also drill on quickly inbounding the ball after a score by an opponent, as often a team relaxes momentarily after they score. Drive that ball down the floor, even though the defense is set.

**7.** Constantly emphasize keeping the head and eyes up and getting the ball down the floor to the man in the most advantageous position as quickly as possible. If you can pass the ball quickly and safely to a man down the floor, do so, but drive it hard on the dribble if there is no one open in a better position to whom you may pass.

**8.** Do not pass to men moving quickly toward a sideline or in to a corner. As a general rule, receivers should be cutting from the sideline or corner to receive a pass on the break.

**9.** Try not to make your cuts in arcs. Sharp angle cutting for a change of direction combined with a change of pace is the best method to set up a defensive man and to get open.

**10.** Balance from a cutting, rebounding, and defensive point of view must be maintained.

## SET OFFENSES

Although I believe in always putting on the pressure immediately and attempting the fast break whenever possession of the ball is obtained, regardless of whether or not the defense appears to be back, I fully realize that a good percentage shot will not be obtained over 50 per cent of the time and that we must have a good set offense on which to fall back. Frankly, I hope to have a set offense the equal of our fast break and a fast-break offense the equal of our set. Each should complement the other.

However, since the fast break will always be tried first and it requires quick reactions and aggressiveness, it stands to reason that our set offense should also be one of aggressive pressure and movement.

In attempting to devise an offense from all the offenses that I have seen and through my experience in the game that would be suitable and adaptable to my basic thinking. I have attempted to come up with a system that will provide each position an equal opportunity to score. The thinking for this has been discussed earlier, but, since repetition is said to be the secret of knowledge, some of the previous discussion will be re-emphasized here.

My self-analysis indicates that I have three basic reasons for this. First, it prevents the defense from concentrating on one or two outstanding scorers, thus making it more difficult to successfully complete your plays. Second, since it is natural for every player to want to score, a finer team spirit is far more likely to exist when the offense provides a somewhat equal number of scoring opportunities. This may not be true for any single game or a few games because of the opposing defenses and individual strengths, but it should equalize in the course of a season. Neither should the offense hold down the better players who might shoot better and be able to get more shots on their own, but the players understand this far better than when it appears that the coach's offense is geared to make a scoring star out of one or two players. Third, it makes it easier to get all five men doing their job at all times and not merely the strong-side men. What you do on the weak side may help free the strong-side men and you want that help when you are on the strong side, and it also will help you get open better, if the ball goes back out from the strong side, for an immediate attack on the weak side.

I like a type of continuity that keeps all of the boys cutting or doing something constantly, but which does not restrict each player too rigidly —in short, a five-man offense that has different options and does not harness individual initiative. I like constant cuts toward the basket to keep drawing the defense back so that you can come up with good-percentage jump shots.

Each man should have the opportunity of passing, driving, or shooting any time he finds an opportunity within the range of his ability. All men must adjust their moves to the moves of the man who has the ball or who just got rid of the ball. Keep your man busy to keep him from helping out or to set him up for your move. Each man must be alert to use any teammate who cuts into their territory as a potential screener on whom they can pick off their defensive man. When you do not have the ball, keep your man busy and try to make him turn his back on the ball. If you do that, he isn't in a very good position to help and he will be much easier for you to elude by a sudden move.

This style of attack demands quick reactions and quick movement, which is in keeping with the initial fast-break attack.

Floor balance and timing are stressed at all times. When a shot is taken from the floor, we should have triangular rebounding underneath with the shooter usually covering the foul-circle area, and a protector between the center and the foul-circle area. He doesn't have to be standing there, but should be moving there and try to stay on a line between the ball and the defensive basket. If a driving shot is taken underneath, I still want the triangle underneath with the front man not quite so close and the driver to get back in the play as quickly as possible. We must always have a man either in or moving to the protecting position.

Different drills are devised to teach each man the specific fundamentals required for his position, and then additional drills are added that have two men working together for possible two-man plays, then three, then four, and finally the five-man unit. However, I want every man to get some work at each position. This helps him to acquire a little more appreciation for the job that a teammate has to do, as well as giving him some preparation in a position in which he may be used on occasion.

The players are given a list of *UCLA Set Offense Possibilities* and are expected to know the moves of each position for every possibility listed. However, they should give first attention to the moves from the position that they are most likely to be playing.

I usually use the single-post attack with variations that I will illustrate. However, I try to drill enough on a simplified double-post attack, which will also be illustrated, to enable us to work it reasonably well when we shift to it on specific occasions.

We also have our zone attack and some special attacks for specific defenses, which will also be illustrated.

Each year, depending upon the individual strengths of my personnel, our emphasis will be placed on certain parts that are shown. Never do we use all of these possibilities in any one season.

The following discussions and diagrams will illustrate the principal set offense that I teach while keeping in mind the basic principles that have been discussed previously.

Please remember that we try to work the plays an equal number of times from each side of the floor and that, although our post man is diagrammed as being set on the foul line, he must keep busy in the vicinity of the deep half of the foul circle in order to free himself in the foul-line area at the proper time.

## UCLA Single Post

**Single Post #1—The Backdoor With Options** (Diag. 4-25). The "Backdoor" should be the first option when the offense sets up. It is the responsibility of the forward on the opposite side of the guard with the ball to set up the play. The "off" forward must be alert to cut to the high post whenever he sees the defense on the off guard playing tight to deny a pass from guard to guard.

As G2 passes to F1, G1 cuts for the basket and F1 has the following options: pass to G1 cutting, to G2 as a second cutter, G1 coming around double screen by C and F2.

If G1 gets the pass coming around the double screen, F1 cuts down lane on opposite side and G2 cuts back out to protect or receive and outlet pass and F2 swings behind C and comes to side of key.

G1 looks for shot or to F2 cutting down lane, or to C on deep post, or to F2 on side post, or back out to G2.

**Single Post #2—Forward Reverse with Three Options** (Diag. 4-26). The forward fakes up to meet the ball and pushes quickly off his outside foot when it is forward, moves quickly for the basket turning toward the inside so that he never loses sight of the ball when the guard starts to dribble toward him. The guard passes to him immediately if he is open. If he isn't open immediately for a pass, he "buttonhooks" at the foul lane and looks for the pass. If he doesn't get the ball on the "buttonhook," he crosses the foul lane and comes around a double screen by the center and the other forward and looks for a pass from the other guard to whom the first guard has passed.

The center pulls to the opposite lane where he will form the double screen with the weak-side forward as soon as he sees the guard dribble toward the strong-side forward.

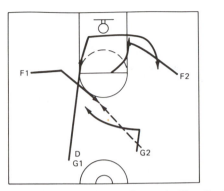

**DIAGRAM 4-25** Single Post #1—The Back-door with Options.

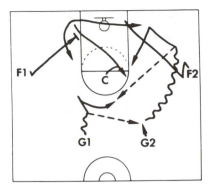

**DIAGRAM 4-26** Single Post #2—Forward Reverse with Three Options.

The strong-side guard may pass to the reversing forward early or on the "buttonhook," may get a good shot himself—jump or drive—or pass back to the other guard who has worked to get open. If he passes to the out guard, he cuts toward the basket and then comes quickly to the side post.

You should be able to visualize each man's possibilities and rebounding responsibility depending on who shoots from the diagram.

This and the next play are two setups that our players may use at any time, but are most effective when the defensive man on the forward is playing him high.

**Single Post #3—Forward Screen and Roll with Three Options** (Diag. 4-27). This play works exactly the same as #1 except the forward initiates it by coming up to screen and roll as the guard received

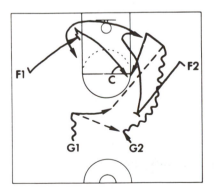

**DIAGRAM 4-27** Single Post #3—Forward Screen and Roll with Three Options.

a pass from the other guard or from the forward himself instead of reversing on the side when the guard dribbled toward him.

In either play if G2 passes back out to G1, G1 may pass to F2 coming around the double screen and cut for the basket, screening G2's guard on the way or getting a screen from G2, or G1 may pass to G2 coming up to the side post and cutting off of him for a two-man play with F2 coming on back as the protector.

**Single Post #4—Guard Passes to High Post** (Diag. 4-28). The guards fake cuts on their sides then cross with the nonpassing guard cutting behind the passing guard. The forwards both reverse sharply looking for a pass from the center when a guard passes to the post and each comes back off a screen by the guard. The center turns and faces the basket when he gets the pass and looks for an open man or makes a move or gets a shot himself. If he passes to the man on the right side or shoots, the forward coming out from the left protects. If the center passes to the left side, the forward coming out on the right protects.

If the defensive guards call "switch," the nonpassing guard doesn't cross, but cuts down the same side as the other guard. G1 and/or G2 may swing out around screens by F1 or F2 instead of screening for them.

**Single Post #5—Guard Passes to High Post** (Diag. 4-29). The guards fake crossing over the top of the center and then cut down their respective sides. The play then proceeds exactly as in #4. After the forwards get accustomed to working with each other, we have them cross underneath at times and come around the opposite guard. When we do this,

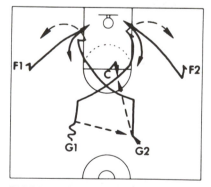

**DIAGRAM 4-28** Single Post #4.

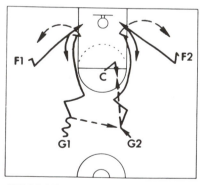

**DIAGRAM 4-29** Single Post #5.

we have each one cross to his right in order to avoid a collision underneath.

G1 and/or G2 may swing out around screens by F1 or F2 instead of screening for them.

**Single Post #6—Most Used Guard to High Post Options** (Diag. 4-30 a, b, c).   G2 to G1 to C who looks for F1 reversing, then for F2 on short post underneath, then for G1 or G2 on wing.

If C passes to either G1 or G2 on the wing, C puts away down the lane and the forward on that side comes off the screen to the side post. The forward on the strong side tries to get open on the deep post and the guard on the wing looks for the deep post, or the high post, or for the other guard coming out.

Of course, the post always has the option of the quick reverse drive down the lane if overplayed as the pass is received.

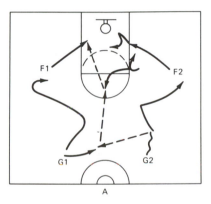

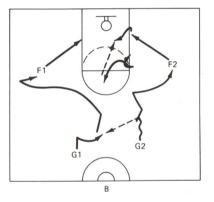

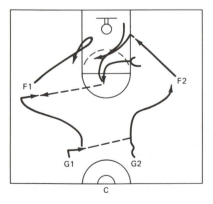

**DIAGRAM 4-30**  Most Used Guard To High Post Option.

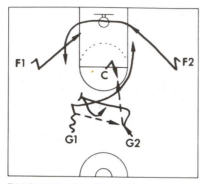

**DIAGRAM 4-31** Single Post #7.

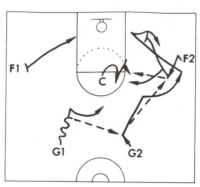

**DIAGRAM 4-32** Single Post #8.

**Single Post #7.** Guard passes to high post, screens for other guard, and moves back out (Diag. 4-31). The center turns and faces the basket and may make his own move, pass to either forward reversing, to the guard cutting off the screen by the passing guard, or to the forward coming around the screen by the other forward, or back out to the protecting guard.

If the center passes back out to the protecting guard, he turns down the lane to screen for the guard that is under, and F2 turns back to screen for F1 to come back off him.

We also vary this play with having the nonpassing guard (G1) make the initial screen for the passing guard (G2). The play then is identical.

**Single Post #8.** Guard passes to forward and cuts outside (Diag. 4-32). Forward passes to center and fakes in and cuts across center or fakes out and goes in to screen for cutting guard coming back. The forward and then the center each face the basket looking for an individual move as soon as they receive a pass.

**Single Post #9.** Guard passes to forward and cuts outside (Diag. 4-33). Forward passes to center moving quickly down the lane and then splits him with the cutting guard.

**Single Post #10.** Guard passes to forward and cuts outside (Diag. 4-34). Forward passes back out to safety guard and forms double screen with the center for the cutting guard. The out guard (G1) can pass to G2 coming back off the double screen and cut for basket off of F1 with F1 coming back to protect, or G1 can pass to F1 and work the side-post options with him as G2 comes out as the protector.

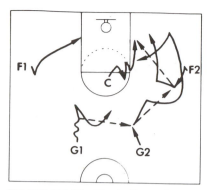

**DIAGRAM 4-33** Single Post #9.

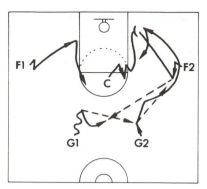

**DIAGRAM 4-34** Single Post #10.

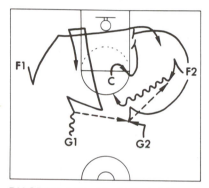

**DIAGRAM 4-35** Single Post #11.

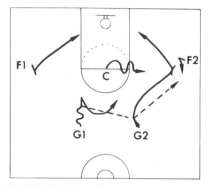

**DIAGRAM 4-36** Single Post #12.

**Single Post #11.** Guard passes to forward and cuts outside (Diag. 4-35). Forward dribbles out. Center goes down in lane to form double screen with G2 for F2 coming across underneath and G1 cuts for basket and comes back on side post. F2 may pass to F1 coming off of double screen or G1 cutting in or coming back to side post and working side-post options with him.

**Single Post #12.** Guard passes to forward, screens inside for forward and rolls for basket, or fakes inside screen and cuts for basket (Diag. 4-36). You have the same options and possibilities that you have in #6, #7, #8, and #9 when the guard cuts to the outside.

**Single Post #13.** Guard passes to forward and cuts off either side of post looking for a pass if he gets open (Diag. 4-37). F2 passes to C after G2 cut by and did not get open. F2 then cuts toward G2 moving toward corner from inside the backboard line and rolls for the basket. C may pass to F2 and move for basket, to G2 and move for basket, get a good move and shoot himself, or pass out to G1 who works weak-side post with F1 as G2 comes back out and C moves down lane and screens for F2 coming back.

**Single Post #14.** Guard passes to forward and cuts off either side of post looking for a pass if he gets open (Diag. 4-38). F2 passes to G2 coming out as he did not get open off C. F2 then screens for C and rolls for the basket, G2 may then pass to F2, or to C, or get a shot himself. Sometimes G2 passes to C who passes on out to G1 who works weak-side post with F1 as C cuts for the basket with F2 coming back around him and G2 comes back as the protector.

**Single Post #15.** Guard passes to forward and cuts to get open off C as he does in #11 and #12 (Diag. 4-39). F2 passes out to G1 and forms double screen with C for G2 to come around. G1 looks for side-post options with F1 and G2 coming off double screen.

**Single Post #16.** Guard passes to forward and cuts off C as in #13, #14, and #15 (Diag. 4-40). F2 dribbles out and G1 cuts toward basket, then screens for F1 coming out as C goes back to screen for G2 and roll for the basket.

**Single Post #17.** Guard passes to forward and fakes cut and steps back as opposite guard cuts off of C (Diag. 4-41). The exact options are available as we had when the passing guard cut off the post as shown in #13, #14, #15, and #16. F2 may get a move or shoot himself, pass to G1 wherever he might be open, pass to C, pass out to G2, or dribble out. The only difference is that G1 and G2 have exchanged places.

**Single Post #18.** Guard passes to forward and cuts off of C as he does in #13, #14, #15, and #16 but when he doesn't receive from F2, he screens on opposite side of foul lane for F1 to come across (Diag. 4-42). We now have exactly the same setup as we had in #13 through #16 except that G2 and F1 have now exchanged places. F2 has all of the possible options that he had in the other.

**Single Post #19.** (#19 through #23 are designed to give a forward and center a little more floor space to work on a one-on-one situation when we think they can beat their particular opponent.) Guard passes to forward and screens for the other guard (Diag. 4-43). All the options

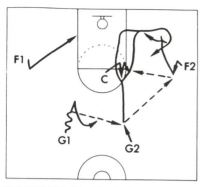

**DIAGRAM 4-37** Single Post #13.

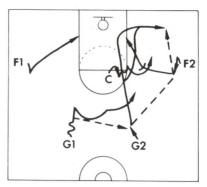

**DIAGRAM 4-38** Single Post #14.

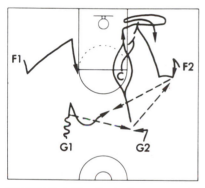

**DIAGRAM 4-39** Single Post #15.

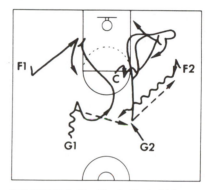

**DIAGRAM 4-40** Single Post #16.

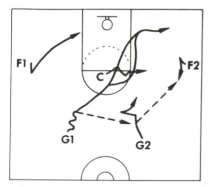

**DIAGRAM 4-41** Single Post #17.

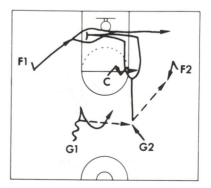

**DIAGRAM 4-42** Single Post #18.

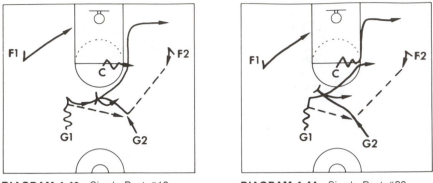

**DIAGRAM 4-43**  Single Post #19.    **DIAGRAM 4-44**  Single Post #20.

are available that were available in #13 through #14 with G1 and G2 merely having now exchanged positions.

**Single Post #20.**  Guard passes to forward and screens for other guard (Diag. 4-44). Center moves down lane quickly looking for pass from forward and G1 takes the post spot. Once again F2 has all the possible options in #13 through #16 with C now in the position of G2, G1 now in the position of C, and G2 now in the position of G1.

**Single Post #21.**  Guard passes to forward and screens for other guard (Diag. 4-45). Forward (F2) dribbles across toward foul line and pivots and hands off to G1 who has come off screen by G2. C moves to opposite lane to screen for F1 when F2 starts the dribble across. F2 rolls for the basket after handing off to G1. If G1 is forced to pivot and pass out to G2, G2 may pass to F1 coming around C or to F2 who also has continued on around C.

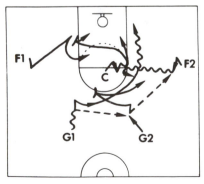

**DIAGRAM 4-45**  Single Post #21.

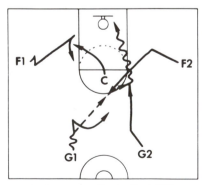

**DIAGRAM 4-46**  Single Post #22.

**Single Post #22.** (This setup is often tried when the center is not yet in position or when F2 notices that G2's guard is overplaying him.) F2 fakes a reverse toward the basket and breaks to the top of the foul circle to receive a pass from G1 (Diag. 4-46). G2 used a quick change of pace and a slight change of direction to break at the time when his guard may turn his head to look at the ball as G1 passes to F2. F2 looks for G2, then for F1.

If F2 doesn't get open for the pass, he may screen G2's guard from behind as G2 breaks for a possible lob pass.

**UCLA Double Post.** This is not intended to be our primary set attack, but merely an attack that we might shift to occasionally for a change of pace or when we might have five men playing for a while that are particularly adapted to this offense.

It is kept extremely simple and with very few options as I do not devote much time to teaching it. We may occasionally work on it when I feel a change is needed during the practice period to break the monotony of our regular offense.

The post men work to the opposite sides of the foul-circle area where the foul line reaches the circle. Although the diagrams appear to have them stationed there, they actually have considerable territory around that area in which to work to get open, but they are trying to time themselves to be open at the foul-line intersection as the middle man or flanker is ready to pass to them.

*Furthermore, the three outside men are not stationary, but constantly faking, or weaving, or interchanging positions* while keeping floor balance.

As in the single-post attack, you must devote the same amount of time toward the development of the attack on each side of the floor if you expect to have a balanced attack that will be difficult to defense properly.

**Double Post #1.** The middle man passes to the post man, fakes straight down and cuts toward the outside, and splits the post with the flanker on that side (Diag. 4-47). The opposite post man cuts sharply across the lane for the basket looking for the ball and opening up the floor for the flanker coming through the foul-line area. The opposite flanker fakes outside and comes back to protect.

The post man with the ball may get a move or shot himself, pass to the other post man, pass to one of the two splitting the post, or back to the safety man. If he passes back out to the safety man, he fakes back toward the basket and comes to the opposite post. The cutters who split

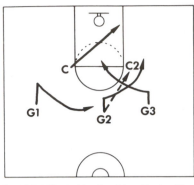

**DIAGRAM 4-47** Double Post #1—
Middle Man to Post.

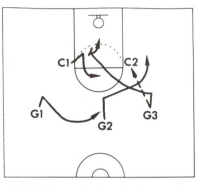

**DIAGRAM 4-48** Double Post #2—
Flanker to Post.

the post come back wide, and the post man who crossed under comes up to the post on the opposite from his original side.

**Double Post #2.** A flanker passes to the post man on his side, fakes down, and then crosses and splits the post with the middle man (Diag. 4-48). He then continues and screens for the opposite post man who fakes back in and then comes around the screen. The weak-side flanker fakes outside, then comes back to the middle to protect.

The post man has approximately the same options as in #1.

**Double Post #3.** A flanker (G3) passes to a post man moving out wide (Diag. 4-49). As G3 passes to the post man, G2 goes the opposite way and screens for G1 and then comes back off a screen by G3 who comes over after passing to the wide post (C2). C2 may pass to C1, or G1, or G2, or back out to G3.

If the pass goes back out to G3, he may work the weak-side post with G1 coming up, or pass to C1 coming around a double screen by G2 and C2.

**Double Post #4.** A flanker passes to the middle man and follows his pass to screen and roll down the lane (Diag. 4-50). The post man on the strong side screens for the post man on the weak side. The middle man may get away for a shot, or pass to the flanker rolling for the basket, or hit C1 coming off screen by C2, or pass back out to the protector with everyone rotating logically to start over.

**Double Post #5.** As a flanker passes to a middle man, each post man comes up and sets a blind screen for the flanker on his side (Diag. 4-51). If neither flanker gets open for a pass from the middle man, the

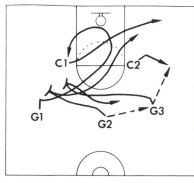

**DIAGRAM 4-49** Double Post #3—
Flanker to Post Moving Out.

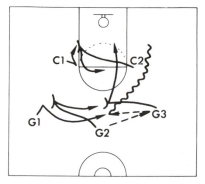

**DIAGRAM 4-50** Double Post #4—
Flanker to Middle Man and Screen.

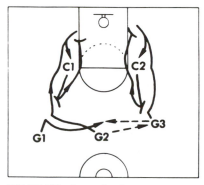

**DIAGRAM 4-51** Double Post #5—
Post Man Screen for Flanker.

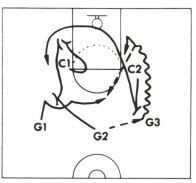

**DIAGRAM 4-52** Double Post #6—
Post Man Screens and Rolls.

post men turn right back and go set a screen for the flanker coming back. If they fail to get open now, they come on back in position to try something else.

**Double Post #6.** A post man comes up to set a blind screen as a flanker receives a pass (Diag. 4-52). As the flanker drives, the post man rolls and the same procedure is followed that we use in our single-post screen and roll.

**Double Post #7—Off-Side Cut** (Diag. 4-53). As a flanker receives a pass from the middle man, the opposite post man makes a quick move to the top of the foul circle to receive a pass. As he makes this move, the strong-side post man moves down his lane to keep his man busy, and the middle man fakes away to try to prevent his man from bothering

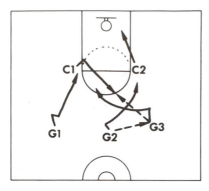

**DIAGRAM 4-53** Double Post #7—
Off-Side Cut.

the pass. As the pass is made, the opposite flanker breaks fast and looks for the pass.

The passer and the middle man split the post and one of them may receive the pass, if the first cutter did not. If they do not get it, they screen for the two men under to come back out.

## ZONE ATTACK

Every team must have a special offense to use against a zone defense or they will find themselves in constant trouble. However, there are so many types of zones, that it is impossible to have an offense for each one that will work well and still perfect your regular offense and the other specific offenses that are a necessity. Therefore, I feel that it is wise to have a zone attack, if it is at all possible, that doesn't require a great amount of adjustment from your regular offense regardless of the particular type of zone.

Since all zones are based on the same principle of playing the ball and a territory rather than a man, except when the man has the ball within your territory, it seems that it should be possible to do this. If time were available to permit having a special offense for every type of zone, it is quite natural to assume that it would be better, but you should never sacrifice your work on fundamentals or your principal offense and defense to do this.

A true fast-breaking team will immediately have a strong point to combat the zone, because it has been a general maxim or axiom since the zone defense first came into being that the best offense against it is to fast break them before the players can get into their set positions.

The ball should be kept moving and, contrary to an old maxim, you must keep cutting toward the basket in order to draw the defense deeper to free you for good percentage shots over them. Different types of zones will have different weak spots that you must find and exploit. Fast clever passing and little dribbling are important facts to keep in mind. You should be able to pass faster than the defense can move, but even more important is the fact that, once you get them moving in one direction, you can come back quickly and hurt them.

Many teams have a tendency to get frantic against a zone, because they may not see very many of them, and that is playing right into their hands. If you pass and cut and a man does not follow you through, you know immediately that it must be some type of zone. The thing to do is to find out what kind and go to work on it.

The 2-1-2 zone will be stronger in the post, but weaker on the sides. The 2-3 zone should be easy prey for the post and short jumpers from the key area. The 3-2 zone should be weak in the corners. The 1-3-1 is very weak in the corners and short angles. A little analysis of any zone will reveal its weakness, so do not get frantic. Analyze it and work against it.

Good outside shooters will hurt any zone—or any other defense, for that matter—but good outside shooters are not easy to find or develop. Furthermore, they are not an absolute necessity if you work the ball properly and quickly and keep penetrating it to draw the defense back. Do not depend upon merely quick passing around it until someone gets free to take a long shot. That is a rather sure way to get beaten.

Once a lead of a few points is acquired, any zone can be forced to come out after you if you wish to hold the ball. I do not like to do that until late in the game, but I know many coaches who will hold it whenever they have a lead and try to force them into a man-to-man defense. Some coaches want a three-, or five-, or seven-point lead before holding the ball.

Since I like an aggressive offense and an aggressive defense, holding the ball is not in keeping with the habits that I have tried to drill in the players: I prefer action. Furthermore, it isn't fair to the fans who support the game by their attendance to refuse to try to play because the team is playing a zone defense. You should continually be trying to get good shots regardless of the score or the defense. It is an entirely different matter to refuse to take anything but a very high percentage shot late in the game when you are protecting a lead, from quitting even trying to get a shot earlier in the game.

We try to beat the zone down and get a good shot before it gets set, but once the zone is set we try to attack it by the following basic patterns with the only initial change from our single-post principal offensive setup being to place the center deep. Remember, however, that all

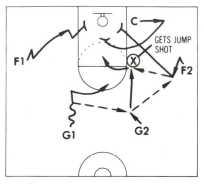

**DIAGRAM 4-54** Zone Attack #1.

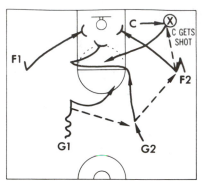

**DIAGRAM 4-55** Zone Attack #2.

of the possible ideas require judgment in adjusting to the particular type of zone being played and how well the individuals are performing within it.

Furthermore, the basic fundamental principles of both individual and regular team offense must be followed if you expect any offense to function successfully.

**Zone Attack #1.**   G1 advances the ball as far as possible to draw the defense over, then snaps a pass at a backward angle across to G2 who immediately passes to F2 and cuts for the spot where the foul line meets the foul circle (Diag. 4-54). C moves halfway out from the foul lane to the sideline. F2 passes to G2 if he gets open and G2 may shoot or he may pass down to F1 who has cut for the basket, or to C if he is open. F2 cuts for the basket when he passes to G2. Note the natural rebounding areas that they fill.

**Zone Attack #2.**   The play starts as in #1, but F2 passes to C halfway out and cuts for the basket in an attempt to get open and to draw the defense back and away from C (Diag. 4-55). F2 doesn't get open and C takes the shot. Please note the natural rebounding positions, remembering that a jump or outside shooter usually rebounds the foul-line area.

**Zone Attack #2A.**   The play starts as in #2, but C passes to G1 who has moved to the area at the side of the foul line that G2 has just vacated and G1 gets the shot from there (Diag. 4-56). Note the natural rebounding rotation.

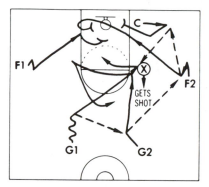

**DIAGRAM 4-56**   Zone Attack #2A.

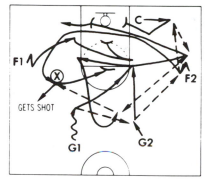

**DIAGRAM 4-57**   Zone Attack #2B.

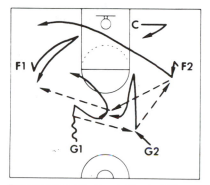

**DIAGRAM 4-58**   Zone Attack #2C.

**Zone Attack #2B.**   The play starts as in #2A, but C passes to G1 who has now moved to the side in the area that F2 vacated when he cut after passing to C (Diag. 4-57). G1 would pass to F1 in the area that G1 just vacated, but in the diagram G1 passes back out to G2 who passes quickly to F2 who has cut all the way under and come out on the opposite side.

**Zone Attack #2C.**   The play starts as in #1, but F2 passes back quickly to G1 and cuts for the basket (Diag. 4-58). G1 passes to F1 quickly and we have almost the same possibilities with an exchange of some positions that we had in the previous options.

**Zone Attack #3.**   G2 starts the play by passing to F2 as in the previous setups, but G1 and G2 exchange the assignments they had from #1 through 2C (Diag. 4-59). Everything else remains the same.

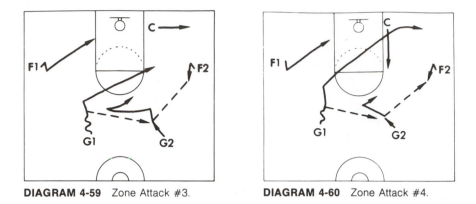

**DIAGRAM 4-59**  Zone Attack #3.          **DIAGRAM 4-60**  Zone Attack #4.

**Zone Attack #4.**  G2 starts the play by passing to F2 as in the previous setups, but G1 and C exchange the assignments they had from #1 through 2C (Diag. 4-60). Everything else remains the same with the same possibilities.

**Zone Attack #5.**  G1 passes to F1 who is on the weak side or the side opposite the center and fakes a cut and steps back (Diag. 4-61). G2 breaks to F1's side to the spot where the foul line meets the foul circle. F1 may pass to G2 for a shot or a pass down. If G2 shoots, F1 would rebound the left side, F2 the right side, C the front, and G2 the foul-circle area.

If G2 doesn't get the ball there, he cuts down the lane and then moves out the baseline looking for a pass. C fills in the spot that G2 left and may receive the pass from F1 for a shot or a pass down to F1 or F2 cutting. If C should shoot, F2 would rebound the right side, F1 the front, G2 the left side, and C the foul-circle area.

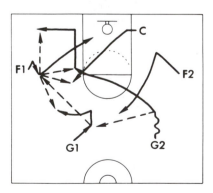

**DIAGRAM 4-61**  Zone Attack #5.

F1 may pass to G2 late as he comes out toward the sideline from the basket and the play would proceed with the possibilities as shown in #2, #2A, and #2B.

F1 may pass back out to G1 and make a quick cut. G1 may snap the ball to F2 for a good shot, or F2 may hit C or F1 who has cut across and come out for a shot.

## PRESS ATTACK

In recent years the pressing defense has become more and more popular. A number of coaches have had good luck with it as their principal defense. Many others have had excellent success by using it at various times during a game or during a season.

Since more and more teams are using it, you are not properly preparing your players unless you have an offense to counteract it.

There are as many different types of pressing defenses as there are zone defenses; therefore I am merely going to present some general ideas that I believe are important in neutralizing it.

We try to keep the floor spread without getting bunched and give and go a lot looking for the return pass.

If we have a good dribbler, we may try to give him the ball and give him room in which to work against the man-to-man press, but we want very little dribbling against the zone press.

Against the zone press, be sure not to waste your dribble. Look the situation over before you ever put the ball on the floor and try to get the quick pass forward.

We want our center to get to the center circle and then break back to form an outlet in the middle of the floor. We also want a man to break well down on the side away from the ball and another man to break past the center line and turn back on the strong side. If we can hit these men and cut while combining them with sharp reverses, we can make it difficult to contain us.

Since the most effective press is usually immediately following a score, I shall try to diagram our actions against a possible press after our opponents have scored.

**Zone Press Attack #1.** One of the guards (G1) takes the ball out-of-bounds and steps back about three feet behind the end line and faces the floor, one forward (F1) goes to the foul line and faces the passer, the other guard (G2) lines up back of the foul circle about six feet, the other forward (F2) faces the same way just inside the center circle, and the C moves near the sideline out from the center circle (Diag. 4-62).

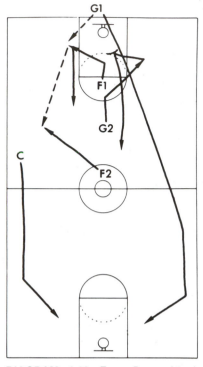

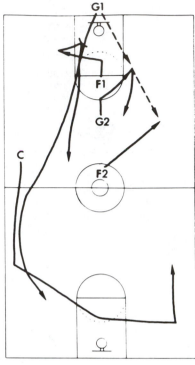

**DIAGRAM 4-62** Zone Press Attack #1.

**DIAGRAM 4-63** Zone Press Attack #2.

F1 moves forward and then breaks quickly either right or left, G2 moves forward at the same time as F1 and breaks the opposite way, F2 breaks out toward the side to which G1 passes. G1 passes to F1 and cuts down the floor off of G2. C breaks down the floor. F1 passes quickly to F2 who looks for C or G1 and then possibly G2.

**Zone Press Attack #2.** Everyone lines up as in #1, but G1 inbounds the ball to G2 (Diag. 4-63). The attack then proceeds in approximately the same manner as in #1 to advance the ball quickly by the pass and to keep the floor spread. C crosses over and comes out on the opposite side for balance. If G1 has trouble in hitting either F1 or G1, F2 is alert to provide an outlet.

**Man-to-Man Press Attack #1.** The players line up in the same manner as they do against the zone press and break the same way to get open (Diag. 4-64). However, G1 fakes to get open for a quick return

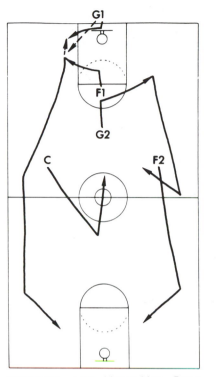

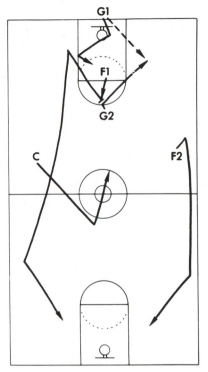

**DIAGRAM 4-64** Man-to-Man Press Attack #1.

**DIAGRAM 4-65** Man-to-Man Press Attack #2.

pass when he inbounds the ball to F1 or G2. The receiver in turn looks down the floor first and then returns the pass to G1 and reverses. Others break to open up the floor, but stay alive to "buttonhook" back to meet a pass.

**Man-to-Man Press Attack #2.** The players line up the same as before except F1 lines up inside the foul line and G2 on top of the circle (Diag. 4-65). F1 turns quickly to screen for G2 and then breaks quickly to the opposite side of the lane. If F1 receives a pass, he looks for G1 as before and the play proceeds the same as in #1. However, if G2 receives the ball from G1, F1 then reverses and moves to the spot from which F1 reversed and stays alive for an outlet pass from G2 or clears the floor for him.

C and F2 must stay alive to meet the ball for potential outlets if F1 or G2 are having trouble staying open. If either C or F2 receives the pass in, the other one reverses quickly.

Against either the zone press or the man-to-man press, we caution our players to be alert, not to panic, and to keep the floor spread. The passes must be quick and crisp and we must use our fakes, changes of pace, and changes of direction to advantage. Do not run away from the ball to force lob passes; just work together as a unit.

## SINGLE SPECIAL OFFENSE

When we have an excellent guard who is an outstanding dribbler and passer, we will use a special offense occasionally during the course of a game.

It starts out as our regular single-post offense, but we work only a few plays from it. Please remember that we are not trying to develop a regular offense, but merely providing a setup to take advantage of a particular strength.

G2 is the special guard and the play is usually determined by the position in which the C lines up on the foul line.

**Single Special #1.** The C takes a position on the foul line toward the F1 side. G1 passes to G2 and cuts off C looking for a lob pass from G2 (Diag. 4-66). After G1 passes him, C turns down the lane to screen for F1 who has reversed. G1 comes back off a screen by F2 who has reversed.

G2 may pass to an open man or get open himself.

**Single Special #2.** The C takes a position in the center of the foul line (Diag. 4-67). G1 passes to G2 and cuts across in front of the center who joins him and goes down the lane to form a double screen for F2

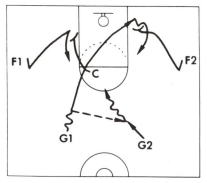

**DIAGRAM 4-66** Single Special #1.

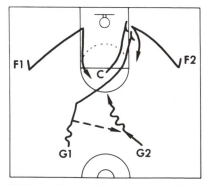

**DIAGRAM 4-67** Single Special #2.

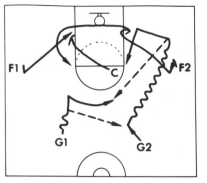

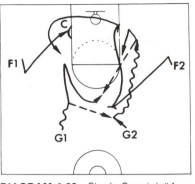

**DIAGRAM 4-68**  Single Special #3.          **DIAGRAM 4-69**  Single Special #4.

coming back from his reverse. F1 comes to the weakside post after his reverse.

G2 again may pass to an open man or get open himself.

**Single Special #3.**  The C takes a position on the foul line toward the F2 side (Diag. 4-68). The play is our reverse play with the three options as shown previously.

**Single Special #4.**  The C takes a position outside the lane under the basket on the F1 side (Diag. 4-69). The play is our screen-and-roll play with the three options as shown previously except for the C starting from the deep position.

## LEAD-PROTECTION OFFENSE.

Regardless of whether you refer to it as a ball-control game, stall game, or merely protecting a lead game, this is one of the most important, exasperating, and frustrating of all offenses.

There are almost as many methods or ideas of protecting a lead as there are coaches, and I have yet to meet a coach who has developed an attack that has been consistently pleasing.

It seems that what may work very satisfactorily for a while may suddenly become ineffective. The individual abilities and temperaments of the players of both your own team and that of your opponent seem to be the main factors that determine a successful or unsuccessful lead-protecting game. However, I have had teams and have seen teams use something very effectively in one game and then have it be a complete failure later or vice versa.

I have almost come to the conclusion that the surest way to protect a lead is to start pressing your opponent at the same time that they feel they have to start pressing you. Since you are ahead, you do not have to gamble quite as much and, therefore, might have an advantage providing that you do not get wild.

This is one phase or aspect of the game where the mental and emotional balance is even more important. Although you should not gamble with a lead, neither should you become overly cautious and lose your drive. There is such a thing as picking up and losing momentum in every sport and it is particularly true in the highly competitive, emotional, fast-moving game of basketball.

I feel that it is best to keep the pressure on, but take only the high percentage shots rather than just good percentage shots. Keep the floor spread, the ball moving, driving toward the basket, and, above all, keep your poise and emotional balance.

The ideas that I will illustrate rather briefly have all worked well for my teams on occasions and have failed to work on others.

First of all, we must be alive for our fast-break attack and for our offense against the press if they are taking us all over the court.

**Lead Protection #1.** Once we get the ball near the center line and we are meeting tight pressure, we look first for the "back-door" play (Diag. 4-70). The forward (F1) on the opposite side of the ball fakes back and breaks quickly to the top of the foul circle to receive a diagonal pass from the opposite guard (G2). The nonpassing guard (G1) times his quick start with the pass to the F1 at the top of the circle and breaks to get open. F2 reverses sharply as F1 receives the pass. F1 looks for F2 and G1 and passes to either one if he gets open, but must not force a pass. The C watches F1 from underneath and moves across

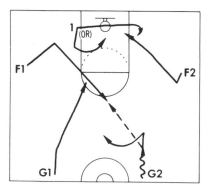

**DIAGRAM 4-70** Lead Protection #1— "Backdoor."

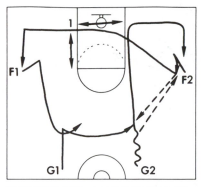

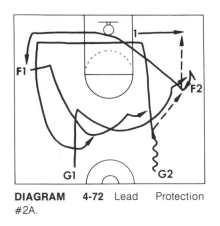

**DIAGRAM 4-71** Lead Protection #2.

**DIAGRAM 4-72** Lead Protection #2A.

underneath if F1 passes to G1, swings up the lane a few feet and turns back in front of the basket if F1 passes to F2, or crosses the lane to a position underneath if F1 passes back out to G2 or dribbles it out.

If the ball is passed back out to G2, F1 and F2 move to the forward spots toward which they are headed, C stays under, and G2 crosses under and comes back out. G2 looks for any opportunity to pass and cut or get away.

**Lead Protection #2.** Once we get fairly well set we try to get the C underneath. In this setup G2 passes to F2 and cuts for the basket and, since the C is on the opposite side of the floor, G2 swings out the baseline on the side of F2 (Diag. 4-71). F2 looks for G2 or G1 who has moved over into the spot that G2 left and cuts for the basket when he passes. There is a natural rotation that can move clockwise or counterclockwise depending upon whether the pass is in from the left or right. The C stays alert for a sudden move as an outlet either up the lane or out the baseline at any time.

**Lead Protection #2A.** This is exactly the same as #2 except the C is now on the strong side and G2 cuts down the lane and then crosses to the opposite side in the rotation (Diag. 4-72).

**Lead Protection #3.** This setup starts from a three-out-and-two-in setup (Diag. 4-73). F2 passes to C and G2 cuts for the basket and breaks to the opposite side if he does not receive the pass. F2 crosses over and screens for G1 coming over as an outlet and looks for a chance to roll down the center of the floor. F1 comes up to fill in the G1

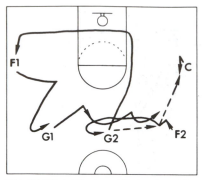

**DIAGRAM 4-73** Lead Protection #3.

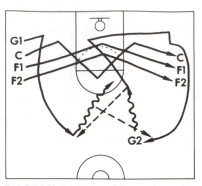

**DIAGRAM 4-74** Lead Protection #4—"Special."

spot and G2 fills the F1 spot. The players must stay constantly alert to exchange positions or get those of the best advantage.

F1 and C must be alert to break up to the top of the circle to set up the "back-door" play whenever it appears open.

This setup is also varied with G1 occasionally making the cut that G2 is illustrated making either directly or off a screen by G2 and with F2 making the cut either directly or after screening for G2 and rolling down the center of the floor.

**Lead Protection #4.** This is a special setup for a player with outstanding ability as a dribbler and passer (Diag. 4-74). He is encouraged to have the ball on one side of the floor with the other four players lined up as shown on the opposite side of the floor.

At the least sign of trouble for G2, the others break toward the basket with G1 faking in and coming back out off the other three and looking for a pass. The center does the same thing and comes off the back of the two forwards. If G2 passes to G1, he cuts for the basket and then comes around the center and forwards to get open for a pass from G1 who takes the position behind the other three on the opposite side of the floor. All must stay alert to help out or to get an easy basket if the defense slips.

**Lead Protection #4A.** This starts out exactly the same as #4, except the C and forward break to the foul line and stay close together facing the center circle (Diag. 4-75). G2 passes to G1 and cuts behind the three men and then comes around them to get open for a pass back from G1 who cuts for the basket and then moves to the opposite side of the floor with his three teammates.

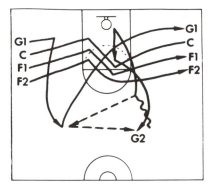

**DIAGRAM    4-75**  Lead    Protection
#4A—"Special."

## Other Methods

On occasions we have used a simple four-man weave with a free-lance post man or a basic five-man weave. As a matter of fact, we practice both of these every year, if only for ball-handling and to learn something about defensing such setups when we come up against them.

# SPECIAL SET AND OUT-OF-BOUNDS PLAYS

Although I am firmly convinced that most coaches and young coaches in particular are far too concerned about plays, every team, regardless of their style of offense, needs a few set and out-of-bounds plays.

As I have repeatedly stated, I do not believe in taking away the individual initiative of the players, but I do believe in having some specific set plays, with options, to use on special occasions, such as—the first time we have the ball at the beginning of any period of play or immediately following a time-out for any reason when the team has been together at the bench.

The success of any set play from an offensive point of view depends largely upon timing and upon decoying the defense or lulling some individual defensive man into a false sense of security. Usually, it will require some type of screen, but many times the sudden, quick move works because the defense will be waiting for a screen or block and you will take them by surprise by a quick thrust or cutback. The play that looks excellent on paper sometimes is not nearly as effective as another that is based merely on exploiting the natural human tendencies.

I believe in having at least one special play for each position and any plays necessary to capitalize on some outstanding talent of a specific individual. It is normal for every player to want to score and I feel that it is conducive to better team spirit to, at least, work on a set play from which the guards have the first option to score, another for the forwards, and another for the center.

As there are hundreds of plays that can be found in various basketball books and publications from which a coach can select to meet his particular style and personnel needs, it would be rather foolish for me to list very many. The ones that I shall illustrate are plays that we have used at one time or another or plays that I have seen worked successfully by other teams either against us or some other opponent.

The plays are set up by a special call or some special key and the players are generally free to set them up at any time. However, I call the play to use when play is resumed following any time-out period and we usually have one or two particular plays that we will never use except in the last three minutes of a game when we might be trailing or leading by two points or less. These are the plays that we feel have the best chance of working against a particular opponent and we do not want to show them except in a very crucial spot.

In addition to some of the plays that will be illustrated in this section we also use various parts of our regular offense as set plays on occasion—for example, the forward reverse, the forward screen and roll, and the "back-door" cut for the guard are often called specifically when we feel that the defense is particularly vulnerable to one of them.

**Set Play #1—Forward Cutback.** G2 passes to F2 and fakes toward C and then goes by him on the opposite side (Diag. 4-76). As G2 goes by, C turns and joins him to form a double screen for F1 who sets his man up to be vulnerable for the screen. G1 cuts close off of G2's back as he cuts toward the basket. F1 dribbles out and passes to G1 or F1, if they get open. If neither gets open, F1 screens for G1 at the right side of the lane underneath and C comes around G2 looking for a pass.

**Set Play #2—Guard Cutback.** G1 passes to F1 and cuts outside of him, hesitates when he does not receive the ball back, and then cuts on for the foul lane (Diag. 4-77). F2 passes out to G2 and cuts back toward the foul lane deep and is joined by C to form a double screen for G1 to come back around. G2 passes quickly to F2 who has faked toward basket and then come out half-way between the foul circle and the sideline. F2 looks for G1 around screen by F1 and C, and then for F1 coming around off of C. If neither gets open, F2 looks for any good possibility, then passes out to G2 and crosses to the other side of the floor,

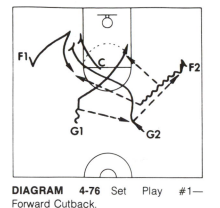

**DIAGRAM 4-76** Set Play #1—Forward Cutback.

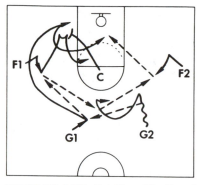

**DIAGRAM 4-77** Set Play #2—Guard Cutback.

as F1 comes out to his side, G1 comes back out to a guard position, and C gets set deep or on the high post to run something else.

**Set Play #3—Weak-Side Guard Cut.** G2 passes to F2, takes one step forward, then steps back to receive a return pass from F2 (Diag. 4-78). When F2 returns the pass to G2, he starts toward the foul circle area and calls for the ball from G1 to whom G2 has just passed. C times himself to come directly off the back of F2 to receive the pass from G1 (with proper deception the pass may look as if it is being made to F2). G2 starts fast as the pass is made to C and looks for the quick pass if he gets the break. F2 goes down the lane on the opposite side to screen for F1, or comes around the screen by F1. If neither G2 nor F1 gets open and C doesn't have a good move, C passes out to G1 and he and F1 form a double screen down the lane for G2 to come back

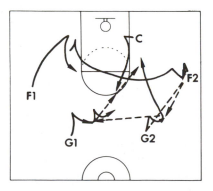

**DIAGRAM 4-78** Set Play #3—Weak-Side Guard Cutback.

around as F2 comes back up the lane on the opposite side for possible options on the side post.

**Set Play #4—Center Around.** The play is run exactly the same as #1 except C now comes around the screen by G2 and F1 instead of F1 coming back around a screen by C and G2 (Diag. 4-79).

**Set Play #5—Forward Under.** G2 passes to F2, fakes inside him, and goes outside. When F2 starts to dribble out, G1 cuts toward him and then uses a quick change of direction and pace and goes toward the basket, G2 moves to a position along the foul lane about even with the front of the basket as C moves down the lane to join him (Diag. 4-80). F2 looks for G1, then F2, then G1 coming back to side post.

**Set Play #6—Forward Cutaway.** G2 passes to F2, fakes inside him, and goes outside and receives the ball from F2 who starts across toward the foul line and then suddenly moves quickly toward basket off C who started toward him from the side post area (Diag. 4-81). G2 looks for F2, or C, or out to G1.

**Set Play #7—Guard Lob.** This is for a good jumping guard (Diag. 4-82). G2 passes to G1 and moves a step or two toward him, then suddenly breaks for the basket off a double screen by C and F2 who comes across as if to meet a pass when G2 passes to G1.

Other options from this are—G2 and C screen for F2 coming across and G1 passes to F1 wide who looks for F2; and F2 receives pass at top of key and G2 cuts as in the back-door play as C moves across and down the lane on the opposite side.

**Set Play #8—Guard Screen and Comeback.** G1 passes to G2, follows his pass, and screens for him (Diag. 4-83). G2 dribbles off screen by G1 and passes to F1 who has moved back and up in the side-post area to get open. G2 moves back to screen for G1 as soon as he passes to F1. When F1 receives the pass from G2, he takes a dribble or two across the foul line as G1 comes by him and C goes down the lane to screen for F2 coming back.

**Set Play #9—Forward Clear.** This may give F2 a little floor space and time to beat his man on a one-and-one situation if he happens to have him outmatched (Diag. 4-84). G2 passes to F2 and takes a step or two forward and then stops for a moment. G1 cuts toward the lane on his side and forms a double screen with C for F1 to come across. As

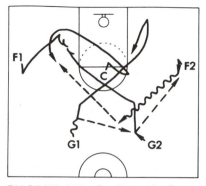

**DIAGRAM 4-79** Set Play #4—Center Around.

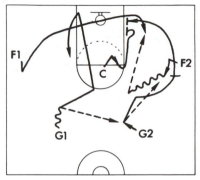

**DIAGRAM 4-80** Set Play #5— Forward Under.

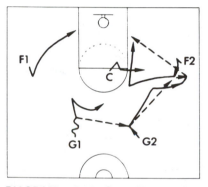

**DIAGRAM 4-81** Set Play #6— Forward Cutaway.

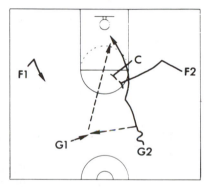

**DIAGRAM 4-82** Set Play #7—Guard Lob.

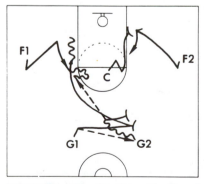

**DIAGRAM 4-83** Set Play #8—Guard Screen and Comeback.

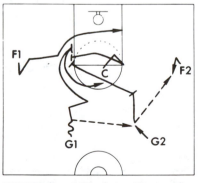

**DIAGRAM 4-84** Set Play #9— Forward Clear.

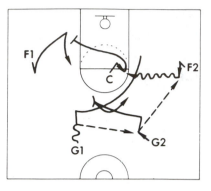

**DIAGRAM 4-85** Set Play #10—Forward Dribble and Pivot.

soon as F1 clears the screen over the top or behind, G2 crosses to screen for G1 coming back.

**Set Play #10—Forward Dribble and Pivot.** G2 passes to F2 and crosses to screen for G1 (Diag. 4-85). F2 dribbles across toward the foul line and looks for a pivot to pass to G1 coming around him. C screens down the opposite lane for F1 coming back.

**Set Play #11—Jump Shot for Guards.** The C is deep for this play (Diag. 4-86). G2 passes to F2 who passes to C coming toward sideline from foul lane deep. G2 moves across to screen for G1 as F2 passes to C. F2 then follows G2 to form a secondary screen for G1 and then screens for G2 coming back.

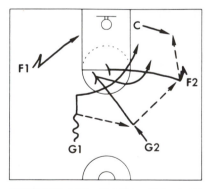

**DIAGRAM 4-86** Set Play #11—Jump Shot for Guards.

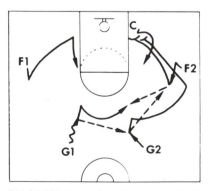

**DIAGRAM 4-87** Set Play #12—Short Jump for Center.

**Set Play #12—Short Jump for Center.** The center is deep again (Diag. 4-87). G2 passes to F2 and cuts outside of him. F2 fakes to G2 and then passes out to G1. As soon as F2 passes to G1, he turns and cuts with G2 to form a double screen for C. F1 has cut to foul lane deep and moves out for side-post options when F2 passes out to G1.

## Out-of-Bounds Plays

All of the end-line and sideline out-of-bounds plays that will be discussed are illustrated from the right side of the floor, but are practiced from both sides of the floor as are the previously illustrated set plays.

The player selected to be the inbounder should have good vision and poise. Since I wanted him to be rather tall and handle the ball on all inbound situations, I almost always trained a tall forward for this. Of course, a back-up player was also trained for this duty.

After the players get their positions, the play starts on a signal by the man with the ball. The signal may be given by orally calling out a name or number, by slapping the ball, or by raising the ball over his head.

The player inbounding the ball must stand about three feet back of the boundary line and must keep perfect balance without leaning. This is equally important for inbounding the ball against a pressing defense.

**Out-of-Bounds #1.** The inbounder looks for 2 on a lob pass to be caught high and put in the basket, for 3 who fakes in and comes around 2, for 5 who tries to pick his man off on 4, and for 4 who backs out for an outlet after 5 has cut around him (Diag. 4-88). 1 moves in quickly to rebound or to get open around a screen.

**DIAGRAM 4-88** Out-of-Bounds #1.

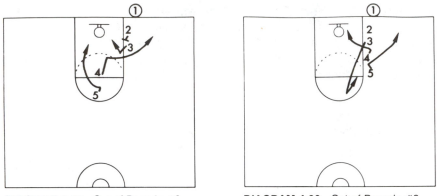

DIAGRAM 4-89   Out-of-Bounds #2.          DIAGRAM 4-90   Out-of-Bounds #3.

**Out-of-Bounds #2.** The inbounder looks for 2 on a lob pass to be caught high and put in the basket, for 5 who has cut off of 4, for 4 who has cut off of 3, and for 3 who rolls after screening for 4 (Diag. 4-89). All are alert to protect or provide an outlet as the play develops. 1 moves into the play quickly after passing.

**Out-of-Bounds #3.** The inbounder looks for 2 as in the first two plays, for 5 cutting outside off of 4, for 4 breaking inside after 5 clears him, and for 3 backing up quickly (Diag. 4-90). 1 moves in quickly after passing.

**Out-of-Bounds #4.** The inbounder looks for 2 as in the other plays, then for 3 who walks slowly toward him and then quickly cuts around 2, then for 5 who cuts around 4, then for 4 as the outlet (Diag. 4-91). 1 moves in quickly after passing.

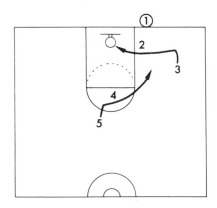

DIAGRAM 4-91   Out-of-Bounds #4.

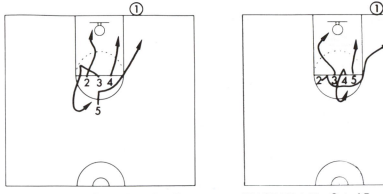

DIAGRAM 4-92  Out-of-Bounds #5.          DIAGRAM 4-93  Out-of-Bounds #6.

**Out-of-Bounds #5.** The inbounder looks for 5 cutting from behind 2, 3, and 4, for 4 moving quickly for the basket if his man shifts to cover 4, for 2 cutting in off of 3, then for 3 backing out (Diag. 4-92). 1 must move in quickly as in the others.

**Out-of-Bounds #6.** This operates on the same principle as the last play (Diag. 4-93). 1 looks for 2 cutting around 3, 4, and 5, then for either end man of the remaining three moving in quickly, then for 4 backing out. 1 moves in quickly after passing. If the man guarding 2 goes between 2's teammates and the basket, 2 stops in back of them for a pass.

**Out-of-Bounds #7.** The inbounder tries to hit 5 breaking in and over and then comes around 2, 3, and 4 and looks for a pass from 5 (Diag. 4-94). All must be alert for a mistake by the defense.

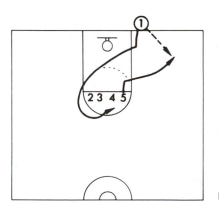

DIAGRAM 4-94  Out-of-Bounds #7.

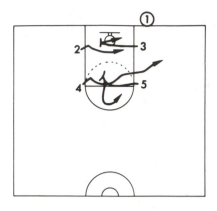

**DIAGRAM 4-95** Out-of-Bounds #8.

**Out-of-Bounds #8.** 1 looks for 2 coming off the screen by 3, for 3 rolling after screening for 2, for 4 coming off the screen by 5, then for 4 backing out (Diag. 4-95). 1 then moves alertly into the play.

**Out-of-Bounds #9.** 1 looks for 4 coming off a screen by 3, for 3 rolling after screening for 4, for 5 moving in and out, then for 2 moving back out (Diag. 4-96). He then moves into the play quickly after his pass.

**Out-of-Bounds #10.** The inbounder looks for 5 coming off of 4—then off of 2, for 2 rolling after his screen, for 4 cutting off of 3, then for 3 backing out (Diag. 4-97). He then moves into the play quickly.

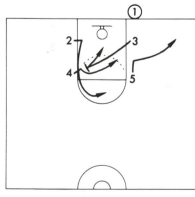

**DIAGRAM 4-96** Out-of-Bounds #9.

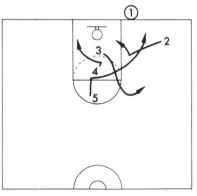

**DIAGRAM 4-97** Out-of-Bounds #10.

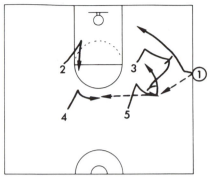

**DIAGRAM 4-98** Out-of-Bounds #1—
Side.

**DIAGRAM 4-99** Out-of-Bounds #2—
Side.

**Out-of-Bounds #1—Side.** 1 passes to 5 who fakes in and comes back and cuts for the basket off of a screen by 3 (Diag. 4-98). 5 passes quickly to 4 who fakes in, comes back (or interchanges with 2), and then cuts off of a second screen by 3. 4 looks for 1, then 5, then for the side-post options with 2.

**Out-of-Bounds #2—Side.** 1 passes in to 4 who fakes in and comes back off of 5 (Diag. 4-99). After passing in, 1 joins 3 to form a double screen for 5 to come back around as 2 fakes in and comes back to the side post. 4 passes to 5 or to 2 for the side-post options.

**Out-of-Bounds #3—Side.** 1 passes in to 5 who fakes in and comes toward him (Diag. 4-100). 5 returns the pass to 1 who fakes in and then comes around him. 1 takes a dribble or two and tries to pass to 2 com-

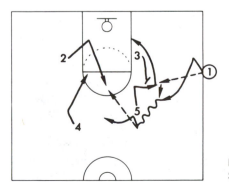

**DIAGRAM 4-100** Out-of-Bounds #3—
Side.

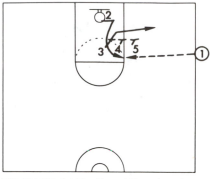

**DIAGRAM 4-101** Out-of-Bounds #4—
Side.

ing up across the foul line. 2 looks for 5 cutting off of a screen by 3 or
for 4 who makes a quick "back-door" cut as 2 receives the ball from 1.

**Out-of-Bounds #4—Side.** 1 looks for 2 coming up the lane around 3,
4, and 5, then for 3 breaking out the opposite side (Diag. 4-101). He
then moves quickly into the play.

# OTHER OFFENSES

It is quite natural that there are many styles of offenses, since practically every coach likes to incorporate his own ideas into the offense
with which he is most familiar. Then, as the years go by and he becomes more familiar with other offenses that appear to be successful,
he incorporates a part of them into his own until his original offense
becomes so changed that it is almost an offense of its own.

However, as I have continually stressed, it is not what you do but how
well you do it providing that it is constructed on sound, valid principles
of floor balance and movement and the players are, first of all, well
grounded in the fundamentals, are well conditioned, and have the
proper team attitude.

Human nature being what it is, coaches have a habit of adopting
what is recently most successful. In some cases this is true of what has
been most successful on a national scale and others on a regional
plane.

The following pages will present a few diagrams of each of several
different types of offenses that have met with varying degrees of success at various times and places.

Please remember that only a few of the basic patterns and ideas of each will be shown without any attempt to develop a total offense. However, I feel that an imaginative coach would have no problem of developing a complete offense from the basic diagrams that are shown.

Although the diagrams will show the attack from only one side, please remember that the same play is available on the opposite side of the floor.

## CINCINNATI STYLE IN 1962

Four possibilities of their setup with a forward set deep near the foul lane behind the center who is halfway down the lane from the foul line to the board and four possibilities of the center on the high post will be shown. Of course, there are options from each of these.

**Cincinnati #1** (Diag. 4-102).   G2 passes to G1 who passes to F1 timing himself to use C as a screen as G1 is ready to pass to him. F1 may get a quick shot from behind C, may drive inside and get the shot or pass back to C who rolls for the basket on the F2 if his man leaves him open, or may drive outside and work the roll play with C.

**Cincinnati #2** (Diag. 4-103).   G2 passes to F2 who angles up quickly to the high post. G2 cuts quickly as G1 passes to F2 and continues on around the double screen by F1 and C if he does not get open for a pass on his cut. G1 fakes to the outside and then cuts off of F2 and looks for pass if G2 did not receive the ball going by F2. F1 may occasionally come around C looking for a pass from F2 as soon as F2 receives pass from G1 and then moves back by C to rebound or form a double screen for G2 coming on if neither got open.

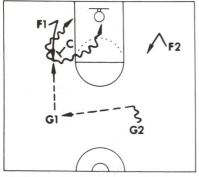

**DIAGRAM 4-102**  Cincinnati #1.

**DIAGRAM 4-103**  Cincinnati #2.

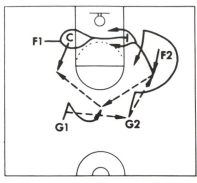

**DIAGRAM 4-104** Cincinnati #3.

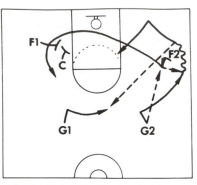

**DIAGRAM 4-105** Cincinnati #4.

**Cincinnati #3** (Diag. 4-104). G2 passes to F2 and cuts outside. F2 looks for F1 coming off C. If F2 passes back out to G1, F1 crosses lane to screen for F2, C moves up and out a little for a pass from G1, and F2 cuts off a screen at the lane by F1. G2 also comes around a screen by F1 as he comes on out.

**Cincinnati #4** (Diag. 4-105). G2 passes to F2 and cuts outside of him and receives the ball back. F2 steps up and then quickly moves for the basket. If F2 does not get open for a pass from G2, he continues on around a double screen by F1 and C and looks for a pass from G1 to whom G2 has passed. G2 cuts for the basket and then to the side post after passing out to G1. F1 may swing around C for a pass from G2 or G1 if he sees an opening.

**Cincinnati #5** (Diag. 4-106). The center is now on the high post. G2 passes to F2 and G1 cuts off of C looking for a pass. C pulls to weak side and screens for F1 coming off of him. If F2 passes to G1 late, he cuts for the basket and screens for F1 on his way. If F2 passes to F1 coming across, he cuts for the basket and screens for G1 on his way. If he passes out to G2, he and F1 both screen for G1 coming back.

**Cincinnati #6** (Diag. 4-107). G2 passes to F2 and gets a return pass as he cuts outside. F2 cuts for basket and C moves downlane off of F2's back. If G2 passes back out to G1, he and F1 form a screen for C coming back and F2 comes up on the opposite side post.

**Cincinnati #7** (Diag. 4-108). G2 passes to F2 and G1 cuts off of C looking for a pass and then crosses lane to opposite side. C cuts downlane looking for a pass from F2. F1 comes across the key. If F2

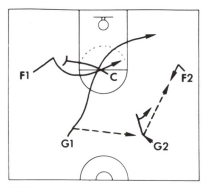

**DIAGRAM 4-106** Cincinnati #5.

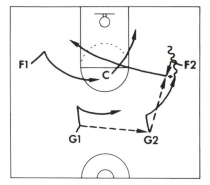

**DIAGRAM 4-107** Cincinnati #6.

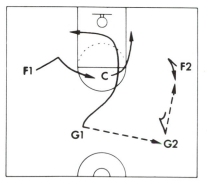

**DIAGRAM 4-108** Cincinnati #7.

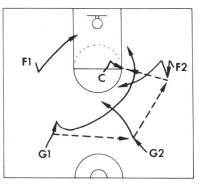

**DIAGRAM 4-109** Cincinnati #8.

passes out to G2, he and F1 screen for C coming back and G1 comes back on the opposite side post.

**Cincinnati #8** (Diag. 4-109). G2 passes to F2 and screens for G1 (or fakes a screen for G1) for one of them to split the post if F2 passed to him. F2 has little time for a one-on-one situation before passing to C if the situation warrants it.

## CENTER AWAY

This offense has the center either on the opposite side from where the first pass is made forward, or pulling to the opposite side as soon as the first forward pass is made. Of course, you must mix it up to make it work effectively by having some options with the center staying on the strong side.

The University of California at Berkeley used a similar offense when

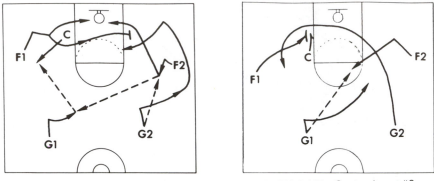

**DIAGRAM 4-110**  Center Away #1.          **DIAGRAM 4-111**  Center Away #2.

they won the national championship in 1959 and many other fine teams have used a variation of this through the years.

**Center Away #1** (Diag. 4-110).   G2 passes to F2 and cuts outside. F1 cuts off of C who is stationed on the opposite foul lane. F2 passes to F1 for a shot or back out to G1 who passes to C as C pulls out and up. F2 cuts off of F1 who forms a screen at the lane when he does not receive the pass. G2 also cuts off of F1 after F2.

**Center Away #2** (Diag. 4-111).   G1 passes to F2 who fakes toward the basket and comes toward the top of the key. G2 cuts quickly as G1 passes to F2 and, if he does not receive a pass going by F2, he continues on around a double screen by F1 and C. G1 fakes in and then cuts by F2 if G2 does not receive a pass from F2.

**Center Away #3** (Diag. 4-112).   G2 passes to F2 and cuts outside of him and receives a return pass. F2 starts across the floor and then quickly cuts for the basket off of C who has come up from the weak side. G2 gets open for a shot, or passes to F2 for a shot, or to C and screens for F2 coming back.

**Center Away #4** (Diag. 4-113).   To open up the floor for a moment for F2 to beat his man on a one-on-one, G2 passes to F2 and cuts across and goes around C who pulls up to foul line on opposite side of circle. F1 fakes back and comes across top of circle of back of G2 and screen by C. G1 goes all the way for a pass if he is open, or pulls back out for an outlet if he isn't.

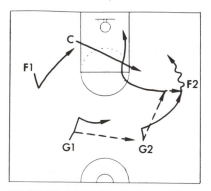

**DIAGRAM 4-112**  Center Away #3.

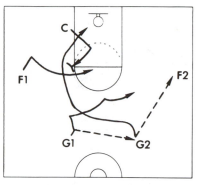

**DIAGRAM 4-113**  Center Away #4.

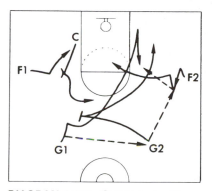

**DIAGRAM 4-114**  Center Away #5.

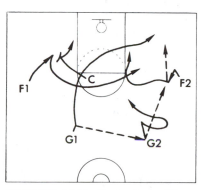

**DIAGRAM 4-115**  Center Away #6.

**Center Away #5** (Diag. 4-114).   G2 passes to F2 and screens for G1 who cuts for the basket and then comes back up toward side post if he does not get open on the way in. F2 passes to G1 on the side post and splits the post with G2. C and F1 keep their men busy on the weak side.

**Center Away #6** (Diag. 4-115).   G2 passes to F2 and G1 cuts off C on the opposite side of key. C pulls away to screen for F1 coming across as soon as G1 clears him. F2 may pass to G1 cutting in, or to F1 coming across and then screening for G1 as he cuts for the basket, or to G1 late coming toward the side and then going across and cutting down lane off of F1, or out to G2 and forming a double screen with F1 for G1 coming back out.

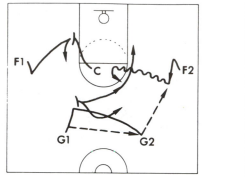

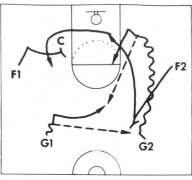

**DIAGRAM 4-116** Center Away #7.　　　**DIAGRAM 4-117** Center Away #8.

**Center Away #7** (Diag. 4-116).   G2 passes to F2 and screens for G1. F2 dribbles across toward foul circle and looks for G1 coming by him. If G1 doesn't get open going by, he may continue on around a double screen by F1 and C. F1 may cut up off C if he sees the opportunity and G2 may cut off of F2 after G1 if it looks good.

**Center Away #8** (Diag. 4-117).   This is the forward and guard screen and roll with the three options that have been shown in other setups.
    The forward reverses to receive a pass from the guard and works in an identical manner as has been shown in other setups.

## NO POST OR THREE OUT

This offense or variations of it have been used with good success in all sections of the country by many fine coaches.
    It is sometimes used to offset the lack of an outstanding post man, or to utilize the abilities of two pretty good post men at the same time, or to utilize the abilities of three good guards at the same time in an effort to open up the floor better for a give-and-go or cutting game, or for a combination of any of those ideas.

**No Post #1** (Diag. 4-118).   G2 passes to F2 coming to the side post and then "splits the post" with G3 as F1 cuts for the basket and G1 fakes an outside cut and comes back to protect. If F2 passes back out to F1, he and F2 may change sides as G2 and G3 move back out to set up again, while also looking for an opening as they do.

**No Post #2** (Diag. 4-119).   The same as #1, except G3 makes the initial pass to F2.

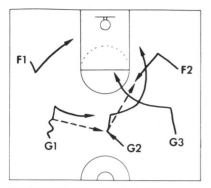

**DIAGRAM 4-118** No Post #1.

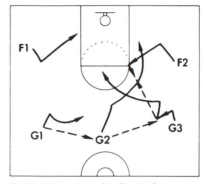

**DIAGRAM 4-119** No Post #2.

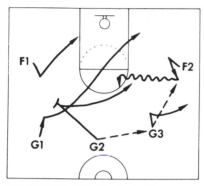

**DIAGRAM 4-120** No Post #3.

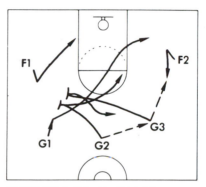

**DIAGRAM 4-121** No Post #4.

**No Post #3** (Diag. 4-120). G2 passes to G3 and screens for G1 as G3 passes to F2 wide. F2 dribbles across if G1 does not get open and looks for a pivot and pass to G2, cutting off of him.

**No Post #4** (Diag. 4-121). G2 passes to G3 and screens for G1. G3 passes to F2 and screens for G2 and, perhaps, also screens for G1 if G1 did not get open from the screen by G2.

**No Post #5—Screen-and-Roll Play with Three Options** (Diag. 4-122). F2 screens for G3 as he receives a pass from G2 and rolls for the basket. G2 screens for G1 after passing to G3 and then moves on down lane to join F1 in a double screen for F2 if he comes on through. If G3 cannot get open or pass to F2 on the roll or on the "buttonhook," he may pass back to G1, fake toward the basket, and come back toward the side post.

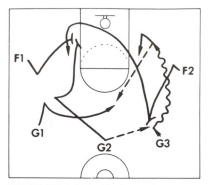

**DIAGRAM 4-122** No Post #5.

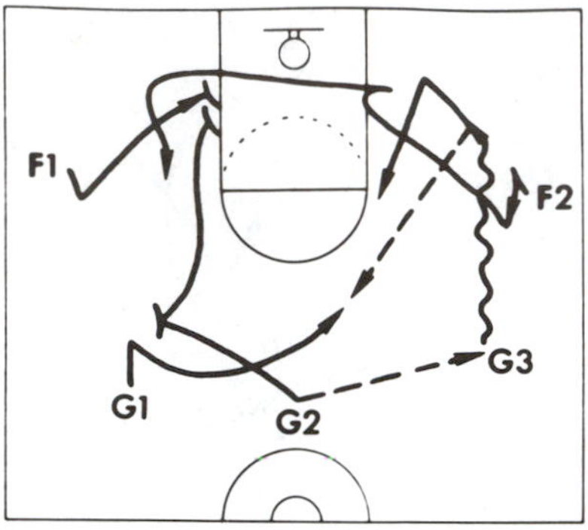

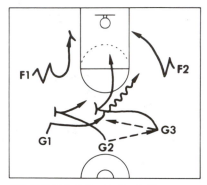

**DIAGRAM 4-123** No Post #6.

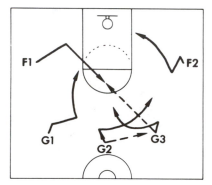

**DIAGRAM 4-124** No Post #7.

**DIAGRAM 4-125** No Post #8.

**No Post #6** (Diag. 4-123). This is the forward reverse play that works exactly as #5, except that G3 starts it by dribbling toward F2 who makes a quick reverse in an effort to get open.

**No Post #7** (Diag. 4-124). G2 passes to F1 who fakes back and comes quickly toward the top of the key. G1 cuts quickly as G3 passes to F1 and F2 reverses quickly on the opposite side. G3 passes to F1 and F2 reverses quickly on the opposite side. G3 fakes outside and then screens for G2 coming across. All must keep looking for screens when they fail to receive a pass.

**No Post #8** (Diag. 4-125). G2 passes to G3 and screens for G1. G3 passes to G1 coming off the screen by G2, follows his pass, and screens and rolls. F2 reverses to look for a pass or to keep his man busy. If F2, G1, or G3 does not get open, G1 may pass back out to G2 who looks for F2 coming on around F1, or for G3 for whom G1 screens after passing back out to G2.

### ONE-THREE-ONE

Although this offense has not been used as much as some of the others, it has been used with excellent results by some very fine coaches.

It enables you to utilize the talents of two different types of post men at the same time, but also needs a good all-around ball player in the #5 position and an outside threat in the #2 and #4 positions for best results.

**One-Three-One #1** (Diag. 4-126).   5 passes to 4 and cuts off of 3 as 4 passes to 1. 4 starts across and screens for 3, then rolls down the lane after passing to 1. If nothing happens, 5 comes in back out to his starting position to receive a pass from 2 who has received a pass from 1 after having exchanged sides with 4.

**One-Three-One #2** (Diag. 4-127).   The play starts the same way as 1, but 3 moves to the opposite side of the lane after 5 cuts by him and 4 cuts for the basket or cuts across and screens for 2.

**One-Three-One #3** (Diag. 4-128).   The play is almost like 1, but 4 cuts off of 3 and goes down the lane, rather than screening for 3 and rolling down the lane.

**One-Three-One #4** (Diag. 4-129).   5 who passes to 4 who passes to 3 and then splits the post with 5 as 1 reverses under and 2 pulls out.

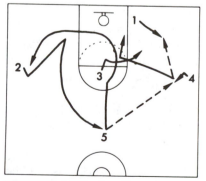

**DIAGRAM 4-126**  One-Three-One #1.

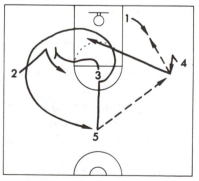

**DIAGRAM 4-127**  One-Three-One #2.

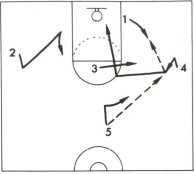

**DIAGRAM 4-128** One-Three-One #3.

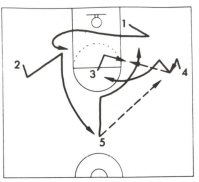

**DIAGRAM 4-129** One-Three-One #4.

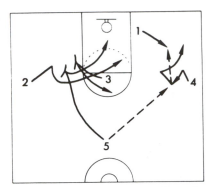

**DIAGRAM 4-130** One-Three-One #5.

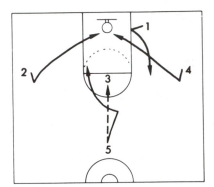

**DIAGRAM 4-131** One-Three-One #6.

**One-Three-One #5** (Diag. 4-130). After 5 passes to 4, he and 3 screen for 2 coming across for a pass from 1 to whom 4 has passed. 3 also makes a secondary screen for 5 coming back.

**One-Three-One #6** (Diag. 4-131). 5 passes to 3 and cuts off of him as 2 and 4 reverse for the basket. 1 sets his man up for a screen off of 4. Either 2, 5, or 1 may get open initially, and 4 might get open late by crossing underneath and coming around off of 2 and, perhaps, 5.

**One-Three-One #7** (Diag. 4-132). 5 passes to 3 and cuts off of him and then forms a double screen with 4 for 1 to cut around. 2 starts a reverse and then comes back out if he isn't open quickly.

**One-Three-One #8** (Diag. 4-133). 3 screens for 5 and rolls for the basket. 2 reverses sharply and stops on the opposite side of the lane for 3 to continue on around if he does not get open. 5 may pass back

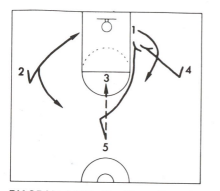

**DIAGRAM 4-132** One-Three-One #7.

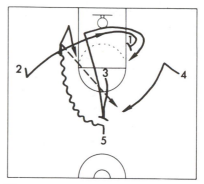

**Diagram 4-133** One-Three-One #8.

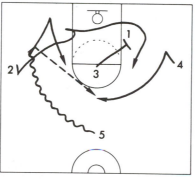

**DIAGRAM 4-134** One-Three-One #9.

out to 4, fake on, and come back to side post if he did not get a pass to 2 or 3 or get a shot himself.

**One-Three-One #9** (Diag. 4-134). This play develops the same as the forward reverses in the other types of offensive setups. 2 reverses to get open, "buttonhooks" at the lane for a second chance, and then continues under and around the double screen by 1 and 3 for a third possibility.

## WEAVES

Many coaches in all sections of the country are partial to an offense that features some type of a weave. As a matter of fact, practically all offenses will use some type of a weave at times.

The weaving offenses demand good movement and ball-handling as well as extreme alertness to take advantage of quick cuts and reverses and to avoid offensive fouls.

Critics of the pure weaving offenses contend that they are too easily defended by the use of zone defenses and that too much energy is expended in movement toward the sidelines.

Regardless of the particular type of weave being used, the passer usually follows his pass to screen and then makes a quick move toward the basket or moves away to open up the floor for a teammate to make the move. They may cause the defense to continue backing up until the offense gets a comparatively short shot over them or may get the defense waiting for them and thus become vulnerable to a quick cut between them or a quick reverse behind them.

The three-man weave may utilize: (1) the guards and one forward when the center is either deep or on the normal post, (2) the three outside men or the middle outside man and the two men on either his right or left when the three-out offense is being used, or (3) the three outside men with the post men working in screens when the high double post is being used.

The four-man weave utilizes men in the guard and forward positions with the center a "roamer" in the foul-lane area for screens or an outlet for a quick pass and cut.

The five-man weave uses no post and is run from the three-out-and-two-in setup. All five men enter in to it and are constantly alert to get open down the middle or by reversing the outside.

The following diagrams merely give an idea of the initial setup and make no attempt to continue the development.

**Weave #1** (Diag. 4-135).    This shows the start of the three-man weave using the two guards and one forward on the side opposite the center.

**Weave #2** (Diag. 4-136).    This shows the start of the setup with the three outside men weaving when you are using either the double post in the side-post areas or the forwards wide.

Considerable screening can be done in the double-post setup, while quick reverses by the forwards with some screening are exploited when the forwards are wide.

**Weave #3** (Diag. 4-137).    In this four-man weave style the center may stay deep to keep the middle open and work up occasionally to the foul lane for a quick outlet or to form a screen.

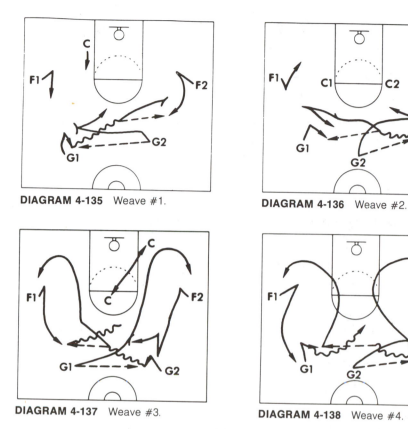

**DIAGRAM 4-135**   Weave #1.

**DIAGRAM 4-136**   Weave #2.

**DIAGRAM 4-137**   Weave #3.

**DIAGRAM 4-138**   Weave #4.

**Weave #4** (Diag. 4-138).   This is the true full-team weave that keeps every one busy and alert. You try for cuts down the middle or quick reverses, but pull out to open it up for the next cut in case you do not get open and receive a pass.

## SHUFFLE

Bruce Drake from the University of Oklahoma is generally given credit for, if not originating at least popularizing, the shuffle offense. Many coaches in both the scholastic and collegiate level have adopted the idea and improvised on it to suit their own ideas. Coach Joel Eaves of Auburn has had excellent success with the shuffle and has written a very fine book in regard to it.

The offense got its name from the fact that it features a change from side to side in its continuation or continuity. It requires excellent movement and has constant cuts that usually first exploit a sharp cut coming off a screen on the weak side and coming toward the ball and the basket.

Although certain changes may be made to take advantage of particular individual strengths of your personnel, the offense requires all five men to play all five positions. Therefore, it has the value of requiring complete teamwork and providing balanced scoring opportunities. The teams who use it well and have patience will usually end up with a very high field-goal percentage as they will get the good shot before shooting and will usually have good scoring balance among the team.

It is quite effective against man-to-man defenses as it forces many shifts and compels the defenses to be able to guard different men in different positions on the floor. Therefore, defensive specialists in certain areas may be forced from their specialized area and may make more defensive errors.

Some of its critics contend that it is not effective against many zone defenses and the players who can work it most effectively are usually players who will not provide you with the best defensive rebounding and general defensive balance.

Since an entire book has been written in regard to this offense, I will not attempt to explain my conception of it any further.

The following diagrams will give a general idea of some of the play setups that come from its use.

**Shuffle #1—Setup** (Diag. 4-139). The initial setup of the players finds them overbalanced to one side as shown here. 1 takes his position five or six feet from the sideline and five or six feet deeper than the foul line extended. 2 sets up near the foul lane opposite from 1 as deep as possible to get open for a pass from 5. 3 lines up just outside the circle at the foul line extended on the strong side. 4 lines up in an outside position in an area that would be midpoint between 1 and 3 from the side and about five or six feet closer to the end line than 5. 5 takes a position in a direct line between the two baskets and five or six feet nearer to the center line than 4.

**Shuffle #2—Change of Side** (Diag. 4-140). This shows how the sides are reversed in one particular setup. 4 cuts off of 3 as soon as 5 passes to 2 and continues on through if he does not get open or no shot is taken and ends up on the opposite side of the floor in 1's spot. 5 cuts down lane and screens for 3 coming to outer half of circle and then rolls for the basket and comes back to the original 2 spot. 3 comes out to the original 5 spot and 2 dribbles out to the spot that 4 originally oc-

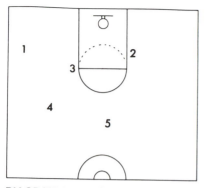

**DIAGRAM 4-139** Shuffle #1—Setup.

**DIAGRAM 4-140** Shuffle #2—Change of Side.

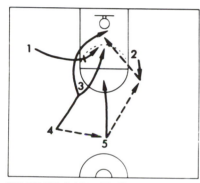

**DIAGRAM 4-141** Shuffle #3.

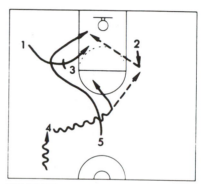

**DIAGRAM 4-142** Shuffle #3A.

cupied. 1 moves toward basket and then up to the side-post spot where 3 was stationed at the beginning. 2 could then pass to 3 or dribble over to the 3 spot (originally #5) as 3 cuts in front of him and comes to the original 4 spot and you are ready to start another play from the identical setup on the opposite side of the floor.

**Shuffle #3** (Diag. 4-141). 4 to 5 to 2. As 5 passes to 2, 4 tries to pick his man off of 3 or 1 and 3. 2 passes to 4 if he gets open.

**Shuffle #3A** (Diag. 4-142). The same as Shuffle #3 except 5 cuts across in front of 4 and becomes the cutter from the weak side as 4 passes to 2.

2 may pass to 1 if his man shifts to 4 and leaves him open moving toward the basket.

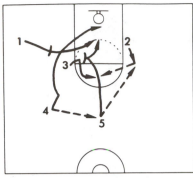

**DIAGRAM 4-143**  Shuffle #4.

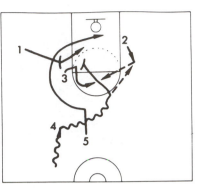

**DIAGRAM 4-144**  Shuffle #4A.

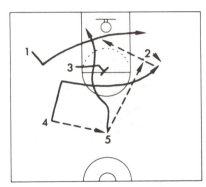

**DIAGRAM 4-145**  Shuffle #5.

**DIAGRAM 4-146**  Shuffle #5A.

**Shuffle #4** (Diag. 4-143).  The same as Shuffle #3 except that 2 passes to 3 coming off screen by 5 instead of passing to 5, 1, or getting a good shot himself.

**Shuffle #4A** (Diag. 4-144).  The same as Shuffle #4 except 4 and 5 exchange starting positions as in Shuffle #3A.

**Shuffle #5** (Diag. 4-145).  4 to 5 to 2 as usual, but 4 fakes a cut out-side 3 and then cuts back across the top and behind 2 for a short pass and jump shot. 1 reverses and goes through and 3 either screens for 5 coming down the lane or comes off a screen by 5. 2 might pass to 4, 1, 5, 3 or get a shot himself.

**Shuffle #5A** (Diag. 4-146).  The same as Shuffle 5 except that 4 and 5 exchange starting positions as in #3A.

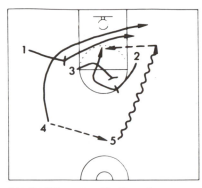

**DIAGRAM 4-147** Shuffle #6.

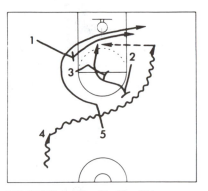

**DIAGRAM 4-148** Shuffle #6A.

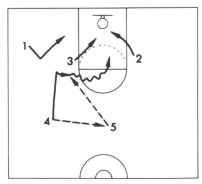

**DIAGRAM 4-149** Shuffle #7.

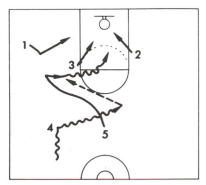

**DIAGRAM 4-150** Shuffle #7A.

**Shuffle #6** (Diag. 4-147).    4 to 5 who dribbles off a screen by 2. 4 cuts for a basket outside of 1 and 3. 2 rolls back downlane off of 3 or screens for 3 and rolls downlane. 5 gets shot or passes to open man.

**Shuffle #6A** (Diag. 4-148).   Same as Shuffle #6 except that the change of starting positions by 4 and 5 as in all of the "A" diagrams.

**Shuffle #7** (Diag. 4-149).   4 passes to 5 and fakes a cut outside of 3 and then receives a pass from 5 in front of 3. He then dribbles toward basket as 3, 1, and 2 move for the basket.

**Shuffle #7A** (Diag. 4-150).   This is Shuffle #7 with the "A" diagram start.

**DIAGRAM 4-151** Shuffle #8.

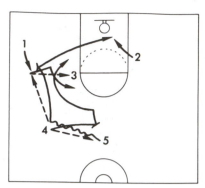

**DIAGRAM 4-152** Shuffle #8A.

**Shuffle #8** (Diag. 4-151). 4 passes to 1 and follows his pass to screen inside and roll for the basket. 1 passes to 3, fakes inside him, and then cuts over the top to split him with 5.

**Shuffle #8A** (Diag. 4-152). The same as Shuffle #8 with the "A diagram start.

**Shuffle #9** (Diag. 4-153). 4 passes to 1 and follows his pass to screen inside and roll for the basket. 1 dribbles across toward the key and hands off to 5 cutting behind him and 3. 1 may occasionally use a change of pace and dribble on around 3 himself.

**Shuffle #9A** (Diag. 4-154). The same as Shuffle #9 with the "A" start.

**DIAGRAM 4-153** Shuffle #9.

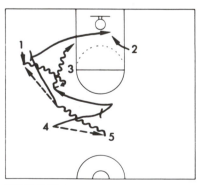

**DIAGRAM 4-154** Shuffle #9A.

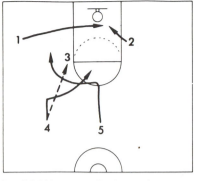

**DIAGRAM 4-155**  Shuffle #10.

**DIAGRAM 4-156**  Shuffle #10A.

**Shuffle #10** (Diag. 4-155).   4 makes a quick pass to 3 and fakes outside, then cuts back inside to split 3 with 5 as 1 reverses.

**Shuffle #10A** (Diag. 4-156).   The same as Shuffle #10 with the "A" start.

There are many other ideas or styles of offense that are used and all coaches should be looking constantly for ways to improve their offense and to take advantage of the strengths of their own individual players, but all should require a lot of movement and good balance.

I would like to close the discussion on team offense by reiterating and reemphasizing that no team offense is any good unless the individuals playing it are properly grounded in the individual fundamentals, are well conditioned, and are imbued with the team spirit or philosophy of always placing the team above self.

Furthermore, almost any offense will be effective if the players possess those three essentials and understand team balance in all of its mental, emotional, and physical aspects.

# 5

## OBTAINING POSSESSION OF THE BALL

Before any offense can be started, you must have possession of the ball. Although gaining this possession is primarily defensive work, since, except for the comparatively small amount of time when the ball is free and in possession of neither team, the opponents have possession of it when you do not, some parts require separate discussion.

We want our players to be eager to gain possession of the ball and to react quickly from defense to offense whenever we do gain possession of it. Therefore, since we want to aggressively seek possession of the ball when we lose it while on offense, it seems rather logical that a discussion of obtaining possession of it should be between the offensive and defensive discussions.

## FROM THE BOARDS

More opportunities for possession will come from missed shots than by any other way; therefore offensive and defensive rebounding must receive a great amount of attention. It has been said often that the team that controls the boards will probably control the game and this statement will usually hold true.

It would be impossible for me to overemphasize the three factors that I consider to have contributed the most toward the exceptional rebounding success of my teams over the years. I place tremendous emphasis on the following mental preparedness:

**1.** Getting the players to assume that every shot will be missed and aggressively rebounding their area. Offensively, we want the second, third, and repeated effort until we score, regain possession, or the ball is definitely lost to the opposition.

**2.** Getting the players to automatically bring their hands to shoulder height with the fingers pointed toward the ceiling and the palms of their hands facing the basket as soon as a shot is attempted.

**3.** Getting our defensive players to play the ball rather than the opponent when a shot is attempted. We like our players as they turn to face the basket when a shot is attempted to merely cross over into the path of their opponent and then go for the ball. In other words, we want our main concentration to be on getting the rebound rather than keeping our opponent from getting it. I consider this to be a positive rather than a negative approach toward obtaining possession of the ball.

## DEFENSIVE REBOUNDING

Once you have moved into the path of the offensive player, you concentrate on the flight of the ball as you quickly move toward the board and try to time your jump in such a manner that you will be contacting the ball with both of your hands just as your elbows are extended at the height of your jump. (See Fig. 5-1.)

Immediately upon his gaining possession of the ball, I like the defensive rebounder to get a wide kick of the legs and to bring the ball quickly and forcefully to the chest with the top of the ball at chin height. The head should turn over the shoulder toward the best probable outlet area and the elbows should be well spread. Do not try to protect the ball by extending the elbows and getting it away from the body, but protect it by keeping it close to the body at chest height and rolling the wrists and hands. Try to land with the weight well balanced on both feet, which are well spread.

Remember that a defensive rebounder's job is not completed until he has quickly and safely got the ball away from the defensive board. Most fast-break baskets are a direct result of the defensive rebounder completing a quick pass to the proper outlet man. Since we like to fast break every time we get possession of the ball, it is essential that we give this phase much attention.

If the man you are guarding takes the shot, take one or two quick steps back toward the basket and watch him momentarily, so that you can cross over into his path and then go for the ball. If he makes no immediate move, go for the board without waiting any longer.

If someone other than your man takes the shot, you must be very alert to quickly check the path of your man and then aggressively play the ball in your territory.

**FIGURE 5-1** Bill Walton (#32) high for a rebound against University of San Francisco.

A defensive rebounder must be very careful that he does not get caught too far under the basket. You must go up and to the basket for the ball rather than merely up. A man caught too far under is easy prey for a clever offensive rebounder who will crowd him with his body while keeping the hands up for a clean tip at the ball.

All rebounders must know the probable rebounding angle of the ball depending upon the spot from which the shot is taken and from where it appears that it will hit the board or the basket. They must also know the probable rebounding distance the ball will come off the board according to the spring of the goal or the board and according to the arch of the ball. From the offensive point of view you should be able from experience to have a fairly good idea of the rebounding characteristics of your own and the shots of your teammates. If you do not, it is a clear indication that you are not a very good student of the game.

The defensive rebounder should almost always try for clear possession of the ball and seldom try to tip the ball away.

Rebounders should realize that this is one of the roughest parts of the game and must not permit any excessive contact to cause them to lose their poise or self-control in any manner. They should remember that contact is a two-way proposition and eventually will even up.

## OFFENSIVE REBOUNDING

Many of the same principles that apply to defensive rebounding also apply to offensive rebounding.

Since the defensive rebounder is usually between the offensive rebounder and the basket, the offensive rebounder must try to fake or outmaneuver the defensive man.

The offensive rebounder must be careful of charging over the top of the defensive man and must be especially careful about keeping the hands at shoulder height. There is a strong tendency for offensive rebounders to push or shove unless they keep their hands up and it is also an acknowledged fact that, although there is much shoving done by the body in and around the boards, it isn't observed or called nearly to the extent that it is when the hands are used.

Offensive rebounders may tip away from the board for possession at times when they are not in position to get either an offensive tip or clear possession.

Offensive rebounders should learn to use their wrists and fingers for tipping and not to bat at the ball. They should also keep the palms of their hands toward the basket in order to have better tipping control. (See Fig. 5-2.)

I like all of our players who are likely to be in position to have the opportunity of getting a number of offensive tips to take exercises to strengthen their wrists and fingers as well as their jumping ability.

Many fine jumpers never develop into fine rebounders while many average jumpers develop into fine rebounders. This is usually because of the necessity of their developing their timing while the better jumpers may rely too much on their native jumping ability.

The offensive player must always be alive to give that second and third effort. I have seen many offensive baskets made simply because one or two rebounders refused to give up and kept giving the extra effort until the ball finally went through the basket.

**FIGURE 5-2** Fine offensive rebound after getting through the blockout.

Like the defensive rebounder, the offensive rebounder must try to play through the ball and try to get contact just prior to reaching the peak of his jump and just before the complete extension of his elbow and wrist joints.

I like players who like to rebound, especially those who really enjoy working the defensive boards, and believe in seeing to it that they get plenty of recognition and praise. Although I often praise my good scorers in private, I seldom give them any public praise, but I continually give public credit to my rebounders, my playmakers, and my better defensive players. The scorers get enough without an assist from me, but the rebounders, playmakers, and defensive men may be overlooked if the coach doesn't help out.

# AFTER AN OPPONENT'S SCORE

This is a most undesirable method of obtaining possession of the ball and it would be nice to never be forced to acquire possession in such a manner, but we must be realistic enough to know that we will be obtaining it in this manner about as much as we will from the boards. Therefore, we must be ready to react quickly when we do and get the ball inbounded quickly to put quick pressure on our opponents.

**Inbounding Ball #1—After a Field Goal** (Diag. 5-1).   We like the ball to be inbounded quickly by a designated player, usually a forward with the other forward and center, listed as 2 and 3, breaking to and from the sidelines to get open for a pass.

We want our designated rebounder to get the ball three to four feet back of the end line with his shoulders parallel to the end line as his four teammates move quickly to their assigned positions as shown in Diag. 5-1. The inbounder must have the ball at his chest and must not be leaning or out of balance.

The guards, 4 and 5, break toward the spot where the center line meets the sideline and then cut back toward 2 and 3. They may receive a direct pass inbounds from 1 or the next pass from 2 or 3, one of whom will always be the first or second option for the inbound pass.

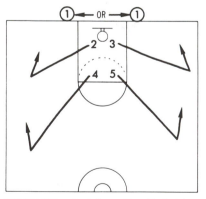

**DIAGRAM 5-1** Inbounding Ball #1—After a Field Goal.

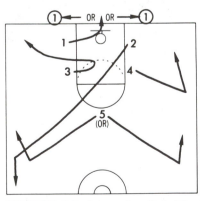

**DIAGRAM 5-2** Inbounding Ball #2—After a Successful Free Throw.

**Inbounding Ball #2—After a Successful Free Throw** (Diag. 5-2). We like the ball to be inbounded quickly by 1 to either 3 or 4 who looks for 5 as soon as he receives the pass from 1. 2 breaks across and down the floor to be the first man down.

It must be remembered and taken into consideration that we like to make fast-break opportunities and stress getting the ball inbounded as quickly as possible after a score in order to keep pressure on our opponents. Of course, we make some changes against pressing defenses, but still like to keep the pressure game ourselves.

## FROM FREE-THROW SITUATIONS

When our opponents are shooting a free throw, we place our two best rebounders on the inside positions and have them get as close as the restraining marker permits to their opponents. We want our best rebounder on the inside of their best tipper. We have our next two best rebounders in the third position on each side and have them crowd the basket side as much as the restraining line permits. In other words we are trying psychologically and physically to squeeze our opponent's most dangerous tippers as much as possible and permissible. Our fifth man lines up directly behind the shooter on the back half of the circle.

**Free Throw #1—Defense** (Diag. 5-3). 1 and 2 are our strongest and best rebounders with our best inside our opponent's most dangerous tipper. 3 and 4—one covers the shooter and the other crowds the most dangerous opponent. 5 is a quick and agile ball handler.

If the offense takes one of the 3 or 4 positions, we have the man he replaces take a spot as close as possible to him and be responsible for the shooter.

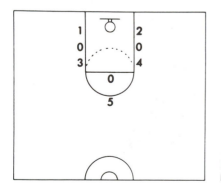

**DIAGRAM 5-3** Free Throw #1—Defense.

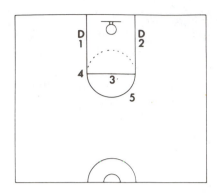

**DIAGRAM 5-4** Free Throw #2—Offense.

The previous section explains our movements when the free throw is made and the ball is in play following it.

**Free Throw #2—Offense** (Diag. 5-4).   1 and 2 are our strongest offensive rebounders with our best attempting to get on the opposite side from the best rebounding opponent, or on the side that he feels best. They should line up in the middle of their restricted area in order that they not feel crowded. Number 5 is probably our smallest nonshooter, who should be quick and agile.

Whenever our inside men feel that they have little or no chance for a tip-in, they are encouraged to tip the ball far out toward 5, who must be ready to get it or to be the protector.

## FROM JUMP BALLS

Although changes in the rules have almost eliminated jump-ball situations during the course of a game, one may occur at a very important time and you should be prepared for that eventuality. As in most situations, when the teams are of near-equal ability the team better prepared in the little details will usually prevail. As I have often said, "Failure to prepare is preparing to fail."

Jump balls become a team affair and all five men must be very alert. There can be a great amount of faking and decoying during jump balls, and clever nonjumpers can be of tremendous value. (See Fig. 5-3.)

The jumper must time himself with the ball and it will be necessary for him to study the ball tossers to be able to do this. Different officials have different mannerisms and methods of tossing the ball and may

**FIGURE 5-3**  Opening tip-off concentration in an actual game.

toss it to a different height. The jumper must neither jump too soon nor be caught waiting. The jumper must go straight up and extend the tipping arm to its full length. The ball must not be slapped or batted, but tipped with a flick of the wrist and the fingers and given impetus by the forepart of the middle, ring, and forefingers and arched to the desired area.

Different jumpers may prefer different stances and I will not change them from what is most natural for them as long as they are getting the job done. (See Fig. 5-4.) However, I prefer to crowd the opposing jumper as much as possible, if it appears likely that he should get the tip, and to prevent being crowded if it appears that the control will be ours or is about even.

When we are certain that our opponent will have the jump, we try to cover every man except one in front or to the side of their jumper. We then encourage him to tip to the man we leave open and have one of our men from behind their jumper time himself to knife in front of their open man and steal the tip that we let him have.

We encourage our jumpers to land in good balance, with their hands

**FIGURE 5-4** Good preparatory balance and position for a jump ball.

up, and alert to move into the play offensively and defensively. If we tip to a man directly in front of our jumper and he is pinched, we often have him tip right back to our jumper over the head of their jumper.

Do not foul your opponent on the jump, but be sure to use and protect the area that belongs to you. Do not get thrown off-balance because you were caught unaware and got crowded.

Since we use and know the value of "roamers" or "free lancers," we must be particularly alert and not get hurt by the same method, especially when it appears that we have tip control.

The following diagrams will illustrate our normal positions for the designated jump ball situations:

**Jump Ball #1—Control Doubtful** (Diag. 5-5).   This concerns a jump in the center circle. 5 is our shortest and should be very quick. 4 should be the quickest of our available tall men. 2 should be our least quick tall man. If we encourage our opponent to tip forward short, or long to the rear, 4 knifes across and tries to tip the ball on back to 5. If successful, 1 may break down the floor off a screen by 2.

**Jump Ball #2—Control Ours** (Diag. 5-6).   This is another center circle jump in which we appear to have control. 1 tips to 2 who tips off to 5 (or 4 if he cuts and 5 stays back). 3 breaks toward the corner on the side of 4 or 5, depending upon which one comes through. 1 cuts off a screen by 2 down the opposite side.

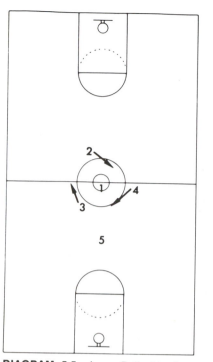

**DIAGRAM 5-5** Jump Ball #1—Control Doubtful.

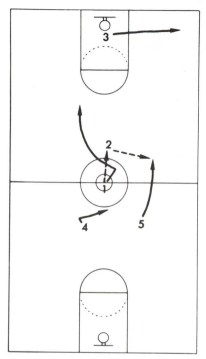

**DIAGRAM 5-6** Jump Ball #2—Control Ours.

**Jump Ball #3—Offensive End—Control Doubtful** (Diag. 5-7). This is a dangerous situation and we must play it carefully. The opponents must two-time our 2 man or we could pick up an easy basket; therefore we must tip to 3 or 4 depending on where the opponents line up and the other one knifes in behind our jumper to get ball or tip it on back to 5 in case they tip forward.

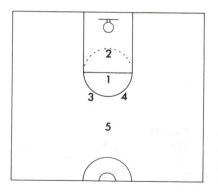

**DIAGRAM 5-7** Jump Ball #3—Offensive End—Control Doubtful.

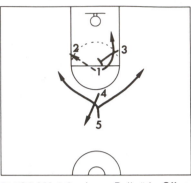

**DIAGRAM 5-8** Jump Ball #4—Offensive End—Control Ours.

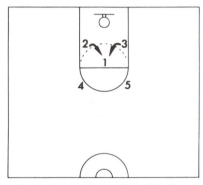

**DIAGRAM 5-9** Jump Ball #5—Defensive End—Control Doubtful.

**DIAGRAM 5-10** Jump Ball #6—Defensive End—Control Ours.

**Jump Ball #4—Offensive End—Control Ours** (Diag. 5-8). Our jumper tips to the outside of 2 or 3 depending upon how our opponents line up. 5 breaks around the outside on the side of the tip and the jumper breaks off of the other front man toward the basket. 4 backs out to protect after 5 breaks off of him.

**Jump Ball #5—Defensive End—Control Doubtful** (Diag. 5-9). 2 and 3 pinch our opponent's front man. 4 or 5 free-lances depending on which one is on the opponent's weak side. The one on the strong side knifes back to help 2 and 3.

**Jump Ball #6—Defensive End—Control Ours** (Diag. 5-10). In this we use the same principle as we use in Jump Ball 2 from the center circle.

## FROM LOOSE BALLS

It takes aggressive players to get the majority of the loose balls and I like aggressive players. "He who hesitates is lost" is an applicable slogan in regard to loose balls, because any hesitation on going after the ball is almost sure to mean that the opposition will get it. Whenever there is a reasonable chance for a loose ball, go after it with full speed and power.

You should go after a loose ball in a crouched position with the knees bent and the hips low. The ball should be scooped up with the forward hand going over it and pulling it to the other hand as you pivot low and quickly away from the opposition.

We use various drills for this with two men going after the ball from different spots. The one who comes up with it drives for the basket and the other one becomes a defensive man against him. This is a fine drill for body balance and permits you to easily recognize the "hesitators," those with poor judgment, those who may shy from contact.

## FROM INTERCEPTIONS

The ball will not be obtained too often in this manner against good ball-handling teams and it is quite dangerous to try it too often. Interceptions may be set up by playing your man safely and cautiously for quite awhile and then suddenly making the quick unexpected move when you have lulled him into a false sense of security.

This requires good footwork and excellent faking. You can use a change of pace and a change of direction in your faking on defense the same as you can on offense.

Teammates must always be ready to cover up and help out in case an attempted interception fails and ready to react to the offensive break in case it was successful. The interceptor must also get back in the play fast in case he failed, as that is no time to feel sorry for yourself or to hang your head.

## FROM OUT-OF-BOUNDS

The new rule in regard to stopping the clock on every whistle and requiring an official to handle the ball on all out-of-bounds except after a score has taken away some of the advantage of getting to the ball and inbounding it quickly. However, I continue to stress getting to the spot where the ball is to be inbounded and passing it into play as soon as the official gives it to you on all out-of-bounds in the back court and in the back half of the front court.

Since we usually set up out-of-bounds plays on every ball to be inbounded on the offensive end line and on the forward half of the front court on balls to be inbounded from the side, we have our designated inbounder taking his time in getting to the ball while the other four hustle to their assigned positions.

We have a designated player inbound the ball on all out-of-bounds on the end line and one forward usually handling the ball on the right side line out-of-bounds and the other forward handling those on the left side.

# DEFENSIVE
# BASKETBALL

## INTRODUCTORY THOUGHTS

Defensive basketball, or playing basketball to the best of your ability when your opponent has the ball in an effort to gain legal possession of the ball without permitting your opponent a good opportunity to score, is every bit as important as trying to score when you are in possession of the ball. Preventing an opponent from scoring a field goal or a free throw means exactly the same to the ultimate outcome of the game as scoring the equivalent yourself. As a matter of fact, from the psychological point of view, it might mean even more, because some players have a tendency to start "pressing" and will make additional errors with the ball when they are temporarily stopped from scoring or getting a good shot.

Since the general public and even the sportwriters and sportscasters tend to overlook defensive play to a great extent and praise the offense, the coach has a natural barrier to break down as soon as he starts teaching defense. It is quite normal for players to get more pleasure from playing offense and scoring than they do from playing defense, and they should not be criticized for it. The base hit in baseball, the touchdown in football, the knockout in boxing—the successful attacker in any sport—are all accorded such acclaim that it would be most unusual for the majority of the players not to be affected without a strong effort being made to counteract it.

Furthermore, the tendency of the rules or the interpretation of the rules to place the defense at a disadvantage and the almost incredible offensive ability of many players in modern basketball have made the playing of defense increasingly difficult. This further complicates the problem of teaching defense and compels the coach to demand complete concentration of the players without a thought of taking a breather when the opponent is in possession of the ball. Every player must remain aggressive but become defensive-minded as soon as the other team gains possession of the ball.

There must be proper balance kept between the offense and the defense and it cannot be attained without the proper mental approach toward each, which is not as easy to acquire as one might think.

I am a firm believer in defense and hope that I emphasize it as much as I do the offense. However, I also believe in the positive approach and never want our players to be too worried about having to stop our opponents for fear of the tendency of becoming overly cautious on our offense as well as on our defense. Overcaution can lead to lack of confidence and make you very vulnerable to the aggressor.

The question is often brought up as to whether as much practice time should be spent on defense as is spent on offense. Although I believe that *equal emphasis* should be placed on both, there is no question in my mind that the execution of an effective offense requires considerably more time to perfect than the development and execution of an effective defense.

The reason for my feeling in regard to this is quite simple—*the basketball.* In addition to the necessity of learning how to fake to get open, other offensive footwork, how to screen, how to take advantage of a screen, the various offense team formations, the set plays, and other offensive team individual and team fundamentals without individual possession of the ball each individual offensive player must learn to do many things when the basketball is in his possession, such as—the execution of a variety of passes and shots, control and speed dribbling, protecting of the ball during quick stops and turns, proper tipping of the ball when rebounding offensively and on jump-ball situations, and proper receiving or catching of the ball.

Therefore, it seems to me that it is quite evident that teaching the successful execution of the many important fundamentals in connection with actual handling of the ball itself, none of which are necessary when on defense, necessitates considerably more practice time being spent on total offense rather than on total defense. In order to be properly understood, however, I want to reiterate that I am speaking of *time, not emphasis. Defense requires equal emphasis, but not equal time.*

An important point that I would like to discuss briefly at this particular time is that defensive averages or the average number of points scored against a team is not necessarily a true and valid criterion for measuring defensive ability. Many coaches use a delayed or stalling type of offense that will naturally keep the score down, and, while this may be excellent strategy and fine basketball, the low score is a result of the of-

A

B

**FIGURE 6-1** The 1-2-1-1 zone press of the 1964–65 champions in action (United Press International Photos).

C

**FIGURE 6-1** *Continued.*

fense and should not be credited to the defense. However, many ball-control teams also play fine defense, but so do many aggressive offensive teams who have considerably more points scored against them.

To consider it as playing defense when your philosophy is based on the fact that your opponent cannot score while you are in possession of the ball is as much of a fallacy as it is to believe that the best defense is a good offense. Neither philosophy is sound, although either might bring effective results at times.

As I have attempted to emphasize previously, there must be good balance between offense and defense if a team is to come close to reaching its potential. Inferior opponents may be outscored without it, but an opponent of equal talent that has balance will outscore another without it and a team with inferior talent but with offensive and defensive balance will outplay one in which it is lacking.

Another point that needs emphasis in any preliminary discussion of defense is the fact that good defense will almost always be more constant and consistent than good offense. There are a number of factors that are extremely difficult and, at times, impossible to control that may have an adverse effect on shooting and passing, which will vitally influence your offense. There are also times when the offense simply seems to have an off or bad night for no particular reason.

This should not be true of defense, because, if it receives the proper emphasis and attention and the players are mentally receptive to its importance and its playing and are in good condition, there are no factors, other than injury, that should keep a team from near peak efficiency.

Therefore, a good defense may be able to "carry you" in the games or parts of games when you are having a difficult time on offense by keeping you from getting too far behind until you can get going offensively or discouraging your opponent to the degree that will keep their offense from being very effective.

The teaching of defense may very well require more psychology on the part of the coach than the teaching of offense. Any player who is mentally receptive to playing defense should be able to improve his defense far more than his offense from a comparative point of view. Most coaches hold to the opinion that an average offensive player can become a good defensive player and a good offensive player can become an excellent defensive player if he will play each with the same concentration and determination. Some players who do not have the ability to become good scorers may have the ability to become outstanding defensive players and team men.

## INDIVIDUAL DEFENSE

As the defense of a team cannot be any better than the defense of the individuals who play it, it is the obligation of the coach not only to make certain that the players are mentally receptive to the importance of playing defense, but also to make sure that they are properly grounded in the individual fundamentals of defense.

Since my introductory remarks dealt primarily with the mental aspects of defense, I shall briefly discuss some of the important individual mental requirements before discussing the physical requirements. It is difficult to say that one is more important than the other, because an effective defense requires both. However, you can say with complete assurance that a player will never execute the physical requirements of defense unless he has the mental requirements.

### MENTAL REQUIREMENTS

**Desire or Determination.** If a player does not have the desire to become a good defensive player and is not determined to accomplish that goal, he will never become one. As a general rule, since it is not as much fun to play defense as it is to play offense the player must have a great desire to offset this natural tendency. Defensive sliding and other defensive drills are hard work from which even fine results will never give you much personal acclaim, so a desire to excel is necessary to keep you bearing down.

**Alertness.** You must always be ready for any eventuality and react to it instantly. The alert player is "alive." He is never caught standing or napping. Remember that the defensive player is the second guesser—you have to stop the offensive player after he makes a move or anticipate his next move and prevent him from making one that will put you at a disadvantage.

**Poise.** The defensive player must maintain his poise if he is to be effective. Once he becomes frantic or rattled he becomes an easy mark for the poised offensive man. Do not get upset or rattled.

**Initiative and Aggressiveness.** These two qualities are combined because they are so closely allied. A player is not likely to have much initiative if he lacks aggressiveness, and, if the offense is more aggressive and takes the initiative, the defense is in for a bad time. The defense can fake the offense just as the offense can fake the defense. Although some players have more drive and are naturally more aggressive than others, those qualities can be improved by encouragement. Ridicule, sarcasm, and public criticism for the less aggressive can only build up false fight, which is neither permanent nor used with judgment.

**Pride.** The players who are really proud of their defensive accomplishments will usually work hard to maintain their pride and to receive credit from the coach. Be sure to give them all possible credit personally and publicly. Try to get teammates to praise the defense of each other when it is deserved. Keep praising improvement even though there may be a long way to go.

**Concentration.** Let nothing distract you when you are on defense. Give it your complete and undivided attention. If you must rest a little or pace yourself, do it when on offense, but never when on defense.

**Confidence.** You must dominate your opponent. If you lack confidence, you will be back on your heels and, if you are overconfident or cocky, you will not play up to your ability. Let your man know by your actions that you are bearing down because of respect, not fear. This requires courage, as a player cannot have true confidence without courage.

**Judgment.** This will come from knowing your own ability and using it in relation to the ability of your opponents. You must know when to gamble and when to bluff and this will vary according to your individual opponent, the style of offense, the score of the game, the position on the floor, and other conditions of a similar nature.

## PHYSICAL REQUIREMENTS

**Quickness.** I consider quickness to be the most important physical asset that any athlete can have. Of course, I want size, especially height, but size without quickness can be neutralized when on offense or on defense by a quick player who is considerably smaller than his opponent.

**Body Balance.** The *weight* should be fairly evenly distributed on the soles of both feet with the heels barely touching the floor and the feet just a little wider than the shoulders.

The *head* should be directly above the midpoint between the two feet with plenty of room between the chin and the chest.

The *knees* should be bent, the *back* straight, the *hips* and *buttocks* low, and *every joint* flexed and relaxed. (See. Fig. 6-2.)

**The Hands and Arms.** One hand should be pointing toward your man and the other toward the ball if your man does not have the ball.

**FIGURE 6-2** Good defensive balance.

The forward hand should be waving in front of the eyes of your man but not reaching and the other feeling behind you toward the basket when your man has the ball.

**The Eyes.** Look through your man at chest level when he has the ball and try to see your man, the ball, and all of the area between him and the ball when he does not have the ball. Never stare at any part of your man—*look through him.* If you must lose sight of your man or the ball, concentrate on the man. If you lose your man, move fast for your defensive basket and be alert for an interception until you find him.

**Voice.** A good defense is almost always a talking defense. Talk to warn your teammates of screens or potential screens, or to help on defense, or to pick up an open man, for encouragement, to disconcert an opponent, or for general psychological reasons and to help yourself and your teammates to remain alert.

**Footwork and Position.** This will be discussed more later according to the position on the floor of the man you are guarding and the ball, but some general ideas are:

**1.** As a general rule, stay between your man and the basket when he has the ball and when he is dangerous as a cutter to receive a pass; and between your man and the ball when he is deep under his basket or when the man with the ball is far away or pressed in such a way that it is difficult for him to pass to your man, or when you are two-timing, or pressing.

**2.** Try to force your man to receive any pass going away from the basket and not toward it in the potential shooting area.

**3.** Do not cross your legs, except when trying to catch up, but slide and glide, bringing the trailing foot up within six inches of the forward foot and then moving the forward foot.

**4.** Keep the head at the same height without permitting it either to bob up and down or to get forward or backward of the midpoint between the two feet.

**5.** Fake hand and some forward foot thrusts from the boxer's stance, but do not lean.

**6.** Split the leg on the strong or danger side of the man you are guarding.

**7.** Judge the distance you should be away from your man according to how far he is from the ball and from his basket.

**8.** As a general rule, the inside leg is kept forward and the outside leg is back when your man has the ball, or when you are guarding a strong-side forward or guard when the other one has the ball.

**9.** Try to maintain a position that will make it as difficult as possible for your man to receive a pass in an area where he can shoot, drive, or pass.

**10.** Try to keep a position where you will never have to give up the easy basket and still make them earn the outside basket.

**11.** Never leave your feet unless the ball or the man with the ball is in the air.

**Hustle.** This could be classified almost as mental rather than physical. Regardless of where it is placed, however, its importance cannot be exaggerated. You must never give up, but continually keep trying. It is often the second and third effort when it seems hopeless that turns the tide. There is an excuse for lack of ability, but there should never be an excuse for lack of hustle. However, remember our hustle must be under control as we want activity with achievement.

**Size and Speed.** These are placed together as one because of their relation to other factors. Size is a relative thing and I am interested in how "tall" a person plays, not how high he measures in inches. I have had 6 foot 3 inch players who played much taller and some 6 foot 6 inch players who played much smaller, but we need good playing size to match our opponents to be the most effective.

The same is true of speed in relation to quickness. If a man is quick and hustles, a lack of speed may go unnoticed and he will appear much faster than he is. On the other hand, a man with fine speed, but who does not have it under control, may not be too effective as he will be out of position too much.

## DEFENSE BEFORE YOUR MAN HAS THE BALL

In my opinion, the most difficult thing to teach in regard to individual defense is to get each defensive player mentally receptive to the fact that he can make his job much easier if he will play aggressive, alert, thinking, defense *before* his man gets the ball.

The defense is definitely the second guesser because they do not know for certain what the offense is going to do. Furthermore, the offensive men have become so adept with the ball in the game today that it is almost impossible to prevent a man from getting a good percentage shot if he can first get the ball in an advantageous position. Yet, *too many players continue to permit their man to receive the ball and then start playing defense.*

Although it is an impossible task to prevent your man from ever receiving the ball, a player can very definitely limit or diminish the number of times his man may receive the ball in the danger area by hard work and concentration.

In all probability the man whom you are guarding will have the ball less than 20 per cent of the total time that his team is on offense and, while how you defend against him during that time is tremendously important, what you do the other 80 per cent of the time is also important and can make the 20 per cent period much easier.

Some important ideas to keep in mind when your man does not have the ball are as follows:

**1.** Try to prevent your man from receiving or having possession of the ball in an area close enough to the basket where he is a threat as a shooter, a dribble driver, or with the give-and-go or pass-and-cut. Eliminate any one of these three options and you have considerably reduced his effectiveness and made your job easier.

**2.** Try to prevent your man from receiving a pass while moving toward the basket. He will not be nearly as dangerous if he receives the ball going away from the basket or toward the sideline.

**3.** Play your man high on his side with your inside hand in front of him to discourage a pass when he is on the same side of the floor as the ball. Use good judgment to prevent being caught by a reverse, but if he does get away on a reverse, turn inside toward the basket and go as fast as you can to play for an interception. You make yourself vulnerable for a quick stop and pull back, but at least he will receive the pass going away from the basket instead of toward it.

**4.** Play in front of your man when he is close to the basket and whenever the man with the ball is not in a favorable position or condition to get the ball to your man.

**5.** Work hard to maintain and increase your peripheral vision so that you may keep both your man and the ball within your sight at all times.

**6.** Keep one hand pointing toward the ball and the other hand pointing toward your man whenever one of his teammates has the ball.

**7.** Study your man constantly in order to learn his favorite moves so that you may be able to anticipate and check them. You must also learn his speed and quickness in order to know how much you may gamble in certain situations.

**8.** Impede the initial progress toward the board of your man when a shot is taken, then go for your board territory and play the rebound.

**9.** Keep moving and anticipating. Never get caught standing still or standing straight up or permitting the head to bob up and down.

**10.** Never relax or "take a breather" either mentally or physically when you are on defense regardless of who has the ball.

**11.** Be alert to avoid a screen, prevent a screen, pick up a loose man, intercept a pass, gain possession of a loose ball, block a shot, discourage a cut, or help in any way to prevent an opponent from gaining a scoring opportunity.

**12.** Earn the right to be proud of your defense and to obtain the respect of your opponents.

## INDIVIDUAL SITUATIONS TO LEARN

Each player must learn the correct stance, position, and individual fundamentals for each of the following situations:

**1.** Against the passer, cutter, dribbler, and potential shooter from various positions on the floor.

**2.** Against the strong-side forward, guard, and center—with and without the ball.

**3.** Against the weak-side forward, guard, and center.

**4.** Checking or blocking out and rebounding.

**5.** Against the side screen.

**6.** Against the blind screen.

**7.** Against men crossing—shifting and scissoring.

**8.** Protecting—one-on-one, two-on-one, three-on-one, three-on-two.

**9.** Against a high- and low-post man—with and without the ball.

**10.** Against a man in various positions on the floor when he has used his dribble and when he is still free to dribble.

**11.** The responsibilities of each position in our man-to-man press.

**12.** The responsibilities of each position in our zone press.

**13.** Jump-ball responsibilities when they are doubtful or against us.

**14.** When either team is at the free-throw line.

## IMPORTANT PRINCIPLES

**1.** Keep between your man and his basket when he has the ball or is in a dangerous cutting area or position with your back generally toward the defensive basket. Stay between him and the ball when he is near the basket or when there is an opportunity for an interception. *Defense is played primarily with the head and the feet*—use them both without trying to save steps.

**2.** Make it difficult for your man to receive or have the ball in his scoring area. The best defense must be played before your man gets the ball.

**3.** Keep the ball and your man within your sight if at all possible. Use split vision with two thirds of your attention on your man and one third on the ball.

**4.** Never cross your legs—slide and glide, unless you are sprinting to catch up from behind.

**5.** Don't charge an opponent. Advance fairly low and cautiously, ready to retreat or to slide to either side.

**6.** Get back fast when you lose possession of the ball. Sprint back, but keep your head over your shoulder.

**7.** Anticipate movements. Study your man. Do not permit him to have that ball in jump shooting range.

**8.** Keep in good balance, relaxed and ready. Do not bob up and down or lean.

**9.** Talk. Warn or encourage teammates and disconcert an opponent.

**10.** Be alert to avoid or shift on screens and warn unsuspecting or vulnerable teammates.

**11.** Open up toward the ball with one hand pointing toward your man and the other toward the ball.

**12.** Make the offensive man commit himself—the offense can be faked as well as the defense.

**13.** The farther your man is away from the ball, the farther you can be away from him.

**14.** Be aggressive and dominate your opponent.

**15.** Do not be caught standing up straight, or flat-footed, or staring.

**16.** Play the ball up underneath the arms with the near hand when guarding the dribbler.

**17.** Change quickly from offense to defense when your team loses possession of the ball.

**18.** Step in front of your man to impede his progress toward the board and then go for your area to rebound when a shot is taken. Do not slap or bat at the ball from the defensive board, but grab it firmly and look for an outlet.

**19.** Keep an arm's distance away from your man when he has the ball and wave your hand in his face if he is a potential shooter. Stay low and in balance.

**20.** Do not leave your feet unless the ball or your man is in the air.

**21.** Force a dribbler away from the basket toward the sideline, corner, or a congested area.

**22.** Back up quickly toward the basket for two or three steps when your man passes, but stay low and keep your eyes on him ready to block his cutting path.

**23.** Keep studying your man to discover his particular strengths and weaknesses and play your defense accordingly.

**24.** Know the system of your opponents and adjust to it.

**25.** Help your teammates. Defend against the short shot. Hustle.

## DEFENSIVE POSITIONS IN RELATION TO THE BALL

A circle drawn around a position in the diagrams will indicate the player in possession of the ball.

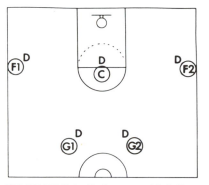

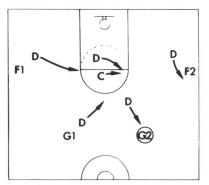

**DIAGRAM 6-1**  Defense vs. High-Post Offense #1.

**DIAGRAM 6-2**  Defense vs. High-Post Offense #2.

**Defense vs. High-Post Offense #1.**  In this diagram (Diag. 6-1) it is assumed that each offensive man has the ball and his defensive man is lined up directly between him and the basket at approximately three feet or arm's length away.

**Defense vs. High-Post Offense #2.**  G2 has the ball with his man splitting his strong side about three feet distance (Diag. 6-2). G1's man floats back toward the post with his right hand pointing toward G1 and his left hand toward the ball. F2's man splits the inside of F2 with his right hand reaching in front toward the ball and his left hand feeling toward F2. F1's man floats over toward where the foul line intersects the circle with his left hand pointing toward the ball and his right hand reaching toward F1, ready to block a pass to F1 at the side post and ready to help on a lob pass to C.

**Defense vs. High-Post Offense #3.**  F2 has the ball with his man splitting his outside leg at reaching distance and protecting the base-line drive (Diag. 6-3). C's man is between him and the basket with his left hand reaching toward the ball in front of C and the right hand feeling toward C. The men guarding G1 and G2 float back with their left hands pointing toward the ball. The man guarding F1 backs up toward the broken line of the circle where he can see both the ball and his man with his left hand pointing toward the ball and the right hand pointing toward F1.

**Defense vs. High-Post Offense #4.**  C has the ball with his man at arm's length directly between him and the basket (Diag. 6-4). The men guarding F1, F2, G1, and G2 have all backed up toward the basket with

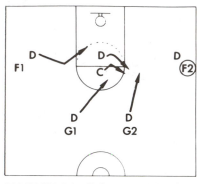

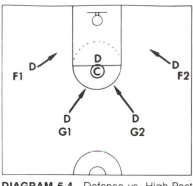

**DIAGRAM 6-3**  Defense vs. High-Post Offense #3.

**DIAGRAM 6-4**  Defense vs. High-Post Offense #4.

the men on F1 and G1 each having their left hands toward the ball and their right hands toward their respective men while the men guarding F2 and G2 each having their right hands toward the ball and their left hands toward their respective men.

**Defense vs. Low-Post Offense #1.**  In this diagram (6-5) it is assumed that each offensive man has the ball in the designated position. The defensive men on F1, G1, F2, and G2 all stay directly between their men and the basket at a distance of about three feet. The man guarding C is as close as possible to C with his right hand up high and his left hand ready to help guard against a drive or turn toward the baseline.

**Defense vs. Low-Post Offense #2, #3, and #4** (Diags. 6-6, 6-7, and 6-8).  All defensive men play their men in approximately the same way as they do in the respective situations in the high-post offense.

**Defense vs. Three-Men-Out Offense #1.**  Here again it is assumed that each offensive man has the ball (Diag. 6-9). Each defensive man plays the man he is guarding directly between him and the basket approximately an arm's length away.

**Defense vs. Three-Men-Out Offense #2.**  G2 has the ball with his man playing him the same as in #1 and with every other defensive man floating toward the basket with the appropriate hand toward the ball and the other toward his respective men (Diag. 6-10).

**Defense vs. Three-Men-Out Offense #3.**  G3 now has the ball and his man guards him as in #1 (Diag. 6-11). The defensive man on F2 splits his inside with his right hand in front of him to discourage a pass

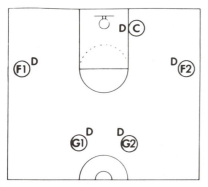

**DIAGRAM 6-5** Defense vs. Low-Post Offense #1.

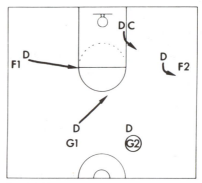

**DIAGRAM 6-6** Defense vs. Low-Post Offense #2.

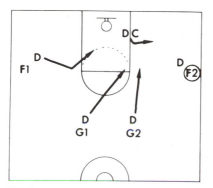

**DIAGRAM 6-7** Defense vs. Low-Post Offense #3.

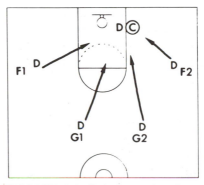

**DIAGRAM 6-8** Defense vs. Low-Post Offense #4.

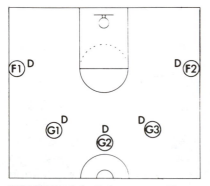

**DIAGRAM 6-9** Defense vs. Three-Men-Out Offense #1.

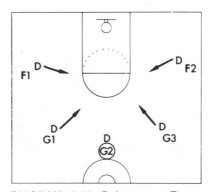

**DIAGRAM 6-10** Defense vs. Three-Men-Out Offense #2.

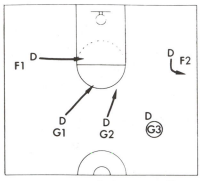

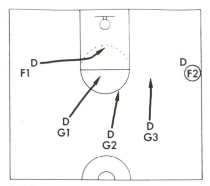

**DIAGRAM 6-11** Defense vs. Three-Men-Out Offense #3.

**DIAGRAM 6-12** Defense vs. Three-Men-Out Offense #4.

and the left foot and left hand between him and the basket. The men guarding F1, G1, and G2 all float away from their men toward the ball and the basket. Their left hands will all be pointing toward the ball and their right hands toward their respective men.

**Defense vs. Three-Men-Out Offense #4.** F2 has the ball and his man guards him as he does in #1 (Diag. 6-12). All of the other defensive men float away from their respective men toward the ball and the defensive basket. The man on F1 plays back a little deeper to prevent the cut behind him. Each man should be deep enough to see both the ball and his man at the same time.

**Defense vs. High Double-Post Offense #1.** As in #1 of the other offensive setups, it is assumed that each man has the ball with his man playing him at arm's distance away directly between him and the basket (Diag. 6-13).

**Defense vs. High Double-Post Offense #2.** C2 has the ball and his man guards him as he did in #1 (Diag. 6-14). The man on C1 floats back toward the basket facing C2 with his right hand pointing toward C1. The men on G1, G2, and G3 all float back toward the ball and the basket.

**Defense vs. High Double-Post Offense #3.** C2 has the ball with his man guarding him the same as he did in #1 (Diag. 6-15). The men on C1 and C2 play them on the inside with one hand in front to discourage a pass and the back arm and leg between their men and the basket.

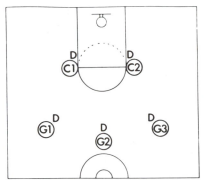

DIAGRAM 6-13 Defense vs. High Double-Post Offense #1.

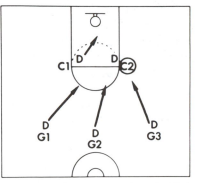

DIAGRAM 6-14 Defense vs. High Double-Post Offense #2.

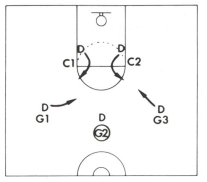

DIAGRAM 6-15 Defense vs. High Double-Post Offense #3.

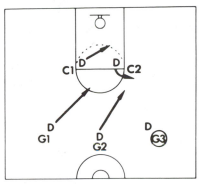

DIAGRAM 6-16 Defense vs. High Double-Post Offense #4

**Defense vs. High Double-Post Offense #4.** G3 has the ball with his man defending him as in #1 (Diag. 6-16). The men guarding G1 and G2 float back toward a line between the ball and C1. The man on C2 splits him inside with his right hand in front to discourage a pass and his left hand and left foot between him and the basket. The man on C1 floats back toward the basket with his right hand pointing toward C1.

## INDIVIDUAL DEFENSE FOR SPECIFIC SITUATIONS

This section will not attempt to cover all situations that exist or may come up in the course of a game, but will discuss briefly a number of the possibilities.

### 1. Defensing a Forward Position.

*a. Without the Ball.* If the near guard has the ball, the defensive man should be about even with the forward and facing him in such a way that he can see both the forward and the ball. He should be quite close to him with one hand waving front of him toward the ball to discourage a pass and the back foot and the other hand between the forward and the basket to guard against a quick reverse. In case his man does get away on a reverse, he turns inside and breaks quickly for the basket to play the interception.

If the away guard has the ball, he floats away near the foul circle where the foul line intersects it and tries to prevent his man from receiving a pass in the foul circle area and from getting open on a reverse.

If the away forward has the ball, he floats even farther to the foul-line area and keeps both his man and the ball in view.

If the post man has the ball, he floats toward the basket to stop any cut for an easy basket, but not so far away that he can not get back out to his man quickly if the post man passes to him.

*When you are guarding any man without the ball,* the distance that you play away from him is directly dependent upon how far he is from the ball and the basket. In every case you are to try to prevent your man from having possession of the ball in an area where he may be a triple threat as a shooter, driver, or passer and cutter.

*b. With the Ball.* If the forward has the ball, you split his outside leg to prevent a baseline drive, wave the inside hand between his eyes and the basket, and keep in balance to block any drive that he may attempt. You play him according to his ability as an outside shooter and as a driver, but keep the hand nearest the sideline down and the other hand up.

When he gets the ball, you advance cautiously in good balance to prevent a drive but able to bother the shot from the floor. Don't reach in to attempt to steal the ball from him, but stay in position on him to prevent an easy scoring opportunity.

If a forward is permitted to drive to the outside or baseline, he will have a more direct line to the basket. He also enhances the possibility that your "helper," often your center on whom you usually can least afford to get into foul trouble, of drawing a foul. By splitting the sideline leg of the forward and forcing him to drive across the floor, you will have more help and also force him to make more of an arc to get to the basket.

## 2. Defensing a Guard Position.
*a. Without the Ball.* If the other guard has the ball, you float back toward the foul-circle area and keep one hand pointing toward your man and the other toward the ball or toward the post depending on the situation. Usually you point with one hand toward your man and the

other toward the ball, but there are some cases where you point toward your man with one hand and toward the passer's target with the other.

If either forward has the ball, you back up where you can see both the ball and your man and point the proper hand at each.

If the post man has the ball, you back up and play your man with one hand pointing at your man and the other reaching behind you toward the post. Usually it will be the outside leg and arm that are back.

*b. With the Ball.*   If your man has the ball and he is within shooting range, you play him at arm's length on his strong side directly between him and the basket. Advance cautiously and stay in balance. Protect against the drive, but bother the set shot.

The particular abilities of our own personnel in the game as well as that of our opponents determine whether or not we try to drive the guard inside or outside.

## 3. Defensing the Post Position.

*a. Without the Ball.*   The principal objective is to prevent the post man from receiving the ball near enough to the basket to get an easy shot. The farther away from the basket that he receives the ball, the easier your job will be.

Although every individual is different and must be played according to his strengths and weaknesses, as a general rule, I feel that you should play slightly back of a post man on the ball side when he is 15 to 20 feet from the basket with the near hand waving to discourage a pass; you should stay close and split his strong side with your hand and foot nearest the ball remaining between him and the ball while the opposite foot and hand keep between him and the basket when he is from 10 to 15 feet from the basket; and you should play between him and the ball when he is within 10 feet of the basket. His exact position will always be determined by the position of his man in relation to the man who has the ball. It will be quite different when the ball is in a forward position from what it will be when a guard has the ball on the outside. Of course, these ideas are based on the assumption that the defensive man is relatively the same size as the post man.

However, you must have help floating from the weak side to guard against a lob pass over your head whenever you are playing high on the side or in front of your pivot man. If the offense has cleared the floor on the weak side, you must be extra careful against lob passes and stay more between your man and the basket with your help coming from men floating back on the strong side.

The defensive man must be very careful and keep the offensive post man from gradually crowding him back deep under the basket. He

**FIGURE 6-3** Good defensive position on post man with the ball.

must keep moving constantly to maintain position on the post man and discourage passes to him inside the foul-line distance. Sometimes it is better to give up the easy one occasionally than to permit him to have the ball at any time in order that you may be certain to protect the very easy one. The defensive man may fake the post man occasionally, just as the post man will be faking him.

He must keep opened up toward the ball side and be alert to pick up any cutters that might get open, protect against the short shot, and check his man off the board when a shot is taken.

*b. With the Ball.* When the post man has the ball, the defense must quickly get to a distance of one arm's length between him and the basket and slightly to his strong side. Keep one hand waving in front of his face and the other hand down on his probable driving side if he is facing the basket. (See Fig. 6-3).

The defensive man must also be alive to pick up any cutter who might get open and to block his man from the board if he takes a shot.

**4. Defensing the Dribbler.** The most important consideration in guarding the dribbler is to drive him away from a straight line toward the basket.

The defensive man must stay low and keep his position by sliding his feet without crossing his legs except when the dribbler gets by him and he has a sprint to catch up. He must also keep in good balance without leaning.

He should never slap down at the ball from over the top, but should play the ball up from underneath with the near hand. This should not only help prevent fouls but also enable the defensive man to keep in better balance and thus maintain position.

You should retreat from the dribbler toward the defensive area and try to drive him toward the sideline, corner, or a congested area. Be very careful about advancing toward him although you may fake and bluff at him to slow him down. Never try to steal or take the ball away from a good dribbler unless he makes a mistake by letting the ball get too far away from him or loses some control of it.

When a dribbler completes his dribble, advance quickly and make him pivot without permitting him an opportunity to shoot or to look the floor over for an open man. Curtail his forward vision. Try to make him turn to the outside.

Be careful of the dribbler who uses a change of pace and be alive to defend against the jump shot. Do not slap down to block the jump shot but try to deflect the ball off line or get the hand moving between the shooter's eyes and the target.

If a dribbler dribbles with only one hand, almost always goes to one particular side, seldom passes off the dribble, usually passes off the dribble, does not like pressure, or has any other particular characteristics when dribbling, then you should play him accordingly. (See Figs. 6-4 and 6-5.)

**5. Defensing the Passer and/or Cutter.**  When an offensive player passes the ball to a teammate, he immediately becomes a dangerous threat as a cutter. If the defensive man relaxes, turns to look for the ball, or straightens up for an instant, the offensive man may gain an advantage and prevent you from blocking his move for the basket.

The defensive man on the passer should immediately take two or three steps backward toward the ball if the pass were to his right or left. He must not take his eyes off the passer and must not raise up. He should open up his stance toward the direction of the ball by quickly dropping back the foot on that side for the first step. The hand on the side to which the ball was passed should reach in the direction of the ball and the other hand should be pointed toward the waist of the passer.

When your man is a potential passer, you should keep your hand down on the side where his is more dangerous as a driver and keep the other hand waving in front of him in the direction to which he is most

A

B

C

**FIGURE 6-4** Defensing the dribbler who makes a good jump stop and turn.

D

E

**FIGURE 6-4** *Continued.*

A

B

C

**FIGURE 6-5** Defensing the dribbler who makes a good one-two stop and a fadeaway comeback jump shot.

D

E

**FIGURE 6-5** *Continued.*

likely to pass. If he has already completed his dribble, then you should tighten up on him and make every effort to destroy forward vision and make it difficult for him to shoot or pass forward.

Before he has passed, you should try to block the more dangerous passing lanes and, after he has passed, you want to block the more dangerous cutting lanes. Remember, too, that the most dangerous pass in most situations is the quick push pass, as a lob or bounce pass takes a little more time to reach the receiver. However, the passer is dangerous after making any kind of pass.

*If the passer cuts away from the ball* after making a pass, he is probably going to screen, or cut back quickly with a change of pace or off a screen. Do not relax and do not follow him away. Float back toward the basket and stay opened up so that you can see both your man and the ball.

Judgment is required, as in every other situation, and a knowledge of the particular abilities of the man as well as his position on the floor is necessary to form a valid judgment as to exactly how he should be defended.

**6. Defensing a Potential Shooter.**   Whenever your man is in an area where he is a reasonably dangerous shooter, every effort must be made to impair his accuracy and still prevent him from improving his position for a higher percentage shot.

If he has already completed a dribble and is no longer a threat to dribble-drive by you, he should be played so close on his strong side that it would be almost impossible for him to take any kind of shot.

If he still has his dribble-drive available, he should be played according to his ability to hit well from his position and according to his particular habits. I do not believe in permitting even a poor outside shooter to shoot completely unmolested if he is within 25 feet of the basket, unless we are floating back to protect the passing lanes to more dangerous inside men.

If he has his dribble available and is within his normal fairly accurate shooting range, I believe in playing him at one arm's length. The foot and arm on the side to which he is most likely to drive are back and the other foot is slightly forward with the arm above that foot waving close to and between the eyes of the shooter and the basket. I also believe in yelling at him in an effort to destroy some of his concentration.

I always want an arm up against a potential shooter, but I want it waving and not stationary over which he might sight.

Players should never leave their feet unless the ball or the man in possession of the ball is in the air. The really good defensive player seldom has a chance to make a spectacular block on his man because he never gets in position where it is necessary. That type of a defensive maneuver may be used when a shift is made to pick up a loose man that has committed himself for a shot or after you have made an error and you have to take a gamble because your man is free.

You must not slap down in an attempt to block a shot whether it be a driving, jump, hook, or set shot, but play across or sometimes up under the arms and ball in an attempt to deflect the shot and/or hinder the vision of the shooter. This greatly lessens the chance of your committing a personal foul and, I believe, also leaves you in a better position afterward while giving you as good or better chance of making a successful defense.

The near hand should be used when you are attempting to block the driving shot and you must avoid contacting the driver with your body.

**7. Defensing the Screen.** The burden of responsibility in defensing the various types of screens is upon the man guarding the screener. Of course, every defensive man must be alert for the possibility of a screen being used against him whenever the man he is guarding is in a position where a screen might make him an immediate scoring threat.

The man guarding the screener must always clearly warn a teammate of a potential screen and a man in a vulnerable position to a screen should always be feeling with one hand toward the direction from which a screener is most likely to come.

*When a man moves away from the ball,* the man guarding him must immediately be alert for a quick cutback and also must warn any teammate in the direction that your man is moving to be alert for a screen. In my opinion, there is no excuse for being screened by a man moving away from the ball because that means that the man you are guarding is away from the ball and you should be floating away from him in the direction of the ball and open up so that you can see him coming and should thus be able to avoid the screen or at least have a comparatively easy switch.

*Whenever a man is advancing from the side to screen you,* you should open up toward him and move one step toward the opposite side of your man. (See Fig. 6-6.) The screener and your teammate who is guarding him will congest the strong-side area and prevent a dangerous cut there when you move over. Thus your moving over and opening up toward the potential screener will enable you to avoid the screen or make possible an easy switch by placing you in a better position to prevent the screener from getting open on a roll if you can not stay with your man. The step away also prevents your man from playing a possible switch and cutting quickly by you on the opposite side.

*When a man is advancing from the rear or from the completely blind side to screen you,* it is necessary to open up the same way as soon as your teammate warns you of the approaching screen. As *it is difficult to screen a man when his body and shoulders are perpendicular to yours,* you should try to get that position against any potential screener and drive your man toward the congested area.

Properly defensing a potential passer to a teammate who has had the

A

B

C

**FIGURE 6-6** Defensing a side screen.

benefit of a screen is also quite important. Regardless of how wide open a man might be, he can never hurt you if he does not have the ball. You should always try to prevent the straight pass and force a lob or bounce if possible. The lob and bounce passes take a little longer to complete and the lob pass is often interceptable by floaters from the opposite side.

**8. Shifting or Switching.** Because our principal defense is the matching man-to-man, *I follow the theory of switching men only when necessary* and then switching back as soon as it is safe to do so. Both men should talk on all shifts with the man who first sees the necessity of it calling it loudly and clearly. The other man answers and completes the switch whether or not he thought it necessary.

No shift should be called merely to save steps or take the easy way at the moment, but only to improve the defense when needed and prevent a potential score or scoring opportunity.

It is often necessary to switch in order to pick up a loose or open man when you are playing a fast-breaking team, and it must be called out and a teammate *notified* to pick up your man. There should really never be the necessity for a switch, unless there is a screen, once the offense has set up, but, if there is such a need, it must be made without hesitation.

**9. Scissoring.** This is usually executed when your man has the ball and an offensive man crosses behind or outside of him. In this case, you take a step back and permit your teammate to go between you and your man. Your teammate waves his near hand at your man as he goes through to discourage a shot and you close to arm's length as soon as your teammate has cleared.

**10. Defensing Specific Combinations**
*a. Guard and Guard.* Each man plays his man according to the explanation under defensing a guard with and without the ball. When one of them passes to the post, both defensive men back up and in. If the guards cross, we usually shift on this, but not until we can touch hands and do not permit either offensive man to cut between us. If one of them fakes a cross and then cuts back, we should be ready for it without having started to shift. (See Fig. 6-7.) We should anticipate the possibility of a shift being necessary on this, but do not make it or call it until it is.

If one guard passes to a forward and cuts away, the man guarding him must warn his teammate on the other guard of a screen and be alive to switch. He must also be alive for the potential screen of the

**FIGURE 6-7** Defensing offensive guards who have hit the post and cross or fake the cross. Do not permit either one to cut between you and stay one good step in front of the post man.

forward dribbling across toward the key to hand off to the guard coming by to the outside. (See Fig. 6-8.)

*b. Guard and Forward* Proper floating on the weak side should eliminate any problem or necessity of making a switch, but the strong side may require adjustments. If a guard passes to a forward and cuts outside the forward, the two defensive men may use the scissoring movement as described earlier or the guard may go behind his teammate guarding the forward. It is better to scissor, if they have the tendency to hand off to the guard.

If a guard passes to the forward and moves for an inside screen on your teammate who is guarding the forward, you should warn your teammate. He should open up as explained earlier, and you should both be alive to switch if necessary. The cutaway by the screener must be anticipated and protected against.

If the forward comes up behind the guard to screen and roll, his man must warn his teammate who should open up as explained previously under screening. Your weak-side men must also be alive to help in this situation.

A

B                                                    C

**FIGURE 6-8**  Defensing the guard who has passed to the forward.

A "split-the-post" or crossing-off-the-post situation may come up at any time a guard or a forward passes to the post. In this situation it is usually the man who makes the pass to the post that forms the initial screen and the danger can be eliminated by blocking his cut. A situation of this type quite often requires a switch.

**11. Defensing the Board or Defensive Rebounding.** Defensive rebounding demands many of the same fundamental principles that were stressed under offensive fundamentals, such as—assuming that every shot will be missed, timing, bringing the hands to shoulder height with the fingers pointed upward and the elbows extended whenever a shot is taken, getting position, getting the ball at the top of your jump, and keeping in good body balance. (See Fig. 6-9.)

Some of my ideas in regard to defensive rebounding vary somewhat from many coaches, but I feel that my teams have had excellent success with them and I see no reason to change my theory.

The difference is that we do not attempt to block our opponent from the board, but merely attempt to check their initial move and then go for the rebound ourselves. I feel that this is the positive approach and that it is, in a sense, negative thinking to place primary emphasis on blocking out the opponent.

The man guarding the outside shooter gets one step away and lets him make the first move. If he starts outside, we make a reverse turn on our outside foot to make him go farther around and then go for the rebound. If he starts inside, we make a front cross-over on our inside foot and then go for the rebound.

When guarding the nonshooter, we move toward him first, if he is close enough to move in and become a potential rebounder, to close our floating gap, and then move in front of him as before and then play the rebound.

It is my belief that this method not only enables us to get more rebounds, but also lessens our danger of fouling. I believe that too much emphasis on blocking out causes the inside men often to get to leaning away and permits the outside men to slide by and improve their position and, as this happens, the defensive men become more likely to foul. It also stresses positive rather than negative thinking and action.

There are far more opportunities to gain possession of the ball from off the defensive board than in any other way and we must be prepared to make the most of them.

We spend considerable practice time on rebounding drills and hope to get the ball out fast to get our fast break functioning. The faster that we get the ball out, the better our fast break will be, and the more

A

B

C

D

**FIGURE 6-9** Defensive rebounder.

rebounds we will get, because this will force our opponents to weaken themselves on the offensive board in order to better defense the fast break. It is sometimes quite amazing how getting the ball out fast from off the board for a couple of good fast breaks can improve your defensive rebounding.

We want our boys to play the ball high, get a wide leg kick, look over their shoulder as they bring the ball in to their chin with their elbows out, and pass the ball out quickly. If there is no outlet pass available, they should drive it out.

*Assuming the shot will be missed, bringing the hands to shoulder height, and crossing in front of the offensive man and then beating him to the ball* are three of the very important essentials.

**12. Defending When Outnumbered.** The main hope of the defense when the offense has them outnumbered in the scoring area is to prevent the easy shot and possibly any good percentage shot until defensive help comes to provide an equal number on defense.

If given enough time, the offense should always be able to get a high percentage shot when they have the defense outnumbered. However, the defense may be able to stall the offense until help gets there by semizoning near the basket to prevent the setup shot and by faking and bluffing at the offense in the hope that they might commit themselves too soon. If you can cause the offense to "hurry," you have destroyed some of their effectiveness.

Since the two-on-one and three-on-two situations are the most difficult to handle as the offense has more working room, they will be the only situations that I shall discuss. As every player should be hustling for defense when the opponent obtains possession of the ball, the numerical advantage of the offense should not exist for over two or three seconds. If it does last longer, then someone is loafing and should soon be seated on the bench.

*a. Two-on-One.* The defensive man should open up so that he can see both men and should try to stop the man with the ball before he reaches the foul line. This may be done by faking, bluffing, and yelling at him, but being very careful not to commit yourself and giving him an opportunity to pass to the other man for an easy basket underneath. Since the man *without* the ball is the most dangerous, the lone defender must be sure that he has him covered. Of course, if the man with the ball gets a little careless and dribbles the ball too high or permits it to get too far away from him, the defensive man might get a steal if he is quick and sees the opportunity.

He must keep the arm and leg back on the side where the extra offensive man is located. Any time he gets the man with the ball to pull up, he should back up quickly and protect against the cutter.

If the defensive man can force the offense to take a quick shot from any distance farther away than the foul line, he has done well and should be commended regardless of whether or not the shot is made.

Remember that the prevention of the easy basket is his principal objective.

*b. Three-on-Two.* When caught in a three-on-two situation, I like a tandem defense with the front man just in front of the foul line and the back man just in front of the basket. If possible, I would prefer the front man to be the quicker and more agile of the two and the back man to be the taller.

The front man tries to stop the man with the ball at the top of the foul circle and overplays him slightly to his strong side. He bluffs and yells at him, but keeps in good balance. When he passes to one side, the front man opens up toward the direction of the pass, but slides quickly toward the cutter on the opposite side and at the same time is alert for a return pass to the middle man. In other words, once he has forced the pass, he immediately becomes responsible for the two men without the ball.

The back man remains about three feet in front of the defensive basket and must not commit himself by leaning or going for a fake. His sole responsibility will be to take the cutter to whom the middle man passes and prevent him from getting an easy shot.

The defense must prevent the really easy or setup shot. If they can force an extra pass or two, they should have help and no longer be outnumbered.

# TEAM DEFENSE

## GENERAL THOUGHTS

Good team defense is like good team offense in that they both require a knowledge of and the ability to properly execute the individual fundamentals. It also comes from the integration into a smooth working unit of individuals who are well grounded in the individual defensive fundamentals. The team defense can be no stronger than the defensive fundamentals of the individual playing it. They must work together as a unit and do a lot of talking regardless of the type of defense played.

Although each type of defense may have many variations, there are three principal types and every team that I have seen in my experience in the game has used some form of one of the three or a combination of any two or all of them.

These three defenses are known as the man-to-man defense, the zone defense, and the pressing defense.

Briefly, the basic principle of each defense is as follows: In the *man-to-man* each player is assigned to an individual opponent and his principal responsibility is to stop him from scoring; in the *zone* each player is assigned a particular area to cover and his principal responsibility is to prevent any opponent from scoring from his area. As a general rule both the man-to-man and the zone defenses require the players to get back fast and play their defense in what their particular coach considers to be the scoring area. The *pressing* defense may be either man-to-man or zone, but the basic idea back of it is to keep contant pressure on the opponents. This pressure might be applied the full length of the court, from three quarters, or at the half court.

Since I have never used a zone defense, I will emphasize the defenses that I do use and then briefly mention other defenses and point out a few of the generally recognized advantages and disadvantages of them.

## UCLA SET DEFENSE

The defense that I use the vast majority of the time is a floating or sagging man-to-man with a zone principle. I like pressure on the man with the ball when he is in the offensive area, except in special cases when we do not consider him to be much of a threat and we stay away from him and protect the passing lanes to more dangerous men, with all others floating away from their men or playing high to block a pass depending on how close their man is to the ball. Strong-side men or men guarding men nearest to the ball and nearer to the basket should be playing tighter to make it difficult for their men to receive the ball in an advantageous position, while men guarding opponents away from the ball should be floating toward the basket and toward the ball and staying ready to help.

The first consideration of each player is to stop his man from scoring, but he must stay alert to help cover any man he can who might become more dangerous than his own man. Actually, each boy must feel a deep responsibility to do everything possible to keep the other team from scoring, and the man to whom he is assigned, while he is his first responsibility, is merely one part of the opposing team. Regardless of who makes the basket, if you could have prevented it, it is your fault.

Shifts are made only when necessary and the shift back to the original man should be made as soon as it is safe to make it. Never shift merely to save steps, but to save scores or possible scores. Talking and pointing are necessary if the shifts are to be made quickly and into the path of the most dangerous threat.

Usually, we believe in picking up the man with the ball at the center line with an occasional one- or two-man surprise press at any place. I do not like to permit the opponents to be able to take their time in setting up their plays or offense. Furthermore, it keeps the game moving a little faster, which I prefer, and helps prevent opposing teams from slowing down the tempo in order to discourage our fast-break attack. This forces our deeper defensive men to play a little higher and tighter to block outlets and yet keep their men from getting open by reversing quickly. They must also be alert when some other man gets loose. This calls for aggressive play, but I feel that it is in keeping with our offensive play and will give us better continuity of offense and defense.

It also places a premium on good condition, and I want our players to be in better condition than any team that we play. Keeping defensive pressure on the opponents as well as offensive pressure may wear down the opposition, if we are in better condition, by the last few minutes of a game and cause them to lose some of their effectiveness at the time when games between two evenly matched opponents are usually won or lost. Other things being equal, the team in the best condition for the "stretch drive" will usually win.

I constantly stress that defense begins as soon as we lose possession of the ball. Our offense is designed to give us defensive balance as we should always have a protector or a man moving to that position with a second man, our key area rebounder, in good position to help. The other players should sprint back toward the area that the man to whom they are assigned usually plays just as soon as we lose possession of the ball. They must be looking back over their shoulders as they sprint for defense. The quick adjustment from offense to defense is the important first move in defensive play.

As has been stressed earlier, strong emphasis is placed on making our players ever alert to the important fact that defense occurs before your man gets the ball. It may be much easier to prevent many players from receiving the ball in a dangerous scoring area than it is to prevent them from scoring after they have the ball in that area.

When the opposing team takes a shot, defense is not forgotten but remains quite important. Take a step across in the path that your man wants to take to go to the board for the rebound, and then, having forced him to run around you, go for your rebounding area. Every man must do his job on this so that you are covering territories as a unit.

Previous diagrams show the position that each man should take in relation to the position of the ball.

## UCLA ZONE PRESS

The 1964 UCLA team, which went through the season without a loss in thirty games and finished the season by winning the NCAA championship despite the fact that in this day of very tall men they had no starter over six feet, five inches, used a two-two-one zone press defense with remarkable effectiveness.

This particular defense was used for several reasons. First, I thought the individual talents of the starting personnel fitted it very well; second, some method was needed in this West Coast area of ball-control teams to prevent our fast-break–minded players from being lulled into a slow tempo; third, I thought our quickness would enable us to play this type of defense quite well; and, fourth, I felt that this type of game would help to neutralize the advantage in height that all of our opponents would have.

Furthermore, I must point out that this type of defense was not designed to take the ball away from the opposition nearly as much as to force them into mental and physical errors on which we hoped to capitalize. We also felt that if we kept constant pressure on them they would be forced to "hurry" their offense, which would be in direct contrast to the style of game that they normally played and, perhaps, this would keep them from executing it as well as when they were able to control the tempo.

We used this zone press only after we scored, but the score could be from either the field or the foul line. Since it takes a couple of seconds for the team inbounding the ball to get it and get out-of-bounds into position to inbound it, we usually had time to move to the positions we wanted. As the players become more accustomed to working together, they would make an occasional shift of position without much difficulty. However, I never encouraged this, except in real emergencies, as I felt each individual was physically best suited to play the position to which he was assigned, and an exchange might weaken both positions. (See Fig. 6-10.)

**Zone Press #1.** The diagram (Diag. 6-17) shows the position to which each man was assigned and how he moved when the ball was inbounded where we wanted it to be.

"A"—Goodrich, a left-handed player with exceedingly quick hands and feet, was assigned to this position. His responsibility was to invite

**FIGURE 6-10** Doug McIntosh (#32) and Mike Lynn (#35) setting the front line of pressing defense.

them to pass the ball in to a man in the area indicated by the dotted line. He then advanced on the receiver but was to keep him from driving by on the sideline. If he started to dribble, Goodrich tried to make him stop and turn away where he would be double-teamed by "B" coming over to help. If the receiver did not dribble, Goodrich would advance on him and try to force him to throw a lob or bounce-pass out rather than a crisp straight pass, and he was not to permit him too much time to locate receivers. If the man were able to dribble by him, Goodrich was to turn and chase him and knock the ball on toward a teammate if possible, or double-team him if a teammate slowed him down or forced him to stop and turn. Whenever the ball got past him down toward our defensive basket, Goodrich was to hustle back while sizing up the proper place to go.

"B"—Slaughter, a 6-foot 5-inch broad (235-pound) but agile center who runs the 100 in ten seconds, was assigned to this position. He was to discourage the pass to his side and then move over quickly to prevent a return pass to the inbounder in the middle of the floor from the man that Goodrich covered. This was a most important assignment for him. He also was to be alert to two-time with Goodrich in case the man who received the inbound pass started to dribble.

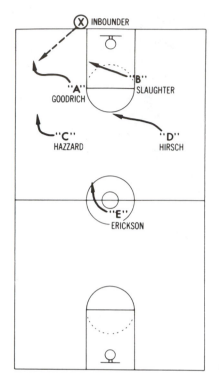

DIAGRAM 6-17 UCLA Zone Press #1.

Slaughter's quickness and speed enabled him to play this spot quite well and his size, both his broadness and his height, made him a rather difficult target to pass over or around.

Whenever the ball was moved past his line of defense and down the floor, he was to turn and sprint for the defensive basket, but analyzing the situation while moving.

"C"—Hazzard, a long-armed, quick-handed, aggressive "ball wanter," was assigned to this position. He was responsible for the area behind Goodrich from the center line to the foul line. He was to stop a driver that might get by Goodrich on that side of the floor and to prevent a receiver from receiving a pass from either the man inbounding the ball or from the man that did receive a short pass from him. He was to intercept any lob pass thrown to a receiver in the area for which he was responsible and to cover any receiver of a crisp, straight pass in that area.

"D"—Hirsch, a left-handed, 6-foot 3-inch tough competitor with unusually quick hands, was assigned to this important position. He was responsible for covering the middle of the floor to his left as he faced the inbounder and for the area on his side from the center line to the foul line or deeper in case Slaughter was pulled over. The middle of the floor area between the center circle and the foul circle became an important responsibility for him as soon as the ball was inbounded into the "A" or Goodrich area. The fact that he was left-handed made him more effective in this area from where the pass was likely to come, just as the fact of Goodrich's being left-handed enabled him to fulfill more effectively the assignment in his area. Like "A," "B," and "C," he was to sprint for the defensive end whenever the ball got past his line of defense down the floor and was to size up the situation on his way and take the logical spot.

"E"—Erickson, a very fast and quick, great jumping, 6-foot 5-inch forward with a lot of fire. He was to get to the center circle as fast as possible and then direct the defense from there. I considered him our "director" once he got into position and expected the "C" and "D" men to follow his directions. He was responsible for any man who went on down the floor and was expected to intercept any pass that was thrown to any spot in the offensive end if it were thrown from any position as far back as the foul line extended. He was a great defender when outnumbered and always got the ball out quickly to start a fast break. This ability often turned what appeared to be a basket for our opponents into a basket for us. This, in turn, sometimes would cause our opponents to become so rattled that we might pick up a few more quick baskets before they could regain their poise and composure.

**Some Important Details.**  The underneath side of the backboard and the net hanging down helped to discourage our opponents from getting the ball in on the "B" side of the floor if they took it out on the "A" side, and our surveys proved that the ball would be inbounded from the "A" side about 90 per cent of the time. However, if they did inbound the ball from the "B" side, the assignments of "A" and "B" were exchanged as were the assignments of "C" and "D".

If they were able to pass the ball in directly from the "A" side to the "B" side, "D" might move up quickly to assume the front responsibility and "B" would move quickly to assume the "D" responsibilities. "A" and "C" would carry out their regular assignments when the ball was inbounded on the side away from them.

An interceptor of any pass in the area of the center of the floor or farther back was to look for Hazzard immediately, and he was to manage to get open. He would drive for the middle of the floor as the side cutting lanes would be filled on the change from defense to offense. Our ability to change quickly from offense to defense often enabled us to capitalize on the errors of our opponents as we might catch them going the wrong way or with their "heads down."

Goodrich set a successful trap and then sprung it on many occasions by lulling the inbounder into a false sense of security by not molesting the pass in for several times as he would size up the situation. Then he would suddenly move up quickly to make an interception and score an easy basket or heave a pass to a teammate for an easy basket.

The players were taught to "tune in" on Erickson, the director of our press, at all times and to follow his commands without hesitation. It is my firm conviction that it is possible to "tune in" and hear one person, regardless of other noises, if you concentrate on his voice. To be truly effective, this defense must have an "Erickson."

The players were taught not to grab, but to pressure just enough to prevent a straight pass and encourage a lob or bounce pass and still try to prevent the dribble by them. If they dribble, try to direct them into a quick double-team situation.

The importance of breaking back quickly whenever the ball moved by you toward your defensive basket and sizing up the situation as you moved was constantly stressed.

Considerable drill time was used in chasing a man from behind and knocking the ball on toward a teammate who was back. We stressed the no-contact-on-him and the fact that you were not trying to get the ball yourself, but, in a sense, deflecting it on to one of your teammates.

It is necessary to give the players considerable work on the man-to-man press before giving them the zone press. This helps their fundamentals a great deal and will enable them to be that much more effective in the zone press.

If a team is hurting our press too much by quick, clever passing, we may go out of the zone press and try a man-to-man press for a while, or change it to a one-three-one, two-one-two, or one-two-one-one zone operated with the same principles.

## Additional Facts To Keep in Mind

**1.** It is a gambling type of defense and requires continued effort and limitless patience if it is to pay dividends.

**2.** The principal value will probably come from demoralizing the opposition and upsetting their game.

**3.** It can speed up the game and, perhaps, force an opponent out of their normal style of play.

**4.** It can cause disharmony and disunity in the opposition.

**5.** Do not reach in to attempt to take the ball away from an opponent, but play position and force errors when the opponents "hurry." This cuts down fouling and helps to establish the proper philosophy.

**6.** Try to permit only lob or bounce passes forward. Passes back toward your offensive basket will not hurt you, but crisp passes the least bit forward cause trouble.

**7.** As soon as the ball passes your individual line of defense, turn and sprint toward your defensive basket and pick up the most dangerous open man. Strong side men should be alive to "two-time" as they go back, and the weak side men should be alert to intercept.

**8.** All players must be well grounded in the individual defensive fundamentals. I use only a man-to-man pressing defense for our freshman, but use zone principles.

**9.** If no opponent is in your zone, close in toward the zone that is being attacked.

**10.** Use tight man-to-man principles if the man in your zone has the ball, and floating man-to-man principles depending upon how far from the ball your man is in the other areas.

**11.** Results often come in spurts, so apply immediate pressure after acquiring the ball through an error. Often they will try to make up the loss "by hurrying" and will make more errors. Our 1964 team had at least one "spurt" in a period of approximately two minutes in all thirty games in which we outscored our opponents from ten to twenty points. Sometimes it did not come until the middle of the second half, but we would usually have at least one spurt before the end of the first half.

**12.** The players must realize the necessity and value of and be willing to make the necessary sacrifices to attain and maintain top condition.

**13.** The players must also be unselfish in regard to scoring as often the scorer when you capitalize will not be the one who caused the error.

**14.** An outstanding player for the important #5 position is essential. He must be quick, alert, courageous, unselfish, able to "read" the man with the ball, very good at handling the deep defense when outnumbered, a fine rebounder who can get the ball out quickly, very aggressive, with judgment that prevents committing himself too soon, and a player who really loves a challenge.

**Zone Press #2.** Diagram 6-18 shows the initial assignment when the ball is inbounded to our right as we face the inbounder.

**Zone Press #3.** Diagram 6-19 shows the possible moves when the ball is inbounded where we want it to be, but is returned to the inbounder who then passes it to the other side. This requires a very quick adjustment. If the opponents are inclined to bring the third man down,

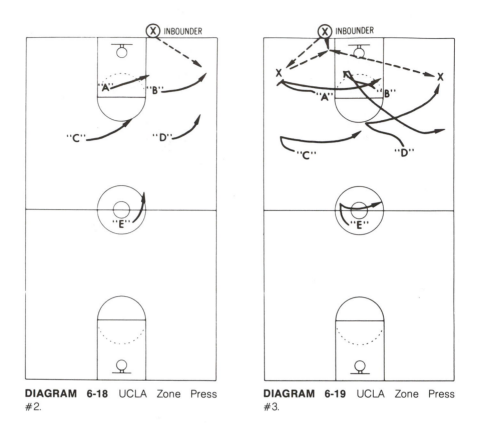

**DIAGRAM 6-18** UCLA Zone Press #2.

**DIAGRAM 6-19** UCLA Zone Press #3.

we often bring our "D" man down to about as far as the free-throw line extends. This throws us out of our 2-2-1, but covers that particular situation much better.

## OTHER UCLA DEFENSES

Since our two basic team defenses have now been fairly well covered and since no defense will work very effectively unless the players are well grounded in the individual defensive fundamentals, and they, too, have been fairly covered, I shall discuss some other defenses in a more cursory manner.

**Defensing the Fast Break.** There are several different methods of defensing the fast break, but I feel that two of these are most common. However, only one of them deals with your actual defense as the other concerns your offense.

The one dealing with your offense is to play a ball-control style of game and handle the ball for several passes before ever attempting a shot. Naturally, we do not use this one.

The principal purpose of this method is an attempt to control the tempo of the game. If you can get a fast-breaking type of team impatient because of your delayed offensive tactics, it may cause them to lose their initial drive or may cause them to try to "hurry" their break, which may result in more ball-handling errors, missed shots, and fewer scoring opportunities. In an effort to offset your delaying tactics, they may change their regular style of offense and (or) defense, which means that you have placed them on the defensive and have them really worrying about you.

Furthermore, the ball-control offense, properly played, will give your opponents fewer defensive rebound opportunities and it is from the defensive board that most fast scoring opportunities originate. They will have fewer rebounds because of three reasons: First, you will be attempting fewer shots, which means there will not be as many opportunities to rebound; second, you should be getting better shots, which means you will be hitting a higher percentage of your shots; and third, you should always be in good position to contest the rebound. Also, this method should enable you to have constant protection back against the break.

The other method deals with trying to tie up the rebounder and make it difficult for him to get a good pass out quickly and (or) by trying to choke off the passing lanes to his favorite or potential receivers. The fast break is usually prevented if the rebounder is not able to pass out quickly. This is the method that we usually attempt against dangerous fast-breaking opponents. It might be described rather accurately as a press with man-to-man principles up front with zone protectors.

If the first pass is made out successfully, you may cause trouble by choking off the logical pass into the breaking lanes. Since the receiver will probably have to receive the ball with his back or side toward his offensive basket, if he is meeting the ball, by hard work and practice you may learn to cause him enough trouble that you may discourage the break.

Occasionally, you will find teams that depend on one principal rebounder or teams that really patternize their outlets to such a degree that you can double-team their key men and cause them difficulty.

I am one who believes in trying to neutralize the strength of an opponent or capitalize on a weakness in a manner that will require little adjustment or deviation from our normal style of play. I believe that spending too much time on trying to stop an opponent may result in failure to develop your own potential and ideas and also may create a defeatist or negative attitude in your own team and I favor the positive or optimistic approach. I prefer to have the other team worrying about us and do not like to take the chance of causing my team to become too worried about them. Confidence without cockiness and respect without fear are our aim with our players.

**Defensing the Weave.** Although a zone defense is most effective against a weaving offense, I have so rarely used a zone defense that I dislike setting it up for the very few weaving offenses that we might face. Therefore, we usually try to pick up a weaving team at the center line thus forcing them to start their weave farther away from their basket. We will hand off, keep the center closed, and try to force them around the outsides. We will stress talking even more than usual. We have our players touch each other as they hand off in order to leave no gaps for the offense to cut or drive through the middle. We stress not getting lazy and waiting for them to come to us or they may knife through the gap we leave. We also caution our players about not getting backed up too far, our outside men constantly to be alive for reverses, our weak-side men to close in toward the ball, and to jump into the path of the weavers when they get careless and we can legally make the move.

**Defensing a Strong Set Blocking or Screening Team.** We use our regular defense, but practice diligently on shifting, scissoring, and rolling. We may also pressure them a bit to keep them from having too much time to set up their offense. Also, since this type of offensive team usually does not like to run, we may press them all the way and try to control the tempo. We must emphasize and review the method of opening up toward the player who is about to screen you and reiterate the importance of warning a teammate of a potential screen.

**Defensing a Strong Pivot Offense.** We use our regular defense once they get set, but float a little more than usual. Against all but the well-known and very good outside shooters, we will float back and block up the passing lanes. From a psychological point of view, this occasionally accomplishes two things and works well. First, the post man who is accustomed to having the ball a lot gets impatient and sometimes goes on his own. Second, the man with the ball is given so much time to shoot that he gets to feeling he should hit, he must hit, and thus may press a little and not hit.

We will also pressure out farther and press down court to limit the opportunities they have to pass to the post. Our floaters on the weak side must really go after all lob passes toward the basket in case we are playing in front of him. We should not play in front of him if they clear the weak side, for then there is no help against the lob. However, we then can float more to block up the passing lane to him as we will have more men on the strong side.

**Defensing Out-of-Bound Plays.** One man should play between the man inbounding the ball and the basket. The other men float back and keep their hands waving over their heads. Be alert for screens and rolls and be sure you protect underneath for the easy one, even if you have to give up an outside shot.

Most teams will have one outside shooter for whom they prefer to set up the shot in case you are protecting well underneath, but you should also know who he is and be alert for a play for him. This sometimes enables you to set up an interception by decoying him. You can fake on defense as well as an offense.

**Team Defensive Rebounding.** The individual fundamentals, physical and mental, of both offensive and defensive rebounding have been discussed previously in the appropriate places and need no further discussion here. However, a few statements regarding team rebounding might prove valuable.

Although the positions of the offensive men when a shot is taken may determine to a great extent the floor position of the defensive rebounders, we like to have team balance on the defensive board just as we do on the offensive board. This ideally would mean that we should have triangular rebounding underneath with each of our other two men responsible for an area around one side of the foul circle and including the half of the circle on his side.

We feel that this gives us better coverage, makes for a better five-man rebounding *team,* puts us in much better position to fast break if we get the ball, gives us more team unity, and poses a psychological as well as a physical problem for the offense. If we can get them worrying about our fast break, we can cut down on their offensive board work and, perhaps, affect their shooting concentration.

Through all of my coaching experience, my teams have seldom been out-rebounded in spite of the fact that we are usually outsized. Furthermore, we seldom have a rebounder who leads our conference or country, but our team will usually be near, or at the top of our conference. Many centers will get more rebounds than our center, many forwards will get more than any of our forwards, and many guards will get more than any of our guards; however, our centers will usually have a creditable number of rebounds, and our forwards' total rebounds usually will exceed the total of the forwards of any of our opponents, with our guards usually showing a similar margin of rebounding superiority over the guards of our opponents.

It is easier to get rebounding balance and be in better position to start a fast break by using a zone defense, but I have never used a zone defense for a full game in over a quarter of a century of high school and college coaching and have only used it for about one half of a game on three different occasions in about eight hundred games.

Therefore, our floating man-to-man defense requires quick adjustment and a great amount of hard work for us to learn to work together as a unit in order to get the team balance that we want on the boards. Our men must learn to cover the five rebounding territories as a unit, which means that, at times, a guard may have to cover one of the triangular spots underneath, a forward may have to cover any of the spots, and, in fact, any player may have to cover any spot. However, the important point that they must all remember is that, as soon as our opponents take a shot, all five of our boys must assume that the shot is missed, momentarily move into the path of an outside opponent, and then—*go get the ball!*

## ADVANTAGES AND DISADVANTAGES OF THE THREE PRINCIPAL DEFENSES

### MAN-TO-MAN

### Advantages

**1.** It enables you to assign each of your men to an opponent whom he may be the most physically and mentally equipped to guard.

**2.** It enables you fairly well to define defensive responsibility to the individual.

**3.** It enables each man to have a better opportunity of studying the strengths and weaknesses of his opponent and thus be better able to combat them.

**4.** It enables you to prepare your players better mentally in regard to their individual opponent. Some players need this very much and can be "built up" to do the job.

**5.** It is a defense that can be played the entire game regardless of the score.

**6.** It is a defense that illustrates to the boys the need for all of the defensive fundamentals.

**7.** It is a defense that permits those assigned to weaker scoring threats to help out readily on the opposing stars.

**8.** It is a defense that permits quick correction and adjustments during time-outs and the half-time periods.

**9.** From my point of view it is a defense that, next to the press, puts a premium on good condition and is in keeping with our hard-driving pressure-type offense.

**10.** It is a defense that helps us to get the press to give more public credit to defensive play.

## Disadvantages

**1.** It requires better condition for most players.

**2.** There is a probability of making more personal fouls.

**3.** Opponents may be able to "work on" a star player a little more and get him to foul out.

**4.** It is more vulnerable to a strong screening or blocking offense.

**5.** It is more difficult to have balanced team rebounding than in the zone.

**6.** It is more difficult to run a fast-break pattern from it than from the zone.

**7.** It is difficult to get some players to play team defense as they get so intent on their own men that they lose sight of the team.

**8.** It requires considerable work on switching and scissoring.

**9.** It is a little more difficult to hide a weak defense player.

**10.** It requires the ability to defend against a man from any spot in the offensive area.

## ZONE

### Advantages

**1.** It lowers the number of personal fouls, which not only cuts down on the number of free-throw attempts of your opponents but also lessens the chances of key personnel fouling out.

**2.** It enables individuals to concentrate on the fewer number of fundamentals necessary for guarding a limited area. For example, some players are much more effective defensing one particular side of the floor.

**3.** It is a strong defense against a screening, blocking, or weaving team.

**4.** It has the players in excellent rebounding position according to their abilities and in position for a patternized fast break.

**5.** It leads to the development of interceptors.

**6.** It enables strong two-timing of individuals or stars.

**7.** It can move deep against a weak outside-shooting team or extend against a good one.

**8.** It can conserve the energy of some.

**9.** It can lead to the development of good team unity.

**10.** Tall, slow men, who could not press, and would be poor in the man-to-man, may be able to play it fairly well.

**11.** Many offensive players let a zone upset them and they start to hurry or force their play and it becomes a psychological weapon.

**12.** It may be more effective against strong rebounders and teams that insist on working in close.

## Disadvantages

**1.** It is weak against outside and angle shooters.

**2.** The fast break may be down on it before they get back and set in their zones.

**3.** It is more difficult to define the individual responsibility.

**4.** Overloading zones can cause trouble.

**5.** Not as good for two-timing stars.

**6.** It may lead to a breakdown of some of the individual fundamentals.

**7.** You can be forced out of it when behind and may not execute the man-to-man fundamentals well enough to have a chance.

**8.** When spread by the offense, it loses some of its strength and may force some man-to-man play.

**9.** It is impossible to cover all the areas adequately on a regulation-sized floor against a good team.

**10.** It hasn't been the principal defense of very many championship teams.

## THE PRESS

### Advantages

**1.** It may keep a ball-control team from controlling the tempo of the game.

**2.** It puts a premium on good condition.

**3.** It can be very effective against slow teams.

**4.** It can be very effective against guards who are not good ballhandlers.

**5.** It may rattle inexperienced teams and cause them to make many errors.

**6.** It is necessary to have an organized press for late in games when you are trailing.

**7.** It forces opponents to spend considerable time to prepare for it.

**8.** It is the greatest demoralizing weapon against most, even good, teams and often gets the individual opposing players to blame each other, causing lack of unity.

**9.** It forces teams who like to rely on set patterns to set them up farther out on the floor or not be able to use them at all.

**10.** It keeps the team aggressive and helps give them the positive approach.

### Disadvantages

**1.** It is a gambling defense.

**2.** It requires great condition, quickness, and aggressiveness.

**3.** It may cause more personal fouls, if not played properly.

**4.** It causes an officiating problem and usually is not as effective on a hostile, foreign court.

**5.** It spreads out the court area to cover and leaves more vulnerable areas.

**6.** It requires every man on the floor to do his job as one weak link may give up an easy basket.

**7.** It is very difficult to set down all the basic rules for the press; therefore it takes extra time to learn it properly and it may be difficult to keep the players from becoming discouraged until they do.

**8.** Some coaches claim that it is too tiring for successful tournament play unless you have a very strong bench.

**9.** It probably requires much harder work in practice to learn it properly, as the drills are tough and the daily preliminary individual fundamentals cannot be slighted.

## STYLES OF THE THREE BASIC DEFENSES

### TIGHT MAN-TO-MAN

This defense really puts the pressure and responsibility on the individual. When it is played properly, each player plays so tight to his man when he has the ball that he is very difficult to screen or block. All players harass their men in the scoring territory and try to keep them from receiving the ball in the dangerous area. They are to switch only when it is absolutely necessary and are taught to feel that they must have done something wrong to cause a switch to become necessary.

This is a "hard-nosed" defense in which there will usually be considerable leg and body checking and quite a few personal fouls. It can be very effective when played properly and often upsets many offensive players.

It naturally requires strict adherence to good footwork, anticipation, alertness, and the other necessary individual defensive fundamentals.

The teams that use this type of defense usually have a great amount of defensive pride, and those that I have known to be the most successful with it have also been teams that use a ball-control type of offense and do not break very much.

## SWITCHING MAN-TO-MAN

This defense requires the use of all the good man-to-man principles and fundamentals.

When the switch occurs, it takes on a zone principle for the moment. However, on crosses out away from the basket involving men of different heights, one defensive man may back up a step to permit his teammate to scissor through and stay with his own man. This prevents a mismatch in height at times on which the offense might be able to capitalize.

The straight switching defense may be a little easier to play, but it takes away individual responsibility and also permits some mismatching. It can enable some quick two-timing and massing, and is more effective against teams that use weaving offenses. It also keeps your men in better assigned rebounding positions and in better position to have a patternized fast break. Although it takes on the zone principle, it is still man-to-man, and you definitely go through with your assigned man until there is a switch called.

It requires a great amount of talking to be effective and proper switching at the right time.

Some important points to keep in mind in regard to the switching defense are:

**1.** When you switch, it should be done quickly without hesitation and should be done forward as much as possible as a lateral switch will keep forcing you back toward the defensive basket.

**2.** A switching defense requires a lot of talking, but I believe that this is a necessity for any good defense.

**3.** Be alert to switch back to your original man as soon as it can be done safely after a switch.

**4.** The deep man should call the switch when it becomes necessary because of a man screening from behind, but the man taking the man with the ball should call it on cross-court or lateral switches. Of course, the other man must answer.

**5.** When a switch is called, *you must switch,* even though it may have been a poor call. However, you can sometimes correct it by immediately calling the switch back.

**6.** Weak-side defensive men or those guarding men away from the ball can often help on a switching situation by floating and slowing down an offensive man enough for the switch to be completed.

**7.** If a small or short man gets taken into the pivot by a tall man, he must call for help and perhaps effect a switch with a weak-side teammate before the offense can capitalize on the mismatch. The weak-side man should always stay alert to help in this situation.

**8.** It is necessary to drill a lot on two-on-two or three-on-three strong-side situations with a lot of screening in order for the defensive men to get away from the habit of depending on weak-side help.

## ZONE DEFENSES

Since the general advantages and disadvantages of the zone defense have been given earlier, I will merely diagram the four most commonly used zone defenses and give some of the more or less recognized facts in regard to them.

The designated zones are merely the spots from which the defense originates. Each man converges toward the ball at all times and in so doing there will be considerable overlapping into other zones.

Most zones can be extended farther away from the basket or withdrawn closer to the basket and this flexibility of coverage is very important in order to better contain various methods of attacking it.

I want to repeat that coaches must always keep in mind that, when the personnel involved is relatively even, there is no defense that cannot be successfully attacked just as there is no offense that cannot be stopped. Therefore, it is imperative that we have a defense that has a certain amount of flexibility and can be adjusted to meet a changing offense.

**Two-One-Two Zone.** Diagram 6-20 illustrates the two-one-two zone, which probably is used more than any other. It is based on good coverage of all the potential scoring area rather than concentration on a particular area to the detriment of the whole.

The principal strengths might be:

**1.** Overall coverage.

**2.** Good coverage of the very important foul-line area.

**3.** Good rebound coverage.

**4.** Excellent position to start a fast-break attack.

**5.** Good coverage against the teams that rely on working inside.

The principal weaknesses could be:

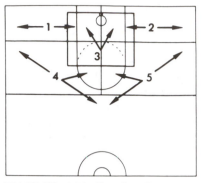

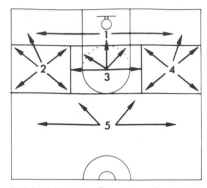

DIAGRAM 6-20 Two-One-Two Zone #1.

DIAGRAM 6-21 One-Three-One Zone.

1. Difficult to cover good outside- and corner-shooting teams.

2. May give up many shots in the high percentage area at the top of the circle.

3. Vulnerable to good baseline shots and moves.

4. Vulnerable in the good jump-shot areas.

**One-Three-One Zone.** Diagram 6-21 illustrates the one-three-one zone, which has been used very effectively by some fine coaches and teams.

The principal strengths might be:

1. Very strong in the foul-line area and really hurts any post offenses.

2. Good coverage against the setup basket.

3. Neutralizes the normal three-man overloading style to a great extent.

4. Requires the offense to make considerable adjustment to their normal zone attack.

5. Good coverage in most of the dangerous jump shot areas.

The principal weaknesses could be:

1. Very vulnerable to good corner shooters.

2. Does not cover the rebounding areas as well as most.

3. Does not complement a fast-break offense very well.

4. Vulnerable to short jump shots along the baseline when set up properly.

5. Gives the wing men a very difficult job and they may be the type that can be worn down.

**Three-Out Two-In Zone.** Diagram 6-22 illustrates the three-out two-in zone, which is one of the oldest of the zone defenses.

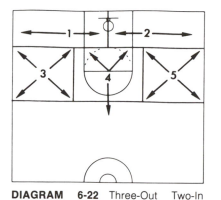

**DIAGRAM** **6-22** Three-Out Two-In Zone.

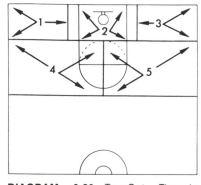

**DIAGRAM** **6-23** Two-Out Three-In Zone.

The principal strengths might be:

**1.** Very strong against good outside shooting teams.

**2.** Very strong against inexperienced or poor ball-handling guards.

**3.** Could make fairly good use of two large but slow men in the deep spots and quick agile men in the three outside positions.

**4.** Could complement a patternized fast break very well.

**5.** Discourages the good drivers from out front.

The principal weaknesses could be:

**1.** Very weak once the front line is penetrated.

**2.** Poor coverage in the corners.

**3.** Not as good rebound coverage.

**4.** Vulnerable in the middle or foul-line area for a pass and quick jump shot.

**5.** Vulnerable to good baseline shots and moves.

**6.** Can be overloaded in the deep and very dangerous areas.

**Three-In Two-Out Zone.** Diagram 6-23 illustrates the three-in two-out zone, which is generally considered to be the first effective zone defense ever used. The two-one-two zone emerged from this by merely moving the middle man in the back line forward and squeezing in the remaining two.

The principal strengths might be:

**1.** Very strong against the easy or setup shot.

**2.** Outstanding rebound coverage.

**3.** Covers corner and baseline operations quite well.

**4.** Complements a patternized fast break very well.

**5.** Very strong against the good deep-post men.

The principal weaknesses could be:

**1.** Very weak in the foul-line and high-post areas.

**2.** Very weak against a good jump-shooting team.

**3.** Front areas are easily overloaded.

**4.** Weak between the two lines of the defense.

**Other Zones.** Other zones that I have seen used on occasion are:

**1.** *The two-two-one.* This is a four-man box formation with a chaser out in front.

**2.** *The one-two-two.* This always keeps one man underneath to protect against the setup shot with a four-man box in front of him.

**3.** *The box and one.* This has one man assigned to individually guard some star player while the other four form a four-man box as in the box with a chaser in front.

**4.** *The T Zone.* This has three men deployed as the three deep men in the three-in two-out zone with a fourth man in the back half of the foul-circle area and the fifth man at the top of the key.

**5.** *The Reverse T Zone.* This has three men deployed as the three front men in the three-out two-in zone with a fourth man between him and middle man of the front three.

## PRESSING DEFENSES

Since I have already discussed the UCLA two-two-one zone press and listed some of the advantages and disadvantages of the pressing defense, I do not intend to devote too much space to it here. Complete books have been written on this topic, as well as many articles. These should be studied by all coaches who are interested in using any form of a pressing defense.

However, every coach should bear in mind that the material with which you have to work should dictate the type of defense, press or otherwise, that you intend to use. Never adopt a certain defense, or offense, simply because some other coach had good success with it. His material and his basic philosophy should be the reason for his style of play and a different philosophy might very well dictate the type of material a coach prefers to use as well as the style of play to which he is most adapted.

In recent years pressing defenses have become more and more popular in both the high school and collegiate ranks and there are those who believe that much of the success of the Boston Celtics is due to the amount of use they devote to the press. Although I do not feel that this is the reason for the success of the Celtics, I feel that it has been effective for them.

At the risk of inviting some criticism I feel that Bill Russell is the principal reason for the success of the Boston Celtics. Up to the 1966 season, they have never lost the professional championship with him, as the year that St. Louis beat them in the final round, he was hurt and either didn't play or wasn't himself for a good part of the series; and I do not believe that they ever won even the first round of the playoffs before they acquired him. Please do not consider this as derogatory or critical as it has been necessary to use him properly to get the results, but no player in the history of intercollegiate or professional basketball has come close to dominating the game as has Russell. Of course, credit must be given to Phil Woolpert, his college coach, who developed his unusual talent and used it so wisely in behalf of the team and to Red Auerbach, who has utilized his talents so magnificently in the pro league. Both coaches recognized his tremendous asset to a pressing defense and capitalized on it and Coach Auerbach has also capitalized on his unmatched ability to get a fast-break attack under way.

Although it takes many ingredients to make up a championship team, I sincerely believe that the pressing defense tactics was the principal contributory factor as far as style of play on either offense or defense is concerned for the NCAA championships won in 1952 by the University of Kansas, in 1955 and 1956 by the University of San Francisco, by the University of California in 1959, by the University of Cincinnati in 1961 and 1962, and by UCLA in 1964 and 1965. It is also noteworthy that other pressing teams were in strong contention throughout that period of years.

## Why UCLA Likes the Press

Earlier I mentioned several advantages and disadvantages of the pressing defense and even before that mentioned some of the reasons for the press when the UCLA two-two-one zone press was discussed.

Although I use some type of a pressing defense at various times in our games every season, it is very seldom that I use it all of the time in any game or in any season. Regardless of the amount of time that I use it, although there are many possible reasons for doing so, my primary reasons are threefold: First, since most of the teams in our conference like to use a slow, ball-control type of offense, I use it to try and speed up the tempo of the game by forcing them out of their deliberate patterns; second, I use it because I feel that it puts a premium on good condition and I like our boys to feel that they are in better condition than any opponent and work them hard to attain such condition; third, I use it to the degree that I feel that I have the type of material to work it effectively. Therefore, the material not only dictates the type of press we will use, but also the amount of time that we will use it whether we are thinking of an individual game or an entire season. I should add at this point that it is very seldom, if ever, that material will be so ideally suited to a specific defense as my 1964 team were to the two-two-one zone press and my 1965 team to changes from an initial one-two-one-one. However, the fact that these same boys had considerable work in the man-to-man set defense in the potential shooting area had given them a fine background in individual defensive fundamentals that proved invaluable to them in the zone press.

## MAN-TO-MAN PRESS

This type of press like the zone press can be applied either full-court, three-quarter court, or half-court. If applied closer to the defensive basket, it becomes a pressure defense rather than a press.

Just as the name implies, the principle is that each man is assigned an individual opponent to whom he must apply the pressing tactics. The front-line men try to drive the men toward the sideline where their passing options will be more limited, but try to keep them from getting by. Whenever you can stop their dribble and force them to pivot to the outside, your nearest teammate on the front line may leave his man and come over quickly to double-team him as he comes out of the turn and before he can size up the floor. The men guarding the back men must constantly keep the man with the ball in their vision and anticipate a pass to their man. The man with the ball may tip off where he is going to pass. Interceptions are tried on lob passes just as they are in the zone press, but men on the opposite side of where a lob or long bounce pass is thrown must go back to protect in case the interception failed.

If a man gets by on a dribble, you should chase him with all speed and try to deflect the ball on forward to a teammate deeper on defense or try to cut him off before he can reach the basket. A real hustler coming from behind and yelling can be a tremendously disturbing influence against most players.

When we apply pressure after we have scored and the opponents are inbounding the ball, we usually turn the inbounder loose and double-team the near potential receiver, but occasionally mix this up by suddenly bothering the inbounder and trying to force him to throw a lob or a bounce pass that will possibly give a defensive teammate an opportunity to intercept.

Every effort should be made to stay between the man with the ball and the defensive basket, but the four men guarding men without the ball play as high up on their man toward the ball as they dare to be in position to intercept a pass. How high they play on their men will, of course, depend on how close they are to the man with the ball and to the defensive basket.

If the press is to be effective, the players must understand and accept the fact that it is a gambling defense and will give up some easy baskets, but the advantages may far offset the easy baskets given up. The coach will have to determine whether or not his personnel can play some type of press effectively enough to make it pay dividends, and his patience and judgment may be severely taxed in trying to make the correct and proper decision.

Some rather basic rules of the man-to-man press are as follows:

**1.** Although we want pressure on the man with the ball, do not overguard him by reaching in and trying to grab the ball.

**2.** Keep in good balance and don't let a man drive by you.

**3.** Try to force the man with the ball to the outside and make him turn his back to the inside and forward part of the floor when he pivots.

**4.** Try to prevent a straight hard pass, but force a lob or bounce pass.

**5.** Whenever a man has used his dribble, force him immediately.

**6.** Always pick up a loose man quickly unless it means leaving a man open for a scoring pass whom no teammate can cover.

**7.** All men quickly converge toward the basket when a man gets open and is headed there.

**8.** In the man-to-man press each man must really be dedicated and have great desire to stay on top of his man and prevent him from getting away when he has the ball and to make it tough for him to receive a pass when he does not have it.

**9.** Although each man is assigned to press an individual opponent, he must always keep in mind that it is a team defense and be alive to help at all times.

**10.** Try to keep the man with the ball out of the middle of the floor as much as possible.

The same basic principles are applied regardless of whether it is a full-, three-quarter, or half-court press. Remember always to keep pressure on the man with the ball and tighten up as much as possible on his potential receivers to make it difficult for them to receive a pass and be alert to intercept or two-time at every opportunity.

## ZONE PRESSES

Zone-press defenses, like the man-to-man press, can be applied full-court, three-quarter court, or half-court, but, unlike the man-to-man, each defensive man is assigned an area to cover rather than an individual opponent. Of course, if there is no offensive man in the area that he is assigned to cover, he slides over toward the danger zone to help out there.

Some of the basic principles of the zone press are as follows:

**1.** Each man must be responsible for his zone, but he is now playing the ball rather than the man.

**2.** When in a front zone and your man has the ball, try to force him to make a lob or bounce pass that will be easier intercepted.

**3.** Try to force the ball toward the sidelines and away from the middle of the floor.

**4.** Men in deeper zones are potential interceptors and should watch the man with the ball. He may telegraph his pass by a look, and you may be able to tell whether or not he can throw a long pass by having his throwing arm cocked back or the leg on his strong side back.

**5.** If a pass is completed over your front-line zones, be tough until you can get regrouped. Front men must retreat quickly and back men must play tough individually.

**6.** Insist on aggressive interceptions. When a player goes for a ball, he must never hesitate. The same kind of movement to protect the basket behind him should be made from a teammate on the opposite side.

**7.** Always be alert to two-time a dribbler, especially when he stops and turns.

**8.** Try to force the opponents to hurry. This will result in more mistakes and loss of poise and teamwork.

**9.** Continually impress on the players that they are not grabbing the ball away, but are forcing the opponents to travel, get tied up, throw a pass that can be intercepted, throw a pass out-of-bounds, commit an offensive foul, or in some way make the error that will give you the ball.

**10.** Teach your boys to continually apply the pressure and be patient for the proper results.

**11.** You must work to capitalize on the error that you effect as this can be very demoralizing.

### Two-Two-One Zone Press

This press has been discussed earlier and is the one used so effectively by the UCLA undefeated national champions of 1964.

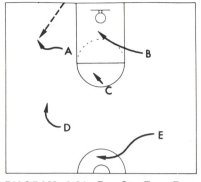

DIAGRAM 6-24 Two-One-Two Zone Press #1.

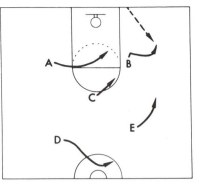

DIAGRAM 6-25 Two-One-Two Zone Press #2.

## Two-One-Two Zone Press

This press has been used quite a bit by a number of coaches who like to augment their regular defense with a press and by some as their principal defense. I have used it with reasonably satisfactory results at times.

When I use this press, I use the same principles that are used in my two-two-one press indicated as follows:

**Two-One-Two Zone Press #1.** If the ball is inbounded on A's side of the floor, A's responsibilities are the same, B's are the same, C is responsible for the territory that D had, D has the responsibility that C had, and E moves too and has the same responsibility that E had in the two-two-one (Diag. 6-24).

**Two-One-Two Zone Press #2.** If the ball is inbounded on B's side of the floor, A and B exchange responsibilities, C is responsible for the same area as he was in #1, and D and E exchange responsibilities (Diag. 6-25).

## One-Two-Two Press

This press has also received some usage and I have used it occasionally with the principles again being compared with those that I use in the two-two-one press. The one-two-two is set in merely the exact reverse manner as the two-two-one.

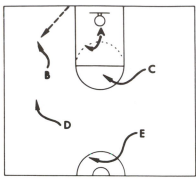

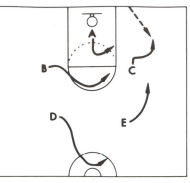

**DIAGRAM 6-26** One-Two-Two Zone Press #1.

**DIAGRAM 6-27** One-Two-Two Zone Press #2.

**One-Two-Two Zone Press #1.** If the ball is inbounded on A's side of the floor, B assumes the duties of A as in the two-two-one, A assumes the duties of B, C assumes the duties of D, D assumes the duties of C, and E moves to and assumes the duties of E in the two-two-one (Diag. 6-26).

**One-Two-Two Zone Press #2.** If the ball is inbounded on B's side of the floor, A has the same duties as in #1, B and C exchange duties, and D and E exchange duties (Diag. 6-27).

Since these are the only zone presses that I have used or observed to much extent, they are the only ones that I will discuss at all. However, I will name and diagram the initial setup of some others that have been used.

### One-Two-One Half Court Press and Three-One-One Full Court Press

These pressing defenses (Diags. 6-28 and 6-29) have been used by the late John Bennington at Michigan State University and by John Ramsay of the Portland Trail Blazers. They have written fine explanations of these and, since I had no practical experience in their use, it would be better for the reader to get their information direct rather than from me.

### One-Three-One Zone Press

I have experimented a bit in practice with this particular type of press, but have never used it or seen it used by another. From using the two-

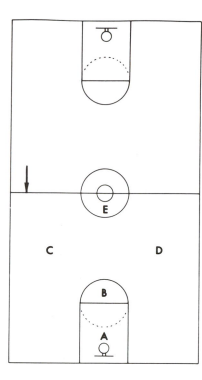

**DIAGRAM 6-28** One-Two-One-One Half-Court Zone Press.

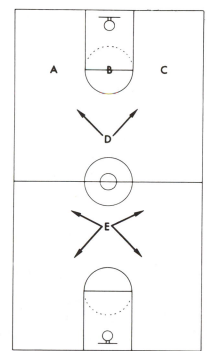

**DIAGRAM 6-29** Three-One-One Full-Court Zone Press.

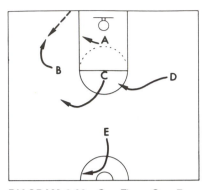

**DIAGRAM 6-30** One-Three-One Zone Press #1.

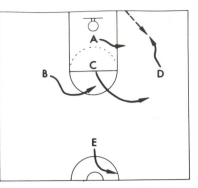

**DIAGRAM 6-31** One-Three-One Zone Press #2.

two-one principles as a basis of comparisons, the initial attack was as follows:

**One-Three-One Zone Press #1.** A assumes the duties of B, B assumes the duties of A, C assumes the duties of B, D assumes the duties of C, and E has the same duties as in the two-two-one (Diag. 6-30).

**One-Three-One Zone Press #2.** If the ball is inbounded on the other side, A performs the same duties as in #1, B assumes the duties of D, C has the same duties except on the opposite side of the floor as are the others, D assumes the duties of B, and E continues with the same duties (Diag. 6-31).

There are many other types of zone presses and combination presses used and perhaps the readers know of others that have been used with good results. However, it may be possible to get some idea that will be helpful from the types that I have discussed.

# 7

# MISCELLANEOUS DRILLS

## INTRODUCTION

The only method of teaching the individual fundamentals, the team offense, and the team defense is by a wise selection of drills and the repetition of them until the desired habits are formed.

There are a countless number of different types of drills, but I believe that every coach can do a better job by devising his own drills to meet his particular requirements. Naturally, many coaches will use many drills that are almost identical, but each will also have some "pet" or favorite drills that he will especially like. I sincerely believe that it is altogether possible that the success of many a coach may be in direct proportion to his ability to devise the proper drills to meet his particular theories or style of play.

Some drills will of necessity deal with one particular fundamental alone, but I try to incorporate several individual fundamentals in almost every drill. For example: Ball handling, passing, and receiving are utilized in practically every offensive drill and in many defensive drills and should never be neglected; dribbling goes together with the stops and turns or pivots, and footwork and other fundamentals must be noted in drills primarily designed for dribbling and pivoting; footwork and body balance should be under inspection in every drill; and, of course, there are many others, but the important thing to keep in mind is the fact you must not permit the players to become careless in the execution of one fundamental merely because the principal emphasis is on some other.

The drills for every fundamental must be varied from day to day to prevent them from becoming monotonous, and not continued for too long a period of time on any day for the same reason. The accomplishment of the purpose of a drill is very likely to diminish in proportion to the enthusiasm with which the players execute it. I also like to make most drills, especially the shooting drills, as competitive as possible once the players have learned the proper method of execution.

The drills also should be progressive in difficulty as the early season moves along, as should their emphasis on conditioning. The players must not become discouraged. The purpose of the drills should be explained early so that the players will see how they fit into the team picture. In teaching an individual fundamental be sure to follow the laws of learning and:

**1.** Explain the drill and either demonstrate or have a capable player demonstrate how it should be properly executed.

**2.** Have the players imitate the proper demonstration where you can observe them carefully.

**3.** Constructively criticize their imitations and show them how to properly correct their mistakes.

**4.** Have the players repeat the correct model daily until the proper habits are formed and then repeat them as frequently as necessary to keep them sharp.

Keep your groups well organized and, once the players know the proper method of executing the drills, focus your attention on the correct execution of the fundamental or fundamentals involved. Good judgment must be used at all times as to how often and how long a drill should be used. Many factors will enter into the making of a wise decision in this, but always keep in mind that a drill is designed for some particular purpose and not merely to use time.

## WHAT-AND-WHEN DRILLS

### MISCELLANEOUS WARMUP

Some of these should be used for a few minutes every day at the start of practice. Many are illustrated in the following section, "Specific Drills."

**1.** Running.
    **(a)** Easy running the length of the floor and back with the arms rotating and every joint loose and relaxed.
    **(b)** Quick change of pace and direction the length of the floor and back.
    **(c)** Defensive sliding the length of the floor and back.
    **(d)** Backward running the length of the floor and back.
    **(e)** Two-man combination the length of the floor and back. One using a change of pace and direction and the other sliding defensively to keep position. Positions are alternated when they reach the center line.

**(f)** Inside turns the length of the floor and back.

**(g)** Reverses without the ball from one side of the floor and then from the other.

**(h)** Reverse drives with an imaginary ball from one side of the floor and then the other, and then with a ball.

**(i)** Alternate foot hopping the length of the floor and back.

2. Dribbling.

**(a)** Control dribbling using the change of pace and direction the length of the floor and back.

**(b)** Speed dribbling the length of the floor and back.

**(c)** Control dribbling with a defensive slider the length of the floor and back.

3. Pivots and (or) stops and turns.

**(a)** Use a control dribble for a few steps, then make a quick stop and turn and hand off to a trailer who comes by late and fast. The dribbler trails him to receive a pass when he makes the stop and turn. Use this up and down the length of the floor.

**(b)** With about three to a line the first man dribbles hard for a few dribbles and makes a quick stop and turn and passes to the next one in line. He then charges the receiver and then goes to the end of the line.

4. Loose-ball recovery. Roll a ball out for the first one in line to scoop up and drive for the basket to score.

5. Five-man weave the length of the floor. Finish with a jump shot and have all five men cover their rebounding areas.

6. Squad defensive sliding to position according to signal.

7. Combination—rebound, passing, and cutting drill in teams.

8. Jumping.

**(a)** Squad jumping as a group. Take two easy jumps and make the third one for height.

**(b)** Imaginary rebound. In squad formation with all hands in rebound position above their shoulders, all boys jump high to rebound properly an imaginary ball that the coach will toss in the air where they all can see.

**(c)** Imaginary jump ball. Everyone takes a jump-ball position and times a jump to the toss of an imaginary ball that the coach tosses in the air.

**(d)** Rebounding ball back and forth across the board above the basket. Five to a basket with the ball starting on the three-man side.

**(e)** Rebounding ball high on the board from a straight line position. Each man rebounds the ball high on the board for the man following him to rebound high for the next one. After rebounding the ball, you move quickly to the end of the line to come in again.

9. Passing.

**(a)** Moving circle and passing across.

**(b)** Double circle with the passes being made back and forth from the outer circle to the inner circle as they move in opposite directions.

## SHOOTING

Since the object of all offense is to get the ball through the basket, some time should be spent every day on drills that teach the proper way to execute the various shots that may be used.

Furthermore, since the vast majority of our baskets will be from hard drives or quick jump shots, we try to spend a proportionate amount of time on the development of those particular shots.

**1.** Squad using quick set shot upon receiving a pass, or a fake set and quick drive of a dribble or two ending with a quick jump shot. Use every day.

**2.** Special drives. *Use every day.* From a dribble drive or from a pass and cut for a return pass.

    **(a)** Fake pass back.
    **(b)** Quick stop and fadeaway.
    **(c)** Hook—right and left.
    **(d)** Layback.
    **(e)** Reachback.

**3.** Position specials. Use every day.

    **(a)** Forwards, centers, and guards work alone on the types of shots that they are most likely to get in game competition.

    **(b)** Forwards and guards combine for the various shots that come from our side-post options, from reverses, and from screen situations.

    **(c)** Free throws. Each player reports on a minimum of fifty attempts each practice day.

## PASS-AND-CUT SITUATIONS

*Use every day.*

**1.** Pass-and-cut situations from front or side positions for all players.

**2.** Pass-and-cut situations that occur in our regular offensive formations with men in their normal positions.

## DEFENSIVE

**1.** One-on-one in their normal situations. *Use every day.*

**2.** Two-on-two. Guard and guard, guard and center, guard and forward, center and forward. *Use every day.*

**3.** Three-on-three.

    **(a)** Strong side—guard, forward, and center. *Use every day.*

    **(b)** Two guards and post man. Pass to the post and cut. *Use twice a week.*

    **(c)** Pressing underneath the basket with the offense trying to inbound the ball and get it past the center line with no long passes. *Use twice a week.*

(d) Defensive checking out two forwards and center with quick set and jump shots being taken from the outside. *Use three times a week.*

4. Four-on-four.

(a) The offense sets up in the normal forward and guard positions without a post man and the offense runs a weave. *Use once a week* or more if needed.

(b) The offense uses a post man who may feed but may not shoot. *Use once or twice a week.*

5. Five-on-five.

(a) The defense works against all types of offenses—weave, high post, low post, double post, shuffle, center to the weak side, etc. *Work against at least one of these every day.*

(b) Work against the ball-control or protecting-a-lead offense *once or twice a week.*

(c) Work a few minutes every day on having the defense check out and rebound the set shot or jump shot.

6. When outnumbered.

(a) Two-on-one from half and full court.

(b) Three-on-two from half and full court.

(c) Three-on-one from half and full court.

(d) Three-on-two conditioner.

7. Special situations.

(a) Vs. side and blind screens—sliding and scissoring.

(b) Vs. strong post man.

(c) All jump-ball situations.

(d) Free-throw situations.

(e) Vs. any type of specialist.

## TEAM FAST BREAK

*Use some every day.*

**1.** From a floorshot, made or missed, and ending with the various options. Without and with some defense.

**2.** From a free throw, made or missed, and ending with the various options. Without and with defense.

**3.** From a half-court scrimmage set up when possession is obtained in any manner.

## REBOUNDING

*Use some every day.*

**1.** One-on-one. From normal position situations.

**2.** Two-on-two. Guard and guard, guard and center, guard and forward, center and forward.

**3.** Three-on-three.
  **(a)** Three inside men (a forward on each side and the center) with two outside shooters or passers.
  **(b)** Strong-side men (guard, forward, and center) with anyone shooting.
  **(c)** Two guards and the center with any one shooting.

**4.** Five-on-five.
  **(a)** Team setup with the offense moving the ball quickly for not over three passes and then taking a quick set or jump shot.
  **(b)** Team setup with the offense running some pattern of their offense for a shot.
  **(c)** Team setup with the offense running an opponent's pattern for a shot.

## REGULAR OFFENSE AND SPECIAL PLAYS

*Use some every day.*

**1.** Work on strong-side patterns.

**2.** Work on weak-side patterns.

**3.** Combine strong side and weak side.

**4.** Zone attack.

**5.** Attacking the press.

## THREE-MAN LANE BALL-HANDLING AND CONDITIONING DRILLS

*Use every day.*

**1.** Parallel lane.

**2.** Tight weave.

**3.** Loose weave.

**4.** Down the middle.

**5.** Front and side.

**6.** Through the squeeze.

**7.** Long pass.

**8.** Dribble, stop and turn, hand off.

## PROTECTING A LEAD

*Use twice a week* beginning a week before the first game and more often if needed.

## PRESSING DEFENSE

*Use every day.*

**1.** Man-to-man.

**2.** Zone.

**3.** Combination.

## SCRIMMAGING

*Use some type every day.*

**1.** Half-court. *Use some every day* to illustrate all types of game situations. Alternate daily the principal emphasis on defense and offense.

    **(a)** Develop the parts of your offense against tough competition.

    **(b)** Have one team stay on offense until they have lost the ball five times and then have the defensive team take the offense. Keep score. A score does not constitute a lost possession. A defensive foul gives either one or two points to the offense without causing a lost possession. An offensive foul constitutes a lost possession.

    **(c)** Have the defense fast break when they obtain possession.

    **(d)** Have the offense press after every score with the defense trying to break the press.

**2.** Full-court. *Almost every day for the first couple of weeks, then twice a week until the first game.* Very rarely after the playing season has opened, but a good one on the day after a game for those who did not get to play too much while the others are shooting free-throw and jump shots.

# SPECIFIC DRILLS

## REBOUNDING

**1.** Mental hints for the players.

    **(a)** The team that controls the boards usually controls the game.

    **(b)** Assume that every shot will be missed, offensively and defensively, and *move* into position to rebound and go up after the ball.

    **(c)** Whenever a shot is taken, your hands should be quickly brought to shoulder height with the palms toward the ball.

    **(d)** When your man shoots, take one or two steps backward with your eyes on your man, and when he makes a move, cross in front of him and go for the ball. If he hesitates, forget him and go for the ball.

    **(e)** When you go for the ball on the defensive board—jump quickly and high, spread the legs with a wide kick as you go up, catch the ball with both hands and bring it forcefully to the chest, take a good look for potential receivers, and get the ball out as quickly as you can do so safely.

**(f)** When you go for the ball on the offensive board—jump quickly and high, keep your fingers spread with the palms forward and tip the ball rather than bat at it, keep the hand up to avoid possible pushing. Make the second and third effort or more if necessary.

**(g)** Never get caught too far under where you are only in position to catch the ball if it goes through the basket and are easily crowded.

**(h)** Keep thinking and faking.

2. The coach should watch for the following things as they might apply in the various drills:

    **(a)** Offensively.

        **(1)** Getting proper position.

        **(2)** Timing.

        **(3)** Quickness of jump.

        **(4)** Keeping hands up.

        **(5)** Making extra efforts.

        **(6)** Wrist and finger flick.

        **(7)** Faking.

        **(8)** Being ready.

    **(b)** Defensively.

        **(1)** Getting proper position.

        **(2)** Moving into path of offense.

        **(3)** Timing.

        **(4)** Quickness of jump.

        **(5)** Spread and kick.

        **(6)** Hands up and elbows out.

        **(7)** Taking the look.

        **(8)** Getting ball out fast.

        **(9)** Aggressiveness.

      **(10)** Being ready.

**Rebounding #1—Three Man Figure Eight** (Diag. 7-1). 1 tosses the ball high off the board, rebounds it, passes to 2, then takes 2's position. 2 dribbles quickly to the front of the board, tosses the ball high off the board, rebounds it, passes to 3, then takes 3's position. 3 continues the same plan and passes to 1.

With three men at a basket, a squad of fifteen can get quite a few rebounds in a period of two or three minutes.

**Rebounding #2—Team Pass and Move** (Diag. 7-2). 1 tosses the ball high on the board, rebounds it, passes to 2, and takes his position; 2 passes quickly to 4 who has faked the other way before moving back to receive the pass. 2 moves out to take the place of 5, who moves up to the 4 position. 4 head fakes back to 2 and passes quickly to 3 who has faked baseline. 4 fakes cutaway after passing to 3 then cuts down

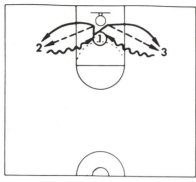

DIAGRAM 7-1 Rebounding #1—
Three-Man Figure Eight.

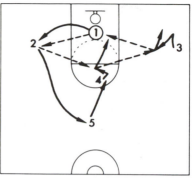

DIAGRAM 7-2 Rebounding #2—
Team Pass and Move.

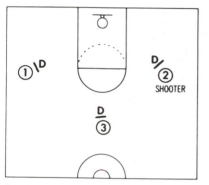

DIAGRAM 7-3 Rebounding #3—
Checking the Shooter.

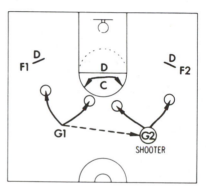

DIAGRAM 7-4 Rebounding #4—Inside Checking.

lane to receive a return pass from 3. He then starts the same procedure over again, but makes the first pass out to 3's side.

You will note that there is a change of position for all except the side man who passes to the man who rebounds.

**Rebounding #3—Checking the Shooter** (Diag. 7-3). The boys pair up with no more than three pair at a basket and work from various spots on the floor. They also alternate offensively and defensively.

The defensive man takes a normal defensive position on the shooter, but permits him to take a set or quick dribble or two and jump shot. He then moves across in his path and goes for the board.

**Rebounding #4—Inside Checking** (Diag. 7-4). The forwards and center take their normal positions with the defense in position on them, G1 and G2 either shoot or pass in to F1, F2, or C who may shoot. When the shot is taken, the inside men rebound with either G1 or G2 covering the key area.

The inside men alternate offensively and defensively.

**Rebounding #5—Offensive Tipping** (Diag. 7-5). 1 and 2 take positions as shown. 3 takes a quick set or jump shot and then rebounds his area as do 1 and 2. The three of them keep after the ball until the basket is made. The ball is then passed out to 4 who has taken the place of 3 with 5 moving up and 1 moving to the end of the line as 2 takes the place of 1 and 3 takes the place of 2.

Keep up the continuity.

**Rebounding #6—Timing Across the Board** (Diag. 7-6). 1 tosses the ball high above the basket and across and off the board to the opposite side and moves over to the end of the 2, 4 line. 2 times himself to rebound the ball at the height of his jump and flicks across high off the board to 3 who has moved up to take the place of 1.

Keep rebounding with each rebounder going quickly to the end of the opposite line as soon as he rebounds.

**Rebounding #7—One Offensive Tipper** (Diag. 7-7). 1 takes a position underneath and rebounds a quick shot by 2 until he scores. If 2 makes the shot, he keeps shooting until he misses. The three men keep alternating positions as indicated.

**Rebounding #8—Across the Board (in Pairs)** (Diag. 7-8). 1 passes the ball high off the board to 2 who times himself and rebounds it high back across the board to 1. They try to keep it in play until each has rebounded the ball five times. 3 then takes the place of 1 and 1 takes the place of 2 and 2 observes.

This is used primarily for the centers, but occasionally for some forwards.

**Rebounding #9—Double Triangle with Pass** (Diag. 7-9). 1 and 2 each toss a ball high on the board and rebound it and pass out to the man on the side, 3 and 4, and take his place, 3 and 4 pass to the front man in the line nearest to them, 5 and 6, who have moved toward the basket, and each moves out to the end of the front line farthest away from them. 5 and 6 rebound their own tosses off the board and continue on the same pattern.

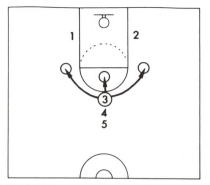

**DIAGRAM 7-5** Rebounding #5—Offensive Tipping.

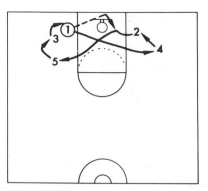

**DIAGRAM 7-6** Rebounding #6—Timing Across the Board.

**DIAGRAM 7-7** Rebounding #7—One Offensive Tipper.

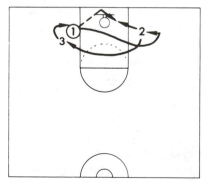

**DIAGRAM 7-8** Rebounding #8—Across the Board (in Pairs)..

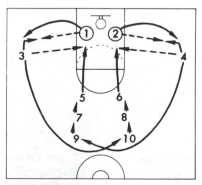

**DIAGRAM 7-9** Rebounding #9—Double Triangle with Pass.

**Rebounding #10—Checking the Drivers** (Diag. 7-10).  1, 2, and 3 take positions near the foul-lane area as shown. 5 dribbles toward the basket and takes a jump shot, or passes to 4 or 6 who takes a quick jump shot. 1, 2, and 3 check out 4, 5, and 6, respectively, for an instant and then go for the ball. When 1, 2, or 3 get possession of the ball, 4, 5, and 6 take the defense and 1, 2, and 3 move to the back of the lines as 7, 8, and 9 move against 4, 5, and 6.

**Rebounding #11—Finding the Receiver** (Diag. 7-11).  3 takes a quick set or jump shot from the jump-shooting area and moves to the back half of the circle for the long rebound area. If he rebounds the ball, he shoots again very quickly. When 1 rebounds the ball, he finds 4, who has faked one way or the other, and gives him a quick pass. 2 moves in from the endline to bother 1 a bit and become the next re-bounder as soon as 1 gets possession. 1 takes the place of 5 when he passes to 4, 4 shoots, 5 takes the place of 4, 3 takes the place of 2, and 2 the place of 1.

**Rebounding #12—Competing for Ball and Completing Pass Out** (Diag. 7-12).  1, 2, and 3 rebound underneath with each trying to get the ball from the other as 4 takes a quick jump shot. The two men who do not get the rebound try to tie up the one who does and prevent him from making a successful pass to 4. The first man to get five rebounds and complete the pass out to 4 exchanges places with 4 and they start over.

**Rebounding #13—Team Checking "A"** (Diag. 7-13).  One team lines up in their regular offensive positions with the defense in position. The coach has a ball and takes a shot from one of the outside positions as indicated by the circles. The offense works for an offensive tip or to regain possession as the defense works to get possession and complete a pass away from the defensive board for what might be the start of a break.

**Rebounding #14—Team Checking "B"** (Diag. 7-14).  The teams line up as in #13. The offense moves the ball quickly with fake cutting for not over three passes and then someone takes a jump shot. The teams then react as in #13.

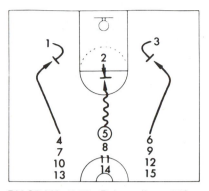

**DIAGRAM 7-10** Rebounding #10—
Checking the Drivers.

**DIAGRAM 7-11** Rebounding #11—
Finding the Receiver.

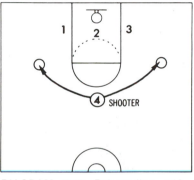

**DIAGRAM 7-12** Rebounding #12—
Competing for the Ball.

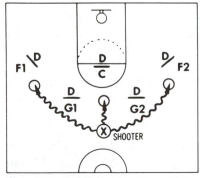

**DIAGRAM 7-13** Rebounding #13—
Team Checking—"A."

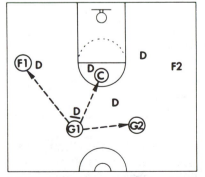

**DIAGRAM 7-14** Rebounding #14—
Team Checking—"B."

## FLOOR LENGTH

These floor-length drills serve a number of purposes and many of them are used every day of practice, almost from the first day of the season to the last. As in the case of most drills, practically every one of these emphasizes the development of more than one fundamental.

The more important reasons for their use are the development of:

1. Physical condition.
2. Quick ball-handling on the move.
3. Body balance and floor balance.
4. Fakes and feints and footwork.
5. Defensive footwork.
6. Timing.
7. Loosening up.
8. Speed- and control-dribbling.
9. Development of some special passes.
10. Fast-break principles.
11. Pressing defense principles.
12. Attacking the press.
13. Offensive and defensive principles for three-on-two situations.
14. The proper execution of all fundamentals.

**Floor Length #1—Start of Organized Practice** (Diag. 7-15).   Since I usually start my organized practice with some loosening-up drills from the three-man lane formation, the squad quickly line up as indicated when I blow the whistle.

**Floor Length #2—Easy Running and Hopping** (Diag. 7-16).   The first men in each of the three lines all start together with each succeeding three starting as soon as the men in front of them are out as far as the foul line extended. They run easily with every joint relaxed and the arms rotating until they cross the opposite end line where they turn and line up ready to start back as soon as the last men have crossed the end line.

We also give them at least one round of alternate foot hopping.

**Floor Length #3—Change of Pace and Direction** (Diag. 7-17).   They line up and move out as they did in #2 except that each man used proceeds with quick changes of pace and direction. The lines on the outside use a third of the width of the floor from their sideline in and the middle line uses the middle third of the floor.

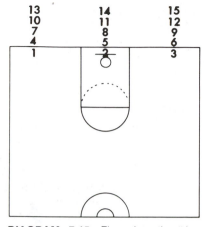

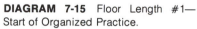

**DIAGRAM 7-15** Floor Length #1—
Start of Organized Practice.

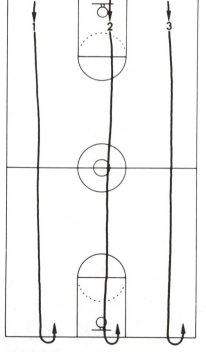

**DIAGRAM 7-16** Floor Length #2—
Easy Running.

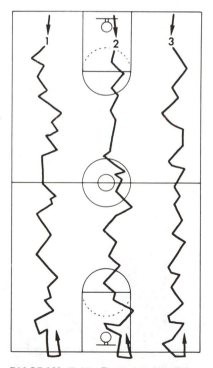

**DIAGRAM 7-17** Floor Length #3—
Change of Pace and Direction.

**Floor Length #4—Half-Court Sprints** (Diag. 7-18). They line up as before and move out three abreast. The purpose now is to sprint to break an imaginary tape across the center line and then ease up and cross the opposite end line. They then line up to return as soon as the last threesomes have crossed the end line.

**Floor Length #5—Control, Speed, and Weak-Hand Dribbling** (Diag. 7-19). The players line up in the three lines as before and, if enough balls are available, each one has a ball. They use a control dribble and work on change of pace and direction until they reach the center line and then use a speed dribble until they cross the end line. When they cross the end line, they make a quick stop and turn and get in position to go the other way as soon as the others have also crossed the end line.

Each group of three try to stay nearly parallel as they use the control dribble to the center line and each succeeding group of three start as soon as the group preceding them pass the foul line extended.

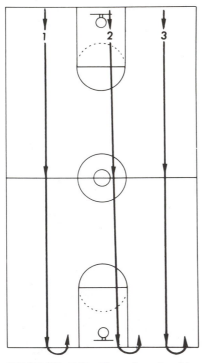

**DIAGRAM 7-18** Floor Length #4— Half-Court Sprints.

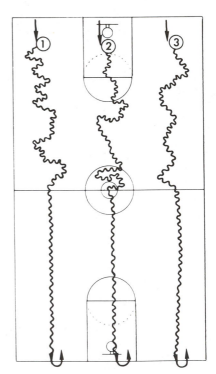

**DIAGRAM 7-19** Floor Length #5— Control, Speed, and Weak-Hand Dribbling.

The dribblers should do considerable work on dribbling with the weak hand.

**Floor Length #6—Defensive Sliding** (Diag. 7-20).   The players line up as before except the first one in each line turns around with his back toward the far basket. They progress backward down the floor defensing an imaginary cutter or dribbler who uses a quick change of pace and direction. They must not get into a pattern, but continue to vary their sliding movements. They try to keep within arms length of the imaginary offensive man, keep the hand down on the side to which they are moving, and have the other hand pointing toward the waist of the imaginary offensive man.

**Floor Length #7—One-on-One (Cutter)** (Diag. 7-21).   The players now work in pairs in their respective lines and change assignments when they reach the center line. It is the responsibility of the offensive man to make the defensive man work. He is not to attempt to outrun

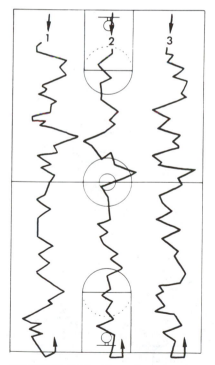

**DIAGRAM  7-20**  Floor  Length  #6—
Defensive Sliding.

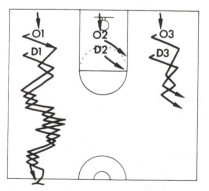

**DIAGRAM  7-21**  Floor  Length  #7—
One-on-One (Cutter).

him, but force him to make quick stops, starts, and changes of direction with a lot of lateral movement as he progresses down the floor.

Each pair must stay in their third of the width of the floor and each succeeding pair must make certain that the defensive man is not forced into the heels of the offensive man in the preceding pair.

**Floor Length #8—One-on-One (Dribbler)** (Diag. 7-22). This runs the same as #7 except each pair now has a ball and the offensive man becomes a dribbler.

**Floor Length #9—Dribble, Stop and Turn, Hand Off to Trailer** (Diag. 7-23). Each middle man now has a ball and works with the corresponding man in the lines on each side of him. The middle man uses the control dribble and moves toward one side or the other and then makes a quick stop and turn and hands off the ball to the man on that side. When the middle man dribbles toward one side, the man on that side times himself with fakes and comes by late and fast to receive the

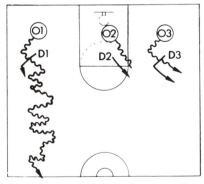

**DIAGRAM 7-22** Floor Length #8—One-on-One (Dribbler).

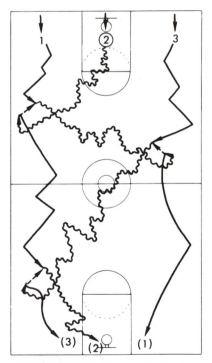

**DIAGRAM 7-23** Floor Length #9—Dribble, Stop and Turn, Hand-off.

hand off at the right time. He then uses a control dribble across the floor where the other side man times himself to come by as the stop-and-turn is made. Each one of the threesome makes one pivot as he proceeds down the floor with the original middle man who started the play receiving the last pass off and driving to score with the other two moving in to rebound.

It is the responsibility of the cutters to time themselves with the dribbler and be moving by at the proper time. They are of little value if they are either too late or too early.

**Floor Length #10—Quick Starts and Stops from Dribbler** (Diag. 7-24). If enough balls are available, each man should have one as he lines up as before. The first threesome move out with a control dribble and come to a quick stop some 20 feet out. They then make a few quick pivots in that position and then suddenly drive forward another 20 feet and do the same thing. This continues the length of the floor.

The next man in each line starts as soon as the man ahead of him continues after making a stop ahead of him.

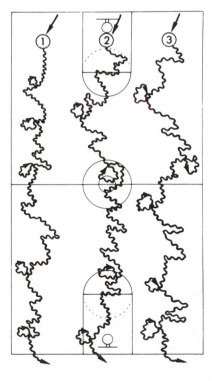

**DIAGRAM 7-24** Floor Length #10—Quick Starts and Stops from Dribble.

**Floor Length #11—Parallel Lanes** (Diag. 7-25). Each middle man has a ball and starts the drill by tossing the ball high on the board and making a good, tough rebound. He then passes to one of the side men and they proceed down the floor as quickly as they can and still maintain good passing control of the ball.

The ball always is passed back to the middle man from the side and is *never* passed across the middle man from one side man to the other.

When the middle man has reached the vicinity of the top of the foul-circle area at the other end, the flanker who receives the next pass takes a driving shot, lands in balance, and turns quickly to get back into the play. The flanker in the opposite side stops quickly to rebound his side. The middle man who made the pass to the driving shooter takes one or two steps toward the receiver with his hands chin-high and looking for a return pass. As soon as he sees that the shot is attempted, he moves to rebound the side of the shooter.

The threesome then clear the floor quickly for the next threesome who always start when the threesome in front of them cross the center line. It is always wise to face toward the court when you move off to the end as

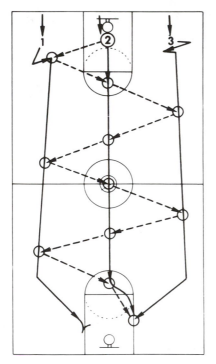

**DIAGRAM 7-25** Floor Length #11—
Parallel Lanes.

a driving man may be injured or cause an injury to the man who gets hit from behind.

Although the last pass to the shooter may be a bounce pass, we usually work on the crisp push pass for the drill. However, we occasionally use the bounce pass entirely.

Keep alternating the middle man.

**Floor Length #12—Weave (Tight and Loose)** (Diag. 7-26).   Start the same as #11 and keep alternating the middle man.

The middle man rebounds the ball and passes to one of the flankers, goes behind him, and cuts back to receive a pass from the man coming from the other side. They proceed down the floor always cutting behind the man to whom they pass and then cutting back to receive a pass. Finish as in #11.

Both the straight push and bounce passes are practiced in this drill. Practice on the close-in hand-off passes is also acquired by making the players close in and use a very tight weave.

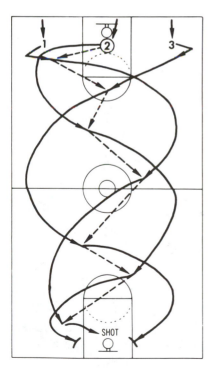

**DIAGRAM 7-26** Floor Length #12— Weave (Tight and Loose).

**Floor Length #13—Down the Middle** (Diag. 7-27).   This starts as in #12, but, when the man who starts the drill (2) gets the ball back, he drives it down the middle and makes a pass off to one of the flankers and all react as in the previous two drills.

**Floor Length #14—Front and Side** (Diag. 7-28).   The middle man starts the drill as in #13, but one of the flankers starts at the top of key instead of on the side. The rebounder passes to the side man (1) who passes to 3 who has faked down the floor and then comes back to meet the pass from 1. In this diagram, 3 passes to 2 who drives the ball down the middle with 1 and 3 filling the lanes. However, 3 may fake to 2 and hand off to 1 who drives it down the middle or passes to 2 who drives it down the middle. In either case, the other men fill the proper lanes. Also, 3 upon receiving the pass from 1 may fake to both 2 and 1 and drive the ball down the middle himself.

A coach may bother 3 and force 1 to adjust by closing the outlet to 3,

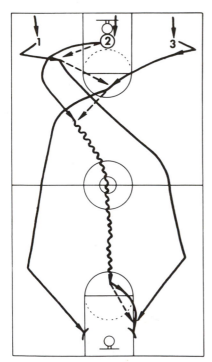

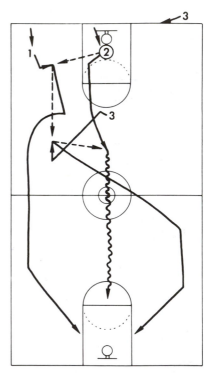

**DIAGRAM 7-27**   Floor Length #13—Down the Middle.

**DIAGRAM 7-28**   Floor Length #14—Front and Side.

or may defense 3 in such a way after he receives the ball from 1 that he is forced to make some specific move.

This is an excellent drill for our style of play.

**Floor Length #15—Turn and Drive Through Pinch** (Diag. 7-29). 2 tosses the ball high on the board and rebounds it. 1 and 3 pinch 2, who lowers his shoulders, pulls the ball in close for protection, and drives between the two down the floor. 1 and 3 cross behind 2 and fill the lanes.

**Floor Length #16—Long Pass (A)** (Diag. 7-30). 2 rebounds his own toss off the board and passes out to one side or the other. The flanker on the opposite side breaks for the basket to receive a long pass from the man who received the pass from the rebounder. The other two men break fast to try and catch the ball before it hits the floor after the shot.

As in the other drills the players must keep alternating positions to get practice from every spot.

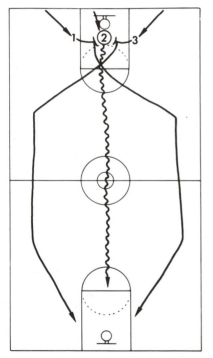

**DIAGRAM 7-29** Floor Length #15—Turn and Drive Through Pinch.

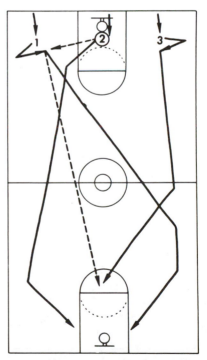

**DIAGRAM 7-30** Floor Length #16—Long Pass (A).

**Floor Length #17—Long Pass (B)** (Diag. 7-31).   The working three-some line up as in #14 with the man at the top of the key (3) faking and breaking to receive a pass as shown.

**Floor Length #18—Three-on-Three with Break** (Diag. 7-32).   This starts with the offensive men starting at the center line. They try to score, but put a press on whenever they lose the ball.

The defense breaks and tries to score at the opposite end when they obtain possession in any manner. However, I usually do not permit a long pass to be used in this drill.

As soon as the 1 and 2 groups pass the center line on the way back, the 3 and 4 groups move into position and the 5 group moves up. The 1 and 2 group move over behind the 5 line when they come off the floor with the 1 group taking the offense against the 5 group when it is their turn.

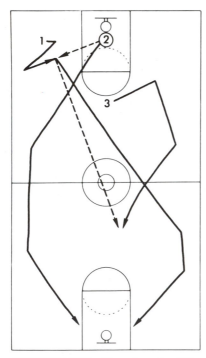

**DIAGRAM 7-31**  Floor Length #17—Long Pass (B).

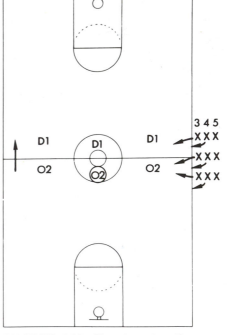

**DIAGRAM 7-32**  Floor Length #18—Three-on-Three with Break.

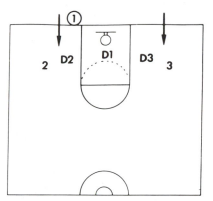

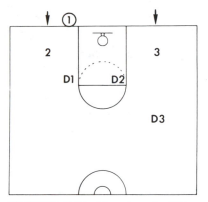

**DIAGRAM 7-33** Floor Length #19— Baseline Man-to-Man Press.

**DIAGRAM 7-34** Floor Length #20— Baseline Three-Man Zone Press.

**Floor Length #19—Baseline Man-to-Man Press** (Diag. 7-33). One threesome tries to inbound the ball against defensive pressure. The long pass is not allowed.

The offensive team tries to score at the far end and all threesomes rotate from the end line as they did in the sideline in #18. Both groups move off the floor and go to the end of the line when the offense loses the ball.

**Floor Length #20—Baseline Three-Man Zone Press** (Diag. 7-34). The defense line up as indicated and the offense try to penetrate past the center line without the use of a long pass. The threesomes keep alternating as in #19 and the defense continue the principles that we use in our regular two-two-one zone press.

**Floor Length #21—Inside Turn (One Line)** (Diag. 7-35). The players line up at one corner of the floor and the coach stands under the basket with a ball. The players start across the floor with each one keeping about ten feet in back of the one in front of him. They run with their hands above their waist, all joints relaxed, in good balance, and never take their eyes off the ball that the coach is holding.

When they get about four feet from the side, they suddenly set the left foot when they are going to the right or the right foot when they are going to the left and push off it with a quick change of pace, to execute the inside turn and go back across the floor.

The coach moves slowly straight down the floor when the last player crosses in front of him to be ready to take a position under the other basket when he is ready to start back.

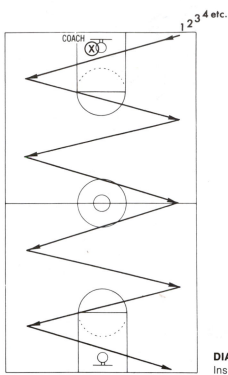

**DIAGRAM 7-35** Floor Length #21—Inside Turn (One Line).

**Floor Length #22—Inside Turn (Crossing Lines)** (Diag. 7-36). The players line up as in #21 except that one half of them are on each corner. The two lines proceed simultaneously down the floor as they did in #21. This requires split vision and quick adjustment to avoid contact with the other line and still keep the basketball within your vision.

**Floor Length #23—Diagonal Long Pass** (Diag. 7-37). The players divide up as equally as possible in the four corners as indicated. The first man in corner 1 and the first man in corner 2 both have a ball. 1 passes diagonally the length of the court to the first man in corner 3 and moves to the end of the line in corner 2, as the first man in corner 2 passes to the first man in line from corner 4 and moves to the end of the line in corner 3. The 3 man passes back to the 1 line and goes to the end of the 4 line as the 4 man passes back to the 2 line and goes to the end of the 4 line.

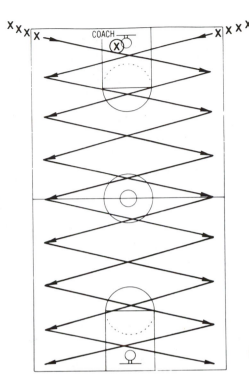

**DIAGRAM** 7-36 Floor Length #22—
Inside Turn (Crossing Lines).

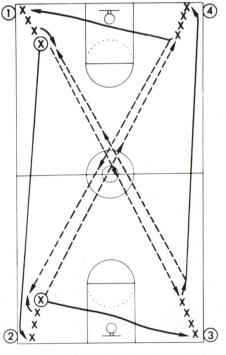

**DIAGRAM** 7-37 Floor Length #23—
Diagonal Long Pass.

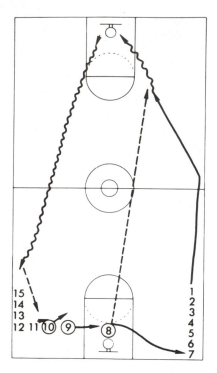

**DIAGRAM 7-38** Floor Length #24—Long Pass from the Board.

**Floor Length #24—Long Pass from the Board** (Diag. 7-38). The players line up as indicated in the diagram with 8, 9, and 10 each having a ball and 1 lined up on the side approximately one step farther out than the foul line extended.

As 8 tosses the ball high on the board, 1 breaks down the sideline and then cuts toward the basket when he gets a few feet past the center line.

8 tries to complete a baseball or long hook pass to 1 and then goes to the end of the line from which 1 broke. 1 tries to receive the pass, score, retrieve the ball, and speed-dribble to the end of the line on the other side of the floor, and pass to the first man in that line without a ball.

As soon as 8 passes, 9 moves over to take his place and 2 moves up to take the place of 1 when he cuts. Each man keeps moving up to take the place of the man who vacates the spot in front of him.

After a while the cutting line should move to the left side of the floor.

**Floor Length #25—One-on-One—Conditioner** (Diag. 7-39). Place a coach with a ball under the basket at each end. The players line up as indicated with the defense about three feet ahead of the offense. When

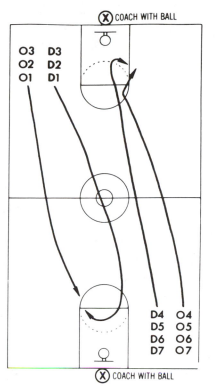

DIAGRAM 7-39 Floor Length #25—
One-on-One—Conditioner.

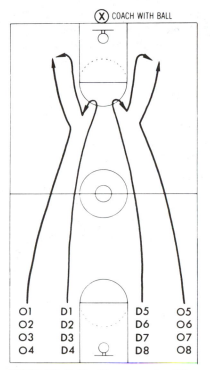

DIAGRAM 7-40 Floor Length #26—
Two-on-Two—Conditioner.

the coach signals the start, the offensive man at each end breaks for the other end to receive a pass from the coach there in an attempt to score. The ball is passed back to the coach when the offensive man scores, when the defensive man gets possession, or when the coach calls for it. The instant the ball is returned to the coach the next pair in line at the opposite end break.

When a pair has finished, they go to the end of the line where they just finished. The offensive and defensive men change assignments after each round, but not after one length.

**Floor Length #26—Two-on-Two—Conditioner** (Diag. 7-40). A coach stands under the basket at one end with a ball and the players line up in four lines at the other end in the offensive and defensive positions as indicated. When the coach signals for the start, the offensive men break for the other end in an attempt to receive a pass and score and the defense break back to prevent that happening. When the ball is returned to the coach under the same conditions as in #25, the next foursome in line break and the foursome who just finished go back down the floor outside the sidelines to the end of the line, but change assignments.

**Floor Length #27—Three-on-Two—Conditioner** (Diag. 7-41). This is a variation of a drill that I saw described by Mike Harkins of Eastern Montana State College and have used to great advantage. It is a fine conditioner as well as providing near-game condition situations for the execution of the finish of the fast break and for defending in the three-against-two situation.

You need at least twelve players for this drill and my squad of fifteen make up a good number for it.

They line up as indicated in the diagram. 1 starts the play by rebounding the ball off the board and passing to 2 or 3 and the three of them fill lanes and advance the ball quickly down the court in any manner. As 1 rebounds the ball, 9 moves out and takes a deep spot near the basket and 10 takes a spot in the outer half of the foul circle. When all three offensive men have passed the center line, 11 comes in from the sideline and touches one foot in the center circle and then comes back to help defensively. This forces the three offensive men to attack the two defensive men quickly and get a good shot before the extra defensive man gets there to make it three-on-three.

When the offense scores or loses the ball in any manner, they get off the floor and go to the end of the line at the side.

The three defensive men, 9, 10, and 11, now become offensive men and break for the other end as 4 and 5 move out on defense at the other end and 6 becomes the late defensive man.

The drill progresses in this manner and the coach must be alert for many things in this fast-moving, action-packed drill. Occasionally, we have the man who scores put on a nuisance one-man press to keep the new offense alert.

**Floor Length #28—Team Weave** (Diag. 7-42). The teams line up five abreast as shown with the man in the middle rebounding the ball off the board to start the movement. He then passes to one of the men nearest to him and goes behind the receiver and one other man and then cuts back toward the center as does every passer.

I like to have them finish with a jump shot at the other end and have all rebounding positions covered. This means a rebounder on each side of the board, one directly in front, one in the circle area, and a protector.

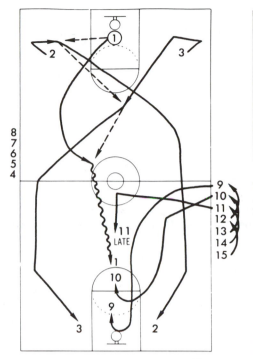

**DIAGRAM 7-41** Floor Length #27— Three-on-Two—Conditioner.

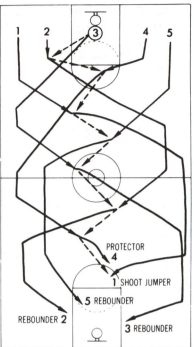

**DIAGRAM 7-42** Floor Length #28— Team Weave.

## PASSING AND RECEIVING

Since all offenses are designed to get good shots and this can be accomplished only through good passing, proper execution of the various passes must be stressed constantly. Almost every drill in which a ball is used involves passing and it must never be taken for granted regardless of the principal purpose of the drill.

Many comments and suggestions in regard to this phase of the game are found in Chapter 3, but I would like to repeat and reemphasize some of them.

1. Passing.

   **(a)** The passes should be crisp and accurate. They should be neither too hard nor too easy and should be above the waist and below the shoulders of the receiver.

   **(b)** The passes should be made quickly through or by the opponent rather than around or over them.

**(c)** Accuracy must be stressed with maximum quickness.

**(d)** Deception must be used, but fanciness and carelessness must be eliminated.

**(e)** As hesitation after making a pass is a major fault, the passer must move quickly after making a pass.

**(f)** The passer must always have a target, such as the outside shoulder, and never merely pass to the man.

2. Receiving.

**(a)** The hands should be kept above the waist with the fingers spread and relaxed.

**(b)** The ball is blocked with one hand with the fingers well spread and the other hand tucks the ball as contact is made.

**(c)** The eyes must follow the ball all of the way into the hands.

**(d)** The potential receiver must work to get open to receive a pass in an advantageous floor position at the right time. Think ahead—don't stand and wait for the ball.

**(e)** The receiver must be ready to do something immediately upon receiving a pass.

3. Some causes of fumbling.

**(a)** The receiver takes his eyes off the ball.

**(b)** The receiver tries to do something with the ball before he catches it.

**(c)** The receiver is too tense and fights the ball.

**(d)** The receiver was not ready.

**(e)** The passer got fancy.

**(f)** The pass was too hard, or too easy, or inaccurate.

**(g)** Loss of temper, self-control, poise, or condition.

In the drills that are to follow the coach should emphasize:

1. Accuracy without telegraphing.

2. Quickness with wrist and finger snap.

3. Crispness.

4. Proper lead and proper target.

5. Timing of passer and receiver.

6. Keeping the hands above the waist, fingers spread and hands ready.

7. Keeping the ball protected.

8. Keeping body balance.

9. Usage of the proper pass.

10. Proper execution.

11. Proper cutting with the necessary fakes and changes of direction and pace.

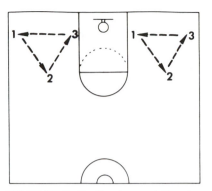

DIAGRAM 7-43  Passing and Receiving #1—Triangle.

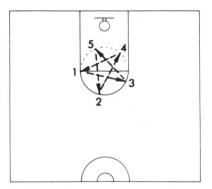

DIAGRAM 7-44  Passing and Receiving #2—Diagonal.

**12.**   The use of a semi-active defensive man to bother the passer in team offensive setups.

**Passing and Receiving #1—Triangle** (Diag. 7-43).   The players divide into groups of three with each group forming a triangle with the players about 15 feet apart. The ball is moved quickly from one to another with the direction being changed frequently.

Various types of passes are used with the coach designating the type that he wants used and when a change is to be made. Some time is spent on the use of the right hand, left hand, and two hands whenever applicable.

**1.**   Push pass.

**2.**   Shoulder pass.

**3.**   Hip pass.

**4.**   Overhead pass.

**5.**   Hand-off pass.

**6.**   Tip pass.

**7.**   Hook pass.

**8.**   Roll pass.

The bounce pass is also practiced where applicable.

**Passing and Receiving #2—Diagonal** (Diag. 7-44).   Five players get evenly spaced around and one step back of each of the three circles. Quick passes are made diagonally across the circle with all types being practiced.

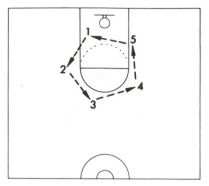 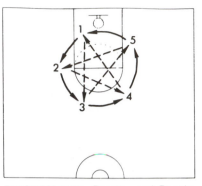

**DIAGRAM 7-45** Passing and Receiving #3—Circle—Around.

**DIAGRAM 7-46** Passing and Receiving #4—Circle—Moving.

**Passing and Receiving #3—Circle Around** (Diag. 7-45). Line up as in #2. The passes are now made around the circle with the passer passing in either direction. Various passes are used.

**Passing and Receiving #4—Circle Moving** (Diag. 7-46). Line up as in #2. The passes are now made across the circle as the players are now on the move. When the coach gives some designated signal, the players quickly change direction.

**Passing and Receiving #5—Double Circle—Moving** (Diag. 7-47). Six men line up around the foul or center circle and nine men form a circle about eight feet outside of them. The circles move in opposite directions and keep two balls moving constantly from one circle to the other. When the coach gives some designated signal, both circles change direction.

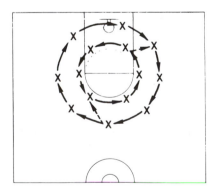

**DIAGRAM 7-47** Passing and Receiving #5—Double Circle—Moving.

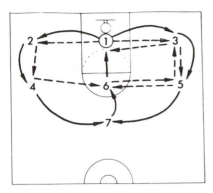

**DIAGRAM 7-48** Passing and Receiving #6—Around and Back.

**Passing and Receiving #6—Around and Back** (Diag. 7-48). The squad lines up as designated in the diagram at two different baskets.

1 has the ball and passes to 2 and takes his place, 2 passes to 4 and takes his place, 4 passes to 6 and moves out behind 7, 6 passes to 5 and moves toward the basket, 5 passes to 3 and holds his position, 3 passes to 6 who rebounds the ball and passes back to 3 and takes his place. The play now proceeds as before, except it is moving the opposite way.

**Passing and Receiving #7—Chaser in the Circle** (Diag. 7-49). Six or seven men space themselves around a foul circle and then move one step back. Another man gets in the center of the circle as a defensive man. Passes are made across the circle with the inside man attempting to deflect or intercept a pass. A passer who fails to complete his pass exchanges positions with the man in the center.

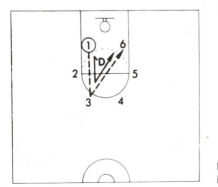

**DIAGRAM 7-49** Passing and Receiving #7—Chaser in Circle.

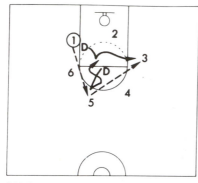

**DIAGRAM 7-50** Passing and Receiving #8—Two Chasers in Circle.

**DIAGRAM 7-51** Passing and Receiving #9—Meet the Bounce.

**Passing and Receiving #8—Two Chasers in Circle** (Diag. 7-50). This drill is the same as #7 except that you place two defensive men inside the circle and make the circle a little larger.

**Passing and Receiving #9—Meet the Bounce** (Diag. 7-51). Using only one half of the court, an equal number of players go to each corner. The first man in the 1 corner and the first man in the 2 corner have a ball. The man with a ball makes a bounce pass to the first man in line facing and then moves quickly to the end of the line to his right. The drill continues with the potential receiver always moving forward to receive the bounce pass.

Good judgment must be used and fakes must be used to prevent the balls contacting each other.

**Passing and Receiving #10—Cross-Court Snap** (Diag. 7-52). Two groups of players line up as indicated and two chairs are placed as indicated. The man with the ball passes across court to the first man in the line facing him, fakes one way, and then cuts back between the two chairs and goes to the end of the opposite line.

The drill continues back and forth in the same manner.

**Passing and Receiving #11—Guard to Reverser** (Diag. 7-53). The squad lines up as indicated with each guard having a ball. As the guard starts dribbling forward, the man in the forward position makes an inside turn for a quick reverse to receive a pass going under. The reverser then moves to pass under. The reverser then moves to the other side of the floor to make the same move from the opposite side

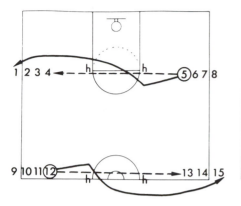

**DIAGRAM 7-52** Passing and Receiving #10—Cross-Court Snap.

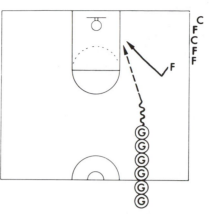

**DIAGRAM 7-53** Passing and Receiving #11—Guard to Reverser.

when the others have had their turn. The guard retrieves the ball and moves back out front to be ready when his turn comes up again.

**Passing and Receiving #12—Guard to Post to Guard to Post** (Diag. 7-54). The three centers line up as indicated and keep changing positions C1 to C2 to C3 to C1. The rest of the squad line up out in front in two lines with the first man in each line having a ball.

The pass is made to the post man and the passer receives a return pass after faking inside and cutting outside. He then takes one or two dribbles and passes back to the post man who fakes a shot and then passes to the guard coming back who passes to the first man in line from where he came and goes to the end of the opposite line.

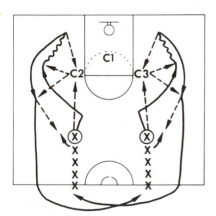

**DIAGRAM 7-54** Passing and Receiving #12—Guard to Post to Guard to Post.

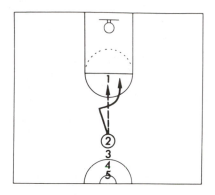

**DIAGRAM 7-55** Passing and Receiving #13—To Post and Alternate.

**Passing and Receiving #13—To Post and Alternate** (Diag. 7-55).   Each of three groups of five line up as indicated. The front man passes to the post man and makes a cut for some potential two man play. After the score, the post man goes to the end of the line out front and the original passer moves to the post.

We often have the next passing guard take a defensive position on the passing guard and bother the passer *some*. Some of the options that can be used are:

**1.**   The cutter may receive a return pass and drive for a shot, make a quick stop for a short jump, fake a shot and pass back to the post man for a shot, make a quick stop and turn and pass back to the post man for a short, or make a quick stop and turn and fake a pass to the post man and take a quick shot himself.

**2.**   The cutter may receive a fake going by the post and then receive a delayed pass underneath.

**3.**   The passer may fake a cut and step back for a return pass and a quick jump shot, or for a quick drive after faking the shot.

**4.**   The post man may fake to the cutter and get some type of shot himself.

**5.**   The post man may make a quick reverse drive for a shot underneath as soon as he receives the pass.

**6.**   The post man may turn quickly and face the basket immediately upon receiving the pass and then maneuver for a shot.

**Passing and Receiving #14—To Post and Screen for Forward** (Diag. 7-56).   The squad lines up as indicated. The centers will keep alternating and the forwards and guards will always go to the end of the line opposite of their respective positions. The guard passes to the post and cuts straight forward for a couple of steps and then moves quickly to set an inside screen for the forward to come across. The guard then

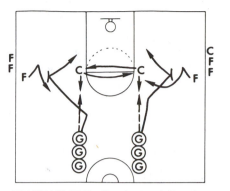

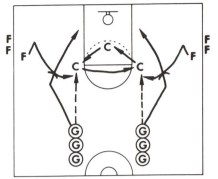

**DIAGRAM 7-56** Passing and Receiving #14—To Post and Screen for Forward.

**DIAGRAM 7-57** Passing and Receiving #15—To Post and Cut Off Forward.

rolls for the basket. The forward must fake back to set up his man for the screen as he comes back quickly.

**Passing and Receiving #15—To Post and Cut Off Forward** (Diag. 7-57).   The squad lines up the same as in #14 and the drill starts the same way. However, the passing guard now moves directly toward the forward spot and the forward comes out to screen for the guard and then rolls across.

**Passing and Receiving #16—To Post and Screen for Guard** (Diag. 7-58).   The guards pair up with one of each pair having a ball. The pass is made to the post man and the passer moves over to set a side screen for the other guard and then rolls back. The post man hits the first one through for a short jump or the out one for a jump from back of

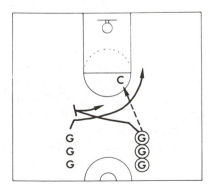

**DIAGRAM 7-58** Passing and Receiving #16—To Post and Screen for Guard.

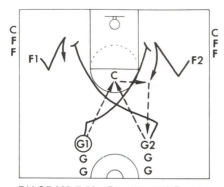

**DIAGRAM 7-59** Passing and Receiving #17—To Post and Screen for Opposite Lane.

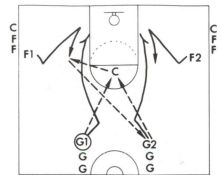

**DIAGRAM 7-60** Passing and Receiving #18—To Post and Screen Down Lane.

the circle area. The post man may move around and be hit on either side of the key.

**Passing and Receiving #17—To Post and Screen Down Opposite Lane** (Diag. 7-59).   The squad lines up as indicated. The centers alternate on the post with the extras working at forward until they take a turn on the post.

G1 passes to post, moves forward slowly, and then suddenly cuts across and screens down the opposite lane for F2 who has reversed. C turns to face the basket when he receives the pass and passes to the forward coming off the screen by the guard who passed to him. The forward who receives the pass from the center turns toward the basket and fakes a shot and then passes out quickly to the first guard in line on his side. This guard quickly passes to the post and the play resumes in the same manner with the center now having received the ball from the guard on the other side. The forwards and guard go to the end of the other line of their respective positions.

**Passing and Receiving #18—To Post and Screen Down Lane** (Diag. 7-60).   The squad lines up as in #17, but the guard who passes to the post now fakes across and then cuts down the lane on his side to screen for the forward who has reversed. C faces the basket when he receives the pass, fakes a shot, and passes to the forward coming off the screen. The forward who receives the pass from the post turns to face the basket and fakes a shot, and then passes to the first guard in line on the opposite side. This guard quickly passes to the post and the drill continues as before.

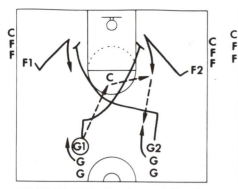

**DIAGRAM 7-61** Passing and Receiving #19—To Post and Guards Cross and Screen.

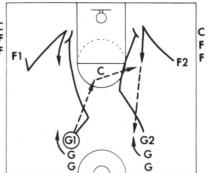

**DIAGRAM 7-62** Passing and Receiving #20—To Post and Guards Screen Down Lanes.

**Passing and Receiving #19—To Post and Guards Cross and Screen** (Diag. 7-61). The squad lines up as in #17, but now both guards cut and both forwards reverse. The guard who passes to the center cuts as he does in #17 and the other guard does the same thing as if he had passed the ball. However, the second guard must cut behind the passing guard as he crosses over to screen down the opposite lane. The post man turns to face the basket when he receives the pass and, after faking a shot, he passes to the forward for whom the passing guard has screened. This forward turns quickly when he receives the pass and fakes a shot. He then passes quickly to the first guard in line on his side. This guard passes quickly to the post and the same procedure as before is followed with the post man having received the pass from the opposite side.

Forwards and guards keep rotating sides and the post man receives about six passes before alternating with one of the centers working at forward.

**Passing and Receiving #20—To Post and Screen Down Lanes** (Diag. 7-62). The squad lines up as in #19, and the drill works the same except that the guard now fakes a cross and screens down his lane. In actual game situations the forward who does not receive the pass from the post becomes the safety man in the #19 and #20 setups.

**Passing and Receiving #21—To Post with Guards Crossing and Forwards Also Crossing Underneath** (Diag. 7-63). This is identical to #19 except that the forwards cross underneath the basket and come around a screen by the guard on the opposite side of the lane. The

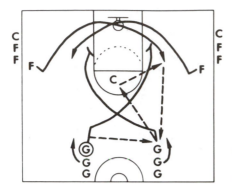

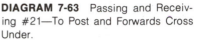

**DIAGRAM 7-63** Passing and Receiving #21—To Post and Forwards Cross Under.

forwards cross *to the right and underneath*. This must be made clear to avoid collisions.

**Passing and Receiving #22—To Post, Guards Cross and Recross** (Diag. 7-64).  The squad lines up as in #21, but the guard who passes to the post now screens for the other guard and moves a step or two away. The guard who cuts off the screen suddenly stops and comes back to screen for the guard who just screened for him and they each go down the lane to which they are nearest to screen for the forwards who have reversed.

In actual game conditions this gives the forwards some time to maneuver against their man underneath to get open for a pass from the post man and a short shot. If they do not get a pass, they come back off the guard screen for a pass.

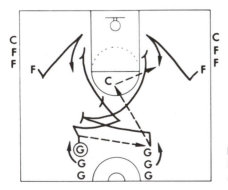

**DIAGRAM 7-64** Passing and Receiving #22—To Post and Guards Cross and Recross.

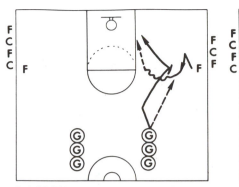

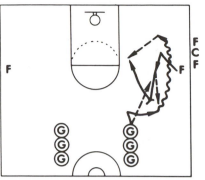

**DIAGRAM 7-65** Passing and Receiving #23—To Forward and Screen and Roll.

**DIAGRAM 7-66** Passing and Receiving #24—To Forward to Guard and Screen and Roll.

**Passing and Receiving #23—Guard Follows Pass to Forward to Screen and Roll** (Diag. 7-65).   The squad lines up as in the diagram with each guard having a ball. The guard passes to the forward, moves forward slowly and then suddenly cuts toward the imaginary guard on the forward, screens as the forward fakes to drive across, and then rolls for the basket to receive a pass from the forward for a shot. The first guard in line on the opposite side passes to the forward as the working pair take the shot and they start.

Although I like all boys to get some work at all positions, usually the boys alternate in the lines of their own position.

**Passing and Receiving #24—Forward to Guard for Screen and Roll** (Diag. 7-66).   The squad lines up as in #23, but the guard who passes to the forward fakes a cut and steps back to receive a return pass from the forward.

When the forward passes back to the guard, he follows his pass to screen, and then rolls for the basket as the guard drives off his screen. The guard now passes to the forward as he rolls for the basket to get a quick shot underneath. The drill continues back and forth as in #23.

**Passing and Receiving #25—Forward to Guard and Reverse for a Return Pass** (Diag. 7-67).   The squad lines up as in #24 and the drill starts in the same way. However, when the forward returns the pass to the guard, he now fakes a step to follow his pass, but suddenly re-

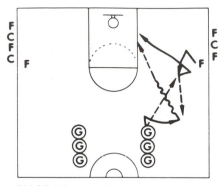

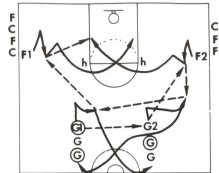

**DIAGRAM 7-67** Passing and Receiving #25—Forward to Guard and Reverse.

**DIAGRAM 7-68** Passing and Receiving #26—Box Exchange.

verses by use of the inside turn as the guard dribbles toward him. The guard then passes to him for a shot.

The continuity is the same as in the others.

**Passing and Receiving #26—Box Exchange** (Diag. 7-68). The players line up as indicated in the diagram with a chair placed in each side of the foul circle just outside the point where the foul line touches the circle. Each pair of guards has a ball with the play starting from alternate sides each time. The quick progression of passes goes as follows—G1 to G2 to F2 to G2 to G1 to F1 to F2.

The players fake away and come back to receive a pass as indicated. When a forward passes back out to the guard, he fakes baseline and then comes back to cut between the two chairs to receive a pass from the other forward. When the forward makes the pass to the other forward who has cut between the chairs, he fakes back and then cuts hard across and between the two chairs.

Both guards and forwards keep alternating in their respective lines.

**Passing and Receiving #27—Guard Outside for a Return Pass from Forward** (Diag. 7-69). The players line up as indicated in the diagram with first one side working and then the other. The working pair always move to the opposite side of the floor after they have shot and retrieved the ball.

The guard passes to the forward and moves forward slowly and then suddenly cuts sharply outside the forward and receives a return pass

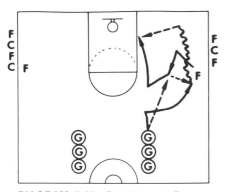

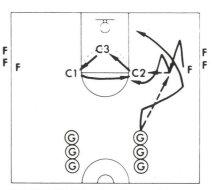

**DIAGRAM 7-69** Passing and Receiving #27—Guard Outside for a Return Pass from Forward.

**DIAGRAM 7-70** Passing and Receiving #28—the Ancient Guard Around.

as he goes by. The forward then moves toward the top of the foul circle, but suddenly reverses and cuts toward the basket to receive a return pass from the guard who has dribbled toward the baseline.

Keep the same rotation and continuity as in #25.

**Passing and Receiving #28—The Ancient Guard Around** (Diag. 7-70). The players line up as indicated in the diagram with the drill working on first one side and then the other and the centers alternating from one post position to the other as indicated.

The guard passes to the forwards and makes his fake and cut as before, but the forward now fakes to him going by and passes to the post, fakes back, and cuts toward the key. The post man may pass to either one for a shot or fake and get the shot himself.

The play is started on the opposite side of the floor as soon as the working group takes the shot.

**Passing and Receiving #29—Guard to Forward to Center to Guard or Forward** (Diag. 7-71). The players line up as indicated in the diagram. The guard passes to the forward and moves forward slowly and then suddenly cuts sharply off the center and down the lane. When the pass goes to the forward, the center immediately crosses over and faces the end line and holds that position until the guard has cut by him. He then fakes toward baseline, but moves to the side of the circle and receives a pass from the forward.

When the forward passes to the post, he cuts toward the end line to form a screen for the guard to come around. The post man may pass to the guard coming around the screen or to the forward rolling for the basket.

The drill continues from one side of the floor to the other and the players keep alternating the sides on which they work.

**Passing and Receiving #30—Guard to Forward to Guard to Center or Forward** (Diag. 7-72). The drill is the same as #29, except that the forward now passes to the guard coming out the baseline and screens for the post man. The guard passes to the post man or to the forward rolling for the basket.

**Passing and Receiving #31—Weak-Side Post** (Diag. 7-73). The players line up as indicated with both sides working at the same time. The guards pass to the side post to the men who have faked and come to that position. The guards fake inside and then cut sharply to the outside of the post as if they are trying to run their defensive man into their side-post teammate. The post men hand off to the cutting guards and raise their hands chin high to receive a quick return pass from the guard. They return the pass quickly to the guard and rotate to the next position as the guard dribbles out to the end of the opposite guard line.

**Passing and Receiving #32—Side-Post Continuity Without Post** (Diag. 7-74). G1 passes to G2 and fakes away before coming back toward the center of the floor. G2 passes to F2 and cuts down the lane with a good change of pace. F2 passes out to G1 and cuts down toward baseline to screen for G2, G1 passes to F1, who has faked back and come to side post, and cuts off of him. F1 passes out to the first guard in the G2 line and he passes to the first man in the G1 line. This man now passes to the man in the forward position and the drill continues.

This is a fine game-condition passing drill for us and is an excellent warmup drill if you gradually increase the tempo.

**Passing and Receiving #33—Team Side-Post Continuity** (Diag. 7-75). This drill works exactly the same as #32 except that the post man has been added and carries out his assignment. We also use only four forwards and one center and have the additional ones make ten free throws at a side basket and then replace someone who then does the same.

Occasionally the team will be permitted to shoot, but the main purpose of the drill is to develop fast and proper ball-handling timed with the cutting in the "bread-and-butter" part of our offense.

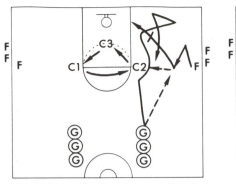

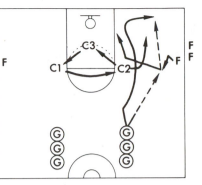

**DIAGRAM 7-71** Passing and Receiving #29—To Forward to Center to Guard or Forward.

**DIAGRAM 7-72** Passing and Receiving #30—To Forward to Guard to Forward or Center.

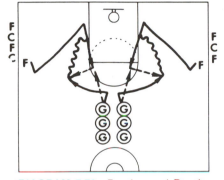

**DIAGRAM 7-73** Passing and Receiving #31—Weak-Side Post Cuts.

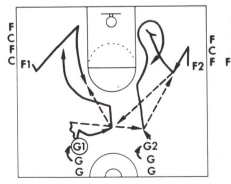

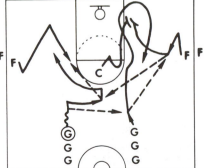

**DIAGRAM 7-74** Passing and Receiving #32—Side Post Without Center.

**DIAGRAM 7-75** Passing and Receiving #33—Team Side-Post Continuity.

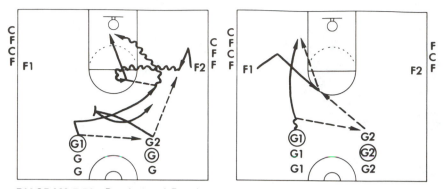

**DIAGRAM 7-76** Passing and Receiving #34—To Forward and Cross Screen.

**DIAGRAM 7-77** Passing and Receiving #35—Back-Door Cut.

**Passing and Receiving #34—Cross Screens** (Diag. 7-76). The squad lines up as indicated in the diagram and work the drill from first one side of the floor and then the other. G1 passes to G2 and fakes away. G2 passes to F2 and crosses to screen for G1. F2 dribbles across to the top of the key and hands off to G2 who dribbles down the lane and then makes a quick pass back to F2 who faked out and cut back toward the basket after handing off.

**Passing and Receiving #35—Back Door Cut** (Diag. 7-77). The squad lines up as indicated in the diagram to start the drill. As G1 passes to G2, F1 fakes back and cuts toward the foul circle to receive a quick pass from G2. As G2 passes to F1, G1 gets a running start and receives a quick pass from F1 as he cuts for the basket. The drill is then continued back and forth from one side of the floor to the other.

## PASSIVE DEFENSE IN THE DRILLS

Although it was not shown in the "Passing and Receiving" diagrams, the next offensive man in line may often be used as a standing or passive defensive man in both the passing and receiving lines to create more gamelike conditions for getting the pass away, getting open, and receiving the pass in drills such as #11, #12, and #13 (passing line only), #14 and #15 (guard and forward lines), #16 through #23 (guard lines only), #24, #25, #26, #27, #29 through #35 (guard lines only).

## FIELD-GOAL SHOOTING

In the final analysis no offense will be effective if the players can not "get the ball through the basket"; therefore, it is important to stress shooting drills every day of practice and shooting practice whenever a shot is taken regardless of any particular drill emphasis.

Many of the drills under "Passing" combine game-condition shooting, and many passing drills in themselves incorporate the fundamentals of shooting.

### Ten Physical Fundamentals To Teach

**1.** Keeping the ball at chest level and close to the body with the elbows in.

**2.** Use of fingertip control, although some parts of the palm may be in slight contact with the ball, and good wrist and elbow action.

**3.** Quickness of getting the shot away.

**4.** Medium arch with natural spin for most shots.

**5.** Eyeing the target, which is the out-of-view top of the rim nearest to the shooter.

**6.** Keeping the back of the shooting hand toward the face and the palm toward the target.

**7.** The forefinger providing the last impetus.

**8.** Maintenance of balance and takeoff on the proper foot, which is usually the opposite foot from the shooting hand.

**9.** Usually, on jump, push, or set shots, you should complete a shot moving slightly forward with the head moving directly toward the target.

**10.** On all driving shots, the shooter must land properly and then get back onto the floor and into the play quickly.

### Five Mental Suggestions

**1.** Confidence and concentration are necessary.

**2.** Practice on game condition shots that you will be able to get and should take. Do not waste practice time on shots that you should not take or will not get.

**3.** Find the form that suits you best and work to develop it. Do not experiment continuously.

**4.** Devote extra time to the development of the shots that you are most likely to get.

**5.** Know your range and ability for a proper selection of shots.

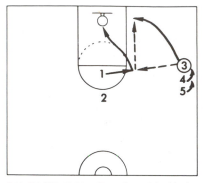

DIAGRAM 7-78 Shooting #1—Under Basket.

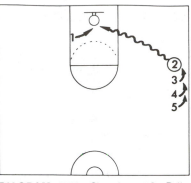

DIAGRAM 7-79 Shooting #2—Dribble Drives.

**Shooting #1—Under Basket from the Move** (Diag. 7-78). The squads line up with five at a basket as indicated in the diagram. The side man passes to the man on the post and cuts for a return pass for the shot. The shooter and passer retrieve the ball before it can touch the floor, pass it back to the sideline, and exchange lines. After a man has worked in both positions, he goes to the opposite side of the floor in order for the drill to continue back and forth from one side to the other.

The following types of shots are practiced from each side of the floor by use of this drill:

1. Quick layup after a head fake to the inside.
2. Quick stop and fadeaway from a few feet out.
3. All the way under for the hook.
4. All the way under for the lay-back.
5. All the way under and from behind the board for the reach-back.

**Shooting #2—Dribble Drives from Side** (Diag. 7-79). The squad lines up with five at a basket as indicated in the diagram. The man underneath rebounds the ball, passes out, and goes to the end of the line. The shooter stays under to rebound for the next driver.

The same shots that were practiced in #1 are also practiced in this drill and from each side of the floor.

**Shooting #3—Dribble Drives from the Front** (Diag. 7-80). The players line up with five at a basket as indicated with one man under to rebound and pass out and the driver remaining under to do the same for the next man.

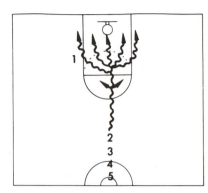

**DIAGRAM 7-80** Shooting #3—Dribble Drives.

The following drives are practiced:

**1.** All the way under to the right or left with a head fake and a quick layup or twister.

**2.** Straight at the basket for a "dunk," if you can do so without undue strain or merely lay the ball over the front rim.

**3.** A semihook from close under.

**4.** A pull-away for a quick shot off the board from just outside the lane.

**5.** A quick stop for a quick jump or a fadeaway from inside the foul line.

**Shooting #4—Set and Fake Set and Drive for a Quick Jump** (Diag. 7-81). The squad lines up with five at a basket and with each group using two balls. The shooter takes a quick shot, retrieves the ball, makes a quick and accurate pass to a teammate, and then moves out to a different spot from where he just shot.

Competition between the three groups of five to see which group can make a designated number first is used a lot.

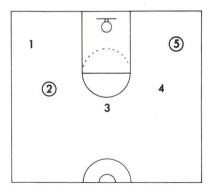

**DIAGRAM 7-81** Shooting #4—Set and Fake Set for Quick Jump.

**1.** The quick medium-distance set.

**2.** The jump after faking the set and making a quick start for one or two dribbles.

**3.** The quick pull back for a quick set after faking a drive.

**4.** The quick fadeaway after a quick stop from a drive. This will be from in a little closer than for the quick stop and jump. The rocker step may be practiced for the start.

**Shooting #5—Set and Jump with Two Rebounders** (Diag. 7-82). The squad lines up with three shooters and two rebounders at each basket and each group uses two balls. The rebounders retrieve and pass out quickly until ten shots have been made and then exchange positions with two shooters. The same shots are practiced as in #4 and it is a competitive drill between the three groups of five. We usually see which group will be the first to make thirty.

**Shooting #6—Quick Spot** (Diag. 7-83). The squad lines up in three groups of five at one basket as indicated with the first man in each line having a ball.

The quick shot is taken with the shooter rebounding his own shot and passing it back to the next man who has moved up to take his place.

This is a competitive drill with fifteen being the magic winning number as a rule.

When one team wins, they exchange positions and start over until each group has had a turn from all three positions. Each line may shoot from a step or two to either their right or left.

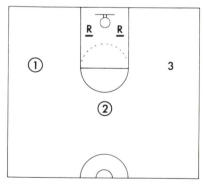

**DIAGRAM 7-82** Shooting #5—Set and Fake Set with Rebounders.

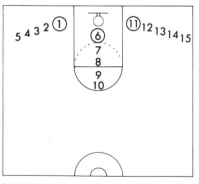

**DIAGRAM 7-83** Shooting #6—Quick Spot.

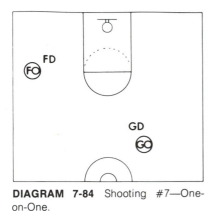

DIAGRAM 7-84 Shooting #7—One-on-One.

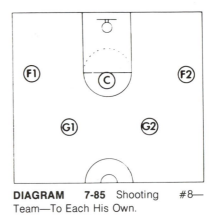

DIAGRAM 7-85 Shooting #8—Team—To Each His Own.

**Shooting #7—One-on-One** (Diag. 7-84).  The squad pairs up with not over two pairs at any one basket. Each pair starts with the shooter in his normal offensive position and the defensive being quite passive. Later the defense will become active.

The offensive and defensive man alternate after every shot until the defense becomes active. Then the offense takes five turns and keeps score before changing, with the idea being to see which one can score the most points in the five turns. A defensive foul gives the offense two points and an offensive foul constitutes one turn.

**Shooting #8—To Each His Own** (Diag. 7-85).  Occasionally each player will have a ball and work for a while on his own on the type of shots that he seems to be getting in game conditions. I prefer having not over three to a basket and try to keep as many different positions represented at each basket as is possible.

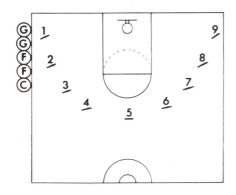

DIAGRAM 7-86 Shooting #9—Team—Nine-Hole Golf—Par 18.

**Shooting #9—Team Nine-Hole Golf—Par 18** (Diag. 7-86). The squad lines up with five at a basket as indicated with each one having a ball. Each man shoots until he scores from each of the nine indicated spots. The three teams are competing against each other for the lowest team score and each player competes with the members of his team for the lowest individual score.

**Shooting #10—Forward Drives** (Diag. 7-87). The forwards line up in the forward positions with half on one side and half on the other. The first man in each line has a ball. If the man on the left side starts first, the man on the right side waits until he takes the shot and then starts. The shooter retrieves the ball after shooting, passes back to the side from which he drove, and then goes to the end of the opposite line.

The drivers use the quick start from a head fake or rocker fake and drive to one of the indicated spots for the shot. They must practice on drives to both the left and right from each side of the floor.

While the forwards are working at one basket, the guards and centers will be at different baskets working on a shooting drill for their position.

**Shooting #11—Forward Drives to the Far Side Underneath** (Diag. 7-88). The forwards line up as in #10, and alternate from side to side as before. The coach designates for one side to fake inside and drive baseline while the other side fakes baseline and drives toward the foul circle and then down the lane to the far side.

The baseline drives work on hooks, lay-backs, and reach-backs and the opposite line works on semihooks, lay-backs, or quick stops combined with a head fake or a pivot before the shot.

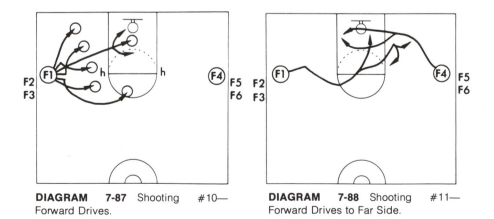

DIAGRAM 7-87 Shooting #10—
Forward Drives.

DIAGRAM 7-88 Shooting #11—
Forward Drives to Far Side.

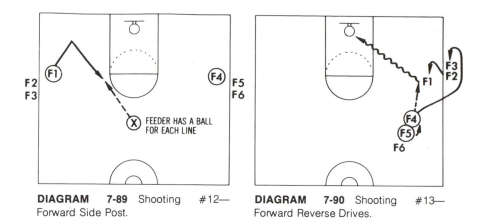

**DIAGRAM 7-89** Shooting #12—Forward Side Post.

**DIAGRAM 7-90** Shooting #13—Forward Reverse Drives.

**Shooting #12—Forwards on Side Post** (Diag. 7-89). The forwards line up as in #10 and #11 with a coach or one of the guards lined up out in front as a feeder with a ball for each line. The forward reverses toward the basket and then suddenly changes direction by a quick push off of the baseline foot and comes to the side post for a shot. The opposite forward makes his move when the active forward takes his shot. The shooter retrieves his own shot and makes a good pass out to the feeder when the feeder is ready to receive and then goes to the end of the opposite line.

The receiver on the side post uses both cross-overs and reverse turns to face the basket and then gets one of the various possible side-post shots after making the proper fake and (or) move.

**Shooting #13—Forward Reverse Drives** (Diag. 7-90). The forwards line up as indicated in the diagram with the first two in the guard position line, each having a ball.

The pass is made to the normal forward position and he swings his outside leg back quickly and drives for the basket to use any one of the driving shots underneath or a quick stop and jump or fadeaway shot. The shooter retrieves his shot and passes the ball out and both men exchange lines.

Work back and forth from one side of the floor to the other after each man has had a shot from one side.

**Shooting #14—Forward Reverse Cuts** (Diag. 7-91). The forwards line up as in #13, but now the outside man starts a dribble toward the man on the side and passes to him as he makes a quick inside turn and cuts for the basket to receive a pass and gets any type of shot that might be applicable.

The cutter pushes quickly off of his sideline foot when it is forward and moves quickly for the basket as soon as he sees the outside man start a dribble.

Keep alternating sides and positions as before.

**Shooting #15—Forward Cutbacks** (Diag. 7-92). The forwards line up as indicated in the diagram with all on one side having a ball. A chair is also placed off the side of each lane as indicated. As the forward with the ball starts a dribble away from his side position, the opposite forward cuts toward the basket and cuts back up as if he were using the chair for a screen to receive a pass and get a quick shot from that area. The passer rebounds underneath with the shooter rebounding the key area. The ball is given to the shooter after the shot and the players go to the end of the opposite line from which they started.

After a while, drill is started from the opposite side of the floor.

**Shooting #16—Forward Cross Under** (Diag. 7-93). The forwards line up as in #15 and the play works exactly the same way except that the chairs are now moved to each side of the foul lane about eight feet out from the end line. The opposite forward now cuts underneath using the chairs as screens to receive a pass for a quick shot.

**Shooting #17—Forwards One-on-One from Side** (Diag. 7-94). The forwards now line up as indicated. An offensive man works against a defensive man while one man stands out. The offensive man becomes the next defensive man, the defensive man stands out, and the man standing out becomes the next offensive man.

Although it causes a bit of congestion at times, I like a pair to be working on each side of the floor at the same time in order to give the players some work on adjusting.

After a few turns from one side of the floor, the players exchange sides.

**Shooting #18—Forwards One-on-One from Side Post** (Diag. 7-95). The players line up as indicated and work on the moves and shots from the side post. The defensive man does not prevent the man from receiving the ball, but plays honest defense when he does receive it.

They alternate positions with the passer becoming the next offensive man, the offensive man becoming the next defensive man and the defensive man becoming the next passer.

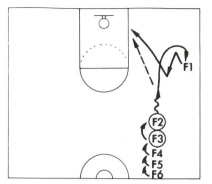

**DIAGRAM 7-91** Shooting #14—
Forward Reverse Cuts.

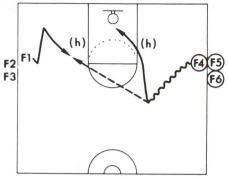

**DIAGRAM 7-92** Shooting #15—
Forward Cutback.

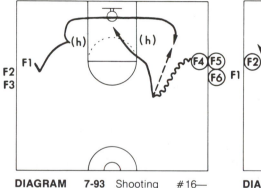

**DIAGRAM 7-93** Shooting #16—
Forward Cross Under.

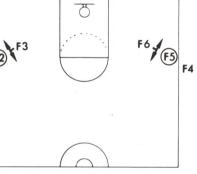

**DIAGRAM 7-94** Shooting #17—
Forward One-on-One (Side).

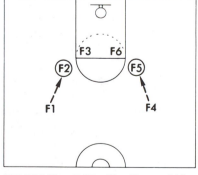

**DIAGRAM 7-95** Shooting #18—
Forward One-on-One (Side Post).

**Shooting #19—Forwards Receiving Return Pass from Post** (Diag. 7-96). The forwards will line up as indicated and a post man alternates back and forth to receive a pass on pass back.

The forward receives a pass, faces the basket by using the proper footwork, passes to the post, fakes one way and cuts the other to receive a return pass and a shot. He then retrieves the ball, passes out to the line from where he received his initial pass, and goes to the end of that corresponding line on the opposite side of the floor.

**Shooting #20—Forward "Dunk" from Lob** (Diag. 7-97). The forwards line up as indicated and a feeder is out in front with a ball for each side. The forward reverses quickly to receive a high lob pass underneath for a "dunk" shot, retrieves the ball, passes back to the feeder after the feeder has passed the other ball to a "dunker" from the opposite line and is ready to receive the pass, and then goes to the end of the opposite line.

**Shooting #21—Guard Dribble and Jump from the Key** (Diag. 7-98). The guards line up out in front in two lines as indicated with a chair placed on each side of the circle in front of where the foul line meets the circle. They drive hard toward the chair and quickly veer to the right or left and take a jump shot. They retrieve their own shot, pass the ball back to the line from which they came, and go to the end of the opposite line.

**Shooting #22—Guard Side-Post Jumps** (Diag. 7-99). The guards line up as in #21 with the first man in each line having a ball and with a post man moving back and forth across the key to receive a pass and feed back from first one side and then the other. The guard passes to the post man and moves forward slowly and then suddenly cuts to the outside by means of a quick change of pace and direction to receive a return pass for a jump shot. The shooter again retrieves his shot, passes back to the line from which he came, and goes to the end of the opposite line.

**Shooting #23—Guard from Jump or Drive** (Diag. 7-100). The guards line up in pairs as indicated with a post man on the lane. A pass is made to the post and the passer screens for the other guard who cuts off of him and down outside the other lane for the basket. The screener moves back in a line between the post man and the defensive basket as soon as his teammate has cut off the screen. The post man mixes up his passes to the cutter for a driving shot and to the back man

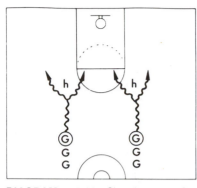

**DIAGRAM 7-96** Shooting #19—
Forward Return Pass from Post.

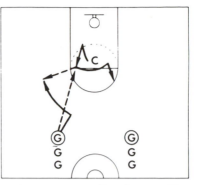

**DIAGRAM 7-97** Shooting #20—
Forward Dunk from Lob.

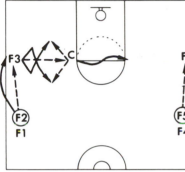

**DIAGRAM 7-98** Shooting #21—
Guard Dribble and Jump from Key.

FEEDER HAS A BALL
FOR EACH LINE

**DIAGRAM 7-99** Shooting #22—
Guard Side-Post Jumps.

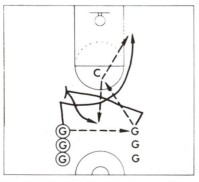

**DIAGRAM 7-100** Shooting #23—
Guard from Jump or Drive.

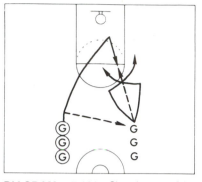

**DIAGRAM 7-101** Shooting #24—Guard Post Return Jumps.

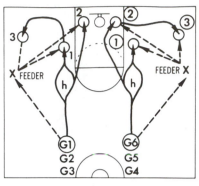

**DIAGRAM 7-102** Shooting #25—Guard from Cutoff High Post.

for a quick set or jump. The guards retrieve the ball and go to the end of the opposite line from which they started.

**Shooting #24—Guard Post Return Jumps** (Diag. 7-101). The guards line up in pairs as indicated. The guard with the ball passes to the other guard, cuts quickly across the foul line, stops and quickly recrosses the foul line to receive a pass from the guard to whom he just passed. He then returns the pass to the passer, who has faked either right or left and comes back the other way, for a quick jump shot.

The jump shooter covers the key area with his buddy rebounding underneath to retrieve the ball. They then move out to the end of the opposite line from which they started.

**Shooting #25—Guard from Cutoff High Post** (Diag. 7-102). The guards line up as indicated with a feeder on each side in the normal position of the forwards and a chair on each side of the foul circle to take the place of a post man off whom they would cut.

The guard passes to the forward who moves a step or two forward and then suddenly cuts close by the chair to receive a pass at one of the three indicated spots for a quick shot. The shooter retrieves his own shot, passes the ball to the line from which he came, and goes to the end of the opposite line.

The drill may be in progress on both sides of the floor at the same time.

**Shooting #26—Guard from Cut In and Back** (Diag. 7-103). The guards line up as indicated in the diagram and with four chairs placed as indicated. The guard passes to the side man and cuts close by the

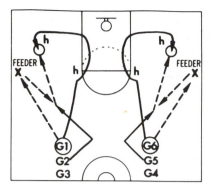

DIAGRAM 7-103 Shooting #26—
Guard from Cut In and Back.

center looking for a pass from the side man. As the side man passes back out to the next guard in line, the cutting guard cuts around the second chair to receive a pass and get a quick shot. The shooter retrieves the ball, passes it back out, and goes to the end of the opposite line.

**Shooting #27—Guard from Lob Pass** (Diag. 7-104). The guards line up as indicated with a chair placed on the foul line.

The guard with the ball passes to the other guard, fakes over toward him, and then suddenly cuts down the lane behind the chair to take a high lob pass for a shot. The passer moves over to the spot from where the shooter originally started and the shooter retrieves the ball, passes back out to him, and goes to the end of the opposite line.

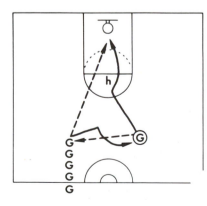

DIAGRAM 7-104 Shooting #27—
Guard from Lob Pass.

**Shooting #28—Dribble Drives** (Diag. 7-105). The guards line up as indicated and dribble hard toward, or between, or around the three chairs placed in the foul circle to get a driving shot of some type from underneath the basket.

The driver retrieves the ball after his shot, passes it out, and goes to the end of the driving line.

**Shooting #29—Guards One-on-One with Post Feeder** (Diag. 7-106). The guards pair up and alternate from offense to defense each time they work. Only one pair works at a time as they take turns.

The offensive man may try to get away on the dribble, or he may pass to the post, but he is not permitted to pick his defensive man off on the post.

The two chairs are placed as indicated on the diagram to give the offense some help as potential screens.

**Shooting #30—Guards One-on-One with Forward Feeder** (Diag. 7-107). The guards work in pairs as indicated and chairs are placed on the floor as indicated. Once again the offensive man may try to free himself on the dribble or he may use the forward as a feeder. The pairs keep alternating and after each player has had a turn on both offense and defense on one side of the floor they move to the opposite side.

**Shooting #31—Guards Two-on-Two with Post Feeder** (Diag. 7-108). The guards line up as in pairs in their normal position with one pair on defense, one pair on offense, and the third pair ready to move in on the next turn. The offense become the next defense, the waiting pair become the next offense, and the defense wait out a turn. They may use the post man as an outlet and a feeder.

**Shooting #32—Guards Two-on-Two with Forward Feeder** (Diag. 7-109). The guards line up as before in #31, but now we have a potential feeder in a forward position on each side of the floor and four chairs placed in possible screening position.

The rotation is the same as in #31.

**Shooting #33—Center Moves from Key** (Diag. 7-110). The three centers line up as indicated with C1 passing to C2 who will be the shooter. After each shot they alternate positions with C1 taking the place of C2, C3 taking the place of C1, and C2 taking the place of C3.

This drill will be used to practice each of the following shots:

**1.** Drives all the way under by turning to both the right and to the left and getting right- and left-handed hooks, lay-backs, layups, "dunks," and twisters.

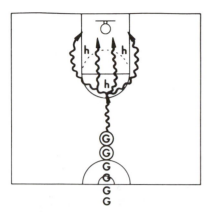

**DIAGRAM 7-105** Shooting #28—
Guard Dribble Drives.

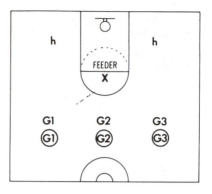

**DIAGRAM 7-106** Shooting #29—
Guards One-on-One with Post Feeder.

**DIAGRAM 7-107** Shooting #30—
Guards One-on-One with Forward
Feeder.

**DIAGRAM 7-108** Shooting #31—
Guards Two-on-Two with Post Feeder.

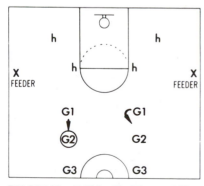

**DIAGRAM 7-109** Shooting #32—
Guards Two-on-Two with Forward
Feeder.

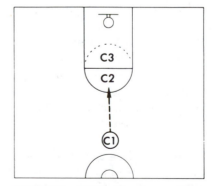

**DIAGRAM 7-110** Shooting #33—
Center Moves from Key.

**2.** Drives to the right or left outside the foul-lane area for quick jumpers or fadeaways after a quick stop.

**3.** Fakes to the right or left and step back for a quick jumper, or fake of a quick jumper and drive for one of the others.

**4.** A quick turn to face the basket by a crossover or reverse turn for a quick shot, a fake of a shot and quick drive for a shot, or a fake of a drive and a quick step back for a shot.

**Shooting #34—Center Returns Pass to Key** (Diag. 7-111). The three centers line up as indicated with a feeder out in front. The feeder passes to the post who passes to one of the flankers who gives him a quick return pass for a shot. All rebound to get the ball in the basket. The ball is then passed out to the feeder and 1 takes the place of 2, 2 takes the place of 3, and 3 takes the place of 1.

**Shooting#35—Center Variety from Key** (Diag. 7-112). The three centers and the feeder line up as indicated in the diagram. The man on the post receives a pass from the feeder, makes his move to face the basket, and then gets some type of shot from the circle area. All rebound until the ball goes through the basket.

They rotate positions as in #34, but not until the middle man has taken five shots.

**Shooting #36—Center After Pass from Forward** (Diag. 7-113). The three centers line up as indicated in the diagram and alternate positions after each turn. 3 passes to 2 who passes to 1 at the side of the key, where he will maneuver for a quick shot, or down the lane, where he will maneuver for a shot.

This is used from both sides of the floor.

**Shooting #37—Center Out Baseline from Forward** (Diag. 7-114). The three centers line up as indicated in the diagram and alternate positions after each turn. 3 passes to 2, who passes to 1 for the shot halfway between the foul lane and the sideline. Like all drills that are applicable on either side of the floor, this shot must be practiced from both sides.

**Shooting #38—Centers One-on-One** (Diag. 7-115). The centers line up as indicated in the diagram and keep a natural rotation of positions after each turn. When the drill is first used, the defense should be passive, but later it must become more active as in game conditions.

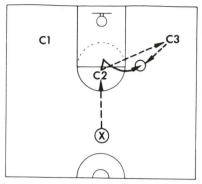

**DIAGRAM** **7-111** Shooting #34— Center Return Pass from Key.

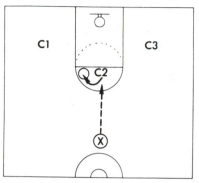

**DIAGRAM** **7-112** Shooting #35— Center Variety from Key.

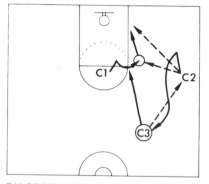

**DIAGRAM** **7-113** Shooting #36— Center from Pass from Forward.

**DIAGRAM** **7-114** Shooting #37— Center Out Baseline from Forward.

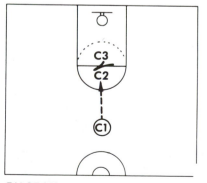

**DIAGRAM** **7-115** Shooting #38— Center One-on-One.

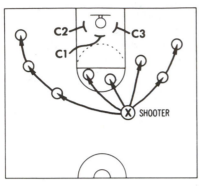

**DIAGRAM 7-116** Shooting #39—Center Offensive Tip-Ins.

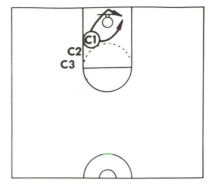

**DIAGRAM 7-117** Shooting #40—Centers—Three Tips and In.

**Shooting #39—Center Tip-Ins** (Diag. 7-116).   The centers line up as indicated with a shooter trying to provide them with tip in opportunities by shots from the various positions much as indicated in the diagram. They should keep alternating starting positions and keep after the ball until the basket is made.

**Shooting #40—Centers—Three Tips and In** (Diag. 7-117).   The centers line up as indicated and run this drill quickly. 1 starts it and goes to the other side when his turn comes up again. The drill starts with C1 passing the ball high off the board to himself on the opposite side where he moves quickly to tip it back across (1), where he moves quickly to tip it back across (2), where he moves quickly to try to tip it in the basket (3), and keeps tipping it until he does score.

## FREE-THROW SHOOTING

Since the outcome of so many games is decided by the free-throw shooting ability of the teams involved, time spent in the practice of this is never wasted time. However, this particular practice takes a great amount of time and I try to have all of my players use any available time they have for practicing free throws. I like to have every boy report on at least fifty attempts every day that have been attempted on his own time.

In addition to the players practicing on their own time, we may have a five- to ten-minute period a couple of times during the practice day for one or both of the following drills.

Techniques and other suggestions have been covered under offensive fundamentals.

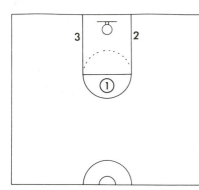

DIAGRAM 7-118 Free Throw #1—
Three-Man.

**Free Throw #1—Three at a Basket** (Diag. 7-118). The players go to separate baskets in groups of three and take positions as indicated. The shooters rotate and do not shoot over two in succession. If a player makes his first shot, he takes a second shot before rotating positions, but, if he misses his first attempt, the players rotate immediately.

This is a competitive drill using five groups of three players each. When any group makes six in succession, they call it out and all groups move to the first basket to the right where they will start immediately. Each group must leave the ball near the foul line before they move.

**Free Throw #2—Team Competition** (Diag. 7-119). The squad is now divided into three teams and the drill is run the same as in #1 except they now are to work for ten in succession before moving.

As a general rule, each team will consist of two forwards, two guards, and one center, but occasionally I will divide the squad into three teams according to their height or use some other method to add variety to the drill.

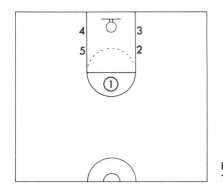

DIAGRAM 7-119 Free Throw #2—
Team.

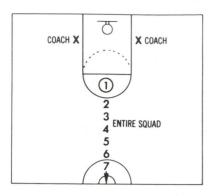

**DIAGRAM 7-120** Free Throw #3—Squad.

**Free Throw #3—Before Showering** (Diag. 7-120). Occasionally I will have the entire squad line up as indicated at the close of practice for a pressure turn at the free-throw line under the scrutiny of the coach and good-natured "heckling" of teammates.

Each player steps to the line in turn to attempt to turn a one-and-one into two points. If he is successful, he is through for the day; if he makes the first one and misses the second, he makes a fast turn around the floor and goes to the end of the line; if he misses the first one, he takes two fast laps around the floor and goes to the end of the line to await another chance.

## DRIBBLING

Many of the drills that have been explained and illustrated under shooting, passing and receiving, and stops and turns or pivots also require dribbling in their execution and it should not be neglected, even when the principal emphasis is on another fundamental.

The players must learn when to dribble as well as how to dribble, as too much dribbling can destroy good team play. The dribble should end with a good pass or shot, either of which may be preceded by a quick stop or stop and turn.

Special emphasis should be placed on the following things during the dribbling drills:

**1.** Keeping the head and eyes up—always.

**2.** Use of the low bounce, keeping the elbow very close to the body, use of change of pace and direction, keeping the hips low and the knees bent, when working on the control dribble.

**3.** Use of the high bounce, pushing the ball away, and running straight up, when working on the speed dribble.

**4.** Control of ball and balance maintained when concluding the dribble with a quick stop, stop and turn, pass, or shot.

**5.** Amount of floor covered with peripheral vision.

**Dribbling #1—Speed Race** (Diag. 7-121). The players line up in five lines of three to a line as shown with the first man in each line having a ball.

They start on signal and must cross the end line at the far end before starting back and must cross the end line on their return before passing to the next man in their line. As soon as a pass is made to the next man in line, the dribbler goes to the end of the line.

If there are an even number in each line, the winner will be the group that first gets back to the exact positions they were in when the drill first started. The drill may be with left hand only, with right hand only, or the dribbler may use either hand or alternate hands.

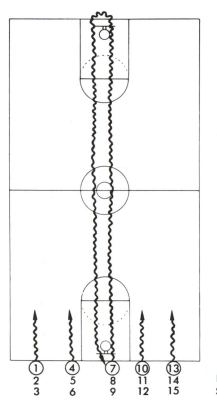

**DIAGRAM 7-121** Dribbling #1— Speed Race.

**Dribbling #2—Speed Relay** (Diag. 7-122). The players line up as indicated in three teams of five each with each team having three men and a ball at one end of the floor and two men facing them at the opposite end. They start on signal and must cross the end line at the opposite end before passing the ball to a teammate there. The winner will be the first team to get back into their exact starting positions.

Get practice in the use of each hand.

**Dribbling #3—Control and Speed Combined** (Diag. 7-123). The players line up in three lines of five as indicated.

They use the control dribble with a change of pace and direction until they cross the center line and the speed dribble from the center

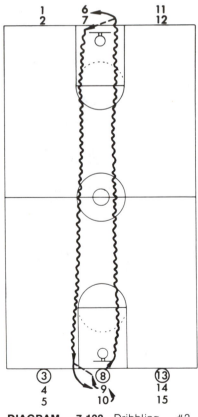

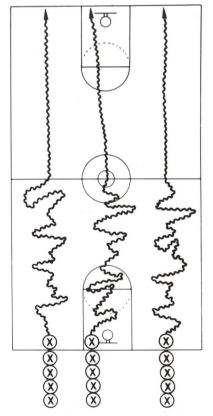

**DIAGRAM 7-122** Dribbling #2—Speed Relay.

**DIAGRAM 7-123** Dribbling #3—Control and Speed Combined.

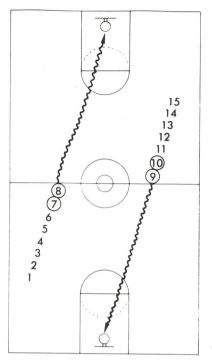

**DIAGRAM** **7-124** Dribbling #4—
Weak-Hand Drive.

line to the end line. After crossing the end line, they wait for all of the others before starting back.

Each succeeding player starts as soon as the player in front of him gets out about 20 feet from the end line.

**Dribbling #4—Weak-Hand Drive** (Diag. 7-124).   Line up as indicated with the first two players in line having a ball.

The first player in each line drives hard for the basket, but must dribble and score with his weak hand. After scoring, he makes a good pass back and goes to the end of the opposite line.

The next man in line should start his drive as soon as the man in front of him scores.

**Dribbling #5—Control** (Diag. 7-125).   The players line up as shown in the diagram in five lines of three each with the first man in each line having a ball.

When the coach blows his whistle, the first man in each line starts

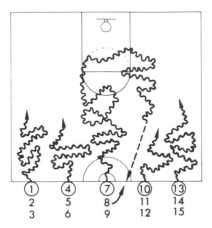

**DIAGRAM 7-125** Dribbling #5—Control.

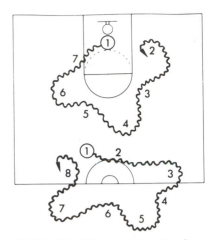

**DIAGRAM 7-126** Dribbling #6—Control—In and Out.

fast and uses a control dribble with a change of pace and direction. They charge at each other, but avoid all contact.

When the whistle blows again, they make a quick pass to the first man in the line from which they started and cut quickly to the end of that line. The next group proceeds in the same manner.

**Dribbling #6—Control—In and Out** (Diag. 7-126).   The squad splits into two groups and half of them form a circle around and in back of the foul circle as the others do the same around the center circle. The man with the ball dribbles in and out around the circle as fast as he can. When he completes the circle, he gives the ball to the next man and takes his place. Use of alternate hands is stressed.

The drill continues with each man doing the same.

**Dribbling #7—Star Exchange** (Diag. 7-127).   The squad splits up into three groups of five each and gets set around each of the floor circles as indicated in the diagram. The man with the ball pivots momentarily and then dribbles fast diagonally across the circle, makes a quick stop and turn, and hands off to the man in that position, and then takes his position as the new man with the ball drives across the circle to do the same.

**Dribbling #8—Two-Line Cross** (Diag. 7-128).   The squad lines up in four groups as indicated with each of the two lines facing each other. The drill is started on a given signal with each man with a ball driving hard across the circle, handing off to the first man in the line, and going

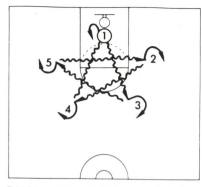

**DIAGRAM 7-127** Dribbling #7—Star Exchange.

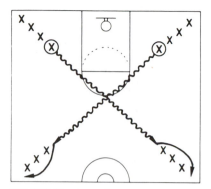

**DIAGRAM 7-128** Dribbling #8—Two-Line Cross.

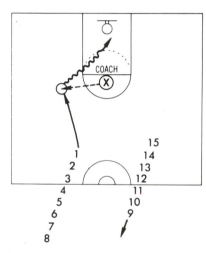

**DIAGRAM 7-129** Dribbling #9—Retrieve and Drive.

to the end of the line. They must be in good control at the crossing point to avoid collision.

Occasionally, I place one or two chairs in the area where the two dribblers will cross to give them some additional control work.

**Dribbling #9—Retrieve and Drive** (Diag. 7-129).   The squad lines up in the two lines indicated with a coach at each foul line. When the coach rolls out a ball, the first man in line retrieves it quickly, makes a quick, low pivot, and dribbles hard for a score. He retrieves the ball, passes it back to the coach, and goes to the end of the opposite line.

Each coach should have an extra ball available, and the driver should not pass to the coach until he has rolled out the other ball.

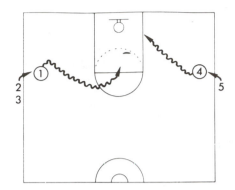

**DIAGRAM 7-130** Dribbling #10—Drive and Pass Back.

**DIAGRAM 7-131** Dribbling #11—Fake Shot and Drive from Side.

**Dribbling #10—Drive and Pass Back** (Diag. 7-130).   The squad lines up with five men at a basket as indicated with one on the post. The man out front with the ball dribbles hard at the post man who moves toward him a couple of steps to screen and roll for a quick pass to provide a stationary post screen combined with a turn to look for a pass. The dribbler drives to his right or left and gives the post man a pass as he rolls for the basket or hits him with a chin-high pass if he stays out. The dribbler becomes the next post man and the post man goes to the end of the line.

**Dribbling #11—Fake Shot and Drive from Side** (Diag. 7-131).   The squad separates into three groups and gets organized at three different baskets as indicated in the diagram.

One side works on a fake drive across and drives the baseline as the other side works on a fake baseline drive and drives across toward the key area. The drives may terminate with a quick stop and turn and pass back or a quick shot. Each driver goes to the end of the opposite line when he has passed back.

**Dribbling #12—Fake Shot and Drive from Front** (Diag. 7-132).   Each group of five now is organized into lines out front in the normal guard positions. They now work on their fakes and drives to both the right and left, shoot or stop and turn, pass back and go to the end of the 'opposite line.

**Dribbling #13—Across Key and Turn In** (Diag. 7-133).   The squad separates into two groups and each group lines up at a basket as indicated in the diagram. A chair is placed on each side of the circle as

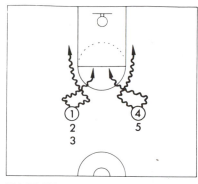

**DIAGRAM 7-132** Dribbling #12—Fake Shot and Drive from Front.

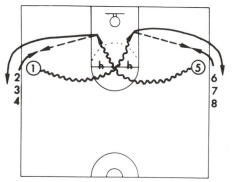

**DIAGRAM 7-133** Dribbling #13—Drive Across Key.

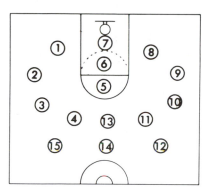

**DIAGRAM 7-134** Dribbling #14—Dribble Tag.

shown. The first man on each side of the floor fakes baseline, drives over the top and between the two chairs, passes to the first man in the line, and moves to the end of that line.

**Dribbling #14—Dribble Tag** (Diag. 7-134). Each player is given a ball and sees how many of his teammates he can touch without losing control of the ball he is dribbling.

They must stay in the half-court area with a teammate receiving credit for a tag if he forces you to touch the center or other out-of-bounds line.

## STOPS, TURNS, AND PIVOTS

Please remember that, as a general rule, *turns* follow a quick stop by the dribbler that was forced by the defense and *pivots* are moves made by the player who has just received a pass to elude the defensive man for a shot or a drive.

For using the quick stop and turn, special emphasis should be placed on:

**1.** Keeping good body balance with the head up, the feet well spread, the knees bent, the buttocks low, and the back straight.

**2.** Hitting the floor flat-footed in order to utilize as much rubber as possible to get good traction, but the forepart of foot will make the initial contact.

**3.** Keeping the ball close to the front of the body on the side away from the defense.

**4.** Expecting some contact and being braced to withstand it without traveling.

**5.** Being alert and ready to get rid of the ball quickly to a potential receiver whenever you have used your dribble.

**6.** Remembering that, almost always, a trailer should be ready to cut by a dribbler, who makes a quick stop and turn, at the proper time. Stress this timing.

**7.** Being careful not to start the turn before making the stop.

For using the pivot after receiving a pass to get position on the defensive man, emphasize the following:

**1.** Keeping your eye on the ball until you have caught it.

**2.** Looking over your shoulder toward your defensive man immediately upon receiving the ball.

**3.** Pivoting on the proper foot.

**4.** Keeping good body balance with the head in the proper position above the feet.

**5.** Keeping the ball close to the body under the chin for protection when you pivot to face the basket and on the side away from the defense but still close to the body when you drive.

**6.** Using ball faking only by a flick of the wrists as the elbows stay in contact with the body and using good head fakes.

A number of drills for shooting, for dribbling, and #9 under "Floor-Length Drills" combine stops and turns or pivots and this fundamental should be observed and executed properly when those drills are being used.

**Stop and Turn #1—Floor Length in Pairs** (Diag. 7-135). The players line up at the end of the floor as indicated with every other one in line having a ball.

The man with the ball uses the change-of-pace-and-direction dribble for a few feet and then makes a quick stop and turn and hands off to his partner who comes by at the right time. The pair continue down the

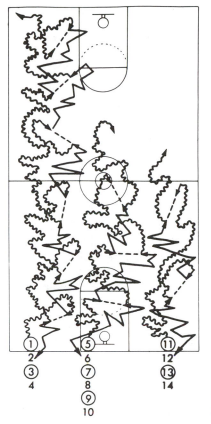

**DIAGRAM 7-135** Stop and Turn #1—
Floor Length (in Pairs).

floor in the same manner with the one receiving the hand off always dribbling a few feet and working on his change-of-pace-and-direction dribble before making the quick stop and turn.

The next pair in each line should let the pair in front of them reach the center line before starting.

Proper timing is always the responsibility of the trailer. He must not come by too soon or too late.

**Stop and Turn #2—Inside Turn and Pass Back** (Diag. 7-136). Five groups of three line up as indicated with the first one in each line having a ball.

They use a hard dribble to about the foul-line distance, make a quick stop, and use the inside turn, take a look across the floor, make a good pass to the next man in their line, and then go to the end of the line.

They should get practice on using both the left foot and the right foot as the pivot foot.

**Stop and Turn #3—Cross-Over and Pass Back** (Diag. 7-137). The squad is divided into two groups and each form two lines facing their basket as indicated with the first man in each line having a ball.

They dribble forward and cross over in the foul-circle area to the opposite side, make a quick stop, take a look, pass to the first man in the opposite line from which they started, and then go to the end of that line.

**Stop and Turn #4—Cross-Over and Pass to Trailer** (Diag. 7-138). The squad is divided into three groups of five and each group lines up at a basket as indicated with the first man in the longest line having a ball. The man with the ball dribbles forward and crosses over to make his stop and turn on the opposite side of the foul circle. The first man in the opposite line fakes outside and times himself to come by the turner at the proper time to receive a pass. He then takes a few dribbles, makes a quick stop and turn, passes out to the first man in the line from where the ball started, and each goes to the end of the opposite line.

**Stop and Turn #5—Straight Line—Pass to Trailer** (Diag. 7-139). The squad is divided into three groups of five and each group line up at their basket as indicated with the first man in line having a ball. The man with the ball dribbles toward the basket, veers off to the right or left at the top of the circle, makes a quick stop and turn, passes to the trailer, and goes to the end of the line. The trailer, who times himself to come by at the right time by proper faking, takes a few dribbles, makes a quick stop and turn, passes to the first man in line, and goes to the end of the line.

**Pivots #1—Reverse Drive from Side** (Diag. 7-140). Groups of five line up at their basket as indicated. 2 passes to 1 and then takes his place. 1 receives the pass at his outside shoulder with his inside foot forward. As soon as 1 receives the pass, he swings his outside leg back and pivots on the inside foot for a quick drive to the basket. The driver retrieves his own shot, passes back to the first one in line, and goes to the end of the line.

Use the drill an equal amount of time on each side of the floor as should be the case in all drills.

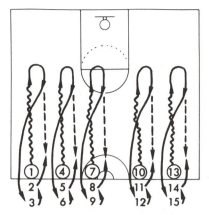

**DIAGRAM 7-136** Stop and Turn #2—Inside Turn and Pass Back.

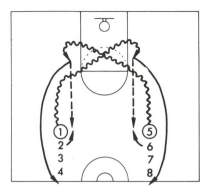

**DIAGRAM 7-137** Stop and Turn #3—Cross-Over and Pass Back.

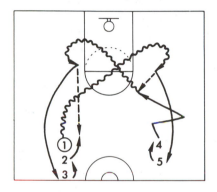

**DIAGRAM 7-138** Stop and Turn #4—Cross-Over and Pass to Trailer.

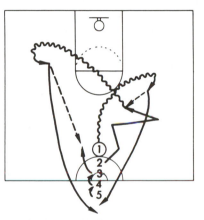

**DIAGRAM 7-139** Stop and Turn #5—Straight Line—Pass to Trailer.

**DIAGRAM 7-140** Pivot #1—Reverse Drive from Side.

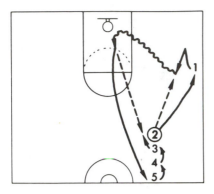

**DIAGRAM 7-141** Pivot #2—Facing Basket from the Side.

**Pivots #2—Facing Basket from the Side** (Diag. 7-141).  The drill works exactly the same as #1, except that the receiver turns to face the basket when he receives the pass, fakes, and drives. The pivoter turns to face the basket while using the left foot as the pivot foot if he is right-handed, and the right foot as the pivot foot if he is left-handed.

This means that a right-handed player will use an inside reverse turn when he is on the right side of the floor and a cross-over step when he is on the left side.

**Pivots #3—Post Moves** (Diag. 7-142).  Groups of five line up at their basket as indicated with a post man on each side of the foul circle. They may also come up from deeper down the lane. They pass in alternates from one side to the other with the passer always taking the place of the post man to whom he passes and the post man who receives the pass going to the end of the line after retrieving the ball and passing out.

The post men work on the reverse-drive move and on the various moves after they have pivoted to face the basket.

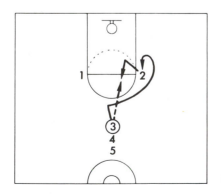

**DIAGRAM 7-142** Pivot #3—Post Moves.

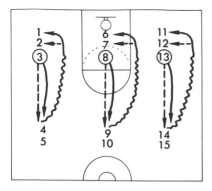

**DIAGRAM 7-143** Forward Pivot and Drive by a Presser.

**Pivots #4—Forward Pivot and Drive by a Presser** (Diag. 7-143). The players line up in three groups of five as indicated with the first man in the longest line of each group having a ball.

The player with the ball passes to the first man in the line facing him and charges after the pass. The pass is received with one foot forward and the back leg is swung quickly around and past the presser, the pass is made to the next man in the line, and the pass is made to the first man in line. The drill is continued in the same manner.

## DEFENSE

Although it must never be forgotten that defense and offense are of equal importance in the proper play of the game, it is also true that more drills are required for offense because of the things that must be done with the ball—various types of shots and passes, receiving, pivoting, and dribbling—in addition to everything else.

It must be stressed constantly that the defense played before your man gets the ball will make your job easier when he does receive the ball. An all-out effort must be made to prevent your man from receiving the ball in an area where he may be a triple threat as a shooter, driver, and passer and cutter. This can be emphasized best during team-situation defensive drills of the half-court scrimmage variety. However, it must also be noted during all defensive drills except those that start with the offensive man having possession within the high danger area.

Special emphasis should be placed on:

**1.** Defense before your man has possession of the ball in the dangerous area.

**2.** Development of pride in defense.

**3.** Proper position and body balance.

**DIAGRAM 7-144** Defense #1—Squad Sliding to Signal.

**DIAGRAM 7-145** Defense #2—Position to Ball.

**4.** Applying constant pressure without relaxing until ball possession is obtained.

**5.** Keeping an open position where you can see both your man and the ball.

**Defense #1—Squad Sliding to Signal** (Diag. 7-144). The entire squad line up facing the coach as indicated. The players all assume a good defense stance as if they were guarding a man and keep watching the coach. The players move in unison while maintaining good body balance as the coach signals by pointing the direction in which he wants them to move.

The coach should work them hard for a few seconds and then give them a breather of a few seconds before continuing.

They must not cross their legs, or bob their head, or lean forward, but must keep good body balance, always keep one foot in contact with the floor, their hands up and ready, and make quick changes of direction without loss of balance.

**Defense #2—Position to Ball** (Diag. 7-145). Using the same formation and principles as in #1, the players move quickly in relation to the ball as the two coaches pass the ball back and forth, fake drives, fake shots, and fake cuts.

**Defense #3—Guarding the Passer Who Cuts** (Diag. 7-146). The squad is divided into three groups of five and each group lines up at a separate basket as indicated. The ball is passed to the post man and the passer makes a cut as fast as the post man with the defensive man backing up quickly, keeping his eyes on the passer, and playing him properly. The defensive man becomes the next post man, the offensive man becomes the next defensive man, and the post man passes the ball out and goes to the end of the line.

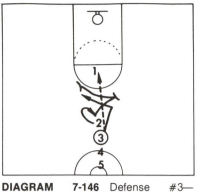 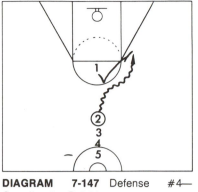

**DIAGRAM 7-146** Defense #3— Guarding the Passer Who Cuts.

**DIAGRAM 7-147** Defense #4— Guarding the Dribbler.

This drill should be used on each side of the floor as well as from out in front.

**Defense #4—Guarding the Dribbler** (Diag. 7-147). Groups of five work at separate baskets as indicated with the dribbler always becoming the next defensive man and the defensive man moving out to the end of the line.

The dribbler should be limited to a driving area of not over 15 feet in width.

**Defense #5—Heading the Dribbler** (Diag. 7-148). The players line up as indicated with the defensive man being on the side of the center line nearest the basket and the dribbler on the other side. The dribbler starts on signal and the defensive man tries to head him off and prevent a good shot. They go back to the ends of the opposite lines when the defense obtains possession.

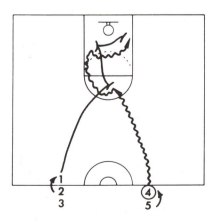

**DIAGRAM 7-148** Defense #5—Heading the Dribbler.

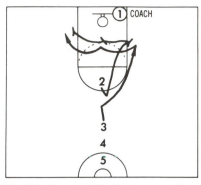

DIAGRAM 7-149 Defense #6—
Guarding the Cutter from Out Front.

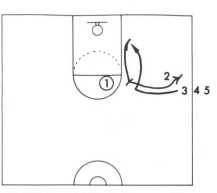

DIAGRAM 7-150 Defense #7—
Guarding the Cutter from the Side.

**Defense #6—Guarding the Cutter from Out Front** (Diag. 7-149). The players line up as indicated and the coach stands under the basket with a ball to feed the offensive man if he gets open. The offensive man will become the next defensive man and the defensive man will go to the end of the line.

**Defense #7—Guarding the Cutter from the Side** (Diag. 7-150). Same principle as #6 with a post man having the ball.

**Defense #8—Guarding Two Cutters from Outside** (Diag. 7-151). Same principle as #6, but using a two-on-two setup.

**Defense #9—Guarding One-on-One** (Diag. 7-152). The players pair up according to the position they play and work one-on-one.

Use two or three pairs at a basket, but only one pair work at a time.

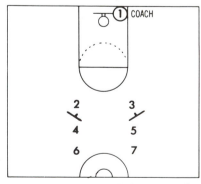

DIAGRAM 7-151 Defense #8—
Guarding Two Cutters from the Outside.

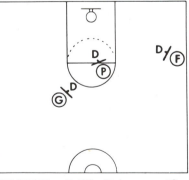

DIAGRAM 7-152 Defense #9—
Guarding One-on-One.

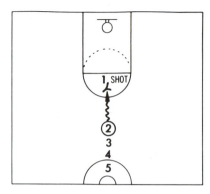

DIAGRAM 7-153 Defense #10—
Guarding the Jump Shooter.

We like to make this drill competitive and have each player see how many points he can score against his teammate before losing possession five times. A score does not count as a lost possession, a defensive foul gives the offensive man one or two points depending on whether or not he was shooting, and an offensive foul counts as a lost possession.

**Defense #10—Guarding the Jump Shooter** (Diag. 7-153). The players line up as indicated in groups of five.

**Defense #11—Guarding the Post** (Diag. 7-154). The three post men work as indicated with 3 feeding from any spot of the arc. They keep alternating positions.

**Defense #12—Two-on-Two (Guards)** (Diag. 7-155). The guards pair up and line up as indicated. The offensive pair become the next defensive pair and the defensive pair wait out one turn as the other moves in.

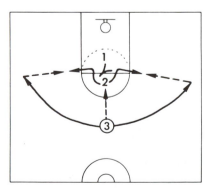

DIAGRAM 7-154 Defense #11—
Guarding the Post.

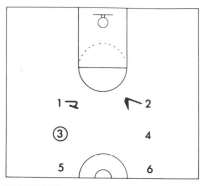

DIAGRAM 7-155 Defense #12—Two-on-Two (Guards).

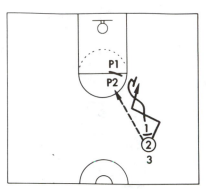

DIAGRAM 7-156 Defense #13—Two-on-Two (Guard and Post).

**Defense #13—Two-on-Two (Guard and Post)** (Diag. 7-156). A guard and a post man now work together on one side of the floor with the offense always becoming the next defense.

**Defense #14—Two-on-Two (Guard and Forward)** (Diag. 7-157). A guard and a forward now work together in the positions in which they normally line up. Keep the usual rotation.

**Defense #15—Three-on-Three (Guards and Post)** (Diag. 7-158). The two guards now work with a post man and rotate as usual.

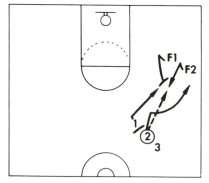

DIAGRAM 7-157 Defense #14—Two-on-Two (Guard and Forward).

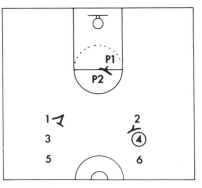

DIAGRAM 7-158 Defense #15—Three-on-Three (Guards and Post).

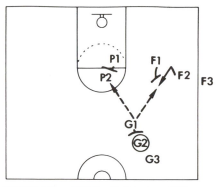

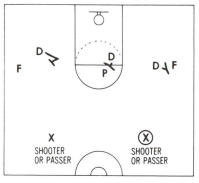

**DIAGRAM 7-159** Defense #16—Strong Side (Guard, Forward, and Post).

**DIAGRAM 7-160** Defense #17—Checking (Deep Men).

**Defense #16—Strong Side (Guard, Forward, and Post)** (Diag. 7-159).   A guard, forward, and post man line up in their normal positions and work against a defense. They may not cross over out of the foul lane.

The offense becomes the next defense each time.

**Defense #17—Checking (Forwards and Post)** (Diag. 7-160).   A pair of forwards and a post man line up in their normal positions with the defense playing them normally. Two other men line up in the guard positions and either shoot or pass in to a forward or the post.

After about five turns, the offense takes the defense, the defensive forwards move out as the shooters or passers, and the offensive shooters or passers move in as the offensive forwards.

**Defense #18—Team Checking** (Diag. 7-161).   One team take the defense, another the offense, and a third stay ready to move in. The offense move the ball from man to man for awhile and take a shot after a few passes. The offense do not cut, but rebound when a shot is taken.

The defense move with the ball and play defense in relation to their man and the ball. They rebound at the time the shot is taken.

Alternate after five shots from offense to defense, defense to standing by, and standing by to offense.

**Defense #19—Blocking the Driving Shot** (Diag. 7-162).   Three groups of five each line up at separate baskets as indicated. The defense permit the man to start the drive and then try to block the shot

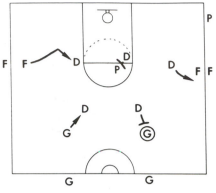

**DIAGRAM 7-161** Defense #18—Team Checking.

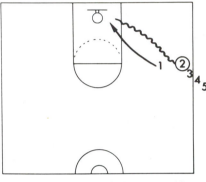

**DIAGRAM 7-162** Defense #19—Blocking the Drive Shot.

**DIAGRAM 7-163** Defense #20—Post Shift to Block Shot.

without fouling. The offense become the next defense and the defensive man goes to the end of the line.

**Defense #20—Post Shift to Block Shot** (Diag. 7-163). The squad is divided into two groups with each one lined up at a separate basket as indicated. When the defensive post man calls the shift, he picks up the driver as the driver's man picks up the post man.

Alternate as usual.

**Defense #21—End-Line Press—Two-on-Two** (Diag. 7-164). Three pairs are utilized in this drill and the guards get more work on it than the others, but all potential court pressers get some work. The rest of the squad work on some specialized drill at the other end of the court.

The defense usually two-time the man in the playing court and turn

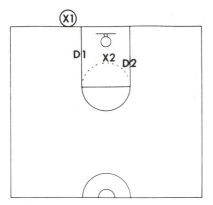

**DIAGRAM 7-164** Defense #21—End-Line Press—Two-on-Two.

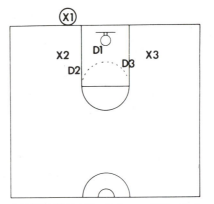

**DIAGRAM 7-165** Defense #22—End-Line Press—Three-on-Three.

the inbounder loose until the pass is made, but occasionally they may vary this and bother the inbounder.

The offensive men try to get the ball across the center line without the use of a long pass. The offensive pair become the next defensive pair, the defensive pair take the place of the waiting pair, and the waiting pair become the next offensive pair.

**Defense #22—End-Line Press—Three-on-Three** (Diag. 7-165). We usually use three groups of three each for this drill and run it the same and alternate the same as we do in the pairs in #21.

**Defense #23—Half-Court Press—Three-on-Three** (Diag. 7-166). We use our entire squad in five groups of three each for this drill and start as indicated in the diagram.

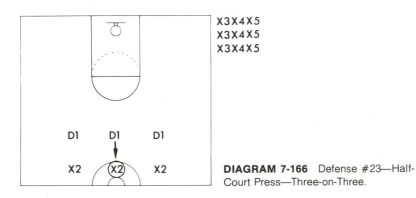

**DIAGRAM 7-166** Defense #23—Half-Court Press—Three-on-Three.

The 1 group pressure the 2 group who try to score. When the 2 group lose possession in any manner, including the scoring of a field goal, they press the 1 group who try to advance the ball past the center line without the use of a long pass. The 3 and 4 groups move on as soon as the 1 and 2 groups reach the center line and the 1 and 2 groups move off to the side in the same order. As they continue in order, it will be 5 vs. 1, 2 vs. 3, 4 vs. 5, or you may change them in any order that you wish.

**Defense #24—Four-on-Four Weave** (Diag. 7-167). We use three groups of four each for this drill, and they keep alternating from offense to defense to waiting.

The defense must work to prevent being forced back, must prevent a roll between any two, and must cover any quick reverse on the outside.

Occasionally, we place a post man in the free-throw area, and he may be used as an outlet for a pass, but not for a screen. On other occasions, we place a chair in the post position to present an additional hazard for the defense to avoid.

**Defense #25—Five-on-Five—Weave and Press** (Diag. 7-168). We alternate three groups of five on this with the offense using a four-man weave and the post man as an outlet and a potential screen.

When the offense scores, they put on our zone press immediately, and when they lose the ball without scoring, they put on our man-to-man press as the other team try to break for a score.

**Defense #26—Five-on-Five Position** (Diag. 7-169). We alternate three groups of five on this and have the offense pass from man to man without cutting. Each offensive man fakes a shot, a drive, and a pass each time he has the ball before passing to a teammate. Each defensive man must assume the proper position on his man at all times, according to the position of the ball and the position of his man.

**Defense #27—Two-on-One—Half-Court** (Diag. 7-170). The players pair up and alternate on defense as soon as each man has had three turns. The defensive man lines up at the free-throw line, fakes and bluffs the man with the ball, but makes certain he has the cutter. His responsibility is to prevent the setup shot and delay the offense, if possible, until help comes.

**Defense #28—Three-on-Two—Half-Court** (Diag. 7-171). We use the entire squad in five groups of three each for this drill.

One group take the defense and stay on defense until they have

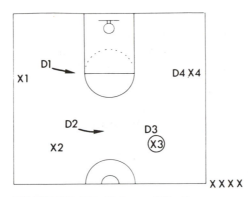

**DIAGRAM 7-167** Defense #24—Four-on-Four Weave.

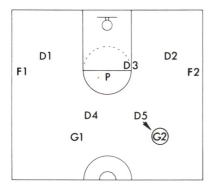

**DIAGRAM 7-168** Defense #25—Five-on-Five (Weave and Press).

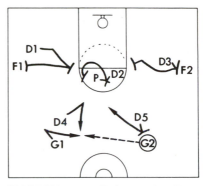

**DIAGRAM 7-169** Defense #26—Five-on-Five (Position).

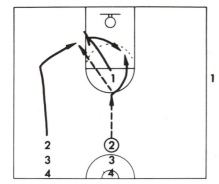

**DIAGRAM 7-170** Defense #27—Two-on-One (Half-Court).

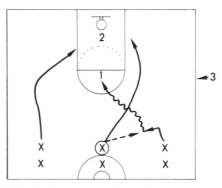

**DIAGRAM 7-171** Defense #28—Three-on-Two (Half-Court).

defensed each of the four offense groups three times. The three defensive men alternate the positions and keep rotating from 1 to 2 to 3 as each new group attacks. The deep man (2) must prevent the setup and the out man (1) must defend against the middle man and the cutter that does not receive the pass from the middle man.

**Defense #29—Two-on-One—Full Court** (Diag. 7-172).   The squad is divided into five groups of three with one group on defense as indicated.

As one offensive threesome start down the floor, one defensive man moves out from the sideline to the center circle and backs up to the free-throw lane area.

The middle man on offense, who starts the attack by tossing the ball on the board, rebounds it and passes to one of the other, drops out of the offense when he reaches the center line, and becomes a protector.

The defensive man comes back to the side of the floor, the offensive men return down the side of the floor to the other end, and a new offensive group start down the floor with another defensive man moving out to defend.

Alternate so that everyone gets a desired amount of work in defense.

**Defense #30—Three-on-Two—Full Court** (Diag. 7-173).   The drill is set up and the players alternate the same as in #29.

However, two defensive men now come out as indicated, and all three offensive men work to get a good shot with not over three quick passes in the scoring area.

The deep defensive man always moves out to the sideline at the center of the floor when the play is completed, the front defensive man becomes the deep defensive man, and the third man moves in to become the front defensive man as the next offensive threesome start their play.

Keep alternating the threesomes as defense to get the desired amount of work you want each group to have.

**Defense #31—Half-Court Scrimmage** (Diag. 7-174).   We do a great amount of half-court scrimmaging and stress defense and offense on alternate days with the top eight players, who play the most in the actual games, getting most of the work on the part that is being emphasized on a particular day.

Some of the situations on which we work are as follows:

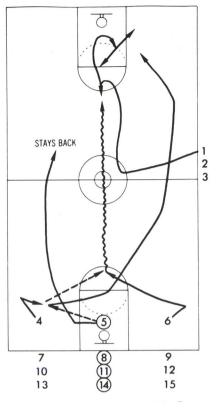

**DIAGRAM 7-172** Defense #29—Two-on-One (Full-Court).

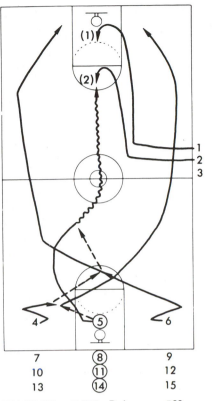

**DIAGRAM 7-173** Defense #30—Three-on-Two (Full-Court).

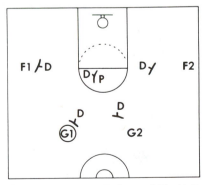

**DIAGRAM 7-174** Defense #31—Half-Court Scrimmage.

1.  Defensing the offense of our next opponent.

2.  Defensing the offense of our most dangerous conference opponent.

3.  Defensing any special type of offense that we are likely to meet, such as a stall or ball control, a double post, a weave, an unusually tall post man, a strong blocking or screening game, etc.

4.  Our pressing defense when we start on offense and put on a zone press when we score and a man-to-man press when we lose the ball without scoring. Occasionally, when we want special work on the zone press, we have the defense permit the offense to score from their regular offense in order that they may apply their press under seminormal conditions, and we can get more work on it.

5.  Defensing our regular offense in order that we may find out and, perhaps, correct what causes our offense the most trouble.

6.  Covering the board after permitting an outside shot of either the set or jump variety.

## Defense—In Other Drills

Rebounding #3—Checking the shooter.
Rebounding #4—Inside checking.
Rebounding #10—Checking the drivers.
Rebounding #13—Team checking "A."
Rebounding #14—Team checking "B."
Floor Length #6—Defensive sliding.
Floor Length #7—One-on-one (cutter).
Floor Length #8—One-on-one (dribbler).
Floor Length #18—Three-on-three with break.
Floor Length #19—Baseline man-to-man press.
Floor Length #20—Baseline three-man zone press.
Floor Length #25—One-on-one conditioner.
Floor Length #26—Two-on-two conditioner.
Floor Length #27—Three-on-two conditioner.
Passing and Receiving #7—Chaser in circle.
Passing and Receiving #8—Two chasers in circle.
Shooting #7—One-on-one.
Shooting #17—One-on-one—forwards
Shooting #18—One-on-one—side post.
Shooting #29—One-on-one—guard with post.
Shooting #30—One-on-one—guard with forward.
Shooting #31—Two-on-two—guards with post.
Shooting #32—Two-on-two—guards with forwards.

## FAST BREAK

Emphasis placed on:

**1.** Getting the ball out fast and making your opportunities.

**2.** Getting speed and quickness without sacrificing accuracy.

**3.** Keeping proper floor balance with a trailer and protector.

**4.** Keeping looking ahead.

**5.** Finishing with a good percentage shot or setup.

**6.** Learning to fill the proper lanes.

**7.** Making the quick change from defense to offense and from offense to defense.

**8.** Learning to adjust to the defense.

Good fast-break drills that have been diagrammed elsewhere will not be repeated here, but some of them are as follows:

**1.** All of the floor-length drills that involve a ball, especially—three-man parallel lane, three-man weave, long pass from board, down the middle, front, and side, turn and drive, long pass (A and B), three-on-two conditioner, and team weave.

**2.** All of the drills that involve getting the ball off the board and getting it out quickly.

**3.** The two-on-one and three-on-two defensive drills.

**4.** The fast-break patterns and possible finishes.

At first, I like to designate how they are to start and finish until all the patterns have been learned and become habit. Then I have someone take an outside shot, and the break is started according to who rebounds it and how. This makes them react, as they do not know in advance where the ball will rebound or if the shot will be made, and they must adjust quickly to whatever happens and get the ball down the floor as quickly as possible.

When they begin to react automatically, it is time to start adding some defense. The defense should block up certain patterns and force the offense to adjust.

Some simple defenses that I use are as follows:

**1.** The man who takes the shot will free-lance defensively.

**2.** The shooter will play defense from foul circle to foul circle and a man at each end will play defense at his end out as far as the center line.

**3.** The same as 2 except use two men at each end instead of one.

**4.** The same as 2 except the three men may freelance defensively all over the court.

**5.** Set up a complete offensive team and have the defense fast break every time they obtain possession of the ball with the offensive team playing defense when they lose the ball, as shown under "Fast-Break Offense" in Chapter 5.

**Fast Break—Five-Man Continuity** (Diag. 7-175). 1 shoots ball off of board and 2 rebounds and passes out to 3 or 5 and 4 screens for the one who does not receive the pass from 2. In the example illustrated here, 2 passes to 3 and 3 passes to 5, who dribbles the ball hard down the middle of the floor. 3 and 4 fill the outside lanes while 1 and 2 come behind 5 with one on each side. When 5 reaches the circle area he passes to a flanker, 3 or 4, and stays out. The opposite flanker rebounds the ball and passes out to 1 or 2, and 5 screens for the one that did not receive the pass. They break back, using the same patterns, but now we have interchanged positions.

With our fifteen-man squad, we like to have one team run this for a few minutes with a second group standing by to come on next and a third group shooting free throws.

**Fast Break—Team Options** (Diag. 7-176). The players must learn to run the patterns and fill the proper lanes whenever the ball is obtained from the board or after a score. These various patterns with their possible options at the start and at the finish are diagrammed under the "Fast Break" part of Chapter 4.

## SCRIMMAGING

This was considered under the discussion of "The Practice Session" in Chapter 2 and in Defensive Drill #31 in Chapter 7 and certainly consists of a vital part of the practice program.

Half-court scrimmage is necessary for the development of:

**1.** The regular team offenses.
**2.** The regular team defenses.
**3.** Floor balance and timing.
**4.** Special offensive plays and setups.
**5.** Special defensive setups.

Full-court scrimmage is necessary for the development of:

**1.** Physical condition.
**2.** Quick reaction from offense to defense and from defense to offense.

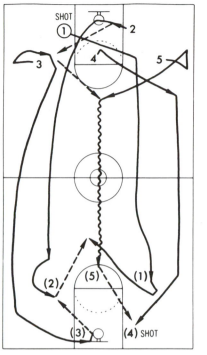

**DIAGRAM 7-175** Fast Break #1—
Five-Man Continuity.

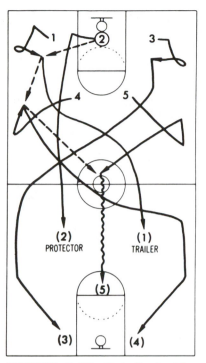

**DIAGRAM 7-176** Fast Break #2—
Team Options.

**3.** Quick adjustment to all changing situations.

**4.** Meeting actual game conditions.

**5.** The fast break.

**6.** All of the points mentioned just previously under "Half-Court Scrimmage."

I would like to re-emphasize some of the things mentioned previously that I consider to be very important to our squad in regard to our scrimmage program.

**1.** Although neither must be neglected, special emphasis is placed on offense one day and on defense the following day.

**2.** When the top seven or eight players have been determined, they should be on offense the majority of the time on the day it is to have special emphasis and the same proportionate amount of time on defense on the days that defense is emphasized.

**3.** It is during the scrimmaging sessions that there is by far the best opportunity for the development of teamwork and it must be stressed continually during these sessions.

**4.** It is during the full-court scrimmage sessions that opportunities are presented for the development of: self-control, acceptance of questionable officiating calls, the habit of acknowledging the receipt of a scoring pass and the complimenting of good plays by a teammate, restraint from criticism of a teammate, adjustment to rules changes, adjustment to the rare or unusual situations.

These mental and emotional adjustments are as necessary for a player to approach his maximum potential as are the physical adjustments.

## THE THREE-POINT GOAL

There has been considerable discussion and experimentation in the last several years in regard to this new rule, which was adopted for the 1986–87 season. Although there seems to be a favorable reaction to the rule by most coaches, many feel the 19-feet, 9-inch distance is too close.

I personally concur with this reaction as I feel the distance should be a minimum of 21 feet. However, the 1986–87 season provided a good test.

If the rule was adopted to discourage the use of zone defenses, then I think it is wrong. However, if it was to diminish some of the physical play in the deep-post area and cut down on fouls, then it certainly was worth adopting. Not only is the latter thought a good possibility, but the rule may help the smaller, quicker player by forcing the defense to extend out a little farther and thus open up more driving room for the more maneuverable player.

Since I think that basketball was meant to be a game of finesse and maneuverability rather than physical strength and brute force, I am hopeful that this rule may lead us back toward that style of play.

# APPENDIX

## OFFICIATING

Section 8 under "General Principles" in a recent *Manual of Basketball Officiating* is entitled, "The Ideal Official." He is described as one who notices everything but is seldom noticed himself; has resourcefulness and initiative; has dignity of voice and manner with no suggestion of pompousness; is considerate and courteous without sacrificing firmness; controls the players effectively and understandingly; has constant concern for the physical (I think it could also include mental) welfare of the players; cooperates fully with fellow officials; is physically able to be—and is—in the right place at the right time; knows what the rules say and what the rules mean.

*The Code of Ethics* in the same booklet states that:

A Good Official Shall:
*Not officiate any game after having had any alcoholic drink on that day.*
*Not converse with crowds at any time before, during, or after game, intermissions included.*
*Not request to officiate a game or games from any coach, league, or official thereof. (No official shall obligate himself to any person affiliated with any game that he might be assigned to officiate.)*
*Be in good physical condition.*
*Be prompt for appointments.*
*Not be overofficious.*
*Not accept league assignments from any school he has attended, coached, or has any relationship with the principal or coach thereof.*
*Not become intimate with coaches or affiliates of teams for whom he might be assigned league games.*
*Never argue with the players. If a player asks a question, he should listen to it, then give a definite and decisive answer, but should not quibble about any situation.*
*Assist players in the interpretation of rules when such request is made at the proper time.*
*Give best efforts in every game officiated. Each team and game is entitled to the official's best efforts, as he is the employed representative to administer the rules of the game.*

Also under "General Principles" and "Important Reminders" additional emphasis is placed on a number of other things, such as:

*Using proper signals.*
*Making decisions firmly without hesitation.*
*Knowing the rules and interpreting them accurately, intelligently, and consistently without provoking resentment or antagonism.*

*Being prepared for anything and everything.*
*Being attired and equipped neatly and properly.*
*Working as a team with your partner.*
*Knowing that you should be rated on your ability to handle games, not through private conversation with coaches or public statements regarding them.*
*Taking great care to be consistent in your calls, in your ball-tossing, in your ball-handling, in your interpretations, etc., throughout the entire game.*

It would seem that any official who could keep reasonably close to the suggestions in the *Official's Manual* would be so nearly perfect that all coaches would be genuinely happy with his work. However, we all know that basketball is a game in which a great percentage of the calls are judgment calls that must be made almost instantaneously with the act and partisan people will "honestly" see the action differently when the call hurts them. The very nature of the action often enables a person from a distance or from a different angle to actually see some types of infractions better than an official who may be right on top of the play. As a result there will always be honest disagreement with many calls as well as the highly unfair disagreements that come from blind partisanship.

The Officials Committee of the National Association of Basketball Coaches, on which I served for several years, is working on ways and means to further improve officiating and the official-coach relationship and recently asked some coaches and officials to submit a separate list of five things, not particularly stressed in other places, that might be desirable from their own particular point of view.

Recognizing the fact that it is almost impossible to mention anything that has not been previously mentioned, at least by inference, I submitted the following:

**1.**   Officials who never decide in advance how they are going to call a game or what they are going to be especially looking for, or strict about, or lenient about.

**2.**   Officials who understand all coaches and realize that the game is the vocation of the coaches and only the avocation of themselves.

**3.**   Officials who know the rules but do not hide behind the technicalities of the rule book. The *purpose* of each rule should be kept in mind as well as the rule itself.

**4.**   Officials who keep all personality conflicts with coaches, players, or fellow officials completely apart from anything related to the game or their officiating.

**5.**   Officials who command, rather than demand, the respect and cooperation of all those associated in any way with the playing or viewing of the game.

The five suggestions of one official were as follows:

**1.** Keep everyone off the team bench with the exception of players in uniform, the coach, an assistant coach, a trainer, and one or two managers.

**2.** Make a better effort to provide more privacy for the officials from the coaches, players, fans, and reporters before, during intermission, and after the game.

**3.** Eliminate all artificial noisemakers, such as—horns, bells, wood blocks, etc.

**4.** Seat the school bands away from the playing floor.

**5.** The school administrators and athletic directors should make every effort to be present at all games.

He also added the following statement:

*Although I do not expect my job to be easy, the coaches can help me to work a better game by—not calling me uncomplimentary names, not questioning my integrity, remaining seated on their benches, remembering that I, too, have feelings, not expecting favors, realizing that it is possible for their players to commit infractions, realizing that it is impossible for the officials to see everything, but we are usually in better position to see things than they are, and giving me the kind of consideration that any man has a right to expect from another.*

As I visit and discuss basketball with coaches from various areas throughout the country, I become more convinced than ever that our main problems are neither the rules nor the interpretation of the rules.

Most of the serious problems seem to be the result of the administration of the rules by the officials and the lack of proper teaching of the rules by the coaches. Too many of us do not teach our players to abide by the rules, but look for ways to beat or "get around" the rules. In other words, we teach evasion of the rules and look for the technicalities that would permit us to beat a rule rather than attempting to teach and live up to the spirit of the rule. Furthermore, it seems to me that most coaches and officials feel that the main problems that arise between the two are not the result of the calls but are due to contrasting personalities.

From the technical point of view, I believe that the particular calls that lead to trouble are almost always the ones that require snap judgment and definitely look different according to the angle or position on the floor from which you view the action. Unfortunately, too, the officials and coaches, because of their proximity and floor-level positions, are not always in the best position to see clearly what happened.

A few of the judgment calls that seem to cause trouble in every section of the country are those involving:

1. Charging or blocking.
2. Traveling.
3. Goal-tending and basket interference.
4. Jump-ball violations and fouls.
5. Foul-lane violations and fouls.

I sincerely believe that, while we constantly must remain alert for improvement in all phases of our game, we could help ourselves tremendously by making improvement in the coach-official relationship. The "soft answer turneth away wrath" philosophy, if practiced by both coach and official, might be a wonderful method of bridging the gap in that relationship.

During a discussion session at a recent coaching clinic, a number of coaches and officials were sincerely, seriously, and conscientiously discussing the officiating problems, and the principal thought that I got from the discussion was the fact that both groups seemed to feel that the main problem was a mutual lack of trust and faith in each other. It was felt that each group was reluctant to honestly recognize and admit any of its shortcomings, but each would give the impression of being persecuted or treated unfairly in one way or another. Although the members of each group felt that they were not biased in their criticism of the other, they were reluctant or unable to accept criticism of themselves in a constructive manner.

No official would admit that it was even possible for him to be affected by a partisan crowd, or that he ever carried a "chip on his shoulder," or had "rabbit ears," or was too officious, or hid behind the rulebook, or carried a grudge, or had any trait that might consciously or subconsciously affect his officiating. The stock reply of the official seemed to be, "I call them as I see them."

The coaches, too, refused to admit to any human weaknesses in regard to their relationship with officials and officiating, but seemed to feel that the officials were out "to take the bread right out of our mouths." It is rather amazing how attitudes can change so much a few minutes later when the outcome of the game was to their satisfaction.

The coach has a grave responsibility toward the official and the official has a grave responsibility toward the coach, but, even more important, they each should have a grave responsibility toward the game in every possible respect.

In the final analysis, perhaps the most important thing we need in all walks of life is more mutual trust, faith, and understanding of the problems of others. If we could acquire and keep that, the coach-official relationship would cease to be a problem.

# POINTERS FOR PLAYER AND COACH

It has long been my practice to distribute considerable miscellaneous material to our boys throughout the season. Perhaps it does little, if any, good in many cases, but I am completely convinced that it helps some boys, and, therefore, it is worthwhile.

In addition to lists of hints or pointers on the various fundamentals of the game, many of which are reproduced in previous chapters, I occasionally distribute applicable poems, slogans, quotations, and general suggestions.

Better than to take the risk of passing out too much at one time and having only a small portion of it digested, I prefer to distribute a small amount every week or two or whenever something seems particularly applicable and needed.

I also have a few separate reminders for the coach that I frequently review to help keep me on my toes. Of course, the coach must be familiar with all of the material in those that are distributed to the players.

Examples of this material follow.

## UCLA BASKETBALL
## JOHN WOODEN, HEAD COACH

### Re: The Coach

The following personal traits and abilities should be possessed or developed by the coach who really wants to reach the top of his chosen profession:

| Primary Traits | Secondary Traits |
|---|---|
| 1. Industriousness | 1. Affability |
| 2. Enthusiasm | 2. Appearance |
| 3. Sympathy | 3. Clear, firm voice |
| 4. Judgment | 4. Adaptability |
| 5. Self-control | 5. Cooperativeness |
| 6. Earnestness | 6. Forcefulness |
| 7. Patience | 7. Accuracy |
| 8. Attentiveness to detail. | 8. Alertness |
| 9. Impartiality | 9. Reliability |
| 10. Integrity | 10. Cheerful, optimistic disposition |
| 11. Teaching skill | 11. Resourcefulness |
| 12. Discipline | 12. Vision |
| 13. Floor organization | 13. Consideration for others |
| 14. Knowledge of the game | 14. Desire to improve |

### Re: The Coach

The coach must never forget that he is, first of all, a teacher. He must come (be present), see (diagnose), and conquer (correct). He must continuously be exploring for ways to improve himself in order that he may improve others and welcome every person and everything that may be helpful to him. As has been said, he must remember, "Others, too have brains."

Some helpful criteria might be:

1. Knowledge of the game of basketball.
2. General knowledge.
3. Teaching skill.
4. Professional attitude.
5. Discipline.
6. Floor organization.
7. School and community relations.
8. Coach-player relations.
9. Warm personality and genuine consideration for others.
10. Desire to improve.

### Re: Coaching—Selecting the Squad

1. Five determining factors.
    - (a) Determining the best players.
    - (b) Determining the proper position for each player.
    - (c) Determining the correct combination for the strongest starting unit.
    - (d) Determining the first line replacements and possible realignment of positions to keep team strength.
    - (e) Determining the proper number and proper players to constitute the full squad.
2. Most important characteristics to consider.
    - (a) Quickness and speed.
    - (b) Size and jumping ability.
    - (c) Ball handling and shooting.
    - (d) Coordination.
    - (e) Experience.
    - (f) Industriousness.
    - (g) Fight, determination, courage, desire.
    - (h) Enthusiasm.
    - (i) Cooperation and team attitude.
    - (j) Self-control.
    - (k) Alertness.
    - (l) Years of eligibility.
3. Give every boy a fair chance and every opportunity he earns.
4. Consider team spirit and morale.
5. Be alert to spot the good competitors and the poor ones.
6. Be alert for potential trouble makers and get rid of them.
7. The coach must select the squad, but should use every available method for help in making an accurate selection, such as statistical charts, conferences, observation, self-rating charts, etc.

### Re: Coaching—Important Principles To Keep in Mind

1. Basketball is a game of habits.
2. Never become satisfied. Basketball is a mental game.

3. Don't give them too much, but teach well.

4. Don't tie them down so rigidly that they lose their initiative.

5. Have an offense that gives equal opportunity to all.

6. Don't overlook little details. You must prepare to win to be a winner.

7. Convince your players of the importance of condition—mental, moral, and physical.

8. Nothing is as important as proper execution of the fundamentals.

9. Confidence comes from being prepared and properly conditioned.

10. Development of team spirit is a must and selfishness, envy, and egotism must be eliminated.

11. Both coach and players must be industrious and enthusiastic if success is to be achieved.

12. Teach respect for all and fear for none.

13. Use the positive approach and develop pride in your own game defensively as well as offensively.

14. Have one team, not regulars and substitutes.

15. Give public credit to your playmakers and defensive men at every opportunity.

16. As over 90 per cent of the playing time of each individual is *without* the ball, teach your players the importance of concentrating on offense when they have the ball and on defense when their man does not have the ball.

### Re: Coaching—Coach and Player Relationship

1. Keep a close personal player relationship, but keep their respect. Be sincerely interested in their personal problems and easy to approach.

2. Maintain discipline without being dictatorial. Be fair and lead rather than drive.

3. Study and respect the individuality of each player and handle him accordingly. Treat each man as he deserves to be treated.

4. Try to develop the same sense of responsibility in all.

5. Analyze yourself as well as your players and be governed accordingly.

6. Approval is a great motivator. Use the "pat on the back," especially after severe criticism.

7. If you teach loyalty, honesty, and respect for the rights of others, you will be taking a big step toward a cooperative team with proper team spirit. Jealousy, egotism, envy, criticism, and razzing of each other can ruin this.

8. Consider the team first, but don't sacrifice a player just to prove a point.

### Re: Coaching Methods

1. Be a teacher. Follow the laws of learning—explanation and demonstration, imitation, criticism of the imitation, repetition until habit is formed.

2. Use lectures, photographs, movies, diagrams, mimeographed material, etc., to supplement your daily practices.

3. Insist on punctuality and proper dress for practice.

4. Insist on strict attention.

5. Permit no "horseplay." Practice is preparation.

6. Show patience.

7. Give new things early in the practice period and then repeat daily until learned.
8. Avoid harsh, public criticism. Use praise as well as censure.
9. Encourage teamwork and unselfishness.
10. Do considerable individual coaching of individuals.
11. Use small, carefully organized groups.
12. Have a definite practice plan—and follow it.

### Re: Coaching—The Practice Plan

1. Start with warmup drills.
2. End with team drills.
3. Vary the drills to prevent monotony.
4. Explain the purpose of the drills.
5. Don't continue the same drill too long.
6. Follow tough drills with easy ones and vice versa.
7. Make drills competitive and simulate game conditions.
8. Give new material early in the practice period then repeat daily until learned.
9. Stress shooting drills every day.
10. Condition players for games.
11. More time for team drills as the season progresses, but never forget, overlook, or neglect the individual fundamentals.
12. Analyze each day's practice while it is still fresh in your mind and plan accordingly for the next day.
13. Early season practices must be progressive in intensity until players have reached top physical condition.
14. Use small, carefully organized groups of from three to five players for the teaching of fundamentals.
15. Combine as many fundamentals as possible in each drill even though emphasis may be on one only.
16. Stress defense and offense on alternate days.
17. Close each practice with a positive, pleasant drill and comment that leaves everyone in a pleasant frame of mind.

## POINTS TO EMPHASIZE IN DRILLS

### I. PASSING AND RECEIVING

1. Accuracy
2. Quickness
3. Crispness
4. Fingertip control
5. Head and eye deception
6. Seeing receiver
7. Receiver watching ball
8. Receiver relaxation
9. Receiver meeting ball
10. Keeping the hands above the waist

### II. SHOOTING

1. Quickness
2. Ball close to body
3. Follow through of hand and head
4. Eye on target—top of rim

**5.** Lightness of shot

**6.** Fingertip control

**7.** Confidence

**8.** Balance—with shoulders square away

**9.** Naturalness for individual

**10.** Competitive

## III. DRIBBLING

**1.** Keeping head up

**2.** Not pounding ball

**3.** Combine with change of pace and direction

**4.** Drive, don't bounce

**5.** Wrist and finger control

**6.** Be ready to pass, pivot, or shoot

**7.** Low dribble when in trouble

**8.** High dribble for speed

## IV. PIVOTS OR STOPS AND TURNS

**1.** Quickness

**2.** Feet spread to shoulder width

**3.** Low body balance

**4.** Ball protection

**5.** Ball control

**6.** Full-sole stop

**7.** Head above feet

**8.** Weight strong near defensive man

## V. PASSING AND CUTTING WITH FAKES

**1.** Deception

**2.** Change of pace

**3.** Change of direction

**4.** Quickness of start

**5.** Quickness of pass

**6.** Meeting the ball

**7.** Timing

**8.** Going through, not around

**9.** Angle cuts

**10.** Setting up your opponent

## VI. TEAM FAST BREAK

**1.** Making opportunities

**2.** Accuracy over speed

**3.** Keeping floor balance

**4.** Looking ahead

**5.** High percentage shots only

**6.** Getting ball through middle

**7.** Getting ball out fast

**8.** Quick change from defense to offense

**9.** Ball-handling on move

## VII. DEFENSE

**1.** Hustle and talking

**2.** Development of pride

**3.** Body balance and position

**4.** Split vision—two thirds man **and one third ball**

**5.** Pointing at man and ball

**6.** Alertness to help—working together

**7.** Keeping pressure on

**8.** Proper footwork

**9.** Never crossing legs

**10.** Getting to position quickly

## VIII. REBOUNDING

**Defensive**

**1.** Getting position

**2.** Keeping hands up and elbows out

**3.** Blocking out

**Offensive**

**1.** Getting position

**2.** Keeping hands up

**3.** Getting around blocks

| | |
|---|---|
| **4.** Timing | **4.** Timing |
| **5.** Height of jump | **5.** Height of jump |
| **6.** Spread and kick | **6.** Good tip or possession |
| **7.** Look | **7.** Develop fingertip control |
| **8.** Quick pass out | **8.** Keep trying |
| **9.** Fake charge. | |

## IX. FULL- AND HALF-COURT DRILLS

**1.** Ball-handling on the move

**2.** Footwork

**3.** Floor balance

**4.** Physical condition

## X. DUMMY SCRIMMAGE AND SCRIMMAGE

**1.** Teamwork

**2.** Floor balance

**3.** Quick adjustment to situations

**4.** Creating game conditions

**5.** Development of out-of-bounds, special set plays, jump-ball situations, and free-throw situations

**6.** Special situations

    **(a)** Attacking zone

    **(b)** Protecting a lead

    **(c)** Using or combating the press

*INDIVIDUAL OFFENSIVE MOVES:*

For Centers:

**1.** Getting open on post to receive pass from guard or forward.

**2.** Feeding from post.

**3.** Various fakes, turns, drives, and shots.

**4.** Screening—weak side and strong side.

**5.** Getting rebounding position and tipping.

For Guards:

**1.** Passing to post and cutting.

**2.** Passing to forward and cutting.

**3.** Passing to forward reversing.

**4.** Setting screen for forward or guard.

**5.** Working with forward on side post (pass and cut; dribble by; dribble by and pass back).

**6.** Working off screen by forward or guard.

**7.** Working on dribble drives ending with a shot, pivot, or pass.

**8.** Advancing the ball under pressure.

For Forwards:

1. Getting open to receive pass on side.
2. Passing to post and cutting.
3. Driving off screen by guard for shot or pass.
4. Reverse drive and straight drive.
5. Reversing without ball.
6. Getting open to receive pass on side post.
7. Moves on side post.
8. Screening for guard.
9. Keeping your guard busy.
10. Getting rebounding position.

*DEFENSIVE MOVES (STANCE, WEIGHT, VISION, HANDS, POSITION):*

1. Against the dribbler from guard and forward position.
2. Against the passer, cutter, and shooter.
3. Against the strong-side forward or guard.
4. Against the weak-side forward or guard.
5. Blocking out and rebounding.
6. Against the blind screen.
7. Against the side screen.
8. Against crossing—shift or scissor.
9. Protector—one-on-one; when outnumbered.
10. Against the post man—strong side, weak side, when he has the ball.

### Re: Player Essentials

1. Skill. The best players will master the following fundamentals and continue practicing them:
   (a) Good shooting—all types for any situation.
   (b) Good passing—all types for any situation.
   (c) Sure receiving and accurate tipping.
   (d) Clever footwork on offense and defense—stops, starts, fakes, feints.
   (e) Clever head, hand, eye, foot, and body fakes.
   (f) Good dribbling, pivoting, jumping, and rebounding.
2. Speed and Quickness
   (a) In shooting, passing, dribbling, pivoting, starting, stopping, turning, reacting.
   (b) Mental alertness—changing from offense to defense and vice versa, picking up open man, getting loose balls and rebounds, spotting advantages.
3. Condition—Mental, Moral, Physical
   (a) Freedom from injuries.
   (b) Endurance.
   (c) Poise and self-control.
   (d) Love of practice and a hard battle.
   (e) Regard for team over the individual.
   (f) Good health—moderation not dissipation.

4. Knowledge of the Game
   - **(a)** Rules.
   - **(b)** Strategy.
   - **(c)** Generalship.
   - **(d)** Systems of offense and defense.
   - **(e)** Special plays and setups.

5. Nerve—"When the going gets tough, the tough get going."
   - **(a)** Ability to do better in competition.
   - **(b)** To play when tired or hurt.
   - **(c)** To take punishment.
   - **(d)** To take criticism constructively.

6. Essential Character Traits: industriousness, enthusiasm, loyalty, cooperation, alertness, intentness, initiative, confidence, integrity, honesty, sincerity, courage, self-control, patience, faith.

### Re: Team Spirit

We want no "man" players, no "stars." We want a team made up of five players at a time, each of whom is a forward, guard, and center combined; in other words, each player should be able to score, outjump, or outsmart one opponent, or prevent the opposing team from scoring, as the occasion demands.

No chain is stronger than its weakest link, no team is stronger than its weakest player. One player attempting to "grandstand" can wreck the best team ever organized. We must be "one for all" and "all for one" with every boy giving his very best every second of the game. The team is first, individual credit is second. There is no place for selfishness, egotism, or envy on our squad.

We want a squad of fighters, afraid of no club, not cocky, not conceited, a team that plays hard, plays fair, and plays to win—always remembering that "a team that won't be beaten, can't be beaten." We want our boys to believe that "a winner never quits and a quitter never wins." Make up your mind before the game that you won't lose, that you can outsmart and outfight the opposing team; in other words, it you have confidence in your team's ability to win, you will be plenty tough to whip.

Others may be faster than you are, larger than you are, and have far more ability than you have—but *no one* should ever be your superior in team spirit, fight, determination, ambition, and character.

### Re: Practice

1. Be dressed, or on the floor, and ready for practice on time every day. There is no substitute for industriousness and enthusiasm.
2. Warm up and then work on your weaknesses and shoot some free throws when you take the floor and until organized practice begins.
3. Work hard to improve yourself without having to be forced. Be serious. Have fun without clowning. You develop only by doing your best.
4. No cliques, no complaining, no criticizing, no jealousy, no egotism, no envy, no alibis. Earn the respect of all.

5. Never leave the floor without permission.

6. When a coach blows the whistle, all give him your undivided attention and respond immediately without disconcerting in any manner.

7. Move quickly to get in position to start a new drill.

8. Keep a neat practice appearance with shirttails in, socks pulled up, hair cut short, clean shaven, and fingernails short.

9. Take excellent care of your equipment and keep your locker neat and orderly.

10. Record your weight in and out every day.

11. Do things the way you have been told and do not have to be told every day. Correct habits are formed only through continued repetition of the perfect model.

12. Be clever, not fancy. Good, clever play brings praise while fancy play brings ridicule and criticism.

13. When group activity is stopped to correct one individual, pay close attention in order that you will not require the same correction.

14. Condition comes from hard work during practice and proper mental and moral conduct.

15. Poise, confidence, and self-control come from being prepared.

## Re: Attitude and Conduct

1. Be a gentleman and do nothing that will bring discredit to you or your school—on or off the floor, when at home or away.

2. Develop great personal pride in all phases of your play—offensively and defensively as an individual and as a team man.

3. The player who has done his best has done everything, while the player who has done less than his best is a failure.

4. Be a keen student of the game. Basketball is a mental game.

5. Truly believe that you are better than your opponent in knowledge of the game, in condition, and in fighting spirit and you will be difficult to defeat.

## Re: Your Education

1. You are in school for an *education*. Keep that *first* in your thoughts, but place *basketball second*.

2. Do not cut classes and do be on time.

3. Do not fall behind and do get your work in on time.

4. Have regular study hours and keep them.

5. Arrange with your professors *in advance* when you must be absent.

6. Do not expect favors. Do your part.

7. Arrange for tutoring at the first sign of trouble.

8. Work for a high-grade point average. Do not be satisfied by merely meeting the eligibility requirements.

9. Do your assignments to the best of your ability, but never be too proud to seek help and advice.

10. Earn the respect of everyone.

### Re: Normal Expectations

Our chances of having a successful team may be in direct proportion to the ability of each player to live up to the following sets of suggestions:

1. Be a gentleman at all times.
2. Be a team player always.
3. Be on time whenever time is involved.
4. Be a good student in all subjects—not just in basketball.
5. Be enthusiastic, industrious, dependable, loyal, and cooperative.
6. Be in the best possible condition—physically, mentally, and morally.
7. Earn the right to be proud and confident.
8. Keep emotions under control without losing fight or aggressiveness.
9. Work constantly to improve without becoming satisfied.
10. Acquire peace of mind by becoming the best that you are capable of becoming.

1. Never criticize, nag, or razz a teammate.
2. Never miss or be late for any class or appointment.
3. Never be selfish, jealous, envious, or egotistical.
4. Never expect favors.
5. Never waste time.
6. Never alibi or make excuses.
7. Never require repeated criticism for the same mistake.
8. Never lose faith or patience.
9. Never grandstand, loaf, sulk, or boast.
10. Never have reason to be sorry afterward.

*The Player who gives his best is sure of success, while the player who gives less than his best is a failure.*

### Re: Criticism

1. If the coach "bawls you out," consider it as a compliment. He is trying to teach you and impress a point upon you. If he were not interested in you, he would not bother. A player is criticized only to improve him and not for any personal reasons.
2. Take your criticism in a constructive way without alibis or sulking. If the coach were wrong, he will find it out in due time.
3. Do not nag or razz or criticize a teammate at any time. It may lead to a bad feeling, which can only hurt the team. We must avoid cliques and all work toward the best interest of the team.

### Re: Expected Criticism for Early in the Season. Please Prove Me Wrong.

*Offensively:*

1. Forwards are not waiting to see what develops on side-post play. The forward should get the shot *only* if the guard does not get open.
2. Forwards are crowding the post man too much. Give him a chance to work.

3. Weak-side men are not keeping their men busy.
4. We are not getting balanced coverage on the boards.
5. We are taking too many chances on both the fast-break and set offense and losing the ball without getting a shot.
6. We are not hustling enough in the back court to fill the lanes for the fast break.
7. Some men are starting the fast break before we get possession of the ball.
8. The centers are making their moves too soon to get open on the set offense and the guards are not showing enough patience.
9. Our ball-handling must improve. It is better to lose a scoring opportunity than to lose the ball.

*Defensively:*

1. We are not talking enough on screens and possible screens, and on helping out.
2. We are not keeping our hand up when our man has the ball in shooting territory or in front of him when he is a potential receiver.
3. We are doing a poor job of blocking out when a shot is taken.
4. We are permitting too many baseline drives.
5. Some are not working hard enough on defense and being ready for anything. Never stand flat-footed. Be loose and moving all the time. Anticipate—don't stand back and wait.

### Re: Game Competition

1. Have courage and do not worry. If you do your best, never lose your temper, and never be outfought or outhustled, you have nothing to worry about. Without faith and courage you are lost.
2. Have respect without fear for every opponent and confidence without cockiness in regard to yourself and our team.
3. Think all of the time. Study your opponent and yourself all of the time for the purpose of increasing your effectiveness and diminishing his.
4. Never be a spectator while in the game. Be doing something at all times, even if it is only being a decoy.
5. Teamwork is essential. Unselfish team play and team spirit are the foremost essentials for a successful team.
6. Be at your best when your best is needed. Enjoy the thrill from a tough battle.

### Re: Game Competition

1. Fundamentals, Condition—mental, moral, and physical, Competitive Spirit, Morale, Industriousness, and Enthusiasm are the cornerstones and heart of any successful team.
2. Never stoop to playing dirty—play hard and don't complain.
3. When you get the ball, react quickly and you may sweep your opponents off their feet, and, when you lose the ball, become defensive minded immediately.
4. Never relax when on defense as you may lose two points that you can never get back. If you must rest, do it when you are on offense.

5. Be sure that you acknowledge and give credit to a teammate each time he hits you with a scoring pass or for any fine play he may make.

6. Be a competitor. When the going gets tough, the tough get going.

### Re: Rebounding

1. The team that controls the boards usually controls the game.

2. When near either board in a potential rebounding position, keep the hands shoulder high with the fingers pointed upward and the elbows out from the body.

3. Assume that every shot will be missed and get into position to rebound—offensively and defensively.

4. When your man shoots, take one or two steps backward with your eyes on him, block his path to the board, and then go for the ball. If someone other than your man takes the shot, check your man out first and then go for the ball.

5. When you go for the ball—jump high, spread and get a good kick, bring the ball in with force, take a good look for potential receivers, and get the ball out quickly.

### Re: Passing

PASSING

1. Make passes crisp and accurate. Not too hard nor too easy.

2. Be quick. Most passes should be through or by the opposition rather than over or around them.

3. Move quickly after you pass. Hesitation after a pass is a serious fault.

4. Passes must be accurate with maximum quickness.

5. Be deceptive, but never careless or fancy.

RECEIVING

1. Work to get open for a pass. Don't stand and wait for the ball. Set up your defensive man.

2. Keep your hands above your waist with fingers spread and relaxed and do not fight the ball.

3. Time yourself to get open at the right time.

4. Keep your eyes on the ball into your hand. Usually meet it.

5. Block the path of the ball with one hand with the fingers well spread and tuck with the other hand.

FUMBLING

1. Taking eyes off the ball.

2. Trying to do something with the ball before you have it.

3. Being too tense and fighting the ball.

4. Not being alert and ready.

5. Loss of temper, self control, poise, or condition.

### *Re: Shooting*

SHOOTING FUNDAMENTALS

1. Keep the ball close to the body, chest high with elbows in.
2. Use fingertip control and wrist action for quickness.
3. Medium arch with natural spin.
4. Eyes on target—top of front rim usually.
5. Back of hand toward face and palms toward target.
6. The head must be moving up and directly toward the basket when the ball leaves your hand.

SHOOTING POINTERS

1. Confidence and concentration are necessary.
2. Quickness to prevent shot being blocked.
3. Practice to develop *your* form. Don't keep experimenting.
4. Extra practice on the type of shots that you are most likely to get.
5. Know your own shooting range and individual ability for proper selection of shots.
6. As a general rule and particularly on jump, push, or set shots, do not shoot unless you can finish with your shoulder squared away toward the basket and the body and head moving up and slightly forward.

### *Re: Dribbling*

1. Too much dribbling hurts team play. There must always be a purpose.
2. Look first for the pass before dribbling. Keep the head up, the ball close to the body and under control.
3. A dribbler needs a trailer.
4. Dribblers should usually keep away from the sidelines and corners.
5. Every dribble must end with a good pass or shot often preceded by a pivot. If you aren't a good passer from the dribble or do not have good floor vision while dribbling, you should not dribble any more than necessary.

### *Re: Pivoting or Stops and Turns*

1. Make a full-sole stop with the feet spread wider than the shoulders.
2. Keep the head up with the knees bent and the "tail" low.
3. Have the ball protected and close to your body away from the defensive man.
4. Don't start your turn before you have stopped.
5. Swing the leg farthest from the defensive man back around while pivoting on the foot near the defensive man.
6. Stop and pass before being driven in a corner and too close to the sideline.
7. Be sure there is a trailer always ready to come late and fast by a potential pivoter.

### *Re: Individual Offense*

1. Weak-side men should keep your men busy.
2. Keep your hands up and ready all of the time.

3. Be quick and clever—with or without the ball—but do not get fancy.
4. *Always* be alive for the pass and cut.
5. Never stand still. Keep the ball moving and you keep moving mentally and physically.
6. Think all of the time. Outsmart your opponent. If he relaxes or turns his head, take advantage of him.
7. Try to put to use all of the hints found under discussions of the individual fundamentals.

### Re: Team Offense

1. Weak-side men try to make your guards turn their back to the ball to keep them from helping. It may also help you to get open if he finds it difficult to divide his attention.
2. Change from defense to offense very quickly when you gain possession of the ball. If you are in the back court, look ahead immediately.
3. The pass and cut must always be a part of your offense. Use it in various ways.
4. Use your teammates for screens whenever they cut into your territory. If you do not get the ball, make yourself available as a screen for a teammate.
5. Keep team floor balance all the time. The weak side is just as important as the strong side.
6. The man with easiest shot should get the pass to shoot.
7. When a shot is taken, try to have triangular rebounding underneath, a rebounder in the circle area, and a protector.

### Re: Five Important Points for Offense and Five for Defense

I want a hustling, fighting team that never has time to crab or complain to anyone about anything.

OFFENSE

1. We must get a good shot every time that we obtain possession of the ball.
2. We must get the ball out fast and fill the lanes to make our fast break work.
3. We must have patience on our set offense when our fast break does not produce a high percentage shot.
4. We must eliminate offensive fouls.
5. We must keep floor balance both before and after a shot is taken.

DEFENSE

1. We must never relax on defense.
2. We must keep good position and cut down on defensive fouls.
3. We must keep pressure on the ball.
4. We must keep our man blocked off our defensive board.
5. We must accept the double responsibility of containing our own man and helping out a teammate.

### Re: 15 Important Suggestions

DEFENSE

1. Usually split your man on the side where you can be hurt the most.
2. When your man passes, back up quickly toward your basket but keep your eyes on your man and get in his path when he cuts.
3. Keep moving. Do not get caught standing still or standing up. Be alert and anticipating when your man does not have the ball. Make it difficult for him to receive the ball in an advantageous position.
4. Block your man out when a shot is taken, then go for the ball.
5. See both your man and the ball whenever possible. Point one hand toward your man and the other toward the ball. Float and help out all you can, but also assume responsibility for your man.

OFFENSE

1. Forwards—go deep toward the baseline in order to free yourself to get open to receive a pass on the weak side post.
2. Look ahead and pass when you have a man open.
3. The fast break must end in a high percentage shot, or we set up and try some option from the weak side post.
4. Be doing something all of the time with or without the ball—cut, fake, drive, screen, decoy, get position, rebound, protect, anticipate, think.
5. Good ball-handling, the use of the change of pace and direction, quick stops and starts, good selection of shots, balanced rebounding, and proper floor balance—insure a good offense.

GENERAL

1. Keep your hands shoulder high when near either board.
2. Assume every shot will be missed and get in position to rebound—offensively or defensively.
3. Good faking is an essential for both offense and defense.
4. Keep the pressure on both offensively and defensively. There is no substitute for hustle.
5. Don't beg, cry, alibi, sulk, or lose your self-control; but do maintain poise, condition, alertness, confidence, industriousness, enthusiasm, fight, and desire.

### Re: Fast Break

1. Try the fast break every time you gain possession. Fast-break opportunities are made in the back court. React quickly every time you get the ball.
2. The break must end with a good percentage shot. It becomes a "fire-wagon" or a "race-horse" game when you take any kind of shot.
3. Keep looking forward and get the ball down the floor as quickly as possible whether that be by pass or by dribble.
4. Balance must be kept from a cutting, rebounding, and defensive point of view. Try for the ball down the middle, a cutter on one side slightly in front of the ball, a cutter

on the other side slightly behind the ball, a trailer ready to come by late and fast in case the middle man is stopped and forced to pivot, and a protector.

5.  More mistakes will be made in the fast game and are to be expected, but hard work and good judgment will help reduce them, which shall be our objective.

### Re: Defense

1.  Play defense before your man gets the ball as well as after he has the ball. Make it difficult for him to receive the ball in the dangerous area. Anticipate and be alert.

2.  Use split vision and try to see both your man and the ball all of the time. If you must lose one, let it be the ball except when you are definitely going for the ball or when you have to shift to pick up a loose man in the scoring area.

3.  A hustling, aggressive, talking defense is likely to be an effective defense. Never rest when on defense, but do not bob around.

4.  Think constantly. When you lose possession of the ball you are a defensive man immediately. Be prepared. React immediately.

5.  The idea of defense is to keep the other team from scoring—not just your man. Work together and help each other.

### Re: Defense

1.  Keep between your man and his basket when he has the ball and is in a dangerous cutting area or position with your back toward the defensive basket. Stay between him and the ball when he is near the basket. Stay an arm's length away when he has the ball.

2.  Make it difficult for your man to receive the ball in scoring territory. The most effective defense is the defense played before your man gets the ball.

3.  By split vision, try to keep both your man and the ball in your sight at all times. As a general rule, give your man two thirds of your attention and the ball one third. Look through your man, not at him.

4.  Never cross your legs—slide, unless you are trying to catch up.

5.  Don't charge an opponent or get your head leaning forward. Keep body low and advance cautiously protecting the most dangerous side and ready to retreat or slide to the right or left.

6.  Sprint back when you lose possession of the ball, but look over your shoulder for guidance.

7.  Anticipate movements. Study your man. Make it difficult for him to have the ball in jump-shooting range.

8.  Keep good balance, relaxed and ready. Don't let the head bob up and down.

9.  Talk. A talking defense is likely to be a good defense. Yell at a shooter and keep a moving hand in his face. Encourage and help teammates.

10. Be alert to avoid or shift on screens and call all shifts. It is better to shift forward rather than laterally and the shift must be made without question when called.

11. Open up toward the ball with one hand pointing toward your man and the other toward the ball.

12. Make the offensive man commit himself.

13. Float when away from the ball. The farther your man is from the ball, the farther you may be from him.

14. Dominate your opponent. Be aggressive. Never relax when on defense. If you must rest, do it while on offense.

15. Don't be caught standing or flat-footed and never stand straight up.

16. Play the ball up underneath the arms of a dribbler or driving shooter and not down across the arms.

17. Change quickly from offense to defense when you lose possession of the ball.

18. Block out your man when a shot is taken, then move aggressively for the ball. Grab the ball and quickly and firmly without tipping it as you may when on offense.

19. Don't leave your feet unless the ball is in the air.

20. Force dribbler toward side, corner, or a congested area. Be sure to stop the base-line drive when guarding a man on the side of the floor.

21. Take two quick steps backward toward basket when your man passes, but keep your eyes on him and try to block his cutting lane.

22. Discover the strong and weak points of your man and play him accordingly. The offensive man may also be faked.

23. Know the system of your opponents and adjust to it.

24. Help your teammates and protect against the easy shot.

25. Earn the right to be proud of your defense.

### Re: Some Thoughts to Consider

1. An unbeatable five consists of industriousness, enthusiasm, condition (mental, moral, and physical), sound fundamentals, and proper team spirit.

2. Never expect miracles. It is steady progress that we want and it will come with industry and patience.

3. Mental, moral, and physical individual and team balance are essential.

4. There is a wonderful mystical law of nature that the three things we crave most in life—happiness, freedom, and peace of mind—are always attained by giving them to someone else.

### Re: Ten Helpful Hints

1. Be quick without hurrying.

2. Show me what you can do, don't tell me.

3. It is the little details that make things work.

4. The harder you work, the more luck you will have.

5. Respect every opponent, but fear none.

6. Hustle makes up for many a mistake.

7. Valid self-analysis means improvement.

8. Be more interested in character than in reputation.

9. There is no substitute for hard work and careful planning.

10. Is it hard for you to keep quiet when you don't have anything to say?

### Re: Many Things

Keep courtesy and consideration of others foremost in your mind at home and away.

Pray for guidance and strength to do your best and then have faith.

Although it may not be possible to determine what happens to you, you should control how you react and respond.

Try to have fun without being funny.

Never try for a laugh at another's expense. Try to laugh with others, never at them.

Our university will be judged by our appearance and our conduct. May we command the respect of all in both.

Good manners should control our actions at all times.

## 1961-62 Varsity Basketball Squad

### Squad Self-Evaluation Chart

Number each of the following players from 1 to 19 in your order of preference as basketball players. Give every player a different number, show no false modesty, and disregard personalities.

| Rating | Name | Rating | Name | Rating | Name |
|--------|------|--------|------|--------|------|
| | Blackman | | Hicks | | Nielsen |
| | Caviezel | | Hirsch | | Rosvall |
| | Cunningham | | Huggins | | Slaughter |
| | Gower | | Johnson | | Stewart |
| | Green | | McFerson | | Waxman |
| | Gugat | | Milhorn | | |
| | Hazzard | | Miller | | |

Rate the following players in your order of preference for the position under which they appear.

| Rating | Forwards | Rating | Centers | Rating | Guards |
|--------|----------|--------|---------|--------|--------|
| | Blackman | | Miller | | Gower |
| | Caviezel | | Slaughter | | Green |
| | Cunningham | | Stewart | | Gugat |
| | Gugat | | Waxman | | Hazzard |
| | Hirsch | | | | Hicks |
| | McFerson | | | | Huggins |
| | Miller | | | | Johnson |
| | Nielsen | | | | Milhorn |
| | Stewart | | | | Nielsen |
| | | | | | Rosvall |

### 1961-62 Varsity Basketball Squad

### Composite Results of Squad Self-Evaluation
### on November 17, 1961

|  |  | Pts | Rank |
|---|---|---|---|
| Blackman |  |  | 4 |
| Caviezel |  |  | 17 |
| Cunningham |  |  | 2 |
| Gower |  |  | 14 |
| Green |  |  | 1 |
| Gugat |  |  | 16 |
| Hazzard |  |  | 3 |
| Hicks |  |  | 9 |
| Hirsch |  |  | 7 |
| Huggins |  |  | 15 |
| Johnson |  |  | 19 |
| McFerson |  |  | 13 |
| Milhorn |  |  | 10 |
| Miller |  |  | 12 |
| Nielsen |  |  | 18 |
| Rosvall |  |  | 11 |
| Slaughter |  |  | 5 |
| Stewart |  |  | 8 |
| Waxman | 7-2-14-6-7-5-6-6-6-7-6-5-6-7-8-6-6-6-7 | 119 | 6 |

|  |  | Pts | Rank |
|---|---|---|---|
| Blackman | Forwards 2-2-2-2 2-2-2-2-2-2-2-2-1-2-3-2-2-2-2 | 38 | 2 |
| Caviezel |  |  | 8 |
| Cunningham | 1-1-1-1-1-1-1-1-1-1-1-2-1-1-1-1-1-1-1 | 20 | 1 |
| Gugat |  |  | 7 |
| Hirsch |  |  | 3 |
| McFerson |  |  | 6 |
| Miller |  |  | 5 |
| Nielsen |  |  | 9 |
| Stewart |  |  | 4 |
| Miller | Centers |  | 4 |
| Slaughter | 2-1-1-1-2-1-2-1-1-2-1-1-1-2-2-2-1-2-1 | 27 | 1 |
| Stewart |  |  | 3 |
| Waxman | 1-2-2-2-1-2-1-2-2-1-2-2-2-1-1-1-2-1-2 | 30 | 2 |
| Gower | Guards 6-5-7-8-6-8-7-6-6-6-8-5-5-6-6-7-7 | 120 | 6 |
| Green |  |  | 1 |
| Gugat |  |  | 8 |
| Hazzard |  |  | 2 |
| Hicks |  |  | 3 |
| Huggins |  |  | 7 |
| Johnson |  |  | 10 |
| Milhorn |  |  | 4 |
| Nielsen |  |  | 9 |
| Rosvall |  |  | 5 |

### U.C.L.A. Basketball Game or Scrimmage Statistics

U.C.L.A. vs _____

Date and Time: _____

Place: _____

Officials: _____

Chart Keeper: _____

Spotter: _____

| Alphabetical Order of Squad Names | Number | Failed to keep man busy on weak side. | Failed to acknowledge a scoring pass from a teammate. | Showed displeasure at a teammate. | Showed displeasure at a coach. | Showed displeasure at an official. | Sulked or got head down. | Lost temper or self-control in any way. | Failed to hustle on either offense or defense. | Failed to get proper rebound balance after a shot. | Appearance to be "cocky", fancy, or "grandstanded". | Failed to see a teammate open for a pass. | Failed to keep hands up around board. | Forced a shot or dribble. |
|---|---|---|---|---|---|---|---|---|---|---|---|---|---|---|
| Blackman | 52 | | | | | | | | | | | | | |
| Green | 45 | | | | | | | | | | | | | |
| Hicks | 24 | | | | | | | | | | | | | |
| Waxman | 32 | | | | | | | | | | | | | |

| | 1961-62 U.C.L.A. Varsity Basketball Scrimmages<br>10/16/61 through 11/24/61<br>Cumulative Plus or Minus Ratings | | | | | | | | | | | |
|---|---|---|---|---|---|---|---|---|---|---|---|---|

| | 1st<br>10/16<br>to<br>10/20 | 2nd<br>10/23<br>to<br>10/27 | 10/16<br>to<br>10/27 | 3rd<br>10/30<br>to<br>11/3 | 10/16<br>to<br>11/3 | 4th<br>11/6<br>to<br>11/10 | 10/16<br>to<br>11/10 | 5th<br>11/13<br>to<br>11/17 | 10/16<br>to<br>11/17 | 6th<br>11/20<br>to<br>11/24 | 10/16<br>to<br>11/24 | Final<br>Rank |
|---|---|---|---|---|---|---|---|---|---|---|---|---|
| Blackman | +17½ | +11½ | +29 | Exc. | +29 | +12 | +41 | +1½ | +42½ | +4 | +46½ | 5 |
| Caviezel | | | | | | | | | | | | |
| Cunningham | +19½ | +19½ | +39 | Exc. | +39 | +19½ | +58½ | +10½ | +69 | +5 | +74 | 1 |
| Gower | | | | | | | | | | | | |
| Green | | | | | | | | | | | | |
| Gugat | | | | | | | | | | | | |
| Hazzard | | | | | | | | | | | | |
| Hicks | | | | | | | | | | | | |
| Hirsch | | | | | | | | | | | | |
| Huggins | −6 | − | −6 | −3 | −9 | − | −9 | −7 | −16 | −5½ | −21½ | 15 |
| Johnson | −10½ | −18½ | −29 | −15 | −44 | | | | | | | Quit<br>11/3 |
| McFerson | | | | | | | | | | | | |
| Milhorn | | | | | | | | | | | | |
| Miller | | | | | | | | | | | | |
| Rosvall | −3½ | +4 | +½ | +½ | +1 | − | +1 | −1½ | −½ | −5 | −5½ | 13 |
| Slaughter | | | | | | | | | | | | |
| Stewart | | | | | | | | | | | | |
| Waxman | | | | | | | | | | | | |

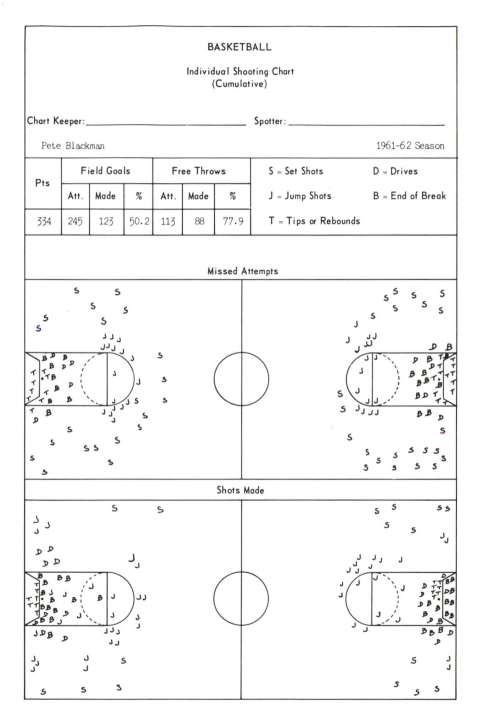

# BASKETBALL

### Individual Shooting Chart
### (Cumulative)

Chart Keeper: _____  Spotter: _____

Pete Blackman                                           1961-62 Season

| Pts | Field Goals | | | Free Throws | | | S = Set Shots        D = Drives |
|---|---|---|---|---|---|---|---|
| | Att. | Made | % | Att. | Made | % | J = Jump Shots       B = End of Break |
| 334 | 245 | 123 | 50.2 | 113 | 88 | 77.9 | T = Tips or Rebounds |

## Missed Attempts

## Shots Made

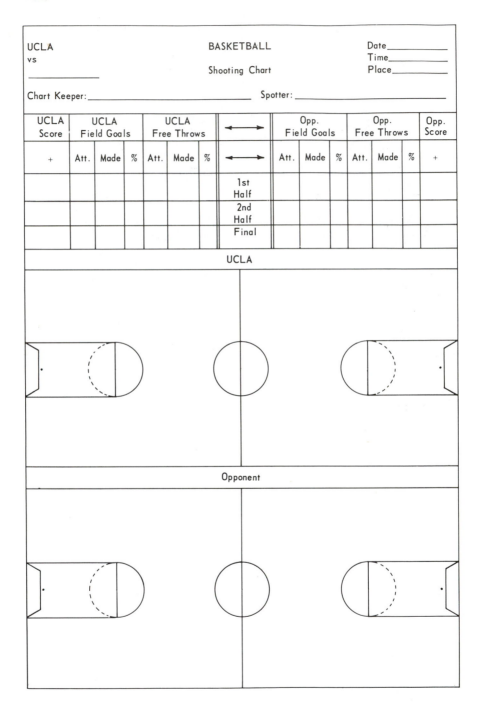

## UCLA BASKETBALL

### Individual Scrimmage Statistics

1961-62 Season  (10/16/61 to 11/24/61)

| Game | Pts. | Field Goals | | | Free Throws | | | Rebounds | Possession | | Assists | Pers. Fouls | D... E... |
| --- | --- | --- | --- | --- | --- | --- | --- | --- | --- | --- | --- | --- | --- |
| | | Att | Made | % | Att | Made | % | | Lost | Gain | | | |
| F | 334-11.5 | 245 | 123 | 50.2 | | | | | | | | | |
| Blackman | 197 | 137 | 85 | 62. | 38 | 27 | 71.1 | 99 | 23 | 22 | 25 | | |
| F | 388-13.4 | 351 | 151 | 43.0 | | | | | | | | | |
| Cunningham | 257 | 171 | 109 | 63.7 | 44 | 39 | 88.6 | 115 | 21 | 13 | 27 | | |
| G | 12-1.1 | 10 | 3 | 30.0 | | | | | | | | | |
| Gower | 120 | 143 | 59 | 41.2 | 7 | 2 | 28.6 | 26 | 29 | 10 | 13 | | |
| G | 559-19.3 | 459 | 179 | 38.9 | | | | | | | | | |
| Green | 202 | 163 | 85 | 52.1 | 41 | 32 | 78. | 103 | 26 | 25 | 42 | | |
| F | 12-0.6 | 11 | 4 | 36.4 | | | | | | | | | |
| Gugat | 87 | 89 | 34 | 38.2 | 30 | 19 | 63.3 | 52 | 21 | 16 | 17 | | |
| G | 370-13.2 | 338 | 134 | 39.6 | | | | | | | | | |
| Hazzard | 252 | 221 | 116 | 52.5 | 38 | 20 | 52.6 | 82 | 42 | 40 | 137 | | |
| G | 38-1.8 | 45 | 18 | 40:0 | | | | | | | | | |
| Hicks | 40 | 55 | 20 | 36.4 | 5 | 0 | 0 | 14 | 17 | 3 | 6 | | |
| F | | | | | | | | | | | | | |
| Hirsch | 77 | 92 | 32 | 34.8 | 22 | 13 | 59.1 | 69 | 9 | 6 | 12 | | |
| G | 5-1-3 | 3 | 2 | 66.7 | | | | | | | | | |
| Huggins | 83 | 124 | 39 | 31.4 | 10 | 5 | 50. | 47 | 37 | 13 | 16 | | |
| F | | | | | | | | | | | | | |
| McFerson | 70 | 112 | 34 | 30.4 | 2 | 2 | 100. | 80 | 15 | 9 | 8 | | |
| G | 17-0.8 | 31 | 6 | 19.4 | | | | | | | | | |
| Milhorn | 156 | 135 | 72 | 53.3 | 19 | 12 | 63.2 | 28 | 21 | 20 | 43 | | |
| F | | | | | | | | | | | | | |
| Miller | 82 | 56 | 31 | 55.4 | 26 | 20 | 76.9 | 67 | 21 | 9 | 12 | | |
| G | 24-1.4 | 34 | 11 | 32.4 | | | | | | | | | |
| Rosvall | 105 | 110 | 52 | 47.3 | 6 | 1 | 16.7 | 42 | 30 | 20 | 37 | | |
| C | 276-7.7 | 196 | 88 | 44.9 | | | | | | | | | |
| Slaughter | 139 | 121 | 65 | 53.7 | 24 | 9 | 37.5 | 89 | 26 | 27 | 30 | | |
| C+F | 83-2.9 | 57 | 26 | 45.6 | | | | | | | | | |
| Stewart | 171 | 145 | 72 | 49.7 | 55 | 27 | 49.1 | 169 | 29 | 10 | 42 | | |
| C | 132-4.7 | 132 | 50 | 37.9 | | | | | | | | | |
| Waxman | 191 | 158 | 77 | 48.7 | 47 | 37 | 78.7 | 121 | 17 | 25 | 25 | | |
| Scrimmage Total | | 2195 | 1020 | 46.4 | 429 | 275 | 64.1 | | | | | | |
| 29 Game Total | 2177 | 1912 | 795 | 41.6 | 813 | 587 | 722 | 1451 | | | | | |
| Ave. | 75.1 | | | | | | | 50. | | | | | |

# MY FAVORITE TEAMS

Although it has been several years since I retired from active coaching, I am continually asked to name the personal favorite of my ten NCAA Championship teams. I have always refused to do this and for the very simple reason that I do not know. It seems that my favorite was the one I was coaching at that particular time.

I also am frequently asked to name my favorite players and that, too, I refuse to do. How can I say that such well-known players as—Lew Alcindor, Keith Erickson, Gail Goodrich, Walt Hazzard, Willie Naulls, Curtis Rowe, Bill Walton, Sidney Wicks, Jamaal Wilkes, and others—are more my favorites than the multitude of comparative unknowns such as Ralph Joeckel, Eddie Sheldrake, George Stanich, Don Bragg, John Moore, Bob Archer, Dick Banton, Ed White, Allen Herring, Conrad Burke, John Green, Pete Blackman, John Ecker, Kenny Washington, Doug McIntosh, Mike Warren, John Vallely, and many others with whom it was a pleasure to work.

I have said that Alcindor (Kareem Jabbar) is the most valuable player that I ever coached, that Bill Walton was the second most valuable and could do more things than Alcindor, that I never coached a smarter player than Mike Warren, nor a better passer than Walt Hazzard, nor more spirited competitors than Gail Goodrich and Keith Erickson, nor anyone who could do more things well and never be a problem in any manner either on or off the floor than Jamaal Wilkes.

Five of my twenty-seven teams while at UCLA probably brought me the greatest personal satisfaction. In chronological order, they were as follows:

**1.** *1948–1949.* This was my first year at UCLA on a three-year contract, and I wanted to get off to a good start. The practice and playing conditions were very difficult, the public acceptance of basketball was entirely different to what I had been accustomed in the midwest, and we were picked to finish last in our conference. Furthermore, I was quite ill at ease in these new surroundings.

Therefore, it was indeed most pleasing to win our conference and finish with the finest season (22-7) that UCLA had ever had. This helped me to become more at ease in an area where the life-style was somewhat foreign to my own.

The players accepted me and a new philosophy of fast break basketball, to which they had never been accustomed, in a fine manner and truly gave their best. Yes, I was and am extremely proud of my first UCLA team.

**FIGURE A-1** Starting five of the UCLA undefeated (30–0) NCAA National Champions, 1963–64. Left to right: Fred Slaughter, Keith Erickson, Jack Hirsch, Walter Hazzard, Gail Goodrich. This is the shortest team to ever win a NCAA championship.

**2.** *1961–1962.* Although a number of teams between my 1948–1949 and 1961–1962 teams gave me much pleasure, I would have to list this one in the top five even though the overall record (18–11) was not nearly as good as some of the others.

We were not very good at the beginning of the year and got off to a very poor start, even though several of our losses were under three points, but made steady progress throughout the year. By tournament time, we probably were as good as any team in the country as attested by the fact that we lost in the semi-final of the NCAA tournament by an 82-80 score to Cincinnati who then won the championship the next night. With the score 80-80 and only a few seconds left, we had the ball and were going for the last shot. However, we lost the ball and a Cincinnati player hit his only basket of the game as time ran out.

This team proved to me how much it is possible to improve during a season as they came from "nowhere" to within a few seconds of a possible national championship.

**3.** *1963–1964.* The fact that this was my first NCAA Championship and had an undefeated (30-0) season is reason enough to make it one of those that gave me tremendous personal satisfaction, but there are other factors that make it particularly significant in my memory.

Comparatively speaking, it was the shortest of all NCAA champions, it used the exciting zone press defense exceptionally well, it was a very colorful and fascinating team, it was one of the few undefeated teams, it exemplified unselfish team play to a remarkable degree in spite of some very diverse and contrasting personalities, and it came as close to realizing its full potential as I believe is possible.

Keith Erickson, Jack Hirsch, Fred Slaughter, Gail Goodrich, and Walt Hazzard started every game, but the contribution of others particularly Kenny Washington and Doug McIntosh, against a fine, big Duke team in the championship game, made this a team in every sense of the word.

**4.** *1969–1970.* This is the team that I chose to call "The Team Without." They will be remembered for the most part as the team to win a fourth consecutive NCAA Championship, but the conditions under which it was won will be most memorable to me.

Very few in the basketball world expected us to be able to overcome the graduation of the dominant Alcindor along with several other fine players, and several opposing coaches had publicly stated that it would be quite different this year.

There was no Alcindor on this team, but we went back to our high post offense which Steve Patterson played very well. Curtis Rowe and

Sidney Wicks made a superb pair of forwards for this offense and John Vallely and Henry Bibby complemented each other very well and made an outstanding pair of guards. Of course, non-starters such as John Ecker, Kenny Booker, and others also had their moments.

I was extremely proud of the manner in which these players adjusted to the loss of a player such as Alcindor and adapted to a completely new style of offense and defense than that which had been used by us since any of them had been on our varsity squad.

Yes, I am and ever will be tremendously proud of these young men and their accomplishments.

**5.** *1974–1975.* Although each of our national championship teams has some special feature that distinguished it from any other, like first and last born children, my first (1964) and last (1975) teams were among the very, very special.

This 1975 team was comprised of as fine a group of young men as any team with whom I have ever had the privilege of working. They gave me no trouble either on or off the floor the entire season and were truly a pleasure to be around. The Championship merely added more "frosting" as they already had established a beautiful memory and permanent niche in my heart.

They were not expected to win the championship, but played as if they did not know that. They showed tremendous courage and determination in battling back from adversity time and time again to win every game that really mattered.

David Meyers was a true All-American at both ends of the court even when seriously handicapped by injury. Pete Trgovich matured and was at his best under extreme pressure. Andre McCarter and Ralph Drollinger steadily improved as the season progressed and gave spectacular performances in the Championship game against a rugged Kentucky team. Marques Johnson and Richard Washington, our youngsters, showed their nettle and indicated what great futures they have in store. Jimmy Spillane and Wilbert Olinde filled in admirably at times, and the "unsung" five"—Casey Corliss, Gavin Smith, Marvin Thomas, Ray Townsend, and Brett Vroman—all contributed day after day in the development of those who got to play the most.

Even though it is sometimes more difficult to do the expected than it is the unexpected, providing the talent is capable, you will note that I did not include any of the teams led by Alcindor or Walton in the five that gave me the most personal satisfaction.

I, too, thought we had a better chance to win it all when we had them, and, although, I personally may have worked even harder in their years, the close of each season came with more of a sense of relief than of satisfaction.

## THE TEN UCLA NATIONAL CHAMPIONSHIP TEAMS

The following comments were made shortly after each championship and reflect my personal feelings in regard to each team at that particular time.

### #1 1964 (30–0)

My remarks in regard to this team were listed in the preceding section and will not be repeated.

### #2 1965 (28–2)

Even though under great pressure all season long as the defending NCAA champions and with only two returning starters, Gail Goodrich and Keith Erickson from the 1964 team, these two with tremendous help from Freddie Goss, Edgar Lacey, Mike Lynn, Doug McIntosh, and Kenny Washington were able to successfully defend our national championship.

A change in pressing defense from the 2-2-1 to 1-2-1-1 worked exceptionally well and Erickson further established himself as one of the truly great safety men in this exciting type of defense.

An opening loss at Illinois and another road loss to the University of Iowa when Erickson was injured were the only setbacks on the road to the championship.

Kenny Washington had another brilliant game off the bench in the championship game against a fine and strong Michigan team which was reminiscent of his performance in the final game against Duke in 1964 and Mike Lynn also came off the bench to play well. The brilliant play of Gail Goodrich was also unforgettable and should have brought him the MVP award.

### #3 1967 (30–0)

This championship was attained by the least experienced and youngest starting five—four sophomores and one junior—ever to achieve such distinction.

It was also very gratifying in that it came through undefeated and

**FIGURE A-2** The 1967 NCAA Championship team; the least experienced team ever to win a national championship. Four players were in their first year of eligibility and one in his second.

made me the only coach to have had two undefeated seasons. Furthermore, I was also pleased to be able to learn that I could work an unusually tall and talented superstar, Lewis Alcindor, into my team-oriented style of play without the other players losing their identity.

The leadership of our 5′ 10″ junior guard, Mike Warren, who is one of the smartest players I have ever coached, was invaluable in creating stability in our four sophomores while they were gaining experience and confidence. Lucius Allen showed remarkable ability, Lynn Shackleford's corner shooting complemented Alcindor's strength very well, and the versatile play of Kenny Heitz proved very outstanding.

## #4 1968 (29–1)

Since all starters from the 1967 champions returned plus the addition of two fine starters, Edgar Lacey and Mike Lynn from our 1965 champions, an excellent team was expected. Nevertheless, the pressure of repeating and internal pressures being assured because the return of Lacey and Lynn meant that two returning starters from a previous championship team would be relegated to non-starting status, pointed to a difficult year from the coaching point of view.

Therefore, I was extremely pleased, in spite of having a 47-game winning streak broken by Houston in the Astrodome (71–69) game before over 55,000 spectators, having Alcindor suffer a serious eye injury, and losing an outstanding player, Edgar Lacey, from the squad, to have this team make UCLA the only school to have won two consecutive championships on two different occasions, 1964 and 1965, and 1967 and 1968.

Once again, the long (Lewis Alcindor) and the short (Mike Warren) provided the most important ingredients—talent and leadership—so necessary at this level for championship play, but Shackleford, Lynn, Allen, Heitz, Nielsen, and others also made their contributions.

### #5 1969 (29–1)

The significance of this championship revolved around it being the first time ever for a team to win three consecutive championships and the fact that we were able to accomplish what was expected in spite of the pressure.

Kansas won none with the great Wilt Chamberlain, Ohio State won only once with the great Lucas, Havlichek, Nowell, and Siegfried teams, USF won only twice with the remarkable Bill Russell and a fine supporting cast, and De Paul won none with the remarkable George Mikan, an all time great. Those facts merely indicate how difficult it is to achieve what is expected at times.

The unusual physical abilities of Lewis Alcindor were a tremendous factor in this accomplishment, but it was his natural eagerness to direct this ability toward the welfare of the team rather than toward individual statistics that really insured it.

Kenny Heitz, Lynn Shackleford, and Bill Sweek completed three fine years, but the play of varsity newcomers John Vallely, Curtis Rowe, and Sidney Wicks made the future look encouraging.

### #6 1970 (28–2)

Discussed in the preceding section.

### #7 1971 (29–1)

Amazing poise, incredible courage, and extraordinary discipline from some highly spirited young men were qualities consistently exemplified by this team throughout the entire season. These qualities, along with a fine, aggressive defense and outstanding rebounding, enabled us to reach the pinnacle to which we aspired and which had been reached by the last four and six of the last seven UCLA basketball teams.

Although the headlines usually, and deservedly, went to Sidney Wicks and Curtis Rowe, both of whom performed superbly, Steve Patterson (what a championship game he had against Villanova!), Henry Bibby (his clutch steal saved a game at Oregon as did his fine shooting on other occasions), Kenny Booker (his play in our first game against USC averted defeat), Terry Schofield (his outside shooting against zones and key steals were instrumental in many victories), John Ecker (pressure free throws in Oregon and fine defensive play on other occasions), Larry Farmer (his critical rebounds in the closing minutes against Long Beach State in the NCAA regional assured our victory), and the daily practice contributions of Rick Betchley, Jon Chapman, Andy Hill, and Larry Hollyfield were all very important in the ultimate accomplishments of this team.

Yes, this was a team in the finest sense of the word.

### #8 1972 (30–0)

Considering their extreme youth, their inexperience, and, certainly, the unrealistic pressure placed on them due to the remarkable success of recent UCLA teams, no knowledgeable basketball person could possibly have foreseen or expected the success of the 1972 Bruins.

The undefeated championship was a result of their development of excellent teamwork, their youthful enthusiasm for hard work, and the unselfish play of another superstar, Bill Walton, who, like Alcindor before him, truly personifies the team concept.

They became quite proficient in the options of our set offense, outlet the ball quickly and accurately for our break, played good team defense, and utilized the pressing defense very well. They became the most versatile of any of my teams.

Bill Walton meant a strong inside while Henry Bibby, Greg Lee, and, at times, Larry Farmer and Tommy Curtis, gave us outside strength. Walton and Keith (Jamaal) Wilkes, two of the finest all around college players I ever had, not only provided the nucleus for an excellent rebounding team, but their unselfishness was an inspiration to their team-mates.

Henry Bibby provided stability and hustle, Tommy Curtis was a real spark at times, Sven Nater toughened Walton and kept the team loose, Larry Hollyfield showed occasional brilliance, and the daily work of Vince Carson, Jon Chapman, Gary Franklin, and Andy Hall all made a contribution.

I should also mention our head manager, Les Friedman, who did an outstanding job in the tradition of a number of his predecessors.

### #9 1973 (30–0)

A mild heart problem which caused me to miss my first game in 38 years of coaching, the problems involved with maintaining a long, con-secutive, game winning streak which had now reached an unbelievable total of 75, the normal pressures from being "at the top" for such an un-precedented period of years, and the additional burden brought on by the publication of several books pertaining to UCLA basketball and my personal life all contributed to making the 1973 season one of the most "trying" in my experience.

However, the end result was extremely gratifying and made this one of the most cherished of all our championships.

How can I ever forget the magnificent performance of Bill Walton in the championship game against Memphis State, the inspirational and effective play of Tommy Curtis on many occasions and especially in the NCAA tournament games against USF and Indiana, the always smooth and often brilliant play of Keith (Jamaal) Wilkes, the fine all-around and consistent performances of Larry Farmer, the many brilliant steals and outstanding plays of Larry Hollyfield, the beautiful lob passes of Greg Lee to Walton and Farmer, the steady improvement and productive play of David Meyers, the good humor and constant effort of Sven Nater, and the unheralded daily contributions of Vince Carson, Casey Corliss, Ralph Drollinger, Gary Franklin, Pete Trgovich, and Bobby Webb?

### #10 1975 (28–3)

Discussed in the preceding section.

In addition to the players who made up these great teams, the mana-gerial staffs and assistant coaches were of immeasurable assistance in their development and ultimate success.

I will not attempt to name all of the managers, but I must give tribute to the many talented and loyal assistants, each of whom played an important part in the success of at least three of these teams—Jerry Norman, who played for me in the early 1950s; Denny Crum, who played for me in the late 1950s; Gary Cunningham, who played for me in the early 1960s; Frank Arnold; and Jay Carty, who, as a graduate student, worked out daily with our great freshman prospect, Lewis Alcindor.

# INDEX

**443**